OXFORD COGNITIVE SCIENCE SERIES

WAYS OF SEEING

D1556575

OXFORD COGNITIVE SCIENCE SERIES

General Editors
Martin Davies, James Higginbotham, Philip Johnson-Laird,
Christopher Peacocke, Kim Plunkett

Published in the series

WAYS OF SEEING

The Scope and Limits of Visual Cognition

PIERRE JACOB AND MARC JEANNEROD

OXFORD

UNIVERSITY PRESS

OXFORD
UNIVERSITY PRESS

Great Clarendon Street, Oxford OX2 6DP

Oxford University Press is a department of the University of Oxford.
It furthers the University's objective of excellence in research, scholarship,
and education by publishing worldwide in

Oxford New York

Auckland Bangkok Buenos Aires Cape Town Chennai
Dar es Salaam Delhi Hong Kong Istanbul Karachi Kolkata
Kuala Lumpur Madrid Melbourne Mexico City Mumbai Nairobi
São Paulo Shanghai Taipei Tokyo Toronto

Oxford is a registered trade mark of Oxford University Press
in the UK and in certain other countries

Published in the United States
by Oxford University Press Inc., New York

A catalogue record for this title is available from the British Library

ISBN 0-19-850920-0 (Hbk)

ISBN 0-19-850921-9 (Pbk)

10 9 8 7 6 5 4 3 2 1

Typeset by Newgen Imaging Systems (P) Ltd., Chennai, India
Printed in Great Britan
on acid-free paper by
Biddles Ltd, Guildford & King's Lynn.

We are very grateful to Jean Bullier, Ruth Garrett Millikan and Chris Peacocke, who read and sent us comments on our manuscript. We are also grateful to Chris Peacocke for having nurtured our project and provided many advices from the very beginning. In addition, we wish to thank Roberto Casati, Jérôme Dokic, Jean-René Duhamel, Mel Goodale, John Marshall, François Michel, Alva Noë, Elisabeth Pacherie, Giacomo Rizzolatti, Georges Rey, Yves Rossetti, Charles Travis, Anne Tüscher and Semir Zeki for useful reactions and conversations. Much of this book originated from interactions between the two authors at the Institut des Sciences Cognitives in Lyon (France).

Contents

Introduction: What is human visual cognition?

Humans can see a great variety of things. They can see tables, trees, flowers, stars, planets, mountains, rivers, substances, tigers, people, vapors, rain, snow, gases, flames, clouds, smoke, shadows, flashes, holes, pictures, signs, movies, events, actions (including people seeing any of the preceding). They can see properties of things such as the color, texture, orientation, shape, contour, location, motion of objects. They can see facts, such as the fact that a given object exemplifies a set of visual attributes and/or stands in some visual relation to other objects. Sight, visual experience or visual perception, is both a particular kind of human experience and a fundamental source of human knowledge of the world. Furthermore, it interacts in multiple ways with human thought, human memory and the rest of human cognition.

Many of the things humans can see they can also think about. Many of the things they can think about, however, they cannot see. For example, they can think about, but they cannot see at all, prime numbers. Nor can they see atoms, molecules and cells without the aid of powerful instruments. Arguably, while atoms, molecules and cells are not visible to the naked eye, unlike numbers, they are not invisible altogether: with powerful microscopes, they become visible. Unlike numerals, however, numbers—whether prime or not—are simply not to be seen at all. Similarly, humans can entertain the thought, but they cannot see, that many of the things they can think about they cannot see.

Museums are institutions purposefully designed to promote the exercise of human sight and the enjoyment of visual experience. If you visit the Louvre in Paris, for example, you can see a famous painting by the late eighteenth-century French painter, Jean Siméon Chardin, called *Le gobelet d'argent* ('The silver goblet') (Fig. 0.1). Facing this picture, you will see three red and yellow apples, a silvery beaker, a large brown dish with a silver spoon in it and two brown chestnuts lying on a brown table. Of course, what you call 'brown' in English is not one but many different color shades: although you call them 'brown', your visual experiences of the colors of the table, the dish and the chestnuts are all different. Nor do you see the full spoon: you merely see a tip of the handle emerging from the dish, but you do take it that what you see is the handle of a spoon the rest of which is being hidden by the dish in which it is resting. The central apple partly occludes the other two. The apple on the right partly occludes the brown dish. As the light is coming from the top left corner of the canvas, it is reflected in the silvery beaker and falling sideways onto the apples, the chestnuts and the top of the spoon. The apples cast their shadows on the table. So do the chestnuts. The dish casts a shadow on the wall. If you look closely, you will discover incredibly subtle reflections of the apples in the silvery beaker. You will also see a rich network of spatial relationships between the objects: the silvery beaker stands to the left and slightly behind the

Fig. 0.1 *Le Gobelet d'argent* by Chardin, Jean Baptiste Siméon (1699–1779),
Louvre © Photo RMN – Hervé Lewandowski.

apples. The large brown dish with a spoon in it stands to the right of the beaker and
behind the apples. The chestnuts are to the right of everything else. Everything lies on
the table.

Your visual experience of the painting raises a number of fascinating issues for cognitive science. First of all, you will not perceive the red and yellow apples, the silvery
beaker, the brown dish, the silvery spoon, the brown chestnuts and the table, unless your
visual system is in good working condition. Some brain lesions can result in visual-
form agnosia, i.e. the inability to perceive visually the shapes of objects. Others can
result in achromatopsia, i.e. the inability to visually perceive the colors of objects.
In the presence of the painting, neither a visual-form agnosic patient nor an achromatopsic patient will see what a normal human being can see. Similarly, there is
evidence that akinetopsic patients, who, as a result of a brain lesion, cannot visually
perceive motion, will not react like normal subjects to the perception of static images
of human bodily postures that convey dynamic information about the movement of, for
example, an athlete throwing a disc. Unlike normal human subjects, even though a
prosopagnosic patient may know the person who served as a model for a portrait, she
might not be able to recognize, in seeing the painting, who the portrait portrays. Second,
it soon emerges that the normal visual experience of the shapes, contours, orientations,
textures and colors of objects depicted by a painting far outstrips the power to impose
conceptual and/or linguistic labels or categories.[1] Third, however, the human power
to parse and categorize the visual scene in terms of concepts of objects is striking.
One can count the objects depicted. If so, then in Chardin's painting, one will find
nine objects: the beaker, the three apples, the dish, the spoon, the pair of chestnuts
and the table. Arguably, unlike the other three artifacts (the beaker, the dish and the
spoon), the table is not so much an object as it is part of the background, together with
the wall standing behind everything else and perpendicular to the top of the table.
Furthermore, one can easily group the objects into meaningful sets or classes: the
three apples and the two chestnuts together make five fruits. Unlike 'fruit' and 'artifact',

---

[1]At least, visual experiences outstrip the power to impose non-demonstrative concepts, where a demonstrative concept is expressible by such English expressions as '*that* shape' or '*this* shade of color'.
See Chapter 1, Section 3.2, for a discussion of why demonstrative concepts are not suitable to capture the
content of visual experiences of, for example, a shape property.

'apple' and 'spoon' are names of what psychologists call basic concepts. Whether 'apple' and 'chestnut' are names of natural kinds, 'spoon', 'beaker' and 'dish' are certainly not. Furthermore, what 'apple' and 'chestnut' name are living things.

These fascinating issues arise on the assumption that one is indeed perceiving a visual array consisting of nine objects with their shapes, contours, orientations, textures, colors and intricate spatial relationships. But, of course, none of this is literally true. Your visual system with the rest of your brain is playing a trick on you: there is no apple, no chestnut, no silvery beaker, no brown dish, no spoon, no table, no wall. All there is is a canvas with two-dimensional shapes and patches of colors drawn on it. How on earth does one see three apples, two chestnuts, a silvery beaker, a brown dish and a spoon when there are no such things to be seen? Or are there after all? This is the puzzle of visual art.

There is evidence that non-human animals (e.g. monkeys) can see things (e.g. plants or animals) in pictures (i.e. in photographs). However, there is also evidence that when they do, they believe that there is a plant or an animal in front of them. They do not think that what they are seeing is a representation. They react to the plant or the animal represented, not to a representation of a plant or an animal. Human beings are different. They too can be fooled by *trompe-l'œil* representations, but they have the joint ability to see what is in a picture and to see a picture as a picture. In seeing Chardin's painting, a normal person can both see the depicted objects as if there were objects to be seen and see the picture as a representation of objects. Only humans can both produce and enjoy pictures such as René Magritte's famous painting depicting a pipe and entitled *La trahison des images* ('The betrayal of images') (Fig. 0.2). The painting is a pictorial representation of a pipe. It includes a French sentence that says correctly—if ironically—of the painting that it is not a pipe. The puzzle of visual art is not restricted to figurative visual art. It arises with abstract painting as well. If one looks at an abstract piece of painting, one will perceive, for example, a red circle located in front of a black rectangle. The puzzle is: Why does one perceive the red circle as being in front of a single black rectangle rather than as being flanked by two black shapes? Alternatively, why does one perceive a single black rectangle partly hidden by a red circle, rather than two black shapes surrounding the red circle?

Fig. 0.2 *La Trahison des Images*, c. 1928–9 by Magritte © ADAGP, Paris and DACS, London 2003.

We think that the beginning of an answer to the puzzle of visual art lies in the idea that in seeing what any normal person takes himself or herself to be seeing in, for example, Chardin's painting, one is pretending, or in Walton's (1990) terms, one is 'playing a game of make-believe'. One pretends that one is being presented with, for example, apples, chestnuts, a dish, a spoon and a beaker, while one knows that there are no such things. One knows that instead there is a representation of these things. Although the puzzle of visual art is genuine and fascinating, in this book, we shall not explore it any further because arguably pretence or make-believe is not a perceptual phenomenon or not merely a perceptual phenomenon: it involves thinking about a work of art and it relies on knowledge of the world. We shall, however, investigate aspects of visual perception. In particular, we shall examine how visual perception can yield knowledge of the world. On the one hand, seeing is connected to thinking about the world. On the other hand, seeing is connected to acting upon the world. In fact, in this book, our goal is to assess what we shall call the 'dualistic' (or dual) model of the human visual processing of objects, i.e. the idea that one and the same objective stimulus can undergo two basic kinds of visual processing according to the task. Now, what we call the dualistic model of human vision refers to the anatomical and functional duality between the ventral and the dorsal pathways in the primate visual system, i.e. the 'two visual systems'. It has no ontological implication whatsoever with respect to the mind–body problem.

Some of the things humans can see, i.e. objects, they can also touch, grasp and manipulate. According to the dualistic model of the human visual processing of objects, seeing an object can and often makes one visually aware of it. But it need not. Human vision does not reduce to sight, the enjoyment of visual experience or visual perception. Sight is, as we said above, a particular kind of human phenomenal experience and a fundamental source of knowledge of the world. However, such behaviors as the pupillary light reflex, the synchronization of circadian rythms and the visual control of posture depend entirely on the visual system. The processing of visual information involved in such non-intentional activities does not lead to sight, visual experience or the visual perception of objects. Furthermore, often enough human beings act efficiently upon objects of which they are dimly aware, if at all. When acting on or away from an object, one sees it, but one is not *ipso facto* visually aware of each and every of its visual attributes. Someone screams! You duck, and you thereby avoid being hit by a threatening missile that you could not identify as you ducked. Alternatively, you catch a ball on the spot. You saw something coming but you remained unaware of its color when you caught it. Perhaps you did not identify what you caught as a ball. The concept of vision must be broad enough to encompass visual perception and the human ability to act efficiently upon objects on the basis of visual information.

Evolution has endowed primates in general and humans in particular with upper limbs involving a hand whose thumb is separated from the rest of the fingers. The dexterity of their hands allows humans to grasp and manipulate a variety of objects. Some objects (e.g. a hammer or an axe) require a power grip engaging the whole hand and the palm. Others (e.g. a pencil or the handle of a cup) require a precision grip between, for example, thumb and index finger.

Consider an artist painting a copy of three apples. She is alternatively attending to the shapes, colors, texture, relative orientation of the apples and to the canvas on which she can see her own sketch of two of the three apples. Suddenly, she moves her right hand and picks up a thin brush between her thumb, index and middle fingers. As the brush rests between her right thumb, index and middle fingers, she moves it accurately back and forth between her palette and the canvas on which she delicately applies light patches of yellow. Before grasping it with a precision grip, of course she saw the brush. She may have been visually aware that the brush, which she intended to grasp, was lying to the left of a tube of black paint. But arguably she was not visually aware of the distance between the brush and her chest. However, in order to allow her to reach the brush, her visual system must have computed the distance between the brush and the axis of her chest. Nor presumably, at any point in the course of grasping it, was she visually aware of three distinct landing sites on the brush where to position respectively her thumb, index and middle fingers. However, her visual system must have computed and selected three points where to locate the grip of each of her three fingers so as to allow her hand first to lift the brush and then to manipulate it deftly towards and away from the canvas. She is visually attending to and perceiving the apples, their sketch on her canvas and her palette. She saw but did not attend to the brush that she swiftly picked up from the table. Nor did she visually perceive the three points on the brush where to apply her fingers. Note that there are brain-lesioned patients (namely optic ataxic patients) who cannot either reach an object or grasp it.

In the present book, we argue in favor of a version of the dualistic approach to human vision. On our view, one and the same objective stimulus can give rise to a perceptual visual representation—a visual percept for short—and to what we shall call a 'visuomotor representation'. Visuomotor representations, which are visual representations of those visual aspects of a target that are relevant to the action to be performed, result from what we shall call the 'pragmatic' processing of objects. In normal human beings, visual perception and the visual control of actions work in tandem. Humans can switch from the perceptual mode to the visuomotor mode as skillfully as an experienced driver can change gears. Nonetheless, the two modes can be dissociated either by lesions in the visual system or by carefully designed experimental tasks.

The main job of visual perception is to provide what philosophers often call the 'belief box' with relevant visual information. In the belief box, which interacts with human memory, are stored mental representations of facts or actual states of affairs, which are themselves the outputs of various sensory mechanisms (including the human visual system, the human auditory system, the human olfactory system, and so on). In particular, perceptual representations formed by the visual system constitute an important source of knowledge about the spatial relationships among objects in one's environment. One may see an apple to the left of a banana. Seeing an apple to the left of a banana is a special sensory experience with a distinctive phenomenology. One is thereby made aware of a pair of objects, their spatial relationship, colors, texture, shapes, and sizes. Presumably, one can see an apple to the left of a banana even if one does not have words for, or concepts of, apples, bananas and spatial relationships. If one does not, then presumably one cannot form the belief that the apple is to the left of the banana. If one does, however, then presumably from one's belief that the apple is to the left of the banana, one can derive the belief that one fruit stands to the right of the other. The perception of colors too is an important source of knowledge about whether objects are edible or not. Thus, visual percepts are distinct from, but they interact with, thoughts and beliefs.

The main job of the visuomotor system—the visuomotor transformation—is to provide what we call the 'intention box' with relevant visual information. An agent's beliefs and desires may cause some of what he or she does. But not everything an agent does is caused by his or her beliefs and desires. Unlike reflexes and non-intentional behaviors, however, all human actions depend on some intention or other.[2] Unlike beliefs, intentions do not represent facts: they represent goals of actions. A goal is a possible state of affairs: if and when it obtains or becomes actual, one of its causes is the agent's intention. We shall argue that visuomotor representations are suited to furnish visual information to motor intentions that initiate, control and monitor object-oriented actions. In a nutshell, we claim that grasping the handle of a cup is an object-oriented action, one of whose causes is the agent's intention to grasp the cup. In the course of the action, the agent's intention draws visual information from the visuomotor component of the visual system. The latter delivers a visuomotor representation of the cup that highlights the visual features of the cup relevant for grasping it. One such feature might be the location of the cup coded in so-called 'egocentric coordinates', i.e. in a frame of reference centered on the agent's body. Other such features might be the shape, size and orientation of the cup or its handle so as to allow the formation of the finger grip necessary to lift the cup. The color of the cup, however, is not relevant.

Thus, the present book as a whole is a sustained argument for a dualistic approach to human vision. The dualistic model of human vision applies to the vision of objects, i.e. things with a spatial location that can both be perceived and acted upon (e.g. manually reached and grasped). As we have already pointed out, humans can also see other things, e.g. holes, shadows, substances and events, that cannot be grasped with one's fingers. The visual perception of some of the things that cannot be manually reached and grasped—human actions—will be discussed in detail in the last chapter of the present book. Leaving the perception of actions aside, the dualistic model of the human visual processing of objects has important revolutionary implications for the philosophy of mind and perception. For several decades now, the question whether perception in general and visual perception in particular has a distinctive kind of content—non-conceptual content—different from the conceptual content of thought, has been a central topic of contention among philosophers.[3]

In this book, we do accept the distinction between the non-conceptual content of visual experience and the conceptual content of thoughts. At this early stage though, we want to stress one important respect in which our acceptance of the dualistic model of the human visual processing of objects leads us to reject one thesis generally accepted by non-conceptualist philosophers who subscribe to the conceptual/non-conceptual content distinction.

Three kinds of considerations are generally adduced in favor of the distinction between the conceptual content of thought and the non-conceptual content of conscious perceptual experience: the distinctive fine-grainedness and informational richness of perceptual experience relative to thought, the ability to enjoy perceptual experiences

---

[2] Arguments for the previous three statements can be found in Chapter 1, Section 5, and in Chapter 6, Section 8.

[3] Dretske (1969, 1981, 1990b, 1995a), Evans (1982), Peacocke (1989, 1992a, 1992b, 2001), Crane (1992), Tye (1995) and Bermudez (1998), are notable advocates of the distinction. McDowell (1994) contains a powerful rebuttal of the distinction.

that one is not able to conceptualize and the alleged distinctive link between the fine-grained content of perceptual experience and the fine-tuning of bodily actions directed towards objects. In agreement with other non-conceptualists, we both think that visual perceptual experiences are more fine-grained and informationally richer than thoughts and that a creature may enjoy visual experiences for which she has no corresponding concepts. The dual model of human vision, however, is not consistent with the alleged link between the non-conceptual content of visual experiences and the fine control of action.

Since they insist that the conceptual content of thought and language fails to capture the fine-grainedness of the non-conceptual content of visual experiences, it is natural for non-conceptualist philosophers to assume that the non-conceptual content of visual experiences must match the requirements of bodily actions. From a non-conceptualist standpoint then, the natural temptation is to link the fine-grainedness of conscious visual experiences to the fine-tuning of bodily movements. For example, consider Peacocke's notion of a 'scenario content' designed to capture part of the non-conceptual spatial content of a visual percept. Peacocke (1992a: 93), who thinks of scenario content as 'an intermediary between perception and action', argues that 'in supplying a subject with information about the location of things relative to bodily axes, perception supplies that non-conceptual information in a form immediately usable if the subject wants to move his body or some limb toward, from, or in some other spatial relation to what he perceives'. Similarly, according to O'Shaughnessy (1992: 231–33), the task of conscious visual experiences is to 'assist', or 'cooperate' with, one's bodily movements: 'sight guides an instrumental act to its target'. The temptation is to assume that the richness and fine-grainedness of sight or the non-conceptual content of visual experiences is at the service of the fine attunement of bodily movements. A version of this temptation has recently been expressed by Clark (2001) as what he calls 'the assumption of experience-based control' (EBC), i.e. the view that 'conscious visual experience presents the world to the subject in a richly textured way; a way that presents fine detail (detail that may [...] exceed our conceptual or propositional grasp) and that is, in virtue of this richness, especially apt for, and typically utilized in, the control and guidance of fine-tuned, real-world activity'.

What seems to lend prima facie support to some version of the thesis of 'experience-based control' is the contrast between the computational requirements made upon the human reasoning and memory systems about objects, and upon the system dedicated to acting on objects, respectively. The job of the former is to encode more abstract information about the enduring properties of objects in a format that is object-dependent and viewer-independent (so as to ensure object-recognition from different subjective viewpoints). The job of the latter is to keep track, and regularly update, the representations of the constantly changing features of visual objects, within an egocentric frame of reference suitable for the guidance and monitoring of finely adjusted bodily movements. We do agree that the fine-tuning of bodily movements involved in reaching and grasping objects does require the computation of visual information about objects different from the visual information relevant for the purpose of categorizing objects, reasoning and memorizing information about them. Indeed, one cannot visually reach and grasp an object unless one's visual system has computed the location of the object within an egocentric frame of reference centered on the axis of one's body. But we do not think that the viewer-dependent perspective that is efficient for reaching and grasping objects is an efficient system for memorizing information about an object's properties so as to maximize the likelihood of object-recognition over time.

In fact, the body of experimental research that supports the dual model of the human visual processing of objects, shows that the human visuomotor transformation at work in the guidance of visual actions directed towards objects is an automatic system that is largely independent from the system that subserves the visual perceptual system. In the everyday life of a normal human being, the visuomotor system and the visual perceptual system collaborate and work in tandem. But brain lesions can disrupt this cooperation. And so can carefully designed psychophysical experiments in normal human subjects. Even normal daily life can provide numerous dissociations between the fine-grainedness of conscious visual experience and the fine attunement of the automatic control of bodily movements: the artist is immersed in the visual conscious experience of the shapes, colors and textures of the fruits she is copying. Her conscious focus onto the visual experience of the fruits in no way interferes with her hand movement: with the fingers of her right hand, she deftly grasps and swiftly lifts her brush onto the canvas. Contrary to the assumption of experience-based control (EBC), the non-conceptual content of visual experiences is not geared towards the guidance and control of action. Rather, as Clark (2001) aptly puts it, it is geared towards the 'selection' of objects that can be either goals for visually guided actions or food for thought. Nor does the alignment of the perceptual visual system with higher cognitive functions (thought, reasoning, the belief-box and memory) force us to assume that the content of visual perceptual experiences is itself conceptualized. The non-conceptual content of visual experiences is poised for conceptualization. To say that it is poised for conceptual use is not to say that it *is* conceptual content.

The structure of the book is as follows. Part I, entitled 'The purposes of vision: perceiving, thinking and acting', is constituted by Chapter 1, in which we try to offer a general representational framework for thinking about the puzzles of human vision. There, we lay the groundwork for the rest of the book by sketching a teleosemantic framework for thinking about the notion of mental representation, which, we think, is, if not required by, at least consistent with, the practice of cognitive neuroscience. We also examine the dynamical processes by which visual percepts give rise to more detached thoughts and visuomotor representations feed motor intentions. We claim that both visual percepts and visuomotor representations are mental representations with non-conceptual content, but they differ significantly from one another. Visual illusions provide an interesting example of the dissociation between the way things may visually look and one's considered judgment. The visual appearances are to some extent immune to what one knows. Conversely, one's considered judgment may diverge from the way things look. Percepts provide no more than evidence for thoughts. Many recent experiments have revealed a still further dissociation: one and the same visual stimulus can give rise to a size-contrast illusory percept and to a different visuomotor representation of a target of prehension, whose content differs in some important respects from the content of the percept. In Chapter 4, we review these experiments. In Chapter 1, we also discuss the arguments offered by philosophers on behalf of the distinction between the conceptual content of thoughts and beliefs, and the non-conceptual content of perceptual representations. As we emphasize, these arguments draw on the fine-grainedness and the informational richness of the phenomenology of perceptual experiences. In a way, our book is an argument for the introduction of a new kind of non-conceptual content: the content of visuomotor representations. The content of visuomotor representations is not conceptual, but it is not perceptual either. As the book makes clear, the argument for dividing non-conceptual content into perceptual and visuomotor content cannot, for principled reasons, rely on the phenomenology of visual experience because, as we said above, vision is broader than sight and, unlike visual perception, the visuomotor processing of a target for action does not give rise to visual awareness of the world.

Part II, entitled 'Empirical evidence for the duality of visual processing', comprises Chapters 2, 3 and 4. There, we review much experimental work ranging from electrophysiological recordings of single cells in the brain of macaque monkeys and behavioral experiments on animals to psychophysical experiments on normal human subjects, through the neuropsychological study of human patients with a brain lesion in their visual system. In Chapter 2, we contrast the responses of single neurons located, respectively, in the anterior intraparietal area (AIP) and in the inferotemporal area (TE) of the brain of macaque monkeys. The former respond to the geometrical properties of objects relevant in the context of grasping tasks. The latter respond to more complex visual properties of the same objects. In Chapter 3, we examine various degrees of visual impairment caused by lesions in the ventral pathway and in the dorsal pathway of the human visual system. In particular, we contrast visual-form agnosias and optic ataxia. In Chapter 4, we review a rich body of psychophysical experiments in normal human subjects that reveal many dissociations between perceptual and visuomotor processing. In particular, we try to assess the complex experimental situation in the study of some size-contrast visual illusions. Succinctly put, we argue that this rich and diverse body of experimental work reveals that much visual processing in the human brain is designed, not so much for the benefit of visual awareness and visual knowledge of the world, as for the guidance of visual actions towards neighboring objects.

In Part III, entitled 'Perceiving objects and grasping them', constituted by Chapters 5 and 6, we try to provide a detailed analysis of the differences between visual percepts and visuomotor representations. In Chapter 5, we examine the modularity of visual percepts: visual percepts are so informationally encapsulated that some of the things that can be thought cannot be perceived. We accept the distinction between non-epistemic and epistemic vision. For example, one can see a scarlet diamond without seeing that it is a scarlet diamond. Seeing that the displayed object is a scarlet diamond is epistemic seeing. Seeing that an object is a scarlet diamond is coming to believe by visual means that a perceptually salient object is a scarlet diamond. One cannot come to have this belief—hence see that an object is a scarlet diamond—unless one has the concepts *scarlet* and *diamond*. There is, however, something it is like to see a scarlet diamond that is different from seeing a red circle or a green lettuce, even for someone who lacks both the concept of a diamond and the concept of scarlet. Seeing a scarlet diamond without seeing *that* it is a scarlet diamond is non-epistemic seeing.[4] An interesting case of weak epistemic seeing is seeing an object *as* a scarlet diamond.[5]

---

[4]It is important to emphasize that the distinction between epistemic and non-epistemic seeing does *not* entail that only a creature who lacks the concept of a diamond and the concept of scarlet can have non-epistemic vision of a scarlet diamond. It merely claims that possession of these concepts is not required for non-epistemic vision.

[5]See Chapter 5 for discussion.

By further distinguishing between primary and secondary epistemic seeing, we try to analyze the subtle ways in which an individual's knowledge arises from visual perception and how visual knowledge interacts with non-visual knowledge. In Chapter 6, we argue that the key towards understanding the modularity of visuomotor representations is that in a visuomotor representation of a target for action, the visual information about the shape, size and orientation of the target is trapped in a representation of its location coded in an egocentric frame of reference. Only by recoding the location of an object in allocentric coordinates can the visual information about the shape, size and orientation of an object be available for perceptual processing.

In the early 1980s, electrophysiological and behavioral evidence from macaque monkeys demonstrated the existence of two separate pathways in the primate visual system: the ventral pathway and the dorsal pathway. Then in the early 1990s, the in-depth neuropsychological study of brain-lesioned human patients provided evidence for the view that the former underlies visual perception, whereas the latter underlies the visuomotor transformation. We depart from the earlier model of the distinction between vision-for-perception and vision-for-action in several respects. First of all, as we have already said, humans can see a great variety of things (including, rivers, substances, clouds, vapors, smoke, movies, events and actions), only a few of which they can also grasp and manipulate. On our view, the dualistic model of human vision, according to which one and the same object can be visually processed either for the purpose of visual perception or for the purpose of visual action, primarily applies to the vision of *objects* that can be perceived, reached and grasped. As it turns out, seeing human actions raises issues that cannot be properly understood on the basis of the restricted duality between the visual perception of objects and the visuomotor transformation. Second, we emphasize the fact that, in the visual life of normally sighted human adults, perceptual and motor processing of visual inputs do almost always collaborate. Thirdly, we think that the anatomical distinction between the ventral pathway and the dorsal pathway, which, according to the earlier dualistic model, underlies vision-for-perception and vision-for-action, must accommodate the distinction between the visuomotor transformation and the perceptual processing of spatial properties and relations among objects. In particular, it must accommodate the dual role of the parietal lobe, which is both involved in the visuomotor transformation and in the perception of spatial relationships. Finally, in our view, the visuomotor transformation is but a first lower level component of the human 'pragmatic processing' of objects. We contrast this lower level pragmatic processing with a higher level pragmatic processing of objects involved in the skilled use and manipulation of complex cultural tools and artifacts.

Thus, in our view, there is a parallelism between levels of semantic processing and levels of pragmatic processing. Lower level visuomotor processing stands to higher level pragmatic processing of objects somewhat as non-epistemic seeing stands to epistemic seeing on the perceptual side. This parallelism is corroborated by the neuropsychological evidence. The term 'agnosia' was coined by Sigmund Freud to refer to a visual perceptual impairment. Neuropsychologists make a distinction between 'apperceptive' agnosic patients and 'associative' agnosic patients. Apperceptive agnosic patients have a deeper perceptual impairment than associative agnosic patients: the former fail to process the elementary visual attributes of objects. Although the latter can process most of the elementary visual attributes of objects (such as their size, shape and orientation), they fail to map their percept onto the appropriate object-category. At the lower level, optic ataxic patients fail to reach and/or grasp objects. At a higher level, apraxic patients fail to use tools and/or pantomime the use of tools required by skilled actions.[6]

Finally, in Part IV, 'The perception of action', which comprises the final and seventh chapter of the book, we turn our attention away from the vision of objects and examine the visual perception of human actions. Clearly, the distinction between the visuomotor transformation and visual perception does not apply any more. The evidence from cognitive neuroscience, brain imagery, neuropsychology, psychophysics and developmental psychology points towards a different distinction. In Chapter 7, we argue that there are two broad circuits in the human brain for the visual processing of human actions. One is devoted to the perception of human actions directed towards objects and artifacts. The other one is devoted to the perception of human actions directed towards conspecifics. At the heart of the former, we argue, is the famous 'mirror system' (first discovered in the premotor cortex of the brain of macaque monkeys). We call the latter the 'social perception' system because it is the human visual perceptual entry into the understanding of intentions involved in actions directed towards other humans.

[6]See Chapter 3 for extensive discussion.

Part I

The purposes of vision: perceiving, thinking and acting

1 The representational theory of the visual mind

In the present chapter, we sketch and argue for a view, which we call the 'representational theory of the visual mind' (RTVM). RTVM is not so much a scientific theory that leads to testable predictions, as a picture or a framework. According to the representational theory of the mind, the mind is at bottom a representational device: in Dretske's (1995b: xiv) terms, 'all mental facts are representational facts'. On this view, mental processes consist of the formation and the transformation of mental representations.

In Section 2 of the present chapter, we shall contrast our version of RTVM (which we call 'visual intentionalism') with two alternatives: 'sense-datum theory' and 'disjunctivism', the latter of which is advocated by some contemporary 'direct realists'. Visual intentionalism, as we conceive it, will turn out to offer a middle course between sense-datum theory and disjunctivism. At the end of Section 2, we shall face the challenge that any representational approach must face, namely the challenge of the homunculus. In our view, RTVM is a framework for thinking about two main puzzles: the puzzle of the visual perception of objects and the puzzle of object-directed actions.

The puzzle of visual perception is the puzzle of how a purely subjective visual experience can provide us with objective knowledge of the world. This puzzle will be taken up again in more detail in Chapter 5. In the present chapter, we call attention to two features of visual percepts. First, in Section 3, we sketch our reasons for thinking that visual percepts have non-conceptual content: we examine the paradigmatic arguments from philosophers who appeal to the distinctive phenomenology of visual experience in order to justify the distinction between the conceptual content of thoughts and the non-conceptual content of visual experiences. Second, in Section 4, we sketch the basis of an approach that we label 'cognitive dynamics', whose purpose is to provide a systematic understanding of the dynamical mapping from visual percepts to thoughts and from more 'engaged' to more 'detached' thoughts. Thus, much of the present chapter is a detailed exploration of the resources of RTVM. One goal of Section 4 on cognitive dynamics is to show that RTVM is not committed to the view that all mental representations are detached descriptive concepts. Not all mental representations need have purely conceptual descriptive content.

The puzzle of visually guided actions is the puzzle of how so many human actions directed towards a target can be accurate in the absence of the agent's visual awareness of many of the target's visual attributes. In Section 5, we turn our attention to three implications of RTVM for the control of visually guided actions. We shall argue that RTVM has the resources to clarify the puzzle of visually guided actions. First, we examine the nature of actions and argue that actions involve mental representations. In Chapter 6, we shall further characterize the specific content of 'visuomotor' representations. Second, we examine the ineliminable role of intentions in the etiology of actions. Third, we discuss the intentionality of intentions. We argue that what is distinctive of intentions is that they have a world-to-mind direction of fit, and a mind-to-world direction of causation. This combination explains the peculiar commitment of intentions to action. In Chapter 6, we shall rely on these ingredients of RTVM to argue that there is a basic asymmetry between visual percepts and visuomotor representations. While the former is input to a process whose output is stored in the 'belief box', the latter is at the service of the 'intention box'.

1   A teleosemantic account of visual percepts

Tokens of mental representations are best thought of as tokens of an animal's brain states or states of its central nervous system. Not any internal physiological state of an animal, however, is a mental representation. States of an animal's digestive system, of its cardio-vascular system, of its respiratory system or of its immune system are not mental representations. Mental representations are neurophysiological states with *content*. Nor are all representations mental representations. The evolution of human cognition has given rise to cultural artifacts, i.e. to non-mental representations of various sorts, such as linguistic utterances, mathematical and logical symbols, diagrams, road-signs, maps, states of measuring devices (e.g. gauges, thermometers, scales, altimeters, etc.), paintings, drawings, photographs and movies. Thoughts, judgments, beliefs, desires, intentions, perceptual experiences, memories and mental images are mental representations. Whether mental or non-mental, all representations have content. They may also have computational properties: as emphasized by many philosophers and cognitive scientists, mental and non-mental representations are typically things to which computations apply and which can be studied from a computational point of view.[1]

We assume, along with many philosophers, that artifacts (i.e. non-mental representations) derive their contents from the contents of the mental representations of the human beings who create and/or use them. We therefore subscribe to the distinction between the *primitive* intentionality of mental representations and the *derived* intentionality of artifacts.[2] Although artifacts derive their contents from the primitive contents of the mental representations of their creators and users, unlike mental representations, they are publically observable. Non-mental representations are physical structures, and as such they have intrinsic physical and chemical properties. What makes them representations is that they have contents. In our view (much inspired by Dretske 1988, 1995b), representations are physical structures with informational function, i.e. with the function to carry information.[3]

A physical signal S can be said to carry information about property F if S tracks instances of F or if S is reliably (or nomically) correlated with exemplifications of F.

---

[1] See Fodor (1975, 1987), Chomsky (1980, 2000), Marr (1982), Pylyshyn (1984), Peacocke (1994).
[2] The distinction is accepted by Fodor (1987), Searle (1992), Dretske (1995b) among others. It is rejected by Dennett (1987).
[3] For elaboration, see Jacob (1997).

Thus, the informational relation between S and F is taken to be the converse of the correlation between F and S. For example, tracks, fingerprints, states of measuring devices and symptoms all carry information. Information so conceived is what Grice (1957) called 'natural meaning'. Perhaps a signal that carries information about a property could be called a 'natural sign'. A track in the mud carries information about the kind and the size of the animal that left it. A fingerprint carries information about the identity of the human being whose finger was imprinted. A gas-gauge on the dashboard of a car carries information about the amount of fuel in the car tank. Spots on a human face carry information about a disease. In all such cases, a signal carries information about some property because the activated signal is correlated with the property in question, and the correlation is reliable and not purely accidental. Informational semantics (i.e. semantics based on non-coincidental correlations) is an essential tool of cognitive neuroscience. Cognitive neuroscientists try to map the activation of neurons in selected areas of the visual system with particular visual attributes instantiated by objects in the environment. To discover that neurons fire in response to (or 'code') the presence of a visual attribute, is to discover that the pattern of neuronal discharge carries information about the attribute in question. Thus, the length of a simple metal bar carries information about the temperature because the length of the metal bar nomically covaries with the variations of the temperature. If so, then the metal bar is a reliable indicator of the temperature. For two connected reasons, information so defined falls short of representation: on the one hand, information is ubiquitous; on the other hand, natural signs cannot misrepresent.

First, if S carries information about F and F is correlated with G, then S carries information about G. The informational relation being transitive, information is ubiquitous and, unlike semantic content, informational content is indeterminate. For example, the length of the metal bar carries information about the temperature. But if variations in temperature are in turn correlated with variations in atmospheric pressure, then the length of the metal bar carries information about atmospheric pressure. Representing the temperature, however, is not representing atmospheric pressure. Hence, given that the length of the metal bar carries information about both the temperature and atmospheric pressure, it cannot *represent* the temperature at all. Similarly, there are many stages on the way from the retina through the optic nerve to the higher levels of information-processing in the visual cortex. Each such stage carries some information about the distal stimulus and about everything the distal stimulus stands in some non-accidental correlation with. However, neither the retina nor the optic nerve represent everything they carry information about.

Second, unless a signal could *mis*represent what it indicates, it cannot represent it. Unlike mental and non-mental representations, natural signs cannot fail to mean or carry information. As Dretske (1988: 56) puts it, 'a person can *say*, and *mean*, that a quail was here without a quail's having been here. But the tracks in the snow cannot mean (in the natural sense of 'meaning') that a quail was here unless, in fact, a quail *was* here'. Unlike a metal bar, a mercury thermometer may represent the temperature. What is the difference? Unlike a simple metal bar, a mercury thermometer does misrepresent the temperature if it misfunctions or if it does not work according to its design. For example, if the glass pipe containing the mercury is broken, then the thermometer may misfunction and misrepresent the temperature. Similarly, the gas-gauge in a car is a representational system whose function is to indicate the amount of gas in the car's tank. Since it has the function to carry information about the amount of fuel in the tank, it too can misfunction and therefore misrepresent how much gas is left in the tank. First, as Fodor (1987) has put it, no representation without *misrepresentation*. Second, 'teleosemantic' theories add: no misrepresentation without a *function*. At the heart of the teleosemantic conception of content is the claim that a representational device owes its content to what Millikan (1984, 1993) calls the device's 'proper' function, where proper function is a teleological, not a dispositional notion. Third, a device's proper function derives from the device's *history*.

Arguably, unless a device has a function, it makes no sense to say that it is misfunctioning. Unless it has a function, a device cannot be defective, damaged or dysfunctional. Thus, unless its function is to carry information about some property, a device cannot be said to misrepresent the exemplification of the property. Unless a device has the function to indicate the temperature, it cannot misrepresent the temperature. A microphone is an electro-acoustical device whose function is to convert the energy of acoustic waves into electrical energy. So is the human ear. They both contain a diaphragm that responds to acoustic vibrations. Unless they had this function, they could not fail to transmit information about sounds. Hence, they could not be said to represent sounds.

Arguably, nothing can have a function unless it has a history. More precisely, nothing can have a function unless it results from some historical process of selection. The historical process of selection is the source of the device's design. Selection processes are design processes. Thus, according to 'teleosemantic' theories, design is the main source of function and content depends on informational function. Such theories are called teleosemantic theories in virtue of the connection between design or teleology and content.

Now, selection processes can be intentional or non-intentional. Mental representations derive their informational functions from a *non*-intentional selection process. The paradigmatic non-intentional process is the mechanism of natural selection by which Darwin explained the phylogenetic evolution of species: natural selection sorts organisms that survive, but no intentional agent is responsible for the sorting. The process of natural selection, is, as Kitcher (1993) puts it, a design process 'without a designer'. The sensory mechanisms of human and non-human animals have informational functions: the visual system, the auditory system, the olfactory system, the tactile system are complex biological systems. They have been recruited by natural selection because they carry information about different specific sets of properties that were instantiated in the environment of human ancestors and early humans in the course of evolution.

In fact, according to the so-called 'etiological' theory of functions—argued for by Wright (1973) and defended by many teleosemanticists such as Millikan (1984, 1993) and Neander (1995)—functions are selected effects. The function or functions of a device must be effects of the device: they must be things that the device can do. What a representational device represents depends on its informational functions. Its informational functions in turn depend on what properties the device can carry information about. The properties a device carries information about are properties the device is nomically correlated with.

An artifact containing a column of mercury responds to pressure. Knowing this, we can use such a device to represent variations in altitude. But variations in the height of a column of mercury are correlated with variations in atmospheric pressure. Which properties an animal's sensory system responds to is not up for us to decide.[4]

Since it cannot reliably discriminate between flies and the movements of lead pellets, the frog's visual system represents small black moving dots, not flies. Frogs feed on flies, not on lead pellets, but they catch flies by means of the visual representation of small black moving dots. The point was made by Fodor (1987: 131–2) in relation to the perceptual environment of male sticklebacks. Male sticklebacks detect sexually active male competing sticklebacks by their characteristic red spot. Upon detecting the characteristic red spot on a sexually active male stickleback, another male stickleback will respond by a no less characteristic display of territorial behavior. But, as Fodor (*ibid.*) puts it, 'the stupidity of the whole arrangement is immediately manifest when an experimenter introduces an arbitrary red object into the scene. It turns out that practically anything red elicits the territorial display; a breeding stickleback male will take Santa Claus for a rival'. The visual system of male sticklebacks represents the presence of red spots, not the presence of other sexually active male sticklebacks.

The sand scorpion is a nocturnal animal: at night, it emerges from its burrow to feed and to mate. It feeds on anything that it can hold onto long enough to paralyze with its neurotoxic sting located at the end of its tail. As discussed by Brownell (1984), it lacks sophisticated visual, auditory and olfactory detection mechanisms: 'covering all eight of the animal's eyes with opaque paint had no effect on either the scorpion's sensitivity to threatening stimuli or on the accuracy with which it turned toward them. Inserting sound-absorbent tiles between the stimulus and the scorpion also did not affect its responses'. A moth held squirming in the air a few centimeters from a scorpion fails to attract its attention. Brownell (1984) reports that the sand scorpion has tarsal hairs and basitarsal slit sensilla at the end of its legs, whose sensory neurons detect vibrations produced in the sand by either prey or predators. Insects cause vibrations in the sand. But so do gentle disturbances of the sand intentionally produced with a twig by an experimental scorpion-psychologist. Vibrations in the sand produced by the motion of a twig do trigger a scorpion's attack. The sensory mechanisms available to the sand scorpion do not allow it to discriminate the vibrations produced by an insect from those produced by a twig. Although the sand scorpion feeds on insects, not on twigs, nonetheless what the sand scorpion's receptors represent are vibrations in the sand, not the insects that cause them.

Dolphins are known to have a sonar system that is sensitive to the geometric shapes of objects. Suppose with Dretske (1990a) that we train a dolphin to discriminate shapes exhibited in water. Suppose that the dolphin learns to recognize all, and only, cylindrical objects in the water. Suppose, further, that all and only the cylindrical objects that have been included in the sample to which the dolphin has been exposed are made in plastic. The dolphin has learned to discriminate cylindrical objects and although all the cylindrical objects that the dolphin is able to recognize are made of plastic, still the dolphin has not learned to recognize plastic objects. Why? Simply because the sensory

---

[4]Some philosophers, e.g. Dennett (1987) and Searle (1992), disagree and argue that there is no fact of the matter as to what the function(s) is of a biological organ.

mechanism that allows the dolphin to recognize shapes is a sonar system. This sensory mechanism is sensitive to the shape, not to the chemical structure of objects.[5]

All four examples—the frog, the stickleback, the sand scorpion and the dolphin— show the need for careful investigation of the sensitivity of an animal's sensory *mechanisms*. It is not enough to know what a predator feeds on in order to know how its sensory system represents its prey. Property G matters to the survival of the animal (e.g. a sexually active male competitor or an insect to capture). The animal's sensory mechanism, however, responds to instantiations of property F, not property G. Often enough in the animal's ecology, instantiations of F coincide with instantiations of G. So detecting an F is a good cue if what enhances the animal's fitness is to produce a behavioral response in the presence of a G. But the animal does not represent G as such. The correlational or informational part of the teleosemantic account of mental representations is precisely designed to take into account the capacities of the sensory mechanisms.[6]

Only if a system is tuned to respond reliably to instantiations of F will it be able to tell if F is being instantiated. In fact, as we said above, the correlational or informational component of the teleosemantic approach underlies the practice of much cognitive neuroscience, whose project is to map the electrophysiological activity of some selected brain area onto the instantiation of some specific property. As we said above, when cognitive neuroscientists speak of the pattern of neural discharge as 'coding' for a given property, they rely on a correlational or informational relation between some brain area and the exemplification of a given property in the brain's environment. Reliability, however, does not mean infallibility: misfiring may occur at some stage in the system.

Thus, the primate visual system evolved because it had the ability to carry information about the size, shape, orientation, internal structure, contours, texture, color, spatial position, distance and motion of objects. Ancestors of humans with such visual abilities survived in the competition against creatures with different visual abilities. As a result of natural selection, the human visual system has acquired the biological function to carry information about such properties. As much contemporary cognitive neuroscience of vision has taught us (see, e.g. Zeki 1993), different visual attributes of objects are processed in separate cortical areas in the visual brain of primates: neurons in area V3 respond to moving shapes; neurons in area V4 respond to colors; neurons in areas MT and V5 are specialized for the processing of motion. Each of these distinct brain areas has been shaped by evolution and selected for responding to specific

---

[5]Here we are claiming that the contents of the representations delivered by such a sensory system as a frog's visual system or a dolphin's sonar system are sharply constrained by the psychophysics of the sensory mechanisms. As we shall see in Chapter 5, although the contents of human visual perceptual representations too are constrained by the kinds of properties (size, shape, texture, orientation, color, etc.) that the human visual system has been designed to process, it does not follow that humans cannot visually represent the cheerfulness, sadness, threat or anger of a conspecific's face. No doubt one can come to believe through visual perception that a face is cheerful, sad, threatening or angry. One can visually represent a face *as* (or see *that* a face is) cheerful, sad, threatening or angry (see Chapter 7). Humans can do this because they have the resources to move from non-epistemic to epistemic visual perception (see Introduction and Chapter 5).

[6]According to *pure* teleological views, such as Millikan's (1984, 1993), the animal's sensory mechanism represents what enhances the animal's overall fitness, i.e. property G, not F. By not taking into account the mechanisms involved in the production of sensory representations, such accounts adopt an exaggerated version of adaptationism. See Jacob (1997, 2001) for more details.

visual attributes. As a result of a lesion in one area of the visual system, the visual system may fail to perform one of its particular informational functions: it may fail to carry reliable information about the shape, color, texture, position or motion of objects. As a result of a lesion in a highly specific brain area, a human patient will fail to experience, e.g. color in the case of achromatopsia, shape in the case of visual-form agnosia, motion in the case of akinetopsia.

According to RTVM then, the phenomenal qualities of an experience are the properties that objects are represented as having in the experience. The phenomenal properties of a visual experience are the 'intentional' properties the visual stimulus is represented as exhibiting by the experience itself. Visual experiences have a distinctive phenomenology different from the phenomenology of experiences in different modalities because the human visual system has been selected to respond to basic properties of objects that are different from the basic properties of objects to which the other human sensory systems have been selected to respond. Visual perception makes us aware of such fundamental properties of objects as their size, orientation, shape, color, texture, spatial position, distance and motion, all at once. So colors can be seen but they cannot be smelled, heard or touched. By contrast, sounds can be heard but they cannot be seen. Pressure can be felt but it cannot be seen either.[7]

What are crucial to *visual* phenomenology are those attributes of objects that can be processed visually and not otherwise (i.e. not by audition, smell or touch). One and the same object (e.g. a violin) can exemplify properties that can be processed in different modalities. Obviously, one thing is to see a violin. Something else is to hear the sound of a violin.

Now, the question arises: are there not properties of objects that can be processed in more than one sensory modality? For example, the shape of an object can be seen and it can also be touched or felt. Nonetheless, it might be objected, seeing the shape of a cube and touching it are very different phenomenal experiences. What it is like to see a cube is clearly different from what it is like to touch it. If so, then does it not follow that the phenomenology of sensory experience cannot be identified with the property the object is represented as having in the experience? No, it does not because there is indeed a difference between the way vision and touch present the shape of a cube. A normally sighted person will not see the shape of the cube without seeing its color. But by feeling the shape of a cube, one does not thereby feel its color. So although the shape of an object can be both seen and felt, still the phenomenal experience of seeing the shape differs from the phenomenal experience of feeling it because only the former will reveal the color of the object whose shape is being seen.[8]

Hence, the difference in the phenomenal character of seeing a shape and feeling it can be made to square with the representational view of the visual mind: the difference in phenomenal character arises from a difference between the visual and the tactile representation of the shape. Indeed, although the property represented by vision and by touch might be the same, the visual perceptual mode of perceiving shape differs from the tactile perceptual mode of perceiving it.

---

[7]As it will turn out, in order to capture the fine-grained non-conceptual content of a visual perceptual representation, which property is being represented will not suffice. We shall introduce the notion of a visual perceptual mode of presentation.

[8]See Chapter 5 for an extended discussion.

2   Visual intentionalism, sense-data and disjunctivism

According to RTVM, visual perception consists in forming and transforming mental representations. Now, the appeal to mental representations is traditional in the philosophy of visual perception: it is at the core of 'sense-datum' theories. Conversely, several contemporary philosophers, who subscribe to direct realism, have expressed scepticism towards the appeal to mental representations in cognitive science. Thus, Putnam (1994: 453) writes:

[...] in contemporary cognitive science, for example, it is the fashion to hypothezise the existence of 'representations' in the cerebral computer. If one assumes that the mind is an organ, and one goes on to identify the mind with the brain, it will become irresistible to (1) think of some of the 'representations' as analogous to the classical theorist's 'impressions' (the cerebral computer, or mind, makes inferences from at least some of the 'representations', the outputs of the perceptual processes, just as the mind makes inferences from impressions, on the classical story), and (2) to think that those 'representations' are linked to objects in the organism's environment only causally, and not cognitively (just as impressions were linked to 'external objects' only causally, and not cognitively).

   At one extreme of the spectrum of views in the philosophy of perception, lie sense-datum theories. At the other extreme lie direct realist views. According to the former, visual perception consists in being aware of visual sense-data. Sense-data are mental 'impressions' that bear the properties one is aware of in visual perception. The latter embrace a radical form of externalism according to which we should give up the very idea of an 'interface' between the mind and the world. But, as it will turn out, the price to pay for giving up the idea of an interface between the mind and the world seems to be that the world itself turns out to be mind-dependent. In this section, we want to examine precisely the respects in which RTVM—or visual intentionalism—differs from both of these extreme views.

2.1   Sense-data and the argument from illusion

Visual perception gives rise to subjective experiences with a peculiar phenomenal character and it yields objective knowledge of the world. It is not surprising therefore that issues of visual phenomenology have been, and still are, intertwined with epistemological issues in the philosophy of visual perception. The epistemological goal of much traditional philosophy of perception has been to locate a secure foundation upon which to erect the rest of human knowledge. Many philosophers have assigned this foundational epistemological role to the concept of a *sense-datum*. Thus, Russell (1911) famously distinguished between 'knowledge by acquaintance' and 'knowledge by description'. Since one can be acquainted with individuals or particulars, knowledge by acquaintance is non-propositional knowledge of objects. Unlike knowledge by acquaintance, knowledge by description is propositional knowledge of facts about objects. Thus, being simpler, knowledge by acquaintance is epistemologically prior to knowledge by description. The latter depends or supervenes on the former. According to Russell, however, genuine knowledge by acquaintance is not knowledge of ordinary physical objects: it is knowledge of mind-dependent or mental entities called 'sense-data'. As Russell (1911: 73) wrote:

[...] in the presence of my table I am acquainted with the sense-data that make up the appearance of my table—its color, shape, hardness, smoothness, etc.; all these are things of which I am immediately conscious when I am seeing and touching my table. The particular shade of color that I am seeing may have many things said about it—I may say that it is brown, that it is rather dark, and so on. But such statements, though they make me know truths *about* the color, do not make me know the color itself any better than I did before; so far as concerns knowledge of the color itself as opposed to knowledge about truths about it, I know the color perfectly and completely when I see it, and no further knowledge of it itself is even theoretically possible. Thus, the sense-data which make up the appearance of my table are things with which I have acquaintance, things immediately known to me just as they are.

On Russell's view then, visual sense-data are mental (or mind-dependent) entities. Unlike mind-independent physical objects, they can be directly known by introspection and with full Cartesian certainty. The mind is acquainted with nothing as fully and intimately as it is with itself. Visual sense-data are mental particulars and they have properties such as color and shape. So each of us is directly acquainted with one's visual sense-data and their properties. On the one hand, knowledge of truths about sense-data is indirect and depends on the more primitive introspective non-propositional acquaintance with them. On the other hand, propositional knowledge about mind-independent physical objects is achieved, if at all, by inference from knowledge of truths about sense-data. On Russell's view of acquaintance, the mind cannot be acquainted with mind-independent physical objects at all. Knowledge of, or about, mind-independent physical objects can only be knowledge by description, i.e. propositional knowledge. Knowledge of, or about, mind-independent objects is thus twice indirect: it derives from knowledge of truths about sense-data, which in turn depends on our prior acquaintance with sense-data. The chief epistemological motivation for postulating such mind-dependent entities as sense-data is that the mind can be directly acquainted with them and the process of acquaintance cannot go wrong. Acquaintance with mental entities provides an epistemically secure (though private and non-propositional) foundation upon which to erect the rest of human knowledge about the non-mental world.

Philosophers of perception, however, have had a second convergent motivation for postulating sense-data. As we pointed out in the previous section, only a device that may fail to give rise to veridical representations deserves to be called a representational system. Much traditional philosophy of perception has traded on the fact that the human perceptual system does not provide infallible knowledge of mind-independent objects. Sense-datum theory postulates that knowledge of sense-data is infallible. But perceptual knowledge of mind-independent objects is not. Thus, sense-datum theories have exploited the so-called 'argument from illusion', which, as we shall explain, is misleadingly so-called.

From a subjective point of view, the visual phenomenal appearances may perfectly well, it is claimed, be indistinguishable, whether the visual perception of mind-independent objects is veridical or not. Whether our visual experience of a non-mental object is veridical or not, there is something it is like to have it: something goes on in our minds in both veridical and non-veridical visual experiences. Something, therefore, is 'present to our minds' in both veridical and non-veridical visual perception. Since the visual appearances may be indistinguishable in both veridical and non-veridical visual perception, what is present to our minds, it is argued, must be common to veridical and to non-veridical cases of visual perception. Given that in non-veridical perception, it may be the case that no mind-independent entity is presented to the mind, it follows that what is present to the mind in both veridical and non-veridical cases of visual perception is a mental sense-datum.

As Austin (1962) has pointed out in his devastating criticism of Ayer's (1940) version of the argument from illusion, much of its force depends upon a confusion between two quite distinct kinds of misperception: visual *illusions* and visual *hallucinations* (or as Austin calls them 'delusions'). As it will turn out in Chapter 4, in some circumstances, normally sighted people undergo size-contrast illusions such as the Ponzo illusion, the Müller–Lyer illusion or the Titchener circles illusion. Every normally sighted human being does. As we shall see in Chapter 4, size-contrast illusions arise from the attempt on the part of the visual perceptual system to maintain size constancy across a visual display containing elements of various relative sizes. In Austin's words:

[...] when I see an optical illusion [...] the illusion is not a little (or a large) peculiarity or idiosyncrasy of my own; it is quite public, anyone can see it, and in many cases, standard procedures can be laid down for producing it.

The argument from illusion, which would be better called 'the argument from delusion', can only go through if visual illusions are *delusive*, i.e. if as Austin (1962: 23–5) puts it, having a visual illusion consists in 'conjuring up' something 'immaterial'.

In fact, not only does the argument from illusion seem to involve a confusion between visual illusions and delusions, but it seems committed to subsuming under the category of illusions something that is not an illusion at all, namely seeing one's reflection in a mirror. From the fact that one sees one's face *in* a mirror, it does not follow, as Austin (*ibid.*, 31) notes, that one's face is actually located either in or behind the mirror. A proponent of the sense-datum theory would argue that what one sees then is a sense-datum. Following Tye (1995: 111–12), we would rather argue that this is evidence in favor of RTVM, i.e. that visual perception is *representing*. From the fact that one has a pain in one's left toe, and from the fact that one's left toe is in one's left shoe, it does not follow that the pain is in one's left shoe (or that there is a pain in one's left shoe). Nor does this show that the English preposition 'in' is ambiguous between a spatial and a non-spatial meaning. What it shows rather is that there is, as Tye (1995: 12) puts it, 'a hidden intensionality in statements of pain location'—as talk of pain in phantoms limbs confirms.

In this respect, visual experiences are like beliefs: they are mental representations. All representations are, in Quine's (1953) terms, *intensional* or *referentially opaque*. There are two criteria for referential opacity or intensionality. First, in belief contexts, co-referential expressions are not always substitutable *salva veritate*. Thus, one can believe that Cicero is bald and fail to believe that Tully is bald, even though 'Cicero' and 'Tully' are names of one and the same individual. Second, the rule of existential generalization does not always apply to beliefs: from the fact that someone believes that there are unicorns, it does not follow that there is any unicorn. Similarly, one can have a pain in one's left hand even though one's left hand has been amputated. On Tye's (1995) representationalist account, a phantom limb pain in one's amputated left hand is a mental *representation* of one's left hand. There need not be a left hand for one to represent it. Similarly, seeing one's face in the mirror is evidence that visual perception is forming a visual representation of one's face. From the fact that one sees one's face in a mirror, it does not follow that one's face is located inside the mirror. That there is 'hidden intensionality' in reports of visual experiences, therefore, argues in favor of a representational view of visual experiences.

The argument from illusion starts from a standard case of a visual illusion, e.g. seeing a straight stick partly immersed in water as being bent. It then raises the puzzle of how something could be both 'crooked' and 'straight' without really changing its shape. Finally, it reaches the conclusion that 'at least some of the visual appearances are delusive'. As Austin (1962: 29) incisively writes:

[...] of this case Ayer says (a) that since the stick looks bent but is straight, 'at least one of the visual appearances of the stick is *delusive*'; and (b) that 'what we see [directly anyway] is not the real quality of [...] a material thing'. Well now: does the stick 'look bent' to begin with? I think we can agree that it does, we have no better way of describing it. But of course it does not look exactly like a bent stick, a bent stick out of water—at most, it may be said to look rather like a bent stick partly immersed *in* water. After all, we can't help seeing the water the stick is partly immersed in. So exactly what in this case is supposed to be *delusive*? What is wrong, what is even faintly surprising, in the idea of a stick's being straight but looking bent sometimes? Does anyone suppose that if something is straight, then it jolly well has to *look* straight at all times and in all circumstances? Obviously no one seriously supposes this.

The first crucial assumption in the argument from illusion is that veridical visual perception is the perception of 'material things' or, as Austin (*ibid.*: 8) calls them, 'moderate-sized specimens of dry goods'. The first assumption is that unless one sees a 'material thing', the visual appearances must be misleading or deceptive: the alternative is between the veridical seeing of 'material things' and the deceptive seeing of 'immaterial' (or 'unreal') ones. Either visual perception is veridical or it is not. If the former, then it is of 'material things'. If the latter, then it is of 'immaterial' or 'unreal' things. Thus, what Austin calls the 'bogus dichotomy' between the veridical perception of material things and its alleged alternative is supposed to prepare the ground for the second step in the argument. Whether they count as 'material things' or not, one can see rivers, substances, gases, vapors, mountains, flames, clouds, smoke, shadows, holes, pictures, movies and arguably events.[9]

The second step in the 'argument from illusion' trades on the confusion between visual illusions and visual hallucinations or delusions. Unlike seeing a straight stick partly immersed in water as being bent, seeing pink rats is suffering from a delusion. As Austin (*ibid.*: 23) argues, delusions are entirely different from visual illusions in that they involve high-level conceptual cognitive processes:

Typical cases would be delusions of persecution, delusions of grandeur. These are primarily a matter of grossly disordered beliefs (and so, probably, behavior) and may well have nothing in particular to do with perception. But I think we might also say that the patient who sees pink rats has (suffers from) delusions—particularly, no doubt, if, as would probably be the case, he is clearly aware that his pink rats aren't real rats.

Unlike visual illusions, which are pure perceptual processes and depend on perceptual constancy mechanisms, hallucinations involve (conceptual) belief-forming mechanisms.

---

[9]See Austin's (1962: 8) list.

As Dennett (1991) has noticed, 'reports of very strong hallucinations are rare'. Phantom-limb pains are genuine cases of hallucination. But by Dennett's (1991: 8) lights, they are weak, since they come in a single sensory modality: amputees *feel* their phantom-limbs, but they do not see, hear or smell them. Instances of genuine visual hallucinations, let alone multi-modal ones, are harder to come by than traditional philosophers of perception have been prone to assume.[10]

According to Dennett's (1991: 8–17) model, hallucinations involve a lowering of the subject's epistemic threshold for gullibility. For some reason (e.g. sensory deprivation, acute pain, extreme fear or trauma), subjects may lower their epistemic standards and become epistemically 'passive'. As a result, 'they feel no desire to probe, challenge or query' the incoming information. Instead, 'they just stand and marvel' at it. If so, then 'the brain must do whatever it takes to *assuage epistemic hunger* [...]. If our brains can just satisfy all our particular epistemic hungers as they arise, we will never find ground for complaint'.

Thus, it is one thing to misperceive some actual object as exemplifying a property that the object does not really instantiate (illusion). It is another thing to have a visual experience in which 'something totally unreal is conjured up' (delusion). Only in the latter case, would one fail to stand in some relation to a mind-independent object. Not only does the 'argument from illusion' trade on the confusion between visual illusions and visual hallucinations, but the conclusion of the argument presupposes that in all cases of visual experiences, veridical as well as non-veridical, some 'object' must exist. Since in non-veridical hallucinatory experiences, a mind-independent 'material' object fails to exist, according to the argument from illusion, it follows that some mind-dependent (purely mental) object must be present in non-veridical cases. Finally, since the visual appearances are allegedly indistinguishable whether the experience is veridical or not, the conclusion is that in all cases of visual perception, what one perceives is a mental sense-datum.

2.2 Disjunctivism and the rejection of an interface between mind and world

In virtue of what Putnam (1994: 445–6) calls 'a familiar pattern of recoil that causes philosophy to leap from one frying pan to fire, from fire to a different frying pan, from a different frying pan to a different fire', sense-datum theories have prompted a 'direct' or 'naive' realist response. Once sense-data are postulated as mental intermediaries between the human mind and mind-independent objects, it seems as if knowledge of mind-independent objects will forever remain inaccessible. Thus, the direct realist 'recoil' is a response to the threat of scepticism involved in sense-datum theories. As Martin (2001: 12) puts it, 'a familiar objection to sense-datum theories of perception is that they introduce entities which act as a "veil of perception" between us and the external world; and it is often suggested that the putative presence of such a veil would lead to insuperable sceptical problems'. The threat is that, if all we are aware of in visual perception is the 'veil' of mental representations, then knowledge of mind-independent

---

[10]In some pathological cases, hallucinations can be stronger than Dennett seems to allow. See in Chapter 3 our discussion of somatoparaphrenia subsequent to right parietal lesions.

objects is bound to escape us. As Putnam (1994: 453) says on behalf of direct (or 'naive') realism, 'the disaster is the idea that there has to be an interface between our cognitive powers and the external world—or, to put the same point differently, the idea that our cognitive powers cannot reach all the way to the objects themselves'.

In order to avoid the threat of scepticism, direct realists espouse what they call a 'disjunctive' account of visual experience. The disjunctive account is so-called because it claims that visual experiences differ according to whether they are veridical or not. On this view, there is no common factor between veridical and non-veridical visual experiences. According to McDowell (1982), a leading exponent of 'disjunctivism', so-called 'highest common factor' conceptions of visual appearances are internalist theories: they rely on the alleged subjective indistinguishability between veridical and non-veridical cases of visual perception. What makes the sense-datum theory a 'highest common factor' conception of visual appearances is that, according to the sense-datum theory, there is a unique mental state that is the 'highest common factor' between veridical and non-veridical cases of visual perception. According to the sense-datum theory, there is a common 'narrow' phenomenological subjective content shared by veridical and non-veridical visual experiences, which consists in having in mind or perceiving a mind-dependent entity, i.e. a visual sense-datum.

It is quite clear that McDowell's motivation for espousing a disjunctive account of visual appearances is to circumvent the risk of scepticism involved in postulating a veil of mental intermediaries between the human mind and the world of mind-independent objects. According to disjunctivism, the 'highest common factor' conception of visual appearances leads to scepticism. Thus, it is the task of disjunctivism to deny the existence of mental representations with a 'narrow' content common to veridical and to non-veridical visual experiences in order to avoid the threat of scepticism. The disjunctive account makes a sharp distinction among visual experiences according to whether they make a mind-independent fact manifest to the mind or not. On the disjunctive account, there is a gap between the fact that an object looks a certain way to an observer and its seeming to an observer as if something looks a certain way. As McDowell (1982: 211) puts it:

[. . .] an appearance that such-and-such is the case can be *either* a mere appearance *or* the fact made manifest to someone [. . .] the object of experience in the deceptive case is a mere appearance. But we are not to accept that in the non-deceptive case too the object of experience is a mere appearance, and hence something that falls short of the fact itself. On the contrary, we are to insist that the appearance that is presented to one in those cases is a matter of the fact itself being disclosed to the experiencer. So appearances are no longer conceived as in general intervening between the experiencing subject and the world.

As Snowdon (1980–81: 186) puts it:

[. . .] the disjunctive picture divides what makes looks ascriptions true into two classes. In cases where there is no sighting they are made true by a state of affairs intrinsically independent of surrounding objects; but in cases of sightings the truth-conferring state of affairs involves the surrounding objects.

On this view then, there is a primitive contrast between the veridical perception of a mind-independent fact and cases of non-veridical perception where no mind-independent fact is made manifest to the human mind.

Thus, disjunctivism starts from the radical metaphysical realist assumption that the goal of visual perception it to make mind-independent facts available to the human mind. In order to capture the very idea of a mind-independent fact being made manifest to the human mind, McDowell (1982) appeals to the idea of the mind's 'direct open-ness to the world'. This idea of the human mind being directly open to the world is the precursor of Putnam's (1994) claim that 'the disaster is the idea that there has to be an interface between our cognitive powers and the external world'. Only if human minds are distinct from mind-independent facts can there be an interface between the former and the latter. Only at the cost of denying the interface between the world and the human mind can the latter be 'directly open' to the former. Indeed, in his more recent writings, McDowell (1994) seems to give up the very idea of mind-independent facts altogether: the world has become mind-dependent.

In his recent writings, McDowell (1994) rejects what he calls 'bald naturalism' and argues for what he calls a 're-enchanted' version of naturalism. According to McDowell (1994), 'bald naturalism' relies on the dualism between 'the space of natural law' and 'the space of human reasons'. This dualism has given rise to a picture in which nature turns out to be 'disenchanted'. Against the bald naturalistic dualism between the realm of law and the realm of reasons, McDowell (1994: 85–8) recommends explicitly that we replace the 'disenchanted' picture of nature by what he calls 'second nature', in which 'meaning is not a mysterious gift from outside nature'. Only by projecting the mind onto the world can the limitations of bald naturalism be overwhelmed. Only if the world is itself mind-dependent, it seems, can what Grice (1957) called 'non-natural meaning' be part of the world. But then if non-natural meaning is as much in the natural world as nat-ural meaning is, why call the former *non*-natural? As we argued above, as natural mean-ing and natural signs arise from correlations, they are ubiquitous. Non-natural meaning or the content of representations is not. So it seems as if one would avoid the threat of scep-ticism at the cost of denying both the very notion of mind-independent objects and the very distinction between information and representation. McDowell (1994) does not offer a solution to the threat of scepticism consistent with metaphysical realism. He gives up metaphysical realism. If so, then the question is: how much comfort is it?

If one thinks, as we do, that 're-enchantment' of the kind McDowell (1994) is urging, is simply not compatible with naturalism, then one will better stick to the idea of an interface between mind and the world. We like RTVM precisely because we think that it avoids the pitfalls of both sense-datum theory and disjunctivism. RTVM is often called 'intentionalism' because it makes the basic claim that the content of a visual experience crucially depends upon the 'intentional' properties that the experience represents objects as having. According to the teleosemantic version of visual inten-tionalism sketched above, the human visual system has been selected by evolution for carrying information about (or for processing) a particular class of properties instanti-ated in the environment of early humans. According to visual intentionalism, what matters to a visual experience—what makes it the experience that it is—are the *properties* that are represented in the experience, not the particular objects that happen to exemplify the properties. What matters are the properties to which the visual system has been tuned by evolution. This is why in visual hallucinations, the visual mind can only 'conjure up' the representation of *visual* properties, not the representation of auditive, olfactory or tactile properties. In non-veridical visual experiences, the visual mind can only represent misleadingly the properties that it is its function to carry information about.

Visual intentionalism and disjunctivism advocated by direct realists both reject the two basic claims of sense-datum theory, namely that in visual perception, the mind is acquainted with mind-dependent sense-data and that all knowledge of mind-independent facts is derivative from the mind's acquaintance with sense-data. Furthermore, visual intentionalism and direct realism reject an introspective implication of the sense-datum theory. According to the sense-datum theory, as alluded to in Russell's (1911) quotation above, introspection should make one aware of the subjective qualities of one's visual experiences (or sense-data). But as advocates of visual intentionalism, Harman (1990) and Tye (1992), have pointed out, visual experiences are 'transparent' or 'diaphanous'. As Martin (2001: 3) writes:

When I stare at the straggling lavender bush at the end of my street, I can attend to the variegated colors and shapes of leaves and branches [...]. But I can also reflect on what it is like for me now to be staring at the bush [...]. When my attention is directed out at the world, the lavender bush and its features occupy center stage. It is also notable that when my attention is turned inwards instead to my experience, the bush is not replaced by some other entity belonging to the inner realm of the mind in contrast to the run-down public sphere of North London.

Introspection of one's visual experience does not reveal any intrinsic property of one's experience: what it reveals is what the experience is *about* or what the experience is an experience *of*. So far, visual intentionalism and the disjunctivism of direct realism can agree against the sense-datum theory.

Thus, our brand of visual intentionalism accepts, while sense-datum theory denies, that mind-independent objects *can* be presented to the mind in visual experiences. According to visual intentionalism, unless such visual properties as shape, orientation, color, texture, motion had been instantiated by mind-independent objects in the environment of early humans, the human visual system could not have carried information about them, let alone been selected to do so by evolution. Our brand of visual intentionalism denies, while sense-datum theory asserts, that what is represented in visual experiences *must* actually exist. According to sense-datum theory, what exists in all cases is a mental (or mind-dependent) entity. Visual intentionalism accepts it that in visual delusion (or hallucination), nothing exemplifies the properties that are represented in the visual experience. Disjunctivism agrees with visual intentionalism, against sense-datum theory, that in visual experience, mind-independent facts and objects *can* be represented. According to disjunctivism, however, mind-independent facts and objects *must* be represented for a visual experience to be a genuine visual experience. On this point, visual intentionalism and disjunctivism part company: according to visual intentionalism, visual experiences are *not* required to make mind-independent facts manifest to the mind. They can, but they do not have to.[11]

---

[11]In Section 2.2, our goal has been to dissociate our version of the representational theory of the visual mind ('visual intentionalism') from both 'direct realism' and 'sense-datum' approaches. In particular, we have addressed the worry that 'visual intentionalism' might commit us to some version of the 'sense-datum fallacy'. We have not yet addressed directly the view of anti-representationalist philosophers who think that there are subjective, phenomenal non-representational properties of visual experiences or that its representational properties do not exhaust the phenomenal character of a visual experience. Nor do we claim that anti-representationalism in this sense is committed to the 'sense-datum fallacy'. We shall deal with a version of anti-representationalism, which we call phenomenal realism, at the end of Chapter 5.

2.3 The challenge of the homunculus

Finally, RTVM raises a puzzle: the puzzle of the homunculus. A non-mental representation (an artifact), such as a painting, has both representational and non-representational intrinsic physical and chemical properties. A physical picture will not reveal its non-mental pictorial content unless an intentional observer looks at it and his or her visual system causally interacts with the picture's intrinsic properties. As Ramachandran and Blakeslee (1998: 66) have noticed, the model of the physical picture leads to the assumption that 'there is a screen somewhere inside the brain where images are displayed'. This assumption in turn leads to an infinite regress for 'if you were to display an image [...] on an internal neural screen, you'd need another little person inside the brain to see that image. And that won't solve the problem either because you'd need yet another, even tinier person inside his head to view that image, and so on and so forth, ad infinitum'. So the puzzle for the representational theory of the visual mind is: how could anything in a person's visual brain be a mental representation unless a homunculus sitting in the person's brain looks at it and perceives its intrinsic neurophysiological properties? How could the discharge of neurons in a person's visual cortex represent anything unless something or someone could perceive their intrinsic properties?

The answer to this puzzle is that, according to RTVM, there is a basic asymmetry between mental representations and representational artifacts. Perceiving a representational artifact consists in detecting its intrinsic properties: one will not be aware of the content of a representational artifact unless one perceives its intrinsic properties. To be visually aware of the content of a picture is to come to know a fact about the picture by visual means. To be visually aware of the content of a picture is to know (hence believe) that it represents, e.g. a ship, a tiger, a house or a tree. In Chapter 5, we shall call this knowledge 'primary epistemic seeing'. One comes to know what a picture represents by seeing the picture: i.e. in virtue of non-epistemically seeing shapes, contours and patches of colors on a two-dimensional canvas. The visual experience consists in seeing the two-dimensional shapes, contours and patches of colors. One cannot see shapes, contours and patches of colors unless one is caused to do so in virtue of responding to the intrinsic properties of the canvas.

Like representational artifacts, mental representations too have intrinsic properties. However—and this is crucial—contrary to the sense-datum theory, according to visual intentionalism, when one visually perceives two-dimensional colors and shapes laid out on a canvas, there is literally nothing *in* the perceiver's brain with the properties of the canvas: there is no sense-datum in the perceiver's brain with the colors and shapes of the canvas. In the brain, there is only electrical activity. So in processing a visual stimulus, one becomes aware of properties of the canvas and the processing in the brain is patterns of electrical activity—it is not an inner perception of mental sense-data. In processing a visual stimulus, one does not become aware of one's percept. The percept represents a physical object and the formation of the percept is the result of the electrical activity of the brain.

This is not to say that one cannot become aware of one's mental representations. For one thing, with the use of sophisticated contemporary techniques of brain imagery, it becomes possible to detect the intrinsic properties of mental representations and as a result to visualize the activities of the brain. But visualizing the activity of a brain area during a perceptual task is not visualizing what is perceived in the task. For example, if a subject perceives a visual token of the word 'cat' in a task of brain imagery, by perceiving an image of the subject's brain activity during the task, one will not thereby see that what the subject was perceiving was a token of the word 'cat'. Nor, as Harman (1990) and Tye (1992) have emphasized, does visual perception consist in becoming aware of one's own visual percept: in Harman's (1990) words, it is a fallacy (the 'sense-datum fallacy') to assume that 'one's awareness of the color of a strawberry is mediated by one's awareness of an intrinsic feature of a perceptual representation'. In perceiving a lavender bush, one is aware of the bush, not of the percept. This is what we called above the 'transparency of experience': visual percepts are 'diaphanous'.[12]

The basic asymmetry between mental representations and representational artifacts can be stated thus: one cannot be aware of the pictorial content of a picture unless one detects the intrinsic properties of the picture. One becomes visually aware of a tree by forming a visual percept of a tree. This process would not be possible unless one were detecting intrinsic properties of the tree. As a result, one visually perceives properties of the tree, not properties of one's visual percept. To say, as we did above, that representational artifacts derive their contents from the primitive contents of mental representations, is to accept the intentionalist thesis that the perceptual process, whereby one becomes aware of the pictorial content of a picture, consists in the formation and transformation of mental representations. In this process, however, mental representations themselves are not perceived visually or otherwise by anyone or anything. In ordinary visual perception, one does *not* become aware of one's own mental representations: the formation and transformation of mental representations is the process whereby one becomes aware of things and properties in one's environment. Intentionalists can agree with Putnam (1994: 453) when he says: 'We don't *perceive* visual experiences, we *have* them'.

According to visual intentionalism, one becomes aware of properties exemplified in one's environment by means of the mental perceptual representations supplied by one's visual system. In visual perception, one becomes visually aware of one's environment through the process whereby mental representations are formed and transformed. In this process, one does not become aware of them. This is not to deny that by introspection one may become aware of the contents of one's own mental representations. But if one can and if one does, then, according to the representational theory of the mind, one is not made aware of one's mental representations by perceiving them (visually or otherwise). One does not visually perceive one's visual percepts any more than one hears one's auditory percepts. One can only form higher order beliefs about them. One can only come to believe that one is enjoying such and such a visual experience. In having a visual experience, one sees objects, properties and facts (many of which are mind-independent). One's visual experience itself is not something to be seen—neither by oneself nor by anybody else (unless one uses brain imaging techniques). As argued by Rosenthal (1986, 1993) and Shoemaker (1994), one's introspective knowledge of one's own visual mind is metarepresentational, not perceptual.

---

[12]The claim of transparency is restricted to visual perception. We are not claiming that the human mind is introspectively blind to the differences between perceiving, believing, remembering, desiring and intending.

3 Conceptual and non-conceptual content

Mental representations come in several varieties. As we said above, thoughts, judgments, beliefs, desires, perceptual experiences and mental images all are mental representations. Much recent philosophy of mind and perception has been devoted to the distinction between the conceptual contents of thoughts and the non-conceptual contents of perceptual representations. Although the issue is somewhat controversial, we accept the distinction between conceptual and non-conceptual content.[13]

The paradigmatic arguments in favor of the assumption that perceptual representations possess a distinctive kind of content advert to three basic kinds of considerations: first of all, they emphasize the fine-grainedness and the richness of the phenomenology of visually formed perceptual representations, which cannot be matched by concepts mastered by the person having the visual experience. Second, they reject the requirement that unless a creature possesses appropriate concepts matching the detailed texture of her perceptual experience, she will not enjoy the perceptual experience. Finally, they point towards a distinctive link between the fine-grainedness of the non-conceptual content of perceptual experience and the fine-tuning of object-oriented actions. We accept both the distinction between the conceptual content of thought and the non-conceptual content of perceptual experience, and the first pair of considerations in its favor. We subscribe, however, to the fundamental duality between the visual perception of objects and visually guided actions directed towards objects. Therefore, as we already argued in the Introduction, we do not accept what Clark (2001) dubbs 'the assumption of experience-based control' (EBC), i.e. the idea of a constitutive link between the non-conceptual content of visual perceptual experiences and the fine-tuning of visually guided actions.[14]

3.1 The productivity and systematicity of thoughts

As many philosophers of mind and language have argued, what is characteristic of conceptual representations is that they are both productive and systematic. Like sentences of natural languages, thoughts are productive in the sense that they form an open-ended infinite set. Although the lexicon of a natural language is made up of finitely many words, thanks to its syntactic rules, a language contains indefinitely many well-formed sentences. Similarly, an individual may entertain indefinitely many conceptual thoughts. In particular, both sentences of public languages and conceptual thoughts contain such devices as negation, conjunction, disjunction and conditionals. So one can form indefinitely many new thoughts by prefixing a thought by a negation operator, by forming a disjunctive, a conjunctive or a conditional thought out of two simpler thoughts or one can generalize a singular thought by means of quantifiers. Sentences of natural languages are systematic in the sense that if a language contains a sentence S with a syntactic structure, e.g. *Rab*, then it must contain a sentence S' expressing a syntactically related sentence, e.g. *Rba*. An individual's conceptual thoughts are supposed

---

[13]For opposition to the distinction, see e.g. McDowell (1994).
[14]An idea that Clark (2001) rejects.

to be systematic too: if a person has the ability to entertain the thought that, for example, John loves Mary, then she must have the ability to entertain the thought that Mary loves John. If a person can form the thought that *Fa*, then she can form both the thought that *Fb* and the thought that *Ga* (where '*a*' and '*b*' stand for individuals and '*F*' and '*G*' stand for properties). Both Fodor's (1975, 1987) language of thought hypothesis and Evans' (1982) generality constraint are designed to account for the productivity and the systematicity of thoughts, i.e. conceptual representations. It is constitutive of thoughts that they are structured and that they involve conceptual constituents that can be combined and recombined to generate indefinitely many new structured thoughts. Thus, concepts are building blocks with inferential roles.

Because they are productive and systematic, conceptual thoughts can rise above the limitations imposed to perceptual representations by the constraints inherent to perception. Unlike thought, visual perception requires some causal interaction between a source of information and some sensory organs. For example, by combining the concepts *horse* and *horn*, one may form the complex concept *unicorn*, even though no unicorn has or ever will be visually perceived (except in visual works of art). Although no unicorn has ever been perceived, within a fictional context, on the basis of the inferential role of its constituents, one can draw the inference that if something is a unicorn, then it has four legs, it eats grass and it is a mammal.

Hence, possessing concepts must involve the mastery of inferential relations: the latter is an important part of the former.[15] Only a creature with conceptual abilities can draw consequences from her perceptual processing of a visual stimulus. Following Dretske (1969), what we shall call 'epistemic seeing' in Chapter 5, requires conceptual processing of perceptual inputs. Thought and visual perception are clearly different cognitive processes. One can think about numbers and one can form negative, disjunctive, conjunctive and general thoughts involving multiple quantifiers. Although one can visually perceive numerals, one cannot visually perceive numbers. Nor can one visually perceive negative, disjunctive, conjunctive or general facts (corresponding to e.g. universally quantified thoughts).

As Crane (1992a: 152) puts it, 'there is no such thing as deductive inference *between* perceptions'. Upon seeing a brown dog, one can see at once that the animal one faces is a dog and that it is brown. If one perceives a brown animal and one is told that it is a dog, then one can certainly come to believe that the brown animal is a dog or that the dog is brown. But on this hybrid epistemic basis, one thinks or believes, but one does not *see* that the dog is brown. One came to know that the dog is brown by seeing it. But one did not come to know that what is brown is a dog by seeing it.[16] Unlike the content of concepts, the content of visual percepts is not a matter of inferential role. As emphasized by Crane (*ibid.*), this is not to say that the content of visual percepts is amorphous or unstructured. One proposal for capturing the non-conceptual structure of visual percepts is Peacocke's (1992a) notion of a scenario content, i.e. a visual way of filling in space. As we shall see momentarily, one can think or believe of an animal that it is a dog without thinking or believing that it has a color. But one

---

[15]Not everyone agrees. Fodor (1998b), e.g. vehemently denies it and espouses an atomic theory of the contents of concepts.

[16]For extended discussion of the scope and limits of *visual* knowledge, see Chapter 5.

cannot see a dog in broad daylight without seeing its color. We shall try to capture this feature of the content of visual percepts, which is part of their distinctive informational richness, in terms of the distinctive function of visual perceptual mechanisms to produce states that encode information analogically.

3.2 The fine-grainedness and informational richness of visual percepts

Unlike thought, visual perception has a spatial, perspectival, iconic and/or pictorial structure not shared by conceptual thought. Arguably, one can visually perceive dots with no spatial internal structure, but one cannot visually perceive an object unless it has some spatial location or other. The content of visual perception has a spatial perspectival structure that pure thoughts lack. In order to apply the concept of a dog, one does not have to occupy a particular spatial perspective relative to any dog. But one cannot see a dog unless one occupies some spatial standpoint or other relative to it: one cannot see a dog simultaneously from the top and from below, from the front and from the back. The concept of a dog applies indiscriminately to poodles, alsatians, dalmatians or bulldogs. One can think that all European dogs bark. But one cannot see all European dogs bark, let alone all dogs in the world bark. Nor can one see a generic dog bark. One must see some particular dog: a poodle, an alsatian, a dalmatian or a bulldog, as it might be. Although one and the same concept—the concept of a dog—may apply to a poodle, an alsatian, a dalmatian or a bulldog, seeing one of them is a very different visual experience than seeing another. One can think that a dog barks without thinking of any other properties of the dog. One cannot, however, see a dog in broad daylight unless one sees its shape and the colors and texture of its hairs. Of course, in poor illumination conditions (e.g. at night), one might see the shape of a dog while failing to see its color. In still worse illumination conditions, one may also become unable to see the shape and spatial orientation of a dog.

Thus, the content of visual perceptual representations turns out to be both more fine-grained and informationally richer than the conceptual contents of thoughts. There are three paradigmatic cases in which the need to distinguish between conceptual content and the non-conceptual content of visual perceptions may arise. First, a creature may be perceptually sensitive to objective perceptual differences for which she has no concepts. There may be something it is like to enjoy a visual experience of a shape and/or a color for which the creature has no concept. Second, two creatures may enjoy one and the same visual experience, which they may be inclined to conceptualize differently. Finally, two different persons may enjoy two distinct visual experiences in the presence of one and the same distal stimulus to which they may be inclined to apply one and the same concept.

Peacocke (1992b: 67–8) asks us to consider, e.g. a person's visual experience of a range of mountains. As he notices, one might want to conceptualize one's visual experience with the help of concepts of shapes expressible in English with such predicates as 'round' and 'jagged'. But these concepts of shapes could apply to the non-conceptual contents of several different visual experiences prompted by the distinct shapes of several distinct mountains. Arguably, although a human being might not possess any concept of shape whose fine-grainedness could match that of her visual experience of the shape of the mountain, her visual experience of the shape is nonetheless distinctive and it may differ from the visual experience of the distinct shape of a different mountain to which she would apply the very same concept. Similarly, human beings are perceptually sensitive to far more colors than they have color concepts and color names to apply. Although a human being might lack two distinct concepts for two distinct shades of color, she might well enjoy a visual experience of one shade that is distinct from her visual experience of the other shade. As Raffman (1995: 295) puts it, 'discriminations along perceptual dimensions surpasses identification [...] our ability to judge whether two or more stimuli are the same or different surpasses our ability to type-identify them'.

Two persons might enjoy one and the same kind of visual experience prompted by one and the same shape or one and the same color, to which they would be inclined to apply pairs of distinct concepts, such as 'red' vs. 'crimson' or 'polygon' vs. 'square'. If so, it would be justified to distinguish the non-conceptual content of their common visual experience from the different concepts that each would be willing to apply. Conversely, as argued by Peacocke (1998), presented with one and the same geometrical object, two persons might be inclined to apply one and the same generic shape concept, e.g. 'that polygon', and still enjoy different perceptual experiences or see the same object as having different shapes. For example, as Peacocke (1998: 381) points out, 'one and the same shape may be perceived as square, or as diamond-shaped [...] the difference between these ways is a matter of which symmetries of the shape are perceived; though of course the subject himself does not need to know that this is the nature of the difference'. If one mentally partitions a square by bisecting its right angles, one sees it as a diamond. If one mentally partitions it by bisecting its sides, one sees it as a square. Presumably, one does not need the concept of an axis of symmetry to perform mentally these two bisections and enjoy two distinct visual experiences. Arguably, one and the same object with one and the same shape can be perceived as a diamond or as a square. Arguably, seeing it as a square or as a diamond may depend on its orientation relative to the perceiver. So a square tilted at 45° will look like a diamond. But as Peacocke (1992b: 76) points out, if embedded within a larger rectangle sharing the same orientation, the very same object will look like a square tilted at 45° (Fig. 1.1).

Now, the rotation of an object around an axis preserves its shape. So if changing the orientation of an object may change the content of the visual perception of the object, then presumably the shape property itself is not sufficiently fine-grained to individuate the non-conceptual content of the visual experience of the object. In addition to the shape property, we need what Peacocke (1989) calls a particular 'perceptual mode of presentation' of the shape. We earlier mentioned the fact that the way one and the same shape is presented by visual perception differs from the way it is presented by, e.g. touch. For instance, in a visual perceptual experience, the representation of shape interacts with the representation of colors, texture and orientation in a way that is unique to the visual modality. This special kind of interaction among the representations of specific properties, which is unique to normal visual perception, is part of the visual perceptual mode of presentation of the shape property. Arguably, being a square and being a diamond are two ways of exemplifying one and the same shape property, i.e. the same way of being shaped. In Peacocke's (2001) terms then, 'a way in which a shape property may be perceived is to be [...] distinguished from a way of being shaped'. Again and again in Chapter 4, we shall see instances of visual processing of illusory displays

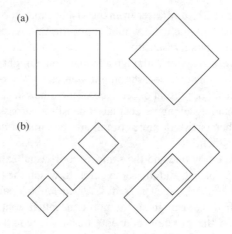

Fig. 1.1 One and the same objective shape can prompt different visual perceptual experiences: (a) the same shape in different orientations is perceived as a square (*left*) or as a regular diamond (*right*); (b) in the proper context, what was perceived as a regular diamond in (a) can be perceived as a tilted square. (From Peacocke 1992a permission sought.)

such that the visual mode of presentation of one and the same shape property (e.g. of a Titchener central disk surrounded by an annulus of either smaller or larger circles than it) varies according to whether the task is a perceptual task or a motor task.

Against this kind of argument in favor of the non-conceptual content of visual experiences, McDowell (1994, 1998) has argued that demonstrative concepts expressible by, e.g. 'that shade of color' or 'that shape', are perfectly suited to capture the fine-grainedness of the visual percept of color and/or shape. We are willing to concede to McDowell that such demonstrative concepts do exist and play an important role in our perceptually based thoughts.

But first of all, we agree with Peacocke (2001) that, unlike perceptual modes of presentation of properties, demonstrative concepts are by their very nature true of the properties of particular objects. In thinking about the shape of an object by means of such a demonstrative concept as 'that shape', one is latching onto a particular object that is demonstrated (or demonstratively referred to) and that happens to exemplify the property expressed by the concept 'shape'. In such a demonstrative thought, the object referred to is being visually perceived, but the shape property is being *thought* about. In fact, the object is not merely being perceived, it is also being *referred* to. The property is being thought about while the object is being visually perceived and referred to. For the concept 'that shape' to be a demonstrative concept, the general concept expressed by 'shape' must apply to the property of a particular object that is both perceived and referred to. Although one cannot perceive the shape of an object unless one perceives the object exemplifying the shape property, what is constitutive of the visual perceptual mode of presentation of the shape of an object is that one represents the shape pictorially. In a visual perceptual mode of presentation, the shape is not thought about; it is visually experienced and pictorially encoded with other visual attributes of the object such as its size, orientation and color. Nor does one have to refer to an object in order to visually experience its shape. Arguably, one cannot visually experience the shape of an object unless one perceives the object. But perceiving an object is one thing; referring to it is another thing. In perceptual experience, information flows from the object towards the perceiver: the object represented causes the representation. Although thought is not always an intentional action, reference in general and demonstrative reference in particular are intentional actions. One's intention to refer causes an object to be referred to. Even attending to an object via visual perception is not the same thing as referring to it. Attending to an object is part of perception. Referring to an object is part of thought.

Second, we agree with Bermudez (1998: 55–7) and Dokic and Pacherie (2001) that such demonstrative concepts would seem to be too weak to perform one of the fundamental jobs that color concepts and shape concepts must be able to perform—namely recognition. Color concepts and shape concepts stored in a creature's memory must allow recognition and re-identification of colors and shapes over long periods of time. Although pure demonstrative color concepts may allow comparison of simultaneously presented samples of color, it is unlikely that they can be used to reliably reidentify one and the same sample over time. Nor presumably could pairs of demonstrative color concepts be used to reliably discriminate pairs of color samples over time. As we shall argue in Section 4, in a perceptual episode, just as one can track the spatio-temporal evolution of a perceived object, one can store in a temporary object file information about its visual properties in a purely indexical or demonstrative format. If, however, information about an object's visual properties is to be stored in episodic memory, for future re-identification, then it cannot be stored in a purely demonstrative or indexical format, which is linked to a particular perceptual context. At a minimum, the demonstrative must be fleshed with descriptive content. This is part of what Raffman (1995: 297) calls 'the memory constraint'. As Raffman (1995: 296) puts it:

[…] the coarse grained character of perceptual memory explains why we can recognize 'determinable' colors like red and blue and even scarlet and indigo *as such*, but not 'determinate' shades of those determinables […]. Because we cannot recognize determinate shades as such, *ostension* is our only means of communicating our knowledge of them. If I want to convey to you the precise shade of an object I see, I must point to it, or perhaps paint you a picture of it […]. I must present you with an instance of that shade. You must have the experience yourself.

Now, if the conceptualist was tempted to turn the tables around and argue that demonstrative concepts (of shapes or colors) are precisely well-suited to capture the fine-grainedness of perceptual experiences on the grounds that they are not designed to achieve recognitional tasks, we would really ask in what sense they would still deserve to be called concepts. If the link between the mental pointer of a shape or a color property and memory is so weak as to preclude re-identification of the shape or the color property, the mental pointer hardly counts as a concept.

The distinctive informational richness of the content of visual percepts has been discussed by Dretske (1981) in terms of what he calls the analogical coding of information.[17]

---

[17]For discussion, see Jacob (1997, ch. 2).

One and the same piece of information—one and the same fact—may be coded analogically or digitally. In Dretske's sense, a signal carries the information that, e.g. a is F in a digital form if the signal carries no additional information about a that is not already nested in the fact that a is F. If the signal does carry additional information about a that is not nested in the fact that a is F, then the information that a is F is carried by the signal in an analogical (or analog) form. For example, the information that a designated cup contains coffee may be carried in a digital form by the utterance of the English sentence: 'There is some coffee in the cup'. The same information can also be carried in an analog form by a picture or by a photograph. Unlike the utterance of the sentence, the picture *cannot* carry the information that the cup contains coffee without carrying additional information about the shape, size, orientation of the cup and the color and the amount of coffee in it. As we pointed out above, unlike the concept of a dog, the visual percept of a dog carries information about which dog one sees, its spatial position, the color and texture of its hairs, and so on.

There are at least two important and related reasons why Dretske's (1981) distinction between the analog and the digital encoding of one and the same piece of information seems unsuitable as a basis for capturing the distinction between the informational richness of the non-conceptual content of perceptual experience and the conceptual content of thought. First of all, in Dretske's (1981) view, what can be encoded either analogically or digitally is *informational* content, *not representational* content. Earlier in this chapter, we expressed our agreement with a teleological view of representational content according to which, to represent the fact that x is F is to have the *function* to indicate (or carry information about) the presence of Fs. Why is this important? Because unlike mere informational content, representational content has *correctness* conditions: unlike a signal carrying information, a representation can be correct or incorrect. If the latter, it is a misrepresentation. As argued forcefully by Millikan (1984, 1993, 2000) and recognized by Dretske (1988, 1995b), unless a system has a function, it cannot misrepresent anything. If so, then Dretske's (1981) analog/digital distinction seems to apply to the wrong kind of thing, namely informational content, not representational content with correctness conditions.

Second, it seems as if any representational state whatsoever can be said to encode some information analogically and some information digitally. For instance, the thought that x is a square can be said to represent conceptually and encode digitally the fact that x is a square and it can be said to encode analogically the fact that x is a rectangle.[18] Presumably, a visual experience can be a non-conceptual representation of, and encode digitally, the fact that, e.g. x presents a certain spatial visual appearance.[19] The same visual experience could also be said to encode analogically the fact that x is a rectangle. Thus, the thought that x is a square and a visual experience can encode analogically the same piece of information, namely the fact that x is a rectangle. If so, then the analog/digital distinction in Dretske's (1981) sense seems to cut across the conceptual/non-conceptual content distinction.

---

[18]As noticed by Peacocke (1989: 315), Millikan (2000) and Pacherie (2000a).
[19]See Peacocke's (1992b) notion of a scenario content.

Perhaps one could nonetheless try to reconcile Dretske's (1981) analog/digital distinction together with a teleological approach to the distinction between the conceptual/non-conceptual content distinction along the following lines. Consider the fact that *x* is a square. Whereas the thought that *x* is a square is a state produced by a mechanism with the function to carry the information that *x* is a square in digital form, one's visual experience prompted by perceiving the very same fact (or state of affairs) would be a state produced by a mechanism with the function to carry information about it (the very same state of affairs) in analogical form. The analog/digital distinction would then serve to capture some of the difference between the non-conceptual content of a visual experience and the conceptual content of a thought within a teleological framework. But the teleological distinction between mechanisms with a function to carry information in analog and in digital form, respectively, would itself be relativized to particular facts (or states of affairs). As we shall argue in Chapters 5 and 6, the teleological distinction between states produced by mechanisms with the function to carry information in analog and in digital form, respectively, is consistent with what we shall soon call the constraint of *contrastive identification*.

To sum up, the arguments by philosophers of mind and by perceptual psychologists in favor of the distinction between the conceptual content of thought and the non-conceptual content of visual percepts, turn on two basic considerations: on the one hand, they rely on the rejection of the claim that unless a creature has the conceptual resources appropriate to conceptualize her experience, she will not enjoy a perceptual visual experience at all; on the other hand, they rely on the distinctive fine-grainedness and the informational richness of visual percepts. Thus, the second considerations turn on the phenomenology of visual experience. In Chapters 2, 3 and 4, we shall provide a variety of evidence from electrophysiological and behavioral studies on macaque monkeys, the neuropsychological examination of brain-lesioned human patients and from psychophysical experiments performed on normal human subjects that point to a different kind of non-conceptual content, which we shall label 'visuomotor' content. In Chapter 6, we shall emphasize the fact that, unlike the arguments in favor of the non-conceptual content of visual percepts, the arguments for the distinction between the non-conceptual content of visual percepts and the non-conceptual content of visuomotor representations do not rely on phenomenology at all. Rather, they rely on the need to postulate mental representations with visuomotor content in order to provide a causal explanation of visually guided actions towards objects. Thus, we submit that the non-conceptual content of visual representations ought to be bifurcated into perceptual and visuomotor content as in Fig. 1.2.

In accord with what Clark's (2001) calls 'the assumption of experience-based selection' (EBS), we emphasize the link between the non-conceptual content of conscious visual experience, conceptual thought and memory: the non-conceptual content of visual experiences is involved in selecting a target for action. But we de-emphasize the connection between the non-conceptual content of visual experiences and visually guided actions towards objects, encapsulated by Clark's (2001) EBC assumption. By so doing, we do not thereby endorse the conceptualist view according to which the content of visual experiences is itself conceptualized. Unlike the content of visuomotor representations, the content of conscious visual experiences is poised for conceptual use, but it is not conceptual content.

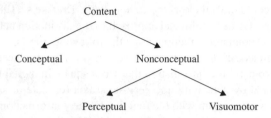

Fig. 1.2 Bifurcation of the nonconceptual content of visual representations into perceptual and visuomotor content.

In the next section, we shall lay the groundwork for Chapters 5 and 6 by examining a process we shall call 'cognitive dynamics'. Cognitive dynamics is a two-fold process: on the one hand, it involves the mapping of visual percepts of objects and locations onto conceptual thoughts. On the other hand, it consists of cognitive adjustments from more engaged to more disengaged thoughts, and vice-versa.

4 Elements of cognitive dynamics

The expression 'cognitive dynamics' was first used by Kaplan (1989) in an influential piece of work (written and widely circulated several years earlier) devoted to the study of such context-dependent linguistic expressions as indexicals (e.g. 'I', 'you', 'now', 'today' 'here', 'there') and demonstratives (e.g. 'he', 'this', 'that', 'there'). Indexicals and demonstratives are linguistic devices whose references change with the context of use. In Campbell's (1994: 42–3) terminology, 'I' and 'you' are personal indexicals; 'now' and 'today' are temporal indexicals; 'here' and 'there' are spatial indexicals. Kaplan was interested in the linguistic adjustments one has to make in order to express one and the same thought at different times or in different places. Indeed, the problem had been raised in the early part of the twentieth century in a famous essay by the logician Gottlob Frege (1918–19) with respect to temporal thoughts: 'If someone wants to say the same today as he expressed yesterday using the word "today", he must replace this word with "yesterday" '.[20]

Evans (1982: 143–76) made an important contribution to the topic of cognitive dynamics by addressing the fundamental issue of what he called 'demonstrative identification', namely the human ability to track objects in one's vicinity through perception and thought. As Evans (1982) emphasized, we may want to distinguish two major cases. During a single visual perceptual episode, one may track the trajectory of an object. Visual perception allows one to create or open a temporary object-file in which one

[20]See Dokic (1997) and Recanati (1997) for further discussion of what cognitive dynamics is about.

stores visual pictorial information about the object (e.g. its shape, color, texture). If and when the visual perceptual relation to the object is momentarily interrupted, the human episodic memory system allows one to recognize and re-identify an object over periods of time of variable length. Arguably, in the perceptual episode, the information gained by visual perception is directly linked to indexical and demonstrative concepts that can be used to refer to the perceived object from within an egocentric perspective. Arguably, in order for information gained by visual perception to be stored in episodic memory for future re-identification of an object, the information about the object must be stored in a more abstract, more descriptive format. One can refer to a perceptible object as 'that sofa' or even as 'that' (followed by no sortal), but presumably when one does not stand in a perceptual relation to the object, information about it cannot be stored in episodic memory in such a pure demonstrative format. Rather, it must be stored using a more descriptive symbol such as 'the (or that) red sofa that used to face the fire-place'.

According to Evans (1982), a 'past-tense' demonstrative concept can be part of what he calls an 'information-based' thought as much as a perceptually-based demonstrative concept. On his view, it seems as if perception, episodic memory and testimony are all on a par at the service of the 'informational system'. It seems to us, however, that there are important differences between the format in which information can be encoded in visual perception and in memory, respectively, as a result of the functional roles of perception and memory. Through perception one gains new information. Through memory, information is retained or preserved, not gained. Arguably, memory can modify the structure of information gained by perception: in memory, perceived items can be recombined so that what one remembers may differ from what one perceived. Memory can contribute to recreate one's representation of one's experienced past; but, if so, what one remembers is not true information. Thus, unlike perception, remembering cannot be a way of acquiring new knowledge.

As Evans emphasizes, one and the same English demonstrative pronoun 'that' can express a perceptually based demonstrative concept or a past-tense demonstrative concept. But on the one hand, language might be slightly misleading here: one and the same word might be used to express different concepts. We might use one and the same English demonstrative 'that' to refer to one and the same object to express slightly different concepts with relevantly different contents. To use an example of Evans (1982: 308), a perceptually based use of 'that bird' has a primarily spatial conceptual content used to refer to a bird accessible to perception. The perceptually based use of 'that bird' serves to direct attention to the spatial location of the perceptually accessible bird. The task of the audience of a perceptually based use of 'that bird' consists in a visual exploration of space to locate the perceptually accessible bird. A 'past-tense' use of the same demonstrative 'that bird' to refer to the same bird years later, as the bird is no longer accessible to perception, has a primarily temporal content. It serves to direct attention to a memory of the bird backwards in time. The task of the audience of a 'past-tense' use of 'that bird' is to search episodes stored in their episodic memory. Arguably, unlike the visual exploration of space, the mental exploration of one's episodic memory, and the retrieval of a particular episode, require use of some descriptive information.

On the other hand, the claim about the difference between the format of the information gained by visual perception and the information stored in episodic memory (for future recall) applies primarily to information about objects (e.g. a bird or a sofa). We are claiming that the content of a demonstrative concept referring to an object supported by a perceptual link to that object must presumably be descriptively enriched in order for the information to be stored in episodic memory for future re-identification of the object referred to by the demonstrative concept. It may be, however, that the use of a 'past-tense' demonstrative (such as 'that dinner party' in the context of a memory retrieval) might serve to express a pure memory demonstrative concept available to one's episodic memory, while one would be at a loss to provide further descriptive conceptual information for uniquely identifying which dinner party one is recalling. If so, we would claim that such pure memory demonstratives made available by the episodic memory experience itself apply to events, not to physical objects. In our view, there is a significant difference between perceiving/remembering a physical object and perceiving/remembering an event. The perceptual link to an object depends on a clear ontological demarcation between the object and the perceiver. By contrast, the perception of an event involves a different mereological relation between the perceiver (or the witness) and the event: the former is part of the latter. So in using a 'past-tense' demonstrative concept for an event stored in episodic memory, one is partly referring to oneself in a way one is not when one uses a 'past-tense' demonstrative concept of an object. This difference, we claim, accounts for why, unlike 'pure' memory demonstratives for events, memory demonstratives for physical objects must be fleshed with more descriptive information.[21]

Perry (1986a) made a useful distinction between vertical and lateral interpretations of sentences containing expressions whose meanings are more or less sensitive to the context. Interpreting a sentence *up* consists in rising above the context by replacing an expression whose meaning is more sensitive to the context by a coreferential expression whose meaning is less sensitive to the context. A person located in Lyon receives a post-card from a friend in San Franciso with the sentence: 'This city has dilapidated cable-cars'. If the person in Lyon writes down in her notebook 'San Francisco has dilapidated cable-cars', she is interpreting *up*. Conversely, consider a person visiting San Francisco who reads the latter sentence in her travel-guide book. If she then writes down the former sentence in her diary, she is interpreting *down*. In other words, she replaces an expression whose meaning is less sensitive to the context by a coreferential expression whose meaning is more sensitive to the context. Lateral interpretation involves replacing an expression by a coreferential expression whose meaning is equally sensitive to the context (e.g. replacing 'you' by 'I').[22]

4.1 Cognitive engagement and the detachment constraint on thoughts

In an interesting discussion of various ways of thinking about space, Campbell (1994: 5–6) distinguishes two broad ways of thinking of one and the same region of space: one

---

[21]Notice that one is not likely to refer to an event, e.g. a dinner party, of which one is both a witness and a constituent, by using the demonstrative 'that' with a spatial content.

[22]See Recanati (1997) for futher elaboration of Perry's distinctions.

way is 'as a participant, as someone plunged into its center [...] with things to do in that space'. The other way is thinking about the same region of space 'as a disengaged theorist'. The former engaged way of thinking about space is the way of thinking 'one uses when sitting at a dinner table, moving and acting in that space'. The latter more detached way of thinking about the same region of space is the way of thinking 'used subsequently by the detective who tries to reconstruct the scene and to establish who did what'. The distinction is that between 'thinking of the space from a particular point of view, as a subject at the center of one's world, and thinking about the space independently of any particular view point on it, in an impersonal or absolute way'.

In Section 3 we argued that thoughts satisfy Evans' (1982) generality constraint and/or Fodor's (1975, 1987) language of thought hypothesis. Thoughts involve concepts. Concepts have inferential roles and they can be recombined in indefinitely many new ways to form new thoughts. Unlike thoughts, visual percepts have non-conceptual iconic or pictorial contents. The pictorial non-conceptual content of visual percepts is informationally richer and more fine-grained than the conceptual contents of thoughts. Thus, the mapping from a visual percept onto a thought involves stripping the percept of much of its informational richness.

To see what is at issue in the mapping between a visual percept and a thought, consider an example adapted from Barwise (1989: 237). Let a visual percept represent a glass to the left of a bottle. The question is: 'How can this visual percept give rise to a thought?'.[23] Notice that the mapping from visual percept to thought is one-way: visual percepts cause thoughts. Thoughts can cause other thoughts, but thoughts do not cause visual percepts.

As we argued above, unlike a thought, in a normal human subject, the visual percept cannot depict the location of the glass relative to the bottle without depicting the orientation, shape, texture, size and content (if any) of both the glass and the bottle. For the mapping to occur, however, the iconic or pictorial content of the visual percept representing the location of the glass relative to the bottle must match the conceptual content expressible by the English two place relation 'being to the left of'. Conceptual processing of the pictorial content of the visual percept may yield a representation whose conceptual content can be expressed by the English sentence: 'The glass is to the left of the bottle'. As we argued above, the conceptual content conveyed by an utterance is informationally impoverished relative to the informational richness of the pictorial content of the visual percept.

Now, once the visual percept has been turned into a thought by a process involving a selective elimination of information, further conceptual processing can yield a still more complex thought involving, not a two-place relation between pairs of objects, but a *three*-place relation between a pair of objects and an egocentric perspective. Once one has formed the thought that the glass is to the left of the bottle, it is a short step to form the more detached thought that the glass is to the left of the bottle from some egocentric perspective, not others. It is a short step to form the thought that, e.g. the glass is to the left of the bottle for someone looking at the fire-place but not for

---

[23]We shall pick up again this question from a slightly different angle in Chapter 5, Section 3, when we examine the scope and limits of visual knowledge and what Dretske calls 'primary epistemic seeing'.

someone with his back onto the fire-place. From the latter perspective, the glass is to the right, not to the left, of the bottle. Here, we reach a fundamental difference between visual percepts and thoughts: one can move upwards from the thought involving the binary relation 'being to the left of', to the more detached thought involving the ternary relation 'being to the left of from one's egocentric perspective'. One can see a glass as being to the left of a bottle. But one cannot see a glass as being to the left of a bottle from one's egocentric perspective, for the simple reason that one cannot see one's egocentric perspective. One's egocentric perspective is something only available to thought or imagination. Someone with his back onto the fire-place can imagine how things would look were he to face the fire-place.[24] One can move, change egocentric perspective at time $t + 1$ and see the egocentric perspective one used to occupy at t. But one cannot see at t one's current egocentric perspective at t.

The shift from the thought involving the binary relation to the thought involving the ternary relation illustrates a fundamental aspect of the cognitive dynamics inherent to conceptual representations. Notice that cognitive dynamics involves both the process of disengagement, whereby one ascends to a more detached thought, and the converse process of immersion, whereby one engages into a less detached thought.[25]

As noticed by Perry (1986b: 221), creatures with the conceptual power to form thoughts can use an n-place predicate in order to represent an $n + 1$-ary relation. If they do, then they have the power to move from a thought involving the n-place relation to a thought involving the $n + 1$-ary relation (i.e a relation taking $n + 1$ arguments). Only conceptual thought can increase the arity of a predicate (i.e the number of its admissible predicates). Following Dokic (2002), we shall call this constraint the detachment constraint:

Creatures with the conceptual power to represent an $n + 1$-ary relation by means of an n-place relation have the power to move from a thought involving the n-place relation to a thought involving the $n + 1$-ary relation.

As the previous example illustrates, unlike conceptual thoughts, visual percepts do not satisfy the detachment constraint. The detachment constraint derives from the generality constraint or the language of thought hypothesis. Thoughts satisfy the detachment constraint because a thought is a structured combination of concepts. Thus, any conceptual parameter implicit in one thought can be made explicit in some further thought.

4.2 Unarticulated constituency

Clearly then, the process of cognitive dynamics is not limited to the transformation of visual percepts into thoughts. It involves shifts from more engaged to more detached or less engaged thoughts and vice versa, as a famous example of Perry's (1986b) will make clear. Let us compare the thoughts expressed, respectively, by the three following sentences all uttered, e.g. in Lyon:

1. It is raining.
2. It is raining here.
3. It is raining in Lyon.

---

[24]In Chapter 3, Section 5.3, we will discuss neglect patients whose ability to imagine spatial perspectives is impaired.
[25]A point emphasized by Recanati (1997).

The meteorological thought expressed by an utterance of (3) contains a city name. Arguably, the meteorological thought involving a city name is more detached than either the thought involving the indexical 'here' or no expression for a place. Using a city name involves the ability to categorize spatial regions in terms of different contrastive cities. It may rain in Lyon, not in London. Furthermore, the use of the proper name 'Lyon' does not mandate a perceptual way of representing the location. Presumably, one may visually perceive parts of the city of Lyon, but one cannot visually perceive the city *per se*—except perhaps either as a dot on a map or from an airplane. But it is unlikely that one can see rain in Lyon either by seeing a dot on a map or by seeing Lyon from an airplane.

The meteorological thought expressed by an utterance of (2) in Lyon involves the spatial indexical concept expressed by 'here'. The ability to identify a location using indexical or demonstrative concepts involves the ability to form perception-based thoughts about locations. Such thoughts are 'egocentric' in the sense that a location can be referred to as 'here' only from some agent's subjective perspective, i.e. relative to the agent's current location. The egocentric contrast between 'here' and 'there' is more engaged or less detached than the spatial contrast drawn by using a city name. One can form the thought expressed by an utterance of (3) while being, e.g. in New York; but one cannot form the thought that it is raining in Lyon by uttering sentence (2) unless one is located in Lyon. Hence, the meteorological thought expressed by an utterance of (2) is more narrowly tied or anchored to the perceptual context than the meteorological thought expressed by an utterance of (3).

Now, the question arises whether an utterance of (1) can express a thought at all, i.e. something that can be true or false. It rains (or snows) at some time, not others. If and when it does, it rains over some area, not others. No genuine disagreement can arise about whether a meteorological thought is true or false until the time and the place of the relevant meteorological event or state of affairs are fixed. Nor can an utterance of (1) be taken to express the thought that it is raining somewhere or other. Assuming that the temporal component of the meteorological thought is expressed by the present tense in (1)–(3), the location is explicitly referred to by a prepositional phrase in (2) and (3), not in (1).

Perry (1986b) argues convincingly that the thought expressed by an utterance of (1) in Lyon involves a tacit reference to some region of space that is supplied by the very fact that the sentence is uttered in Lyon. In Perry's (1986b) terminology, (1) involves an 'unarticulated constituent' for the location: it is anchored in Lyon, not elsewhere. An agent looks out the window and comes to form the meteorological thought expressed by (1). This thought interacts with her action plans to generate her intention to, e.g. grab her umbrella. The agent did not bother to represent in her meteorological thought any contrast between the place relevant to her intended action and some different location—as she would had she instead formed the thought either expressed by (2) or by (3). In forming the thought expressed by (1), the agent lets the very area to which her immediate perception and action are anchored supply the missing location.

Perry (1986b) asks us to consider creatures from an imaginary country, which he calls 'Z-land'. Z-landers, as he calls them, never travel and they are so fixated onto their land that their meteorological thoughts never contain a constituent for a place. Unlike normal human adults' thoughts, the meteorological thoughts of Z-landers contain a one-place predicate 'rain' with one argument for time, none for place. All the mete-orological thoughts that Z-landers ever entertain are spatially anchored to their immediate surroundings, i.e. to the spatial context that is both perceptually accessible and relevant to their immediate actions. When Z-landers think what they express with their use of (1), the semantic connection between their thought and Z-land is supplied by their being in Z-land; but it is not explicitly reflected in their thought. As Perry (1986b) remarks, 'there is a little of the Z-lander in the most-travelled of us'. We adult human beings, however, do have the ability to rise above the limitations of our visual perceptual capacities and reflect on the contrast between the region of space to which our actions and perceptions may be anchored, and other possible places affording different possibilities for perception and action.

Spatial demonstrative and indexical concepts (expressed by 'here' and 'there') lie at the very interface between the visual perception of spatial relations and spatial thoughts.[26] They afford elementary reflective conceptual capacities, which allow normal human adults to rise above the limitations inherent to Z-landers' meteorological thoughts. As we argued above, the spatial egocentric contrast between 'here' and 'there' is more engaged than one made using a city name, but it is a conceptual contrast nonetheless. What shows that indexical and demonstrative expressions like 'here' and 'there' have conceptual contents is that they have inferential roles: if some object is *here*, then it is *not there*. Far more sophisticated is the human reflective conceptual ability to represent e.g. the fact that time is relative to a time zone. When a person living in Paris wakes up in the morning upon hearing her alarm clock, she does not have to represent the fact that it is 7:00 a.m. in Paris, not in New York; but she could. It was a considerable concep-tual revolution to discover that simultaneity is a ternary relation. Rarely if ever, if they are not theoretical physicists, do human beings represent the fact that two events are simultaneous within one frame of reference, not others. But by learning special relativ-ity, they can come to reflect on the fact that simultaneity is a ternary relation involving a pair of events and a frame of reference, not just a pair of events. In all such cases, the mapping of one thought to the next satisfies the detachment constraint: by a process of cognitive disengagement, one conceptual constituent implicit in one thought is made explicit in another thought.

5 Actions and the intentionality of intentions

Unlike plants, animals are agents, at least some of the time. Since they do not have roots, they must act in order to find food, protection, shelter and sexual partners.[27] Humans are no exception. Unlike plants, animals can act because they have a nervous sys-tem made up of neurons, some of which are sensory neurons, some are motor neurons and some are sensorimotor neurons. When an animal is an agent, then, unlike the motion of other physical objects, its action may involve, in Premack's (1990) terms, a 'self-propelled' movement, i.e. a movement one of whose causes is internal to the agent.

---

[26]In Chapter 6, Section 7.2., we shall argue that what Campbell (1994) calls 'causal indexicals' lie at the interface between visuomotor representations and action concepts involved in the contents of prior intentions.

[27]Sponges, oysters, mussels, fetuses might be exceptions.

What is an action? The question is very complex. It has been, and still is, intensely discussed among philosophers. Although there is no settled answer to the question, we shall assume that an action is a special kind of behavior: intentional behavior. Much behavior is not intentional. Although plants do not navigate through space, let alone act, they nonetheless behave. Photosynthesis, e.g. is plant behavior. Deciduous trees shed their leaves in the Fall and flowers blossom in the Spring. Plant behavior is non-intentional. Much of what human and non-human animals do is non-intentional behavior too. Humans breathe, digest, salivate, blush, yawn, shiver, perspire, hiccup, snore, vomit and so on and so forth. If and when they engage in such behaviors, humans do not act. Reflexive behaviors are not actions. The light pupillary reflex produces the contraction of one's pupil. It is not an action. Nor is the visual control of one's posture.

A system S's behavior is something the system does, as opposed to something that happens to S. If a tree loses its leaves because an animal has cut them or as a result of a storm, then losing its leaves is something that happened to the tree. Unlike shedding its leaves, it is not something the tree did. Being bitten by a mosquito is something that may happen to a mammal: it is a piece of mosquito behavior, not mammal behavior. If John raises his hand, then the movement of John's hand is part of his behavior. But if Ann raises John's hand, then the movement of John's hand is part of Ann's behavior, not John's. Of course, a system S's motor output may have many different causes. But unless some internal state c of S did contribute to the process whereby S's motor output m was produced, the motor output m was not part of S's behavior.

On the face of it, however, S's motor output m does not seem to be a necessary condition of S's behavior. First of all, changes other than movements of an animals's limbs (or other bodily parts) may be involved in behavior. Humans, e.g. blush in certain circumstances. Blushing involves a change in the color of the face, not a movement of the limbs. Perhaps it is controversial whether blushing is something one does rather than something that happens to one. Concentrating and/or listening, however, are uncontroversially things one does and they do not involve specific movements of one's limbs. Second, behavior may consist in the lack of limb movement: a prey's behavior may consist in refraining from moving in order to escape its predator's attention. In this case, the prey's lack of movement is indeed controlled by one of its internal states. Producing a lack of movement is different from failing to produce any movement. The latter, not the former, is what a dead animal does—if a dead animal can do anything.

So behavior can be intentional or non-intentional. S's behavior is an action if it is intentional behavior. What makes S's behavior intentional is the peculiar nature of c, the internal cause of S's movement (change or internally produced lack of movement). For S's behavior to be intentional and hence to be an action, the internal cause of S's motor output must be a mental representation. As Fodor (1986: 6) puts it:

[…] some of a paramecium's movements count as 'behaviors' in some sense of that notion that brings them within the explanatory purview of psychological theory. This is to grant that they count as responses but not, of course, that they count as actions. I take it only intentional systems can act.

5.1 The distinctive role of intentions in the etiology of actions

Prior to Davidson's seminal (1963) paper on 'Actions, reasons and causes', many philosophers were inclined to make a sharp distinction between reason explanations and causal explanations. According to this distinction, it is one thing to provide reasons for an agent's intentional action, it is something else to supply the causes of an agent's physical movements. On this view, actions have reasons, not causes. Movements have causes, not reasons. Beliefs and desires can only be reasons for an action, not causes of physical movements. Davidson (1963) argued that an appropriate belief–desire pair can both be a reason for an agent's action and the cause of what the agent does. Subsequently, the question arose whether an agent is required to hold beliefs and desires in order for his behavior to qualify as an action.[28]

First of all, the question arises whether all actions must involve a relevant belief–desire pair. When it is spontaneously performed, or perhaps triggered by an affordance (in Gibson's sense),[29] an action may involve movements that are controlled neither by the agent's beliefs nor by his desires. Still we do not want to count all of them as reflexes.

Among acts that are not reflexes, there is the category that O'Shaughnessy (1980: 58–73) has labeled 'sub-intentional acts', i.e. a class of acts which are intentional under no description. Consider the movement of one's tongue in one's mouth as one reads, the movements of one's fingers as one is attending to a lecture or the tapping of one's feet to the rhythm as one is listening to a piece of music. Arguably, these acts are not instances of reflexive responses to an incoming signal. After all, one can stop to tap one's feet to the rhythm if requested to do so. But one cannot prevent one's pupil from contracting in the light or from dilating in the dark. Nor are these 'sub-intentional acts' intended in the sense that the movements involved in such acts can be causally traced back to an intention of the agent. Arguably, movements involved in 'sub-intentional acts' can be overt or covert: the movements can be executed or imagined. In this respect, the phenomenon discussed by O'Shaughnessy is interestingly related to what cognitive scientists call motor imagery.[30]

As emphazised by O'Shaughnessy (1980: 60), one can come to notice, and thus discover, the existence of such movements. What one so discovers then is the existence of bodily movements for which one is, as he puts it, 'responsible'. One discovers that one is executing or performing such movements. By contrast, the reflexive contraction of one's pupil or the visual control of one's posture are automatic responses to incoming signals for which one does not bear responsibility.

Also, as noticed by Searle (1983: 84), there seems to exist a class of intentional though *non-deliberate* actions: getting up and pacing about a room absorbed in one's thoughts seems to qualify as such a non-deliberate action. Again, the reflexive contraction of one's pupil or the automatic visual control of one's posture do not seem to qualify as non-deliberate intentional actions. Such non-deliberate actions differ from both reflexive behaviors and sub-intentional acts, for they do involve an intention on the part of the agent. Arguably, one cannot get up and pace around one's room without both intending and having decided to do so. One cannot, however, intend, let alone decide, to contract one's pupil. The contraction of one's pupil is the automatic result of the light pupillary

---

[28]See Pacherie (2001) for a detailed discussion.
[29]See Chapter 6, Section 2.
[30]See Chapter 6 for a discussion of motor imagery and Chapter 7 for a discussion of mirror neurons related to O'Shaughnessy's 'sub-intentional acts'.

reflex. Presumably, one does not intend, let alone decide, to move one's tongue in one's mouth while reading. Nor must one intend and decide to tap one's feet to the rhythm in order to do so while listening to a piece of music. One may, however, stop doing so.

On the taxonomy espoused here, one should distinguish reflexes from 'sub-intentional acts'. Although neither reflexes nor sub-intentional acts are intended, unlike the former, one can stop the latter if one intends to. Both reflexes and sub-intentional acts should be distinguished from non-deliberate intentional actions such as pacing around one's room, the existence of which shows that having beliefs and desires is not necessary for acting intentionally. Some intentional actions seem to involve movements caused by an intention alone.

Second, examples of so-called 'deviant' causal chains show that the contribution of a relevant belief–desire pair may not be sufficient for a behavioral process to count as an intentional action. Consider Davidson's (1980: 79) much discussed climber example:

A climber might want to rid himself of the weight and danger of holding another man on a rope, and he might know that by loosening his hold on the rope he could rid himself of the weight and danger. This belief and want might so unnerve him as to cause him to loosen his hold. Yet it might be the case that he never chose to loosen his hold, nor did he do it intentionally.

The climber may feel the urge to loosen his grip on the rope. He may well know that if he did, he would be relieved. But if he happens to loosen his grip without ever intending to do so, then he did it by accident, not intentionally.

Searle (1983: 82) discusses another murderous example: Bill wants to kill his uncle because he believes that by doing so, he will inherit his fortune—something that would please him very much. He is driving his car towards his uncle's house thinking about how to kill him. On his way, he is so agitated by his thoughts that he accidentally hits and kills a pedestrian, who turns out to be his uncle. Although Bill killed his uncle, it was an accident—not something he did intentionally. Given his belief and desire, Bill did intend to kill his uncle, but *not* the way he actually did it. He did it by accident. Bill had what Searle (1983, 2001) calls a *prior intention* to kill his uncle. What he did not have is what Searle (1983, 2001) calls the *intention in action* to kill him by running him over with his car. Arguably, not all actions have prior intentions, but all have an intention in action. Getting up and pacing about a room may not be caused by a prior intention. But it must be caused by an intention in action.

Arguably, no single mental representation having the characteristic intentionality of intentions can play all the functions assigned to intentions in the etiology of actions. Thus, like many theorists who have embraced a dual view of intentions, Searle (1983) distinguishes between prior intentions and intentions in action. In his view, whereas the former represents the whole action, the latter represents the agent's physical movements necessary to achieve the action's goal. As Searle (1983: 93, 2001: 47–9) sees it, the prior intention results from a process of deliberation or reflection on one's own beliefs and desires. It in turn gives rise to the action, which consists of two components: the intention in action and the bodily movement. According to Searle's (1983, 2001) particular view of the matter, the prior intention would seem to stand as the cause of both the whole action and the intention in action. The prior intention would stand as a cause of the whole action by virtue of being the cause of the intention in action, which in turn causes the bodily movement. If so, then it seems to be a consequence of Searle's view that, unlike the intention in action, the prior intention does not belong to the action properly so called: since it causes it, it must be distinct from it. Searle's dual view gives rise to the further question whether the prior intention fades away once the intention in action is formed, as it seems it must once its causal role is achieved. If and when a short-circuit causes a fire, once the fire is on, the short-circuit is over. Similarly, if a prior intention causes an intention in action, the prior intention should give way to the intention in action.

5.2   The intentionality of intentions

Perceptions, beliefs, desires and intentions are psychological states with intentionality: they are about or represent objects and states of affairs under a particular psychological mode or format. Perceptions, beliefs, desires and intentions each have a distinctive intentionality. Anscombe (1957: 56) asks us to consider a 'shopping list'. The list might either be used as a set of instructions (or a blueprint) for action by a customer in a store or as an inventory by a detective whose purpose is to draw a record of what the customer is buying. In the former case, the list is not to be revised in the light of what lies in the customer's grocery bag; but in the latter case, it is. If a mismatch should occur between the content of the grocery bag and the list used by the customer, then the blame should be put on the customer, not on the list. In the case of a mismatch between the content of the bag and the list drawn by the detective, the detective should correct his list. In Searle's (1983, 2001) terminology, beliefs and desires have opposite 'directions of fit'. Beliefs have a mind-to-world direction of fit: they can be true or false. A belief is true if, and only if, the world is as the belief represents it to be. It is the function of beliefs to match facts or actual states of affairs. In forming a belief, it is up for the mind to meet the demands of the world. Unlike beliefs, desires have a world-to-mind direction of fit. Desires are not either true or false: they are fulfilled or frustrated. The job of a desire is not to represent the world as it is but rather as the agent would like it to be. Desires are representations of goals, i.e. possible non-actual states of affairs. In entertaining a desire, it is so to speak up for the world to meet the demands of the mind. The agent's action is supposed to bridge the gap between the mind's goal and the world.

As Searle (1983, 2001) has noticed, perceptual experiences and intentions have opposite directions of fit. Perceptual experiences have the same mind-to-world direction of fit as beliefs. Intentions have the same world-to-mind direction of fit as desires. In addition, perceptual experiences and intentions have opposite directions of causation: whereas a perceptual experience represents the state of affairs that causes it, an intention causes the state of affairs that it represents.

Although intentions and desires share the same world-to-mind direction of fit, intentions are different from desires in a number of important respects, which all flow from the peculiar commitment to action of intentions. Broadly speaking, desires are relevant to the process of deliberation that precedes one's engagement into a course of action. Once an intention is formed, however, the process of deliberation comes to an end. To intend is to have made up one's mind about whether to act. Once an intention is formed, one has taken the decision whether to act. Of course, every intention does not give rise to an action. There are more intended actions than actions performed, for the simple reason that human beings change their minds. We shall discuss the contrast between intentions and desires under five headings.[31]

First, as we said above, intentions, unlike desires, achieve their world-to-mind direction of fit by virtue of their mind-to-world direction of causation. This is what Searle (1983, 2001) calls the 'causal self-referentiality' of intentions. If, e.g. one intends to raise one's arm, then one's arm must rise as a result of one's intention to raise it and not otherwise. If Ann raises John's arm, then the rising of John's arm cannot result from John's intention. John may have wished that Ann would raise his hand, but John cannot intend that Ann raises his arm. In our view, what Searle (*ibid.*) calls the causal self-referentiality of intentions does not require that only creatures with the conceptual resources necessary for representing the causal relation between their intentions and their subsequent movements can be agents and be ascribed intentions.

Although the issue is complex, we would like to suggest that what Searle characterizes in terms of causal self-referentiality is a feature of intending, i.e. the psychological mode of intentions. Assuming that the human cognitive architecture includes an 'intention box', as it includes a 'belief box' and a 'desire box', only some mental representations have the appropriate format for entering each of these 'boxes'.[32]

Thus, when an agent forms an intention, the content of her mental representation is entertained under a mode distinct from both beliefs and desires, whether the agent knows it or conceptualizes it or not. The agent need have no higher order belief about what it takes to form an intention, as opposed to a perception, a belief or a desire. Perhaps, as discussed by Searle (1983, 2001) and by Pacherie (2000b, 2001), what William James called 'the experience of acting' is the non-conceptual phenomenological counterpart of what Searle conceptualizes as the causal self-referentiality of intentions. A patient whose arm has been anesthetized is requested to raise his arm with his eyes closed. Unbeknownst to him, his arm is prevented from moving by being tied to his chair. Although he cannot raise his arm, he has the experience of acting, so much so that, upon opening his eyes, he is surprised to see that his arm did not rise. Conversely, epileptic patients have been stimulated by Penfield (1975) by direct application of a microelectrode onto their motor cortex. The stimulation of the motor cortex caused the movement of the patient's arm. The patient, however, was surprised to see his arm rise and reported no experience of acting. Perhaps James' experience of acting is related to both the sense of agency and to what is called 'motor imagery' (see Jeannerod 1994, 1997).[33]

Second, as already alluded to previously, desires can be about anything or anybody: one can wish or hope that somebody else would do something or other. Unlike hopes and desires, however, intentions are always about the self. One intends to raise one's arm, not somebody else's. One intends to reach a glass of water, to get married or to get elected. The intended reaching, marriage or election must be the agent's own. One can wish somebody else would reach a glass of water, would get married or would get elected. One can intend to contribute to the reaching of a glass of water by somebody else. One can intend to contribute to somebody else's marriage or to somebody

---

[31]Millikan (1996) argues that human intentions are hybrid mental representations with both a directive world-to-mind direction of fit and a descriptive mind-to-world direction of fit. In Chapter 6, Section 8.1, we discuss her view.

[32]The functional terminology of 'boxes' was introduced by Schiffer (1981) and Fodor (1987).

[33]See Chapter 6, Section 8.1 for further discussion of motor imagery.

else's election. But one cannot intend that somebody else reaches for a glass of water. Nor can one intend that somebody else gets married or gets elected. Similarly, a human being can wish she were, e.g. a bird; she can pretend, but she cannot intend, to be a bird.

Third, unlike desires, intentions are tied to the present and to the future. One cannot form an intention about the past. One can wish things had been different in the past, but one cannot intend to have done something in the past. Intentions can be about temporally distant states of affairs lying far ahead in the future or about immediately executable goals. The more the state of affairs intended is temporally remote from the time when the intention is being entertained, the more the content of the intention is conceptual (or conceptualized). Hence, intentions directed towards states of affairs remote in the distant future may and must have conceptual content. The more the goal is accessible temporally and spatially, the less it needs to be conceptualized. The conceptual content of intentions about remote goals involves action concepts (with a world-to-mind direction of fit).

Fourth, like the contents of desires, the contents of intentions are about possible non-actual states of affairs. But unlike the content of a desire, the conceptual content of an intention directed towards the distant future cannot be about a state of affairs that the agent knows to be impossible. An agent may wrongly take a state of affairs to be possible. Contrary to her expectation, the intended state of affairs may turn out to be impossible. But an agent cannot intend to achieve a state of affairs that she knows to be impossible at the time when she forms the intention.

Finally, one can consistently entertain contradictory desires, but one cannot consistently form contradictory intentions. One can consistently have the desire to be at the same time in Paris and in New York city: one can consistently wish one were simultaneously in Paris and in New York city. A man can consistenly have the desire to marry two distinct women at the same time; he may consistently wish to do so. But one cannot consistently form intentions that cannot be carried out simultaneously. One can consistently wish to be, but one cannot consistently intend to be, at the same time in Paris and in New York city. Although he can consistently wish he could get married to two distinct women simultaneously, nonetheless, in many human cultures, a man cannot consistently intend to marry two different women at the same time.

In the rest of this book, we shall review evidence in favor of the hypothesis that the human visual system processes visual information about objects in two fundamentally different ways: one and the same stimulus can undergo perceptual processing or motor processing. For example, one can perceive a cup and one can grasp it. We do not want to suggest that the human visual system is restricted to perceiving objects of prehension: humans can perceive a great many things other than objects that can be direct targets of their hand actions. Nor do we want to suggest that humans can only plan and intend object-oriented actions: humans can intend actions far more complex than grasping an object. In this chapter, we have laid the groundwork for the rest of the argument by emphasizing the contrast between the mind-to-world direction of fit of both beliefs and perceptual experiences, and the world-to-mind direction of fit and the mind-to-world direction of causation of intentions. As we shall argue in Chapters 5 and 6, the output of the perceptual processing of visual inputs serves as an input for further conceptual processing that produces thoughts about objects, which can be stored in the 'belief box'. In Chapter 6, we shall argue that visuomotor representations, which result from motor processing, present visual information about objects to motor intentions. Notice that in our view, visuomotor representations interact with motor intentions. They are not involved in what O'Shaughnessy (1980) calls 'sub-intentional acts', i.e. bodily movements whose causal origins cannot be traced back to an intention of the agent. Although we do believe that 'sub-intentional acts' in O'Shaughnessy's sense do indeed exist, we do not believe that visually guided hand actions directed towards objects are 'sub-intentional acts' in O'Shaughnessy's sense. Visuomotor representations are hybrid representations with a dual direction of fit, or so we shall contend: they represent features of actual states of affairs appropriate for action. We shall further argue that the contents of visuomotor representations can be conceptualized with the help of action concepts and be stored in the 'intention box'. Thus, in the rest of this book, we shall claim that the duality between the perceptual processing and the motor processing of visual objects is the reflection within the human visual system of the duality between the intentionality of intentions and the intentionality of perceptions and beliefs. In a few words: one can intend to act, but one cannot intend to think (or believe), let alone to perceive.

Part II

Empirical evidence for the duality of visual processing

Foreword to Part II

The main thesis of this book is that objects that humans can both see and manipulate can give rise to two kinds of visual representations: visual percepts and visuomotor representations. The former serve as input to higher human cognitive processes, including memory, categorization, conceptual thought and reasoning. The latter is at the service of human action. From the standpoint of our version of the 'two visual systems' hypothesis, vision serves two masters: thinking about, and acting upon, the world.

First, it is worth emphasizing that the two visual systems hypothesis runs both against untutored intuition and against much philosophical tradition. On the one hand, normal human beings can have no introspective awareness of the fact that human vision has two major functions, for in normal everyday life circumstances, perception and visually guided actions march to the beat of a single drummer: perceptual processing and visuomotor processing cooperate harmoniously. On the other hand, contrary to much writing on the philosophy of perception, not all seeing leads to sight, visual perception or visual experience of the world. Much of the human visual system serves the purpose of reaching, grasping and manipulating neighboring objects.

Second, it is equally important to appreciate not only the scope but also the limits of the two visual systems hypothesis. Just as it would be absurd to reduce human visual perception to visual experiences elicited by seeing objects that can be manually grasped, it would be similarly absurd to reduce human actions to hand movements involved in reaching and grasping objects. On the one hand, humans can perceive entities that they cannot manipulate at all, such as shadows, flames, stars, the horizon, events and human actions. On the other hand, humans can plan and execute actions whose goals are not visible at all, let alone graspable with the fingers of their hands.

In Part I, we sketched a general framework, which we called RTVM (the representational theory of the visual mind), for thinking about two basic issues that have been traditionally addressed by philosophers: the issue of the phenomenology of visual experience and the role of vision in the guidance of action. In Part II, we change gears and examine in some details the empirical evidence for the two visual systems hypothesis so construed. The evidence falls into three main categories. The first category is constituted by electrophysiological and behavioral experiments run on non-human animals, in particular on macaque monkeys. The second category is constituted by the neuropsychological study of human patients with a brain lesion in some part of their visual system. The third category is constituted by psychophysical experiments in normal human beings. Electrophysiological experiments on animals, the investigation of human patients with a brain lesion and psychophysical experiments on normal human beings, require very different experimental equipment, empirical methods and expertise. Because the experimental evidence is quite varied and has been gathered using quite specialized tools, we devote a special chapter to each of the three kinds of data. The overall goal of Part II, however, is to show that, notwithstanding its diversity, the empirical evidence points unambiguously towards the two visual systems hypothesis.

In Chapter 2, we tell the story of the progressive discovery of the anatomical bifurcation between the two pathways in the primate visual system. In fact, the very idea that a visual stimulus can be simultaneously processed by distinct neural structures, each serving a different function, is rooted in the neurophysiological tradition. It was explicitly entertained by late nineteenth-century physiologists, who observed the visual behaviors of a variety of animal species. Although amphibians have no cerebral cortex, it was found that in the brain of amphibians, two separate neural structures underlie two distinct visually guided behaviors: respectively, prey-catching behavior and the visual control of barrier avoidance. In mammals (e.g. rodents), in which the visual cortex is substantially more developed, it was again found that two separate neural structures underlie sensitivity to the shape and color of a stimulus, and the detection of its spatial location.

Because much of the early evidence for the two visual systems hypothesis came from the study of animals with no or little visual cortex, early versions of the two visual systems hypothesis tended to emphasize the distinction between vision based on subcortical structures and vision based on cortical structures. A major step was taken when the anatomical bifurcation between the two pathways became firmly located within the primate visual cortex itself. Whereas the ventral pathway links the primary visual cortex to the temporal lobe, the dorsal pathway links the primary visual cortex to the parietal lobe. First, selective experimental ablation of the ventral pathway in macaque monkeys was shown to impair the animal's ability to recognize objects by shape, texture and color. Selective experimental ablation of the dorsal pathway was shown to impair the animal's ability to localize objects in visual space. Then, single-cell recordings demonstrated that neurons in both pathways respond to different stimuli and serve different tasks. Single neurons recorded in the ventral pathway respond preferentially to colors, complex shapes and contours of objects in the context of perceptual tasks. Many parietal areas that are part of the dorsal pathway have been shown to be involved primarily in the localization of stimuli in visual space and in the perception of spatial relationships among visual objects. Some single neurons, recorded mainly in area AIP of the dorsal pathway, respond preferentially to those geometrical properties of objects that serve such visuomotor tasks as grasping them.

Thus, from the behavioral and electrophysiological studies in macaque monkeys reviewed in Chapter 2, three conclusions emerge. First, the primate visual cortex is divided into two pathways: the ventral pathway and the dorsal pathway. Second, study of the dorsal pathway of the primate visual system made it possible to ask questions that are fundamental for the rest of the book: how is the so-called 'visuomotor transformation' effected?; what are the neural mechanisms underlying the conversion of visual information about objects of prehension into motor commands of arm and hand movements? Third, study of the dorsal pathway also shows that the primate visual system faces two fundamentally different computational requirements according to whether it is engaged in a perceptual task or in a visuomotor task. During a perceptual task, an element of a visual array is localized relative to other neighboring items. It must be sorted out from a number of competitors and distractors and segregated from the background. In order to perform these operations, the visual system must localize the relevant object in viewer-independent coordinates centered on some element of the visual array—either the object itself or some other landmark. During a visuomotor task, the target of the visually guided action must be localized in a set of coordinates, which originate on the agent's retina. Then, the retino-centered frame of reference must be adjusted to take into account eye and head movements and transformed into an egocentric frame of reference centered on the agent's body to allow efficient action on the object.

In visually guided hand actions routinely performed by normal human adults, the perceptual processing and the visuomotor processing cooperate harmoniously. As Chapter 2 shows, it is, however, a fundamental discovery of recent cognitive neuroscience that the visual perceptual system and the visuomotor system are subserved by largely distinct areas in the brain of non-human primates. Furthermore, as Chapter 3 reveals, detailed observation shows that brain lesions in humans can selectively impair the visual perception and recognition of objects and leave visuomotor processing largely intact and vice-versa. Finally, as indicated by Chapter 4, carefully crafted experiments show that spectacular dissociations between perception and action can be created in normal human adults. Thus, perception and visually guided actions in humans can be made to march to the beats of two separate drummers.

Chapter 3 is devoted to dissociations between the visual recognition of objects, the perception of spatial relationships among objects and visually guided actions in brain lesioned human patients. Chapter 4 is devoted to the study of dissociations between perception and visually guided actions in normal human beings. Both the neuropsychological study of brain lesioned human patients and psychophysical experiments in normal human adults make use of some of the characteristics of the movements of the human hand in the course of a prehension action. Indeed, the detailed analysis of arm and hand movements in actions of prehension has become the favorite toolkit of both psychophysicists and neuropsychologists.

Thanks to the articulation of their upper limbs and the dexterity of their hands, non-human primates and humans are able to make prehension movements and to grasp objects. The hand consists of a pulpar surface and the opposition between four fingers and the thumb. The hand allows two basic kinds of grip: a precision grip and a power grip. The handle of a tea cup is grasped with precision grip. A hammer is grasped with power grip. Due to the relatively shorter length of their thumb, the precision grip of non-human primates cannot compete with that of humans: non-human primates handle small objects between their thumbs and the middle phalanx of their index finger. In non-human primates, the pulp or the side of the thumb can contact the side of the middle or the terminal phalanx of the index finger; but rarely if ever, in non-human primates, can the pulp of the thumb contact the pulp of either the fourth or the fifth finger.

In the early 1980s, it was discovered that the finger-grip formed by the hand at the instant the hand contacts the object to be grasped is the final stage of a motor process that starts much before the hand touches the object. The action of grasping involves at least three components organized in a parallel non-sequential structure: a selection component, a reaching component and a grasping component.

The selection phase is the true perceptual part of the process: the target of prehension must first be sorted out from a number of competitors. The rest of the process is an automatic visuomotor process in which the visual information is used for the purpose of action. In the selection process, the object is recognized on the basis of its shape, orientation, size, texture, color. During the perceptual phase, the object is spatially located relative to other neighboring objects in the visual array in an allocentric frame of reference. No object in the environment can be grasped unless the agent reaches it.

The action of grasping involves a reaching component guided by a representation of the location of the object, not in an allocentric frame of reference, but in an egocentric frame of reference centered on the agent's body. In order to launch the reaching phase, the perceptual representation elaborated during the selection phase activates 'motor schemas'. The reaching part of an action of grasping involves ballistic movements of the different segments of the upper limb connecting the hand to the shoulder. Importantly, it was found that during transportation of the hand, there is an automatic process of grip formation: the preshaping of the fingers is programmed much before the hand touches the object. Transportation of the hand itself consists first of a progressive opening and then a closure of the fingers. The opening reaches its peak—the so-called MGA (for maximum grip aperture)—at about 60% of the movement of transportation. It has been found that the size of the finger-grip at MGA (though much larger than the object to be grasped) is linearly correlated with the size of the object. This finding shows that the calibration of the finger-grip aperture is made automatically on the basis of a visuomotor representation of the geometrical properties of the object. Measuring MGA during the action of grasping thus provides a unique insight into the human visuomotor transformation.

Reaching culminates when the hand contacts its target. Grasping of the object involves automatic planning of the calibration of the finger-grip and the rotation of the wrist, so as to allow the best grasp upon contact between the hand and the object. Whereas transportation of the hand is guided by a representation of the location of the object in egocentric coordinates, calibration of the finger-grip and rotation of the wrist involve processing of the size, shape and orientation of the object.

The empirical evidence reviewed in Chapter 3 is very different from the evidence reviewed in Chapter 2. Much of the knowledge in the neuropsychological literature reviewed in Chapter 3 revolves around the careful examination and testing of a few patients. Due to a lesion, these patients have been deprived at some level or other of one of the two fundamental capacities whose exercise depends on an intact ventral pathway and on an intact dorsal pathway. In the 1970s, blindsight patients with a lesion in the primary visual cortex, who are deprived of phenomenal visual experience in their impaired hemifield, were discovered to have surprising residual visuomotor capacities. The discovery of blindsight patients raised the fundamental question: 'how important is phenomenal visual experience for visually guided actions on objects in the world?'. As we already noticed, many philosophers of mind and perception, who subscribe to what we earlier called the EBC (for 'experience-based control') assumption, have been tempted to respond that indeed phenomenal visual experience is of crucial importance for acting efficiently on the world.

In Chapter 3, we pursue this question and examine evidence that we take to be inconsistent with a simple reading of the EBC assumption. Thus, we review cases of patients in whom lesions at different levels of the ventral pathway produce impairments of various degrees in the visual perception, recognition and identification of objects.

Conversely, we review cases of patients whose lesions in the dorsal pathway produce impairments in either the visuomotor transformation or in spatial orientation and in the ability to localize objects in space. It came as a great surprise to find that patients with a lesion in the ventral pathway, who could not perceive and recognize the shape of objects, could still accurately grasp them. Some patients with a lesion in the dorsal pathway, whose visuomotor transformation has been damaged, can still perceive and recognize objects that they fail to grasp normally. Furthermore, relying on their favorite toolkit, neuropsychologists have been able to use one and the same effector—namely the distance between thumb and index finger—to test patients' ability either to grasp an object or to visually estimate its size, shape and orientation. The very same patients, who can scale the distance between their index finger and their thumb to the size of an object in one task, fail in the other task.

In Chapter 4, we review numerous psychophysical experiments in normal human adults whose purpose is to establish a dissociation between perception and action. In these experiments, the typical actions can be of two kinds: pointing and grasping. We review experiments that show that normal human adults are able to point accurately their index finger towards a target that just moved and of whose motion they are not perceptually aware. We contrast the temporal properties of the processing responsible for the accurate visuomotor action of pointing and for perceptual awareness. Then much of the chapter is devoted to an examination of a series of experiments using size-contrast visual illusions—some of which involve pointing and some of which involve grasping. A size-contrast illusion, such as the famous Titchener (or Ebbinghaus) illusion, arises from the automatic comparison between the visual computation of the size of the diameter of a central circle and the computation of the size of the diameters of either smaller or larger circles contained in a surrounding annulus. It has been known since the late nineteenth century that the perceptual comparison between two circles of equal diameter, one surrounded by an annulus of circles larger than it, the other surrounded by an annulus of circles smaller than it, gives rise to a robust illusion: the former looks smaller than the former. However, experiments in the mid-1990s, using the toolkit of psychophysics, measured the grip aperture of subjects asked to grasp one of two three-dimensional disks of equal diameter surrounded by different illusory annuli. These experiments showed a dissociation between perception and action: the illusion turned out to be significantly weaker on action than on perception. Some methodological criticisms were leveled against the interpretation of the initial experiment. The experimental situation has become quite entangled. We try to provide a balanced assessment of the situation, which, we believe, corroborates the view that the representations underlying action can be dissociated from the representations underlying perception.

2 Multiple pathways in the primate visual system

The general idea that the same object can be simultaneously processed by different visual pathways is by no means a new one. Indeed, this idea corresponds to the physiological evidence that there is no single act of seeing. First of all, not all animals see the same things or the same properties of things. For example, some see colors, others do not. Second, in the same animal, seeing may vary according to the task: it may have multiple behavioral expressions. Avoiding or catching a visual object might not rely on the same kinds of neural operations as identifying or categorizing it for the purpose of building up a classification. One could even go so far as thinking that these broadly different operations require different anatomical systems with different connections and intrinsic organizations. Our goal in this chapter is thus to review the progressive build-up by anatomists and physiologists of the concept of multiple visual systems with specialized functions. In particular, we will examine the grounds for distinguishing a visual subsystem dedicated to localizing a stimulus (the 'where' system) from a visual subsystem dedicated to its identification (the 'what' system).

1 The where and the what: two visual systems

The idea that the visual system is a heterogeneous ensemble stems from evolutionary theorizing among comparative anatomists at the end of the nineteenth century. Orienting reflexes and simple visuomotor functions were hypothesized to belong to primitive subcortical visual systems well exemplified by, e.g. amphibians. The frog's visual system is based on an isotropic retina and retinotopic projections onto midbrain structures such as the optic tectum, which have close links to the motor system that governs head and limb movements. As illustrated by the work of Ingle (1973, 1982), the study of the frog's visual system has revealed that two distinct neural pathways underlie two kinds of visually guided behaviors. The visual control of prey-catching behavior is mediated by retinal projections onto the optic tectum, while the visual control of barrier avoidance in locomotion is mediated by retinal projections onto pretectal nuclei. By contrast with these simple visuomotor capacities, the analysis leading to the identification and/or recognition of the visual stimulus—something that frogs do not do—were attributed to more recently evolved visual systems, i.e. systems comprising a visual cortex. From an evolutionary point of view, the transition from simple visuomotor functions to more complex operations involved in the identification of a visual stimulus were supposed to be accounted for by the addition of successively more complex layers to the elementary visual competencies of primitive organisms throughout the phylogenetic scale. One such typical evolutionary creation would be the addition of a visual cortex to subcortical visual structures.

In a series of seminal papers, Ingle (1967), Trevarthen (1968) and Schneider (1969) entertained a preliminary version of the dualistic approach to vision. In particular, Schneider (1969) demonstrated that a hamster with a lesion of its optic tectum became unable to orient towards visual stimuli presented in its peripheral visual field. The animal was nonetheless able to discriminate horizontal from vertical stripes—something a hamster with an intact tectum and a lesioned visual cortex cannot do. In this early dualistic framework, there was neither any hierarchy nor any priority given to the 'where' system over the 'what' system: the animal was not expected to be able to local- ize a stimulus in space before being able to identify some of its intrinsic properties.

There is, however, an important difference between the two contrasting kinds of tasks used to illustrate the hamster's 'two visual systems'. Processing the spatial posi- tion of a stimulus consists in turning the eyes and the hand in its direction so as to be able to interact with it. Thus, there is no gap between the visual task and the visuo- motor response: the visuomotor response is congruent with the visual analysis of the stimulus. When the animal discriminates horizontal from vertical stripes, its discrimin- atory ability is also expressed through a behavioral response. In this case, however, there is a gap between the animal's action and the visual task, since the latter consists of a visually based choice (vertical vs. horizontal) made according to some criterion that the animal had to learn. Already at this elementary level of visual cognition, one encounters a primitive version of the opposition between visually guided actions and visual perception (which will play a pivotal role in the rest of this book).

A still different version of the 'two visual systems' framework arose in connection with the study of vision in primates, not rodents. Trevarthen's (1968) model offers a dis- tinction between two complementary systems for visually guided behavior. In this model, subcortical (midbrain) structures, whose job is to ensure 'ambient' vision, mostly controlled by peripheral retinal information processing, match visual loci onto goals for movements via the representation of body-centered visual space. The job of cortical (phylogenetically more recent) structures is 'focal' vision: they underlie more detailed visual examination of small areas of space in order to allow the generation of highly specific acts (small exploratory eye movements, hand and finger movements, etc.) within the central field of vision mediated by the foveal part of the retina.

2 Two cortical visual systems

A crucial step was taken by Mishkin and collaborators, in the mid-1970s, when they firmly located the two visual systems within the visual cortex. The main rationale for this move was that, on their view, the so-called 'where' system in primates ought to be considered as a perceptual, and therefore cortical, system. On this view, the visuo- motor function would be achieved by automatic subcortical structures and would be devoted to the localization of objects in space for the sole purpose of immediately performed visually guided actions. The 'where' system, which would be located in the visual cortex, would be devoted to the perceptual processing and memorization of spatial relationships among visual objects in topological space. Cortical specialization for visual processing of spatial relations should thus have co-evolved with the visual capacities for object identification and with visual experience. In other words, one of the chief motivations behind Mishkin's version of the dualistic model of the visual system was his conviction that the major function of the evolutionary process of cortical specialization is to allow perception. One might wonder why interest in space perception was delayed for so long with respect to other aspects of perception, like the perception of objects, for example. It is a fact that clinical disorders in human spatial perception subsequent to cortical lesions were not systematically investigated by neuropsychologists until the Second World War, whereas object agnosia had already been fully described in the early 1900s (see Chapter 3).

Mishkin and his colleagues were impressed by the visual impairments observed in monkeys following ablation of cortical areas quite remote from striate visual cortex, i.e. areas in the temporal and parietal lobes where, at the time, no connections with the visual cortex had yet been described (Mishkin 1966). Subsequent work led to the progressive disclosure of a vast ensemble forming the extrastriate visual cortex: combined anatomical and electrophysiological studies in monkeys have revealed the existence of over 30 visual areas as defined by their retinotopic organization. The pattern of connections between these areas evokes a largely distributed network with reciprocal connections between most of the areas and many examples of parallel as well as serial connections (Boussaoud *et al.* 1990; Morel and Bullier 1990) (Fig. 2.1).

In spite of this apparent complexity of the visual cortical network, a number of organizing principles seem to emerge, which are summarized here:

1. The connections turn out to be segregated into two main streams: one stream—the dorsal stream—links the primary visual cortex (V1), through the middle temporal area (MT), to the posterior parietal lobe. The other stream—the ventral stream—links the primary visual cortex, through area V4, to the inferotemporal region. However, the contribution of V1 to the two streams is not equivalent. Destruction or temporary inactivation of V1 completely deprives 'ventral' neurons from visual input, while 'dorsal' neurons still remain responsive (Girard *et al.* 1992). This difference can be explained by a contribution of subcortical visual pathways to the dorsal stream, not to the ventral stream (see below). Bi-directional interconnections exist between nearly all areas of the two streams. However, as stressed by Young (1992), areas in a given stream are more connected with each other than with areas outside their stream. A large amount of the integration of information processed in the two streams probably occurs at the level of the prefrontal cortex, which is densely connected with both of them (e.g. Baizer *et al.* 1991). According to Bullier and his colleagues, the projections of the two streams converge only on a small area of the lateral frontal eye field (area 45). The global pattern is that of two networks: one of these networks is associated with the inferotemporal cortex and includes the connections between the ventral bank of the superior temporal sulcus, the ventral peristriate cortex and the lateral frontal eye field. This network underlies central vision, object recognition, exploration of the visual field with small eye movements. The other network is associated with parietal areas in the intraparietal sulcus: it consists of areas in the dorsal prestriate cortex, in the upper bank of the superior temporal

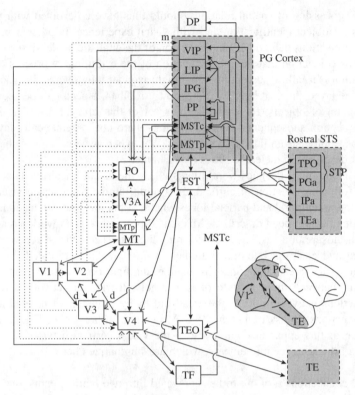

Fig. 2.1 An anatomical view of the 'two visual systems' model. This flow chart outlines the main connections between visual cortical areas. The projections from primary visual cortex (area V1, which receives afferents from the retina via the lateral geniculate body) are organized in two main pathways. The ventral pathway, through area V4, reaches the inferotemporal cortex (areas TE and TEO). The dorsal pathway, through area MT, reaches areas at the parieto-occipital junction (area PO) and areas buried in the intraparietal sulcus (areas VIP, LIP, MIP, etc.). Area AIP, discovered more recently, is not mentioned here.

Note the existence of a putative 'third' pathway reaching the region of the superior temporal sulcus (STS). See Chapter 7 for a description of the role of STS areas. Also note the density of connections between the two main pathways, and the reciprocal nature of nearly all connections. (From Boussaoud *et al*. 1990 permission sought.)

sulcus and the medial part of the frontal eye field. It is involved in peripheral vision and large eye movements (Morel and Bullier 1990; Schall *et al*. 1995; Bullier *et al*. 1996).

2. Retinotopic organization, which is rather strict in areas close to V1, tends to vanish as one gets further away from retino-geniculate projections: receptive fields tend to become larger and larger until they overlap with the whole hemifield, or even the entire visual field, in remote temporal areas, for example.

3. Visual inputs reaching areas located in the parietal lobe tend to originate from representations of the peripheral visual field, whereas those reaching the temporal lobe originate from the more central part of the visual field.

4. The fibers innervating each pathway can be tracked down to different cellular ensembles in the lateral geniculate body. The dorsal stream is irrigated almost exclusively by projections originating from the magnocellular part of the lateral geniculate body, i.e. by large fibers with fast conduction velocities and transient discharge properties. By contrast, the ventral stream receives fibers from both the magnocellular region and the parvocellular region: parvocellular fibers have slower conduction velocities and sustained discharge properties. Also, the organization of the information flow in the ventral stream is more sequential and includes fewer shortcuts than the dorsal stream, which includes direct projections from V1 onto areas MT and V6. These differences may explain why visual latencies in the dorsal stream (40–80 ms) are faster than in the ventral stream (100–150 ms).

5. The parietal areas are heavily connected with motor centers in the frontal lobe, including monosynaptic connections with the premotor cortex. This is not true for temporal areas, which are devoid of direct access to motor centers and can reach the premotor cortex only through prefrontal areas. No doubt, these anatomical and functional differences will impose sharp constraints on the type of information-processing effected by each stream, and on the type of behavioral response that can be expected from each of them.

In the experiments of the Mishkin group on monkeys, attention was primarily focused on the behavioral effects of lesions localized in different extrastriate visual areas. Behavioral effects were measured using a revised version of a test used for measuring memory capacities. In both conditions, a board was shown with two covered food-wells, about 25 cm apart from each other. In the object-discrimination task, two distinct objects with different shapes, colors and textures were each located next to each food-well. The animal had to select the novel object, i.e. the object that had not been previously shown. In the space-perception experiment, an object used as a landmark was located either closer or farther away from one food-well: the animal had to select the food-well closest to the landmark object.

The major outcome of these experiments was that lesions in the temporal and in the parietal visual associative areas, respectively, produced contrasting effects. A lesion in the inferotemporal cortex deprived the animal of both the ability to memorize the discrimination of a novel object made prior to the lesion, and the post-operative ability to make new discriminations. The deficits involved not only color- or brightness-based discriminations, but also discriminations based on three-dimensional shapes (e.g. Gross 1973). By contrast, a lesion in the posterior parietal cortex affected the monkey's performance in the landmark task (see Fig. 2.2). To quote Mishkin's (1972) own terms, these results suggest that 'the inferior temporal cortex participates mainly in the acts of noticing and remembering an object's qualities, not its position in space'. They suggest further that 'conversely, the posterior parietal cortex seems to be concerned with the perception of spatial relations among objects, and not their intrinsic qualities'. Hence, in this framework, the basic contrast is drawn in terms of two kinds of visual attributes of a perceived object: its intrinsic qualities and its extrinsic spatial relationships to other objects in the visual array.

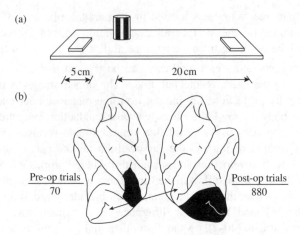

Fig. 2.2 The role of monkey parietal cortex in spatial orientation. (a) The landmark test. The monkey learns that the reward is hidden in the food-well close to the landmark object. The position of the landmark is changed at each trial. (b) Brain lesions shown on external views of the two hemispheres. The critical parietal area is ablated on one hemisphere (*left*). The *right* hemisphere is rendered blind by ablation of the primary visual cortex. Thus, the monkey is left with one hemisphere without parietal cortex. It takes 70 trials for an intact animal to learn the task, but after 800 trials, the lesioned animal still fails. (Rearranged from Ungerleider and Mishkin 1982, in D.J. Ingle, M.A. Goodale, and R.J.W. Mansfield (eds.) *Analysis of visual behaviour* (1982), published by MIT Press, with permission.)

We may thus sum up the main contributions of this model to the elaboration of the concept of specialized (cortical) visual systems under two main headings. On the one hand, this model departs in three respects from the previous versions of the 'two visual systems' model, which involved a distinction between a cortical and a subcortical system:

1. Ungerleider and Mishkin (1982) clearly restrict the role of subcortical (retinotectal) structures and their projections onto the parietal cortex (via the pulvinar) to purely visuomotor functions;

2. they ascribe to subcortical structures a merely ancillary role in the visual perception of spatial relationships;

3. although they acknowledge that misreaching is also a symptom of posterior parietal dysfunction, Ungerleider and Mishkin nonetheless emphasize the fact that parietal lesions prevalently produce visual spatial disorientation.

On the other hand, the aim of their model is predominantly to describe perceptual functions. The job of the ventral pathway is to allow an appreciation of an object's intrinsic qualities, whereas the job of the dorsal pathway is to provide an analysis of the spatial relationships among objects. Mishkin explicitly referred to the ventral and the dorsal pathways, respectively, as the 'object' and the 'space' channels, suggesting their complementary specialization for decoding objects' properties and their spatial relationships.

In the next sections, we will describe the contribution of experiments performed on macaque monkeys in the last 25 years to the concept of specialized visual systems. Given that experimental evidence gathered on animals has enormously grown during this period, and given that it has been used for addressing questions about vision in humans where precise anatomical and physiological data are difficult to obtain, the description of experiments in macaque monkeys is critical for an analysis and evaluation of the dualistic theory of the visual system, its strengths and weaknesses. For the sake of clarity, these data have been classified under three main categories, according to whether they refer to object discrimination, the perception of spatial relationships or the visuomotor transformation.

3 Neural mechanisms for object discrimination: the encoding of intrinsic object properties

The general idea of the Mishkin school was that object discrimination is a sequential process in which information that reaches the striate cortex is transmitted for further processing to the prestriate cortex, and from there to the inferotemporal areas TEO and TE in the superior temporal sulcus. The pioneering work of Gross *et al.* (1972), using cell recordings in anaesthetized monkeys, showed that inferotemporal neurons are preferentially activated by complex visual stimuli (Gross *et al.* used stimuli like a hand, a feather, a leaf, etc.). This view holds that object attributes are processed serially from simpler features to more complex ones. For example, V1 and V2 cells extract oriented edges and contours, V4 cells respond if the stimulus pops out from the background on the basis of its shape or color, whereas inferotemporal cells, and especially TE cells, respond to considerably more complex features of objects presented in a 2D or 3D format.

This hierarchy of cortical visual areas based on the existence of feedforward connections between areas (known as the 'feedforward model', see: Ungerleider and Haxby 1994; Rolls and Deco 2002) tends to overlook the fact that connections between areas are in fact reciprocal. As stressed by Bullier (2001a), the fact that the primate visual system instantaneously identifies complex objects from a noisy visual scene cannot be accounted for by a purely feedforward system. How could such a system interpret the global view of a scene that has been first segmented and analyzed detail by detail at the lower levels of the system? How could it achieve object recognition when occlusions, shadows, luminance edges and the like interfere with the low-level segmentation process? One solution to this problem would be that the analysis of the global scene is returned to the lower level, so that the detailed local analysis is combined with the global interpretation: only then can the occlusion and luminance artifacts be resolved. This dynamical view of visual processing is supported by the existence of fast feedback connections from higher order areas down to the V1 and V2 level. According to Bullier (2001b), an early wave of activation driven by the magnocellular cells of the lateral geniculate nucleus reaches V1 some 20 ms earlier than the activation driven by the slower parvocellular neurons. 'This suggests that the first wave of magnocellular activity conveys a first-pass analysis of the visual scene and that the results of computation done in higher-order areas are rapidly retro-injected into lower-order areas in time for the arrival of the parvocellular wave of activity. Combination of the early feedback activation and the feedforward input from parvocellular neurons may be essential for the proper processing of information by other cortical areas in the hierarchy' (Bullier 2001b: 370).

The stimulus selectivity of individual neurons in the ventral stream of macaque monkeys has been thoroughly investigated in the anaesthetized preparation. Attempts have been made at systematically reducing the stimulus complexity, by simplifying the set of features comprising, e.g. complex biological visual stimuli: the outcome of this procedure is that neurons are activated by moderately complex assemblages of simple features. According to the study of Tanaka *et al.* (1991) (Fig. 2.3), cells in the posterior part of the inferotemporal cortex respond better to relatively simple stimuli like elongated bars or small colored disks (primary cells). Other cells, scattered throughout the

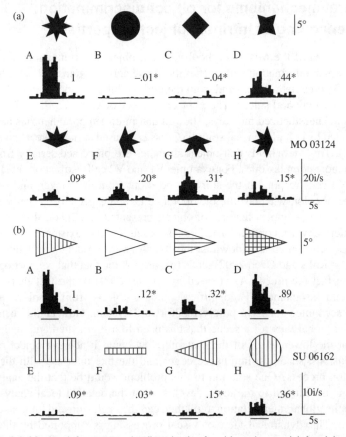

Fig. 2.3 Monkey inferotemporal cells selective for object shapes. (a) An elaborate cell responding to a star shape. Cell response is shown by histograms below the shape. Note maximal response for shapes A, D and G. (b) An elaborate cell that required integration of texture and shape. The critical feature was a vertical grating within a triangle with the apex directed to the right. Note maximal response in A and D. (From Tanaka *et al.* 1991, *Journal of Neurophysiology*)

inferotemporal cortex, are sensitive to textures, e.g. striped or dotted patterns of a given spatial frequency (texture cells). Finally, still another category, elaborate cells, was identified in the more anterior part of the inferotemporal cortex. Elaborate cells responded better to shapes like brushes, pineapple leaves or other stimuli involving multiple projections from a central body. Others were sensitive to a combination of two different or identical shapes (e.g. two disks), or to a combination of a shape and a texture or several textures and/or colors. Consider the example given by Tanaka (1993) where an individual TE neuron was found to fire upon detecting the image of a tiger's head seen from the top down (Fig. 2.4). He showed that a single cell keeps responding to a series of simplifications of the visual stimulus until the tiger's head is reduced to a combination of a pair of symmetrical black rectangles flanking a white square. The cell stops responding when presented with either a picture of the two black rectangles or the white square alone.

Tanaka *et al.* (1991) conclude from their study that the analysis of visual stimuli effected by inferotemporal neurons is not complex enough to specify a particular biological object on the basis of a single cell discharge. Thus, a group of cells with different critical features is necessary to specify a particular natural object. Cells with overlapping, but slightly different, selectivity tend to cluster in modules or columns of roughly 500 μm by 500 μm on average (an organization of cells in TE reminiscent of the columnar structure observed in many other areas of the cerebral cortex). Moderately complex stimuli can thus be detected by the coordinated activities of several cells with overlapping selectivity and organized in such columns. The contribution of several modules may be necessary for representing the whole image of an object. However, because TE receptive fields are too large to discriminate different objects according to their retinal positions, the problem arises of disentangling the activities of several modules for one single object and for different objects respectively. One solution to this problem— one version of the problem of 'binding'—would be that activities of different and sometimes distant modules related to a single object would in some way be synchronized with each other, whereas activities arising from different objects would remain asynchronous (Tanaka 1993). In fact, the role of synchronous processing between interacting

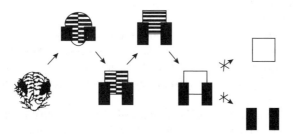

Fig. 2.4 Critical features for the activation of a single inferotemporal cell. The method consists in gradually reducing the complexity of the stimulus, from a real tiger head (*left*) down to a white square flanked with two black bars. Further reduction (white square or black bars alone) does not trigger a cell response. (Reprinted with permission from Tanaka, K. (1993) Neuronal mechanisms of object recognition. *Science*, **262**, 685–8. Copyright 1993 American Association for the Advancement of Science.)

cells located at some distance from one another, for perceptual grouping, has been emphasized by Engel *et al.* (1992) and by Singer *et al.* (1997).[1]

The mechanism for this high degree of selectivity depends on local inhibitory circuits, depending on the role of a neuromediator, GABA. The inhibitory action of GABA can be reversibly blocked by the local injection of bicuculine. When bicuculine is injected in a small area of the inferotemporal cortex, where a population of TE neurons selective for particular object features has been detected, the selectivity of neurons at the injection site is markedly altered: neuron responses to previously effective stimuli will be decreased and neurons will respond to previously ineffective stimuli. This experiment (Wang *et al.* 2000) sheds some light on the role of local inhibition in tuning inferotemporal neurons to specific visual stimuli.

The selectivity of TE neurons is maintained in the absence of the effective stimulus. In other words, the selectivity of TE neurons is not purely tuned to the detection of a visual stimulus, but to its memorization as well. This property can be demonstrated by recording neuron activity during a delay period of a visual short-term memory task, where the monkey must memorize the image of an object. This sustained activity (as well as the activity of the neuron during presentation of the object) can be shown to code pictorial information relevant to the memorized representation of the object and is not directly correlated with the latter's physical attributes: it is uninfluenced by the size, orientation, color or position of the object in the visual field. Thus the sustained activity during the delay period relates to a memorized percept (Miyashita and Chang 1988). A further experiment indicates that these cells might in fact represent the memory store for pictorial information. Tomita *et al.* (1999) further studied this property of TE cells to be selectively activated by the image of a previously learned stimulus, in the absence of the stimulus itself. The monkey performed a stimulus–stimulus association task, where the effective stimulus for a given cell was remembered by the animal when another, ineffective, stimulus was shown. As Tomita *et al.* argue, this cell activation was likely to reflect the influence of the top-down signal originating in other areas, presumably located in the prefrontal cortex. Accordingly, when area TE was experimentally disconnected from prefrontal areas, the cell failed to be activated. Thus, the reciprocal projection between the prefrontal cortex and the inferotemporal cortex appears to mediate the recall of pictorial information stored in TE cells. These data on the selectivity of TE cells and their memory properties fully account for the effects of bilateral inferotemporal lesions as they were performed in Mishkin's experiments. Following such lesions, the animals lost both the ability to memorize the discrimination of an object learned prior to the lesion, and the postoperative ability to make new discriminations.

The fact that TE neurons have large bilateral visual receptive fields, which is itself a consequence of their receiving projections from both hemispheres (Gross *et al.* 1972), explains the fact that they are not sensitive to the stimulus position in the visual field. The latter property provides a mechanism for stimulus invariance across retinal positions and may account for the ability to discriminate and/or recognize an object as the same regardless of its position and orientation in the visual field (Booth and Rolls 1998). Accordingly, the response selectivity of inferotemporal neurons is not influenced

---

[1]We go back to the problem of binding in the last section of Chapter 5.

by the eye position in the orbit, nor by the background retinal stimulation during presentation of the specific stimulus. DiCarlo and Maunsell (2000) showed that the cell response remains unaltered during free viewing, i.e. during the natural condition of form recognition using visual exploration with eye movements. As we shall see below, parietal neurons in the dorsal stream lack this property: parietal neurons tend to have smaller receptive fields than inferotemporal neurons. The former are therefore likely to be more influenced than the latter by the position of the stimulus in the visual field.

When Tanaka *et al.* (1991) concluded that single elaborate cells were unable to specify a complex biological object, they made one major exception. About 15% of elaborate cells that they recorded in the anterior inferotemporal cortex selectively responded to the sight of a face (either simian or human). A few others responded selectively to the view of a hand. This striking selectivity for biologically significant stimuli was extensively studied by Perrett and his group (see review in: Perrett *et al.* 1989; Carey *et al.* 1997). In the STS region, populations of cells are found that are more responsive to the sight of faces than to any other simple or even complex stimuli of interest to the animal (e.g. the picture of a snake or a bird). Some of these cells can be sensitive only to a single facial feature (the eyes). Others respond to the whole face shown in a given orientation: a given cell, e.g. may prefer the front view of a face and stop responding if the face is turned to profile or is rotated upside down. In these populations, cells can be found that respond differentially to different people or monkeys: in that case, they continue to differentiate between individuals for many different views. Perrett *et al.* (1989) also described, in the inferior bank of STS, cells selective to certain hand actions (e.g. reach for, retrieve, manipulate, pick, etc.), with a tendency to generalize their response to different instances of the same action. Hand–object interaction was more effective in firing the cell than object–object interaction and, in the hand–object interaction, the nature of the object itself (e.g. large or small, colored or not) was irrelevant (see Figs 2.5, 2.6). The role of these inferotemporal cells which provide high-level visual descriptions of bodies and their movements will be discussed again in Chapter 7, Section 4.[2]

4 Neural mechanisms for space perception: the encoding of spatial relationships in the posterior parietal lobe

The property of neurons in the dorsal stream to encode spatial parameters is a requirement for the function of posterior parietal areas as a 'space' channel, as demonstrated by the effects of parietal ablations on the landmark test (in Mishkin's experiments). Physiologists, however, are faced with difficulties relative to the role of space in visual perception. Should neurons dedicated to spatial perception be restricted to those that exhibit so-called 'passive' properties, i.e. which encode positions and/or movements of visual stimuli in the environment presented to an immobile observer (in an allocentric

---

[2]Further distinctions between populations of TE cells properties could be made as well. Janssen *et al.* (2000) made a distinction between TE cells in the ventral bank of the superior temporal sulcus, which respond to 2D and 3D shapes, and cells in the lateral TE, which respond to 2D shapes only.

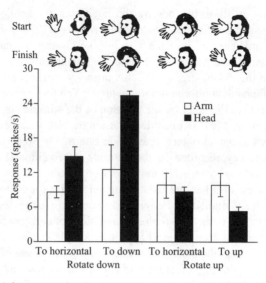

Fig. 2.5 An inferotemporal cell selective for the movement of a human head. The discharge rate of the cell increases when a human head (*black bars*), not a human hand (*white bars*), is moved downwards, not upwards. (Reprinted from Carey *et al.* 1997, with permission from Elsevier.)

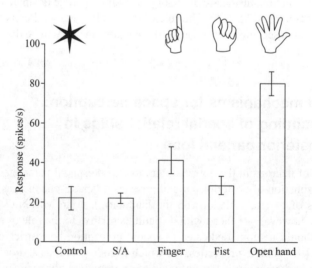

Fig. 2.6 An inferotemporal cell selective for the view of a human hand. The discharge rate of the cell is maximum for the view of an open hand. Other hand shapes or a star are inefficient. S/A: spontaneous activity level of the cell. (Reprinted from Carey *et al.* 1997, with permission from Elsevier.)

frame of reference centered on the observed object and independent from the observer)? Should not one include neurons that exhibit so-called 'active' properties and process spatial visual stimuli in relation to the agent's actions (in an egocentric frame of reference centered on the agent's body)? This distinction is critical since it might represent the boundary between what pertains to space perception in Mishkin's sense and what pertains to the visuomotor transformation during interaction with objects

Before getting to this point, let us first describe the spatial properties of neurons located in areas MT, MST and 7a on the convexity of the posterior parietal cortex (see Fig. 2.7). First, these neurons respond to moving stimuli, i.e. many of them detect the displacement, within their (usually large) receptive fields, of a preferred stimulus (e.g. a square or a disk) along a preferred direction. Note that posterior parietal neurons are much less selective to visual stimuli with a complex internal structure than inferotemporal neurons, mostly because the former cannot detect high spatial frequencies. The moving stimuli, which best trigger the discharges of posterior parietal neurons, are simple objects with well-defined geometric properties. The complexity of the response pattern of these neurons arises from the preferred stimulus motion needed to activate them: some parietal neurons are activated by looming stimuli, e.g. expanding/contracting objects; others are influenced by a rotatory motion, e.g. when an object rotates around its axis in the frontal plane or in the sagittal plane (Fig. 2.8); still others are activated when a stimulus is presented, within a large receptive field, close to the fixation point, not if the stimulus is presented farther away from the fixation point (Sakata *et al.* 1985, 1986).

These neurons 'passively' encode spatial transformations occurring during object motion. They are suited for the perception of spatial cues, such as distance or orientation. They are to be distinguished from other neurons present in more or less the same

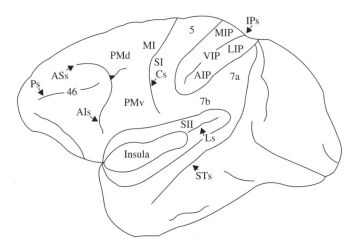

Fig. 2.7 A lateral view of the left hemisphere of a monkey brain. On this lateral view, the lateral sulcus (Ls) and the intraparietal sulcus (Ips) have been open to show buried areas. In the Ips, note area AIP at the tip of the sulcus. Cs: central sulcus. MI, SI: primary motor and somatosensory areas, respectively. PMd, PMv: dorsal and ventral premotor cortex, respectively. (From Jeannerod *et al.* 1995 with permission from the author.)

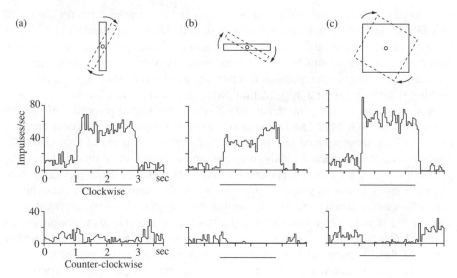

Fig. 2.8 A parietal cell selective for spatial transformations. The cell discharge, shown as post-stimulus time histograms, increases when (a) a vertical bar, (b) a horizontal bar or (c) a square are rotated clockwise in front of the monkey. Counter-clockwise rotation of the same stimuli produces no increase in discharge rate. (From Sakata *et al.* 1985 permission sought.)

areas and which are activated when the animal is active during the presentation of the stimulus. This is the case, for example, of neurons that discharge when a stimulus is presented within their receptive field and the animal is actively looking at a given point in space (Andersen and Mountcastle 1983). Such neurons are likely to encode, not only the presence of some spatial property of a visual stimulus, but also the direction of gaze as well (Sakata *et al.* 1985). As such, they come close to the next category to be described, namely, visuomotor neurons. We call visuomotor neurons those that operate the coordinate transformation needed for the animal to act on the spatially coded visual stimuli.

5   Neural mechanisms for acting in space: the visuomotor functions of posterior parietal areas

The second major step in building the model of specialized visual systems was the discovery of the role of the parietal cortex in the visuomotor transformation. In 1975, Mountcastle and his colleagues published an influential paper on neuron properties in the posterior parietal cortical areas (Mountcastle *et al.* 1975). Quoting from a paper written by this author 20 years later (Mountcastle 1995: 377, 378), these neurons were active:

[...] if and only if the animal 'had a mind' to deal with the stimulus in a behaviorally meaningful way! In *area 5*, there were neurons active when the animal projected his arm toward a target of interest, not during random arm movements [...]. Quite different sets of neurons appeared to drive the transport and grasping phases of reaching movements [...].

In *area* 7, there were neurons active during visual fixation of objects of interest, not during casual fixations; neurons active during visually evoked but not during spontaneous saccadic eye movements [...].

The term 'command neurons' was first used by the authors to indicate the involvement of this mechanism in visually goal-oriented movements. Later, however, they chose to redescribe neurons from areas 5 and 7 as a subclass of visual neurons, responding to specific visual stimuli, following Mountcastle's argument that only neurons directly involved in the perception of seen objects should be categorized as 'visual'. Relevant to this choice is the distinction drawn, at the end of the previous section, between parietal neurons, respectively, with 'passive' properties and 'active' properties. Neurons with 'active' properties, i.e. neurons from areas 5 and 7, which fire in the course of visually guided actions, better correspond to Mountcastle's earlier insight of a category of neurons with visuomotor properties.

Mountcastle's (1975) paper (together with a paper with very similar results published by Hyvarinen and Poranen in 1974) undoubtedly drew attention to the visuomotor function of the posterior parietal cortex. Consequently, a series of lesion experiments were performed, in which the site of the lesion was focused on area 7. Lamotte and Acuna (1978) and Faugier Grimaud *et al.* (1978) found striking effects on the animal's motor behavior mostly limited to the hand contralateral to the lesion: during the first post-operative days, the contralateral hand remained generally unused, although it was in no way paralyzed as the animal could use it, albeit awkwardly, when the other hand was attached. When the affected hand was used by the animal, severe visuomotor deficits became apparent: the animal misreached visual food targets located anywhere in the workspace. In addition, the hand was not shaped according to objects' shape or size, and precision grip was abolished. These visuomotor effects must have been overlooked in the parietal lesion experiments performed by the Mishkin group, which were not designed for the analysis of goal-directed movements.

In the last two decades, the experiment by Mountcastle and his collaborators was followed by a long series of studies aimed at elucidating, at the level of posterior parietal neurons, the mechanisms of what is now designated as the visuomotor transformation. The problem here is two-fold:

1. What are the basic operations for mapping external space onto egocentric space?
2. How is the analysis of an object's intrinsic properties—like shape—transformed into motor commands?

5.1   Neural mechanisms for coordinate transformations in the posterior parietal cortex

Visual stimuli are first coded by the nervous system according to the position of their projection on the retina. This retinocentric space can be described, e.g. in areas V1 or V2, as a set of radial coordinates originating at the fovea, the optical center of the retina. However, in order for a moving animal to get hold of the object that gives rise to its visual experience (to look at it and/or to reach towards it), other cues must be added to the retinocentric map. Signals related to the position of the eye in the orbit and to the position of the head with respect to the rest of the body must be available, so that eye and arm movements can be generated in the proper direction. Indeed, reaching for a visual object requires that the frame of reference in which the object-oriented movement is computed must have its origin on the agent's body, i.e. that its position be determined in an egocentric frame of reference. This constraint stems from the fact that object position in space must be reconstructed by adding signals from eye, head and body positions for the arm to be ultimately directed at the proper location. Determining object position in space by computing its retinal position alone would be inappropriate, because one and the same locus in external space would correspond to different retinal positions according to respective eye, head and body positions (Jeannerod 1988). The following paragraphs describe some of the mechanisms that have been identified in recent experiments in monkeys and which could account for transforming retinal (eye-centered) coordinates into (body-centered) egocentric coordinates. These mechanisms are primarily located in the intraparietal sulcus (see Fig. 2.7).

An influential hypothesis proposes that the basic information about where to reach for an object is the motor command sent to the eyes to move in its direction (the eye position signal). As mentioned earlier, neurons in area 7a have been shown to encode visual stimuli for a specific position of the eye in its orbit, i.e. they fire preferentially when the object stimulates a given location on the retina (the neuron's receptive field), and when the gaze is fixating in that direction (Andersen and Mountcastle 1983). These neurons would provide a representation of visual space by taking into account, not only the retinal projection of the target, but also signals providing information about the position of the eye in its orbit. This representation could subsequently be transferred to the premotor cortex for guiding the arm reach. This mechanism, however, is hardly compatible with the organization of visually guided movements observed during a normal action of pointing directed to a visual target: although the gaze appears to move first to the location of the desired stimulus, followed by the arm movement within about 150 ms, a closer look shows that, because the motor command to the arm muscles anticipates arm displacement by about the same amount, the motor commands to the eye and to the arm are in fact more or less synchronous (Biguer *et al.* 1982). Duhamel and his colleagues found the solution to that enigma. They discovered in area LIP neurons that fire in response to a stimulus briefly presented, not within their receptive field, but within the area of space where their receptive field will project after an eye movement is made. This effect begins some 80 ms before the eye movement starts (Duhamel *et al.* 1992). The retinal position of receptive fields is thus modified prior to the occurrence of an eye movement. This anticipatory remapping of the representation of space in parietal cortex accounts for the guidance of the arm to the target. In addition, it ensures perceptual stability of the visual scene during the eye movement.

In area VIP, neuron discharges testify to a different form of remapping. Their recept-ive fields remain in the same spatial position irrespective of eye position in the orbit. In this case, therefore, the receptive fields appear to be anchored, not to the eye, but to the head, i.e. the receptive fields move across the retina when the eyes move (Duhamel *et al.* 1997). Eye and head position signals, however, should not be sufficient in and of themselves for generating a directional signal for guiding the arm. Besides position of the stimulus on the retina and position of the eye in the orbit, the position of the arm with respect to the body must also be available to the arm motor command. This function is achieved by neurons presenting receptive fields in two sensory modalities.

Neurons in area MIP, e.g. respond to both a localized visual stimulus and a cutaneous stimulation applied to one hand. These bimodal neurons are strongly activated when the monkey reaches with that hand to the visual target within their receptive field (see: Andersen *et al*. 1997; Colby 1998).

These parietal areas directly project onto the premotor cortex (area 6). The dorsal part of area 6, where neurons coding for reaching movements are found, is connected with the rostralmost part of area 7a (Matelli *et al*. 1986), with area MIP (Johnson *et al*. 1993) and with area PO, either directly (Tanné *et al*. 1995), or via the superior parietal lobule (Caminiti *et al*. 1996). Galletti *et al*. (1993) found in area PO a variety of neurons (which they call the 'real position' cells), the receptive field of which keeps the same position, with respect to the head, when the eyes move. It should therefore not be surprising that neurons located in the motor region, outside the parietal cortex, also encode the position of visual stimuli with respect to the body. Indeed, such neurons were found by Graziano and his colleagues in the premotor cortex: they have both tactile and visual receptive fields that extend from the tactile area into adjacent space. For those neurons that have their tactile receptive field on the arm, the visual receptive field moves when the arm is displaced (Graziano *et al*. 1994). These visual receptive fields anchored to the arm encode visual stimulus location in body (arm) coordinates and thus may provide a solution for directional coding of reaching.

A question, which is still open for further discussion, is whether neurons encoding the spatial location of a target are merely linked to execution of the movement toward that target, or reflect plans for movements which may or may not be executed. Many parietal neurons, including in area LIP, have been found to keep firing during a prolonged waiting period after a stimulus has been briefly presented. According to Colby and Goldberg (1999), this prolonged discharge can be an effect of sustained attention on a point of space corresponding to where the stimulus was, in view of execution. Andersen and his colleagues, however, consider that LIP neurons encode, not the stimulus, but the monkey's intention to perform a given movement, based on the argument that the sustained neuronal response is selective for the movement (e.g. eye or arm) called for by the instruction (see Snyder *et al*. 1996). A similar observation was made by Assad and Maunsell (1995). These authors found that neurons from the lateral bank of the intraparietal sulcus responsive to the motion of a visual stimulus kept firing while the stimulus disappeared behind a mask. These observations of a sustained discharge of parietal neurons in the absence of a visual stimulus will have to be reconciled with the current conception of the role of the parietal cortex in the 'immediate' or 'automatic' guidance of movements. The possibility that parietal neurons might entertain an abstract representation of the spatial position of targets must be seriously considered.

5.2   Neural mechanisms for transforming object geometric properties into motor commands

Grasping an object and reaching it rely on quite different systems: the former involves distal segments, multiple degrees of freedom, high degree of reliance on tactile function. Grasping is thus the result of an ensemble of visuomotor transformations that pre-shape the hand while it is transported at the object location, according to object features such as its size, its shape or its orientation. This function is also part of the parietal contribution to visuomotor coordination. Neurons related to active hand movements were first recorded in the inferior parietal lobe by Mountcastle and his colleagues, who identified, besides the 'arm projection' neurons related to reaching, a group of 'hand manipulation' neurons (Mountcastle *et al.* 1975).

More recently, hand movement-related neurons were found by Sakata and his colleagues to be concentrated in a small zone (the anterior intraparietal area, AIP) within the rostral part of the posterior bank of the intraparietal sulcus (Taira *et al.* 1990; Sakata *et al.* 1992). Using a broad variety of 3D graspable objects, including primitive shapes such as spheres, cubes, cones, cylinders, rings and plates of different sizes, they found that individual AIP neurons were active during grasping one particular type of object. The objects were all white in color and they were displayed against a black background (Fig. 2.9). The experimenters compared four different tasks. During the 'hand manipulation task', the object was illuminated and the monkey was required to grasp and manipulate the object in the dark after the light had been turned off. During the 'object fixation task', the monkey was required to fixate the illuminated object without manipulating it. During the 'delayed hand manipulation task', before he could manipulate the object in the dark, the monkey had to wait for 2 s after the light had been turned off. During the 'light interrupted object fixation task', the monkey was tested during eye fixation for 2 s in the dark without any manipulation. On the basis of these four tasks, the experimenters divided the population of AIP neurons into three classes: visual dominant, motor dominant and visual-and-motor dominant neurons. The visual dominant neurons were active during the hand manipulation task in the light, not in the dark. The motor dominant neurons were active during the hand manipulation task in the dark as well as in the light. The visual-and-motor dominant neurons were less active during the hand manipulation task in the dark than in the light. The visual dominant as well as the visual-and-motor neurons were further divided into object type, which were active in response to the sight of an object, and non-object type, which were not active in response to the sight of an object. Hence, the activity of AIP neurons studied by Sakata *et al.* (1995) is modulated by the geometric shape of seen objects relevant for the control of grasping and manipulating them. These latter findings confirm that the activity of AIP neurons relates to distal hand and finger movements (for which an object's spatial position is irrelevant) rather than to proximal movements of the arm—where spatial position is relevant for reaching.

Like TE neurons in the ventral stream, AIP neurons in the parietal lobe can maintain their object-related activity in the absence of the effective stimulus. In other words, they too play a role in short-term memory of geometric features of graspable objects. This property was demonstrated by means of a delayed prehension task in which the monkey first saw the object, and then had to wait in the dark before grasping it. This sustained activity thus represents a working memory for the object's visual attributes relevant for the motor (i.e. grasping) task. Unlike ventral neurons, however, AIP neurons do not encode complex features of objects, let alone complex features of biological stimuli. Rather, they respond to simple geometrical or spatial parameters, like size, or parameters related to primitive shapes, like the presence or the absence of edges (Murata *et al.* 1996). In keeping with the postulated role of the dorsal stream in spatial processing, it can be suggested that these parameters may provide spatio-motor, rather than truly pictorial, information on the objects that are the target for grasping

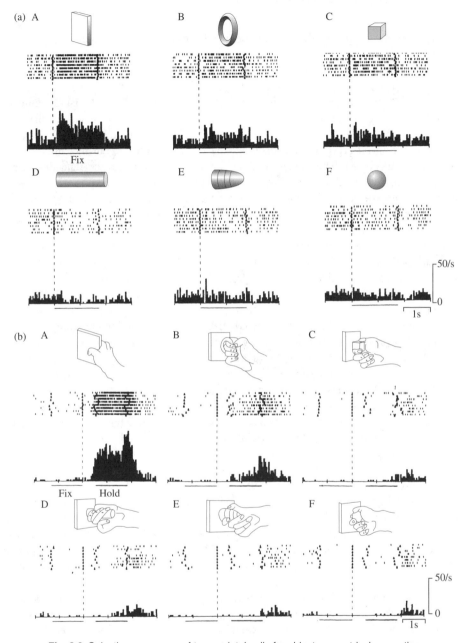

Fig. 2.9 Selective responses of two parietal cells for object geometrical properties. (a) An object-type visuomotor cell. During an object-fixation task, the cell responds selectively to the geometrical properties of objects. Note maximal response in A, B and C. Cell response is displayed both as a raster, where each line corresponds to one trial and each bar corresponds to a spike, and as a histogram. (b) A non-object-type visuomotor cell. The cell response is maximal when the monkey holds an object of a certain shape. Note maximal response for object A. (From Murata *et al.* 2000, *Journal of Neurophysiology*.)

movements. By 'spatio-motor' information, we mean spatial properties of an object that are particularly relevant for grasping it between the fingers of one's hand.

The contribution of AIP neurons to grasping is confirmed by the effects of transient inactivation (by local injection of a GABA agonist such as muscimol) of the AIP region. This injection produces a subtle change in the monkey's performance of visually guided grasping. Lack of preshaping and grasping errors are observed in tasks requiring a precision grip. In addition, there is an interestingly clear-cut dissociation of the effects of the injection on grasping and reaching: the former is altered, but the latter is not (Gallese *et al*. 1994). This result confirms, and usefully refines, the data discussed earlier in this section about the effects of irreversible ablations in the posterior parietal cortex: as the site of the lesions were larger than the localized action of the GABA agonist, both reaching and grasping were altered by the lesions.

Area AIP is directly connected to a subfield of the ventral premotor cortex (Matelli *et al*. 1985). Neurons located in this area of the premotor cortex are related to grasping and they are highly selective for different types of hand grasps, as shown by the Rizzolatti group (e.g. Rizzolatti *et al*. 1988). Selective reversible inactivation of this area also impairs preshaping of the contralateral hand during reach-to-grasp movements (Fogassi *et al*. 2001). Thus, the connection linking the parietal area AIP and the ventral premotor cortex constitutes a specialized visuomotor system for encoding objects' spatio-motor primitives and for generating the corresponding hand-and-finger configuration. A mechanism for the visuomotor transformation has been proposed by Sakata: parietal neurons would contribute to the visuomotor transformation by extracting the properties of 3D objects relevant for manipulation (the role of the visual dominant neurons) and would send this information to premotor cortex. Premotor cortex, in its turn, would retroproject to area AIP and contribute to the activity of motor dominant neurons. This feedback loop from parietal to frontal cortex and back to parietal cortex could be used as a comparator for matching the motor commands prepared for the fingers to the visual properties of the object to be grasped, until the two perfectly coincide (see review in Jeannerod *et al*. 1995).

Neurons in the premotor cortex thus contribute to the visuomotor system, which ultimately produces hand movements adapted to the shape and size of visual objects. At this point, it is interesting to consider the existence, in the same cortical area, of a further population of neurons, which seem highly relevant to the problem of grasping. Di Pellegrino *et al*. (1992) noticed that some of these neurons, which selectively code for finger movements during the action of grasping, were also active during mere observation, by the recorded animal, of the same movements performed by another monkey or by a human subject. The degree of selectivity of activation of these neurons during the movement itself was retained for their activation during action observation. In other words, these neurons are influenced by the mirror image of their preferred movement (hence the term of 'mirror neurons' used by di Pellegrino *et al*. 1992). Subsequent studies showed that mirror neurons encode observed movements performed by real hands, not by tools. Furthermore, these movements have to be directed at objects of interest for the animal (e.g. pieces of food). Pantomimed actions without object performed in front of the monkey are ineffective (see Rizzolatti *et al*. 1995). Thus, the goal of the movements has to be present or at least known to the monkey. As recently shown by the same group of authors, a given mirror neuron may discharge during the observed movement, even if the goal of the movement is temporarily masked to the view of the animal (Rizzolatti *et al.* 2000). These properties of mirror neurons and their function for action perception will be further discussed in Chapter 7.

In previous paragraphs of this section, we discussed the neural organization of reaching and grasping movements. We stressed the fact that the production of these movements rests on segregated anatomical pathways: a connection between the parietal area MIP (among others) and the dorsal premotor cortex for the reaching component, and a connection between the parietal area AIP and the ventral premotor cortex for the grasping component. This anatomical segregation, however, may seem paradoxical, because reaching and grasping cannot be considered as functionally independent: they represent two complementary aspects of the same action, they are components of a single visually guided action directed towards the same object. Nonetheless, visual processing for reaching and grasping address different types of visual information: object location in egocentric space must be determined for guiding the reach component, whereas the geometrical properties of that same object will guide the grasping component. This difference in visual processing will be reflected in the temporal properties of these respective components. Experiments using visual 'perturbations' synchronized with movement onset clearly illustrate this point. Suppose, e.g. that the target object to be reached by the subject jumps by 10 degrees to the right as the subject starts reaching in its direction—an effect that can be achieved by means of an optical device. Then, the subject produces a corrective movement so that the new target is adequately reached. The first kinematic evidence for correction occurs around 100 ms after the perturbation. If, in another experiment, the object keeps the same location, but changes size (e.g. increases) as the subject starts to move, it takes at least 300 ms for the finger-grip to adjust to the changing object size (Paulignan *et al.* 1991). This sharp contrast between the timing of the two types of corrections accounts for the functional differences between the two components of a single action. Although fast execution during reaching has a clear adaptive value (e.g. for catching moving targets), this is not obviously the case for grasping, whose function is to prepare the fine manipulation of the object. As suggested earlier (Jeannerod 1981), the two sets of information—dealing with object localization and object shape—could be hierarchically ordered. The egocentric localization of an object (within an egocentric frame of reference) would have priority over the precise computation of the shape and exact size of the object to be grasped. The fast timing of the former would play a major role in determining the overall temporal frame of the action and would thus constrain the more fine-grained expression of the grasp.

6 Conclusion

As revealed by monkey experiments spreading over more than 30 years, the primate visual system reveals itself as a composite structure with several dissociable functions. Whereas the ventral stream can be assigned a rather clearcut (though highly integrated) function, it does not seem as if the posterior parietal cortex (the dorsal stream) can be assigned a single function. First, the posterior parietal cortex, as emphasized by Ungerleider and Mishkin (1982), does encode spatial relationships between objects, mostly based on motion cues. This processing, as theory would require, is effected in a system of coordinates independent of the perceiver such that, e.g. the position of an object relative to a landmark in the workspace can be determined. Second, the dorsal pathway is involved in the interaction between the perceiver and external objects: visual objects are also targets for visually guided actions of agents. For a visually guided action directed onto an object to succeed, the frame of reference in which the agent represents the object's position in external space must be matched onto the frame of reference in which the position of his effectors is encoded. Given that the dorsal pathway underlies both the perception of spatial relationships and the visuomotor transformation, the question naturally arises how these two functions relate to each other.

3   Dissociations of visual functions by brain lesions in human patients

1   Introduction

In the previous chapter, we described the emergence of a conception of the primate visual system based on a segregation between two distinct pathways with complementary functions. The success of this research program into the primate visual system rested on convergent data from anatomical and physiological studies run on monkeys for several decades. This program originated with behavioral observations on brain-lesioned animals that revealed specific deficits prompted, respectively, by lesions in the ventral stream and in the dorsal stream of the primate visual system. The functional duality of visual information processing was confirmed by single-cell studies focusing on each subdivision of the system. Thus, according to Ungerleider and Mishkin (1982), the task of the ventral pathway is to process pictorial information about objects, irrespective of their spatial position in the work field, and to allow for object recognition. By contrast, the task of the dorsal pathway is to determine the spatial layout of objects by processing their respective position in the visual field. According to the system of coordinates in which this processing is effected in the dorsal system, different outcomes are obtained. When an object's position is encoded in allocentric coordinates, its spatial position is determined relative to other objects. When it is encoded in egocentric coordinates, its spatial position is determined relative to the agent's effector and the object becomes a goal for action. Spatial localization and the visuomotor transformation are thus conceived of as two complementary functions of the dorsal pathway.

The aim of the present chapter is to examine neuropsychological evidence for similar dissociations in human visual capacities based on the examination of lesions in the human visual system. For a long time, the observation of the effects of brain lesions produced by pathological conditions has been the only source of available information. In the middle of the nineteenth century, the earliest neuropsychological studies were based on the anatomo-clinical method, whereby clinical symptoms were confronted with autopsy data. At present, clinical data are still accumulating, although in a new context: on the one hand, patients can now be examined within the methodological framework of cognitive psychology; on the other hand, neuro-imaging techniques have greatly enhanced our understanding by mapping the effects of focal brain lesions onto topographically determined brain functions studied in normal subjects.

Any attempted comparison between human data obtained by neuropsychological methods and neurophysiological evidence gathered on monkeys must proceed with caution for at least two important reasons. First, pathological lesions in human brains almost never produce the destruction of a single anatomically and/or functionally well-defined area. Unlike experimentally produced lesions, accidental lesions observed in pathology may extend over distinct brain areas. They may considerably encroach on the underlying white matter, hence producing disconnection between relatively remote areas. Reconstruction techniques, which allow a good mapping of brain lesions, have been introduced only recently and many 'classical' descriptions were based on cases in which the exact topography and extent of the lesioned area were incompletely known.

The second reason for caution is the lack of a clear homology between monkey and human areas, especially in those brain regions under interest here, like the parietal associative cortex. Furthermore, the human brain is characterized by the development of lateralized structures, which have no anatomical and functional counterpart in the monkey brain. Besides the well-known example of the language areas in the left hemisphere, which are unique to humans, an asymmetrical distribution of functions and pathologies are also frequently observed in humans, though not in the monkey. Neuro-imaging experiments show that cognitive tasks in humans may selectively activate the human right or left parietal lobe. Whether it is located in the right or in the left parietal area of the human brain, a lesion is likely to produce different effects. No such asymmetry, however, is ever observed in the monkey. For example, hemineglect—a typical lateralized syndrome with no known equivalent in the monkey—will typically arise in humans from a lesion in the right parieto-occipito-temporal opercular region, though not from a lesion in the left homologous region.

This chapter will deal with clinical cases of lesions affecting different parts of the visual system. Although no clear description of the behavioral effects of lesions of the visual system beyond the striate cortex was available in monkeys until Mishkin's work, several of the classical human visual syndromes were already described at the end of the nineteenth century. These descriptions clearly emphasized different sites of the visual system underlying different aspects of visual processing. The first influential model was that of a sequential organization of visual functions based on associations between different nervous centers (e.g. Wernicke 1874; Lissauer 1890). This theory was based on an anatomical separation between a primary center of 'sensation' and a secondary center of 'imagination', such that sensations were transmitted to the imagination center to allow the production of a mental visual image that could be stored and compared with previously acquired images. Accordingly, lesions located in the primary visual center were held to affect detection of the most elementary visual features, whereas lesions sparing the primary center but destroying surrounding areas (in the association cortex) were held to produce a disturbance in the recognition of objects.

The possibility that specialized visual areas could be distributed over two visual pathways with complementary roles was also considered early on in human studies. Thus, Holmes and Lister (1916: 365), made a distinction between visual agnosia, i.e. the inability to recognize objects by vision alone, associated with bilateral lesions of the posterior portions of the hemispheres, and another form of visual disturbance, which they described as the 'inability to orientate and localize correctly in space objects that can be perfectly well seen and recognized'. The latter dysfunction is, according to Holmes and Lister, associated with bilateral lesions of the parietal lobes. This is indeed an early formulation of the 'two visual systems' hypothesis that will be further explored and developed in this chapter.

In subsequent sections, the effects of pathological lesions in the visual system on visual behavior in man will be described: we shall examine the effects of lesions in the primary visual cortex, in the ventral pathway and in the dorsal pathway of the human visual system, respectively.

2 Visual impairments following lesions in the primary visual cortex

A bilateral lesion in the occipital lobe involving the primary visual cortex results in so-called cortical blindness. Cortically blind patients behave like completely blind people, except that their pupillar reflex to light is preserved: they do not see objects, they cannot orient in space, they bump into obstacles, etc., even though many of them tend to ignore their blindness and may even report seeing complex visual scenes (e.g. Goldenberg *et al.* 1995; see below). When the lesion is partial (e.g. limited to one hemisphere), the above condition of blindness applies to the retinotopic area corresponding to the cortical lesion, the so-called 'scotoma', i.e. an area in the visual field where visual signals are not processed. If the primary visual cortex is completely destroyed in one hemisphere, the scotoma includes the two homonymous hemiretinae projecting to that hemisphere and it results in an hemianopia involving the visual field contralateral to the lesion.

The question arises of why such patients behave like blind people. This is indeed a paradox, considering the fact that a sizeable part of their visual system may still be functional: despite lesion of the visual cortex, the terminal relay of the main retinofugal pathway, retinal inputs can still reach several subcortical areas. Relying on an analogy with the monkey visual system, we can hypothesize that it is even likely that some of the retinal projections relaying in the optic tectum and in the pulvinar finally reach the parietal cortex. If this hypothesis is correct, then a lesion in the primary visual cortex should result in a complete deafferentation of the ventral pathway from retinal inputs. But the dorsal pathway should still receive retinal information via the indirect subcortical route. In fact, this reasoning was at the origin of the discovery of a remarkable phenomenon, known as 'blindsight'. As first observed in the early 1970s, patients who had lost conscious vision in part of their visual field following a lesion in their primary visual cortex turned out to still be able to produce accurate visuomotor responses to visual stimuli presented in that part of their visual field. This striking phenomenon, however, could not be observed unless patients were placed in a so-called 'forced choice' situation, in which no conscious report about the presence and the nature of the visual stimulus was required, and in which they were invited to produce an 'automatic' response to it.

Early blindsight experiments tested patients' ability to localize targets in their impaired visual field, either by eye movements or by hand reaching (Pöppel *et al.* 1973; Weiskrantz *et al.* 1974; Perenin and Jeannerod 1975). When applied to more complex visual processing, such as visual form discrimination, this method usually led to negative results (see Weiskrantz 1986). We know from a more recent observation, however, that a blindsight patient can respond to the presentation, in his blind field, of objects' physical (or geometrical) attributes, such as their size and orientation. Perenin and Rossetti (1996) examined a patient, PJG, who sustained a lesion of the left occipital lobe severing the primary visual cortex from the optic radiations, following a vascular accident. This lesion resulted in a dense right homonymous hemianopia. While the patient maintained visual fixation on a central visual target, objects were presented within his hemianopic field, at a few degrees away from the fixation point. These objects were a visual slit oriented at different angles and/or a set of quadrangular wooden blocks of different sizes. PJG was requested to produce a hand movement towards these objects: reach the slit with a hand-held card, so as to 'post' the card through the slit, or reach and grasp the blocks. Although the patient claimed that he did not 'see' the objects, he consistently produced adequate visuomotor responses: the orientation of his hand during the reach was modified according to the orientation of the slit and maximum finger-grip size (maximum grip aperture, MGA) during the reach-to-grasp movement correlated with object size. Thus, his visuomotor behavior provided evidence of his correct automatic visual processing of the relevant objects' physical properties. By contrast, when, in other trials, PJG was instructed to provide a perceptual estimate of the very same objects' properties (e.g. by matching the rotation of his hand and the orientation of the slit without transporting the hand-held card to the slit or by matching the block size with his fingers without reaching for and grasping the blocks), then his responses were at chance (see Fig. 3.1). A full description of this mode of testing perceptual functions will be reported in the next chapter.

These results with patient PJG illustrate an extreme case of the dissociation between two distinct modes of processing of one and the same visual stimulus in two different object-oriented situations. On the one hand, assuming that the above hypothesis of a subcortical bypass of the geniculo-cortical pathway to the parietal cortex is correct, and assuming that the ventral pathway was effectively deafferented from visual retinal inputs, the persistence of accurate visuomotor responses in this patient provides a confirmation of the role of the parietal cortex in the automatic visuomotor transformation. On the other hand, however, being based, as they are, on subcortical inputs to the parietal cortex, PJG's responses do not correspond to the normal situation, where parietal areas receive massive cortico-cortical connections from the primary visual areas. The remaining visual functions performed by the dorsal pathway in a patient like PJG are very impoverished, compared to a normally functioning human dorsal pathway. It corresponds to the activity of a 'primitive' system for fast and crude reactions to visual stimuli (see Bullier *et al.* 1994). By contrast, the visuomotor transformation, which is normally carried out by the dorsal stream in an intact human brain, is both more complex and less direct. However remarkable the residual visuomotor abilities of patient PJG, it is important to stress that one would vastly underestimate the complexity of the visuomotor transformation performed by the dorsal stream in an intact human brain if one were to restrict one's evidence to the examination of patients like PJG (see Carey *et al.* 1996). In normal humans, parietal functions do not operate in isolation. Rather, they are embedded in a broader system for producing action, which involves other areas, including those from the ventral pathway (see below).

3   Impairment in visual perception and the recognition of objects following occipito-temporal lesions

Visual agnosia refers to the condition of patients who are unable to perceive and/or to recognize visual objects, while at the same time these patients do not appear to be blind

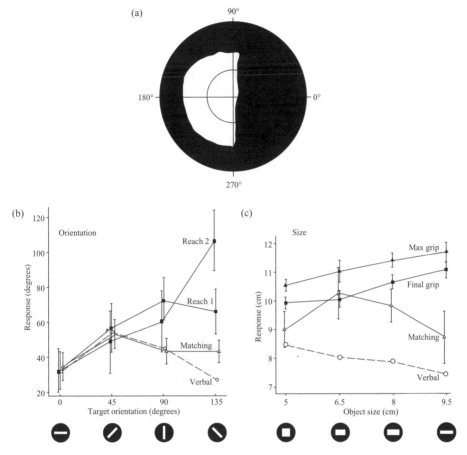

Fig. 3.1 Blindsight responses in a patient, PJG. (a) Binocular visual field of the patient. The black area (*right*) represents the hemi-anopic scotoma due to the lesion of the left primary visual cortex. (b) Reaching hand responses to an oriented slit presented within the scotoma. Note relatively accurate orientation of the hand. By contrast, note complete failure in the matching task (indicate with the hand the orientation of the slit without reaching to it). The same happens if the patient has to verbally describe the orientation of the slit. (c) Scaling of finger-grip during grasping an object of different sizes presented within the scotoma. Note correlation of maximum grip size and final grip size to object size during real grasp. By contrast, note poor responses in the other two conditions. (From Perenin and Rossetti 1996 permission sought.)

since they clearly respond to visual stimuli. The term 'agnosia' introduced by Freud (1891) came to replace the original term 'mind blindness' used by Lissauer (1890).[1]

---

[1]Recently, the term 'mindblindness' has been appropriated in a sense different from Lissauer's by cognitive psychologists and cognitive neuropsychologists to denote an entirely different pathological condition, namely autism, i.e. an impairment in mindreading abilities that has nothing to do with visual impairment (see Baron-Cohen 1995).

Following Lissauer's model of a sequential organization of visual functions, agnosias have been divided into two main types: 'apperceptive agnosias' and 'associative agnosias'. Apperceptive agnosias are those in which recognition of objects fails because of an impairment in visual perception despite preservation of more elementary visual abilities, such as acuity or detection of primitive or elementary visual features (e.g. brightness or colors). Nonetheless, patients with apperceptive agnosia do not perceive objects normally, and hence cannot recognize them. By contrast, in patients with associative agnosia, although visual perception of objects seems adequate, still object-recognition is impaired, as if the 'meaning' of the object could not be 'deciphered'. Associative agnosia involves, in Teuber's (1960) phrase, 'a normal percept stripped of its meaning'. Hence, the classical term 'psychic blindness' used to denote this condition (for review see Farah 1990).

Arguably, the above distinction between degrees of pathological disorganization of visual processing has strong implications for the underlying model used for understanding normal perception. This model will be more fully justified and elaborated in Chapters 5 and 6. For the moment, we will assume that the perceptual process leading to what we call the 'semantic' recognition and the identification of an object involves, but does not reduce to, the generation of a preliminary 'pre-semantic' perceptual representation of the object seen by the subject in front of him. We think of the visual perceptual process leading to the 'semantic' identification of an object as a dynamic perceptual process. The first stage of this process involves the elaboration of a highly contextual visual percept, which is a pictorial representation of a particular object, at a particular location, in a particular context. If needed, this highly contextual 'pre-semantic' pictorial percept can be stored in memory for immediate recall. Arguably, this visual percept in itself is not sufficient for answering all queries about the identity of the object. In the early pictorial representation, there are slots for further identification of the object to be determined by further processing. Determining the identity of the object involves, for example, the comparison of the visual percept with other pictorial data stored in long-term visual memory. Thus, the more elaborate 'semantic' visual percept that results from further processing of the contextual pre-semantic visual percept involves fixing the potential function of the perceived object, as well as the object-category to which the object represented belongs. In our view, determining the function and the object-category stands at the interface between pure visual processing and conceptual processing of information.[2] The underlying idea here is that, in apperceptive agnosia, the highly contextual pre-semantic visual percept is impaired. By contrast, in associative agnosia, only the second stage of visual perceptual processing is altered.

The apperceptive/associative dichotomy of visual agnosia, however, is not universally accepted as a valid framework for describing disorders of visual perception. Ellis and Young (1988), e.g. have used a different classification. They hypothezise a first level of impairment of shape processing, which involves alteration of a viewer-centered

---

[2]As Chapters 1, 5, and 6 should make clear, when we talk of 'pre-semantic' visual processing or 'pre-semantic visual percept' here, we do not mean 'pragmatic' visual processing. In our view, it is important to keep semantic processing and pragmatic processing separate. But within the semantic processing of visual inputs, we distinguish a pre-semantic stage of processing from a fully semantic stage of processing.

representation and an object-centered representation of the same objects. They posit a further level of possible impairment: the semantic system itself. Third, they also consider a higher level of impairment, whereby patients fail to integrate various local details about object shape into a unified percept and cannot generate an object-centered representation. Finally, they supplement the list of agnosias with cases of optic aphasia—a disorder in naming visually presented objects that have clearly been recognized and identified by the patients. This last particular type of verbal conceptual impairment lies outside the scope of the present study.

In the present chapter, we will stick to the distinction between apperceptive and associative agnosias (along with Shallice 1988 and Farah 1995) for the main reason that our discussion of clinical cases will take into account the anatomical basis of visual perception. Both the anatomical location of the lesions producing impairments in visual perception and the functional anatomy of normal visual perception, as described by neuro-imaging techniques, will serve as our basis for describing and for classifying agnosias and other visual disorders, rather than pre-conceived theories.

3.1 Associative agnosia

We will start our description of agnosias with the associative type, which refers to an impairment located at a hierarchically higher level of visual processing than apperceptive agnosia. Since our emphasis in this chapter is on the functional significance of the contrast between ventral processing and dorsal processing, we shall proceed in a top-down (as opposed to a bottom-up) fashion, i.e. we shall examine the higher level recognitional impairment first. Then, we shall move to the more basic perceptual impairment, which we shall be in a better position to contrast in detail with some visuomotor dysfunctions, i.e. with specific impairments in object oriented actions.

A prototypical case may serve as a starting-point for describing the clinical condition of associative agnosia. Rubens and Benson (1971) described a 47-year-old man who was admitted to hospital after being found comatous with low blood pressure. After recovery from coma, he presented a right homonymous hemianopia with macular sparing. On neurological examination, he was found to be close to normal for language, memory and intelligence. His main difficulty was with visual recognition tasks. He was slow but accurate in matching colors, though he had difficulties in naming the colors of objects. He was unable to recognize faces of relatives or of famous people. He could not name objects and showed no evidence for non-verbal forms of object recognition (e.g. by grouping objects according to categories). Furthermore, he could not demonstrate or describe the use of the objects he was shown. Although he could recognize and name simple geometrical shapes, he was unable to recognize pictures of objects. By contrast, he was able to draw copies of those objects he could not identify, and he still failed to recognize his own drawings (Fig. 3.2). He could read (though hesitantly) block letters, but not small print. He could write, but he could not read what he had written. Finally, he performed normally for visual mental imagery and short-term visual recall. The authors demonstrated with several tests that the patient's difficulty was limited to visual recognition: he could immediately identify and name objects presented to him in the auditory or the tactile channel. He was also able to spell words and to recognize spelled words.

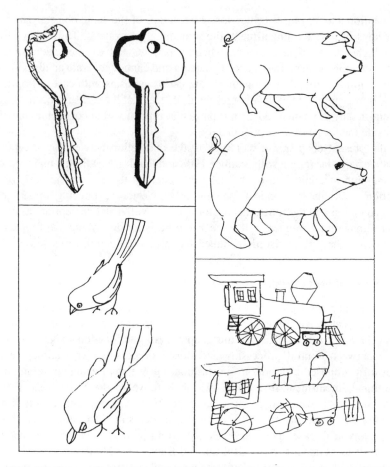

Fig. 3.2 Copy drawings made by a patient with an associative agnosia. (From Rubens and Benson 1971 with permission from the American Medical Association.)

Although in Benson and Rubens' patient, visual mental imagery seems to have been spared, this is not always the case (e.g. Farah 1984). In many patients with visual agnosia, not only the ability to recognize objects, but also the ability to image them is impaired. Farah *et al.* (1988) report a case in which the visual imagery deficit parallels the recognition deficit. Their associative agnosic patient, LH, was deeply impaired in visual recognition for faces, animals, plants, food and many common objects. His capacity for processing more elementary visual features, like orientation or shape, was preserved, as he could correctly copy drawings of many objects that he did not recognize. This patient was tested in a variety of tasks requiring visual imagery, like determining some of the characteristics of well-known objects that are rarely encoded in verbal memory and that require access to iconic memory such as: What is the color of a football? Which, of a popsicle or a packet of cigarettes, is bigger? Do beavers have long tails? and so on. LH was deficient in all these tasks. His deficit in visual imagery stood in contrast with his preserved ability to form images in other types of imagery tasks, such as spatial imagery. Thus, LH was able to perform the mental rotation of letters or other 3D shapes, mental scanning, etc. (see below). The loss of the ability to visually imagine objects in an associative agnosic patient like LH is congruent with findings made in normal subjects using methods for mapping brain activity. These methods reveal that, in a subject engaged in mentally imaging faces or other objects, the activated areas are located at the occipito-temporal junction or in more anterior regions, including the inferotemporal cortex: these areas are the same as those activated during tasks involving recognition and matching of object shapes presented to the subjects (see Ungerleider and Haxby 1994). In addition, according to several authors, the image-generation process would produce a stronger activation in the left than in the right temporal regions (see review in Farah 1995). As will be reported below, these areas are the main locus of lesions in associative agnosic patients. The loss of visual imagery in this condition raises the question of which level of visual processing is altered. Unlike the early visual percept, which is built during visual perception, where the object is present in front of the patient, the representation that is used during visual imagery is purely based on stored memories. A unifying explanation for recognition and imagery impairments observed in associative agnosia could thus be that the specific memory buffers, in which visual information about objects is stored, are damaged. Thus, the patient would have lost access to objects' 'meaning' (i.e. identity) and would not be able to evoke content-specific images.

The question raised by such agnosic patients, who have lost what we shall call the 'visual semantics' of objects (since they cannot recognize them), is the question whether they have kept what is sometimes called the 'semantics of action'. The question is: If a patient cannot recognize objects, can he figure out how they can be used? In Chapter 7, we shall offer an analysis of the 'semantics of action' in terms of a higher-order pragmatic visual processing of objects. From the published literature (see review in Hécaen and Albert 1978), it appears that associative agnosics are often able to describe the shape of an object shown to them, its outline, its internal parts, although they are unable to name it or to describe its usage verbally or by gesture. There are indications, however, that tacit knowledge of the basic functionality of objects can be preserved. This is illustrated by a patient, FB, described by Sirigu *et al.* (1991). FB had severe difficulties in recognizing visual objects, as well as colors, faces and places. His visual imagery ability was apparently correct, as he could draw objects from memory. He could also name objects when their function was verbally described to him. When shown a common object, FB described and performed actions that were congruent with the specific manipulation of that object, even if he could not correctly identify its function verbally. As an example, he described an iron in the following way: 'You hold it in one hand and move it back and forth horizontally (mimes the action). Maybe you can spread glue evenly with it' (Sirigu *et al.* 1991: 2566).

This type of observation is compatible with the fact that patients with object-recognition disorders may still be able to normally use objects and to perform everyday actions. Does this preserved ability reflect some residual representation of 'object meaning', as opposed to a deficit in other semantic categories, e.g. in the knowledge of word meaning? This view was held by Lauro-Grotto *et al.* (1997), following the observation of a patient, who presented a deep impairment in her knowledge about the meaning of words, although her capacity to use information about functional relationships between objects, such as joint use or common function, had remained intact. This specific preservation of the tacit knowledge of the functionality of objects could explain, according to Lauro-Grotto *et al.* (1997), why the patient still succeeded in tasks where she had to use many objects, e.g. in cooking.[3]

This notion of a specific storage of the functional knowledge of objects is not without experimental support. PET experiments in normal subjects reveal that a specific brain area is involved in associating an action word to the picture of an object (e.g. generate the word 'write' when shown the picture of a pencil). This area appears to be located in the middle portion of the temporal lobe on the left side. Activation was also found in the inferior part of the parietal lobe on the same side. A similar task where subjects had to generate color words instead of action words for the same objects activated a different area (Martin *et al.* 1995). Thus, activations in different brain areas were observed in response to tasks involving, respectively, knowledge of object functions and knowledge of object colors. Incidentally, this sort of finding using brain imaging techniques is a good basis for exploring category-specific deficits in object recognition, frequently observed in associative agnosia. For example, some associative agnosic patients fail to recognize manufactured objects and artifacts, while they are still able to recognize biological objects (see e.g. Warrington and Shallice 1984). Also, the recognition deficit may be restricted to the visual processing of written linguistic symbols (pure alexia).

The fact that declarative knowledge of the function of objects is preserved, whereas knowledge of the identity of the same objects is lost, apparently fits with the above idea of category-specific recognition deficits. This possibility, however, has been challenged by an alternative hypothesis according to which the preservation of object use would in fact reflect the activity of another, intact system devoted to pure sensorimotor abilities. This hypothesis was tested by Hodges *et al.* (1999) in two patients with semantic dementia—a loss of the ability to attribute 'meaning' to objects, which includes most of the features of associative agnosia. These patients were unable to name familiar objects. They were also very poor in their functional knowledge about these objects (e.g. they could not associate pictures of two objects jointly used in the same kind of action, such as a lighter and a pack of cigarettes). By contrast, their performance was normal in a task consisting of the manipulation of novel tools and the demonstration of the use of such tools in a meaningless action, i.e. use the right tool to achieve the task of raising a cylinder from the table top (Fig. 3.3). Hodges *et al.* (1999) concluded that this behavior was attributable to the dorsal system, i.e. a system specialized for sensorimotor interaction with the environment and distinct from the system in which knowledge of object function is supposedly stored. This point will be discussed in the section dealing with lesions of the dorsal system.

The cerebral lesion in associative agnosia is classically a predominantly left occipito-temporal lesion. Although in Rubens and Benson's patient the lesion site was not documented, the right hemianopia observed in this patient clearly speaks in favor of a lesion affecting the visual pathways in the left hemisphere. Patient RM and the patients

---

[3]See Chapter 7 for further elaboration of the notion of a higher-order pragmatic processing of objects.

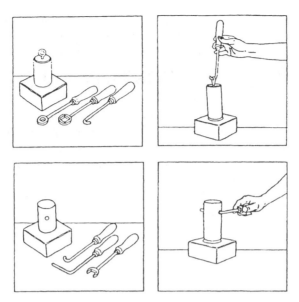

Fig. 3.3 Correct choice of tools for raising a cylinder in a patient with object agnosia. (From Hodges *et al.* 1999. Reprinted with permission from PNAS, vol. 96 © 1999 National Academy of Sciences, courtesy of the National Academies Press, Washington, D.C.)

described by Hodges *et al.* (1999) presented a predominantly left temporal atrophy. In other cases, like LH or FB, the lesion was bilateral: FB presented a bilateral lesion of the temporal poles involving Brodman's areas 38, 20 and 21, as well as medial temporal structures (the hippocampus and the amygdala).

3.2 Apperceptive agnosia

Poppelreuter (1917) compared apperceptive agnosic patients with a normal observer presented with a complex sketch during a very short time (e.g. a few tens of milliseconds): he would report having seen a visual form, but would be unable to identify it. This comparison suggests that visual attributes can be processed and detected but not assembled into a meaningful percept. To qualify this broad statement, we will use the complete description of the case of an agnosic patient, Mr S, reported by Benson and Greenberg (1969) and also studied by Efron (1966–68). Mr S suffered a carbon monoxide overexposure in his bathroom. After a period of cortical blindness lasting for a few weeks, his vision returned, but with a striking characteristic: he was unable to name visually presented objects. By contrast, he could name objects placed in his hand. In spite of this deep visual deficit, Mr S retained a reasonable visual acuity. He was able to make accurate judgments in comparing two objects for their color, brightness and/or size. Physiological tests of visual function (spatial summation, flicker fusion thresholds, visual field) were within normal range.

The failure to recognize and name objects was thoroughly investigated in this patient. His deficit extended to visually presented objects, pictures of objects, body parts, letters, numerical symbols and geometrical shapes. During the recognition tasks, the visual stimulus had to be moved back and forth in front of the patient before he could visually extract anything from the background: only then was he able to trace the contours of the object with his index finger. Mr S was unable to copy drawings of simple objects, letters or numerical symbols (Fig. 3.4). A set of cards containing either two identical squares, or a square and a rectangle of identical areas but with varying degrees of elongation of the rectangle, were used to test his shape perception. Identical shapes were judged 'different' in 60% of cases and very different shapes (the square and the most elongated rectangle) were judged similar in more than 10% of cases. This deficit contrasted with Mr S's preserved ability to verbally describe the shape of simple objects (e.g. a coin or a rod) retrieved from memory.

The authors' conclusion was that Mr S's object-recognition deficit rested on his inability to discriminate objects' shapes. This raises an interesting semantic discussion. According to Benson and Greenberg (1969), identification of shape or form is the only precondition for identifying an object, a letter or a face. Other visual attributes, like color or brightness, are not essential for object identification. Thus, Mr S's inability to discriminate visually presented forms would account, not only for his symptoms of object agnosia, but also for his alexia (inability to read) and his prosopagnosia (inability to recognize faces). Benson and Greenberg (1969) proposed the term

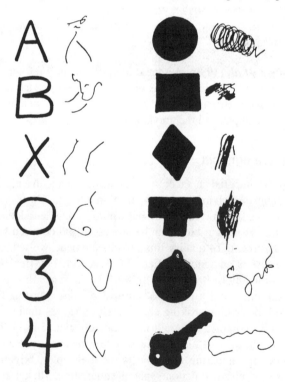

Fig. 3.4 Inability to copy block letters, numbers or simple two-dimensional shapes in a patient with apperceptive agnosia. (From Benson and Greenberg 1969 with permission from the American Medical Association.)

'visual form agnosia' to characterize this condition. An alternative view, held by Poppelreuter (1917), posits that detection of simple shapes should be classified among the preconditions of visual perception, on a par with detection of depth, color or orientation. Poppelreuter (1917) described several cases of apperceptive agnosia where the detection of simple shapes was preserved, but the synthesis of the elements into a coherent whole could not be achieved. More recently, Humphreys and Riddoch (1987) held a similar view. They showed that their agnosic patient, HJA, was able to process local aspects of shapes but was unable to integrate them into a perceptual whole, due to inadequate segmentation of these local features: hence, the term 'integrative agnosia' applied by these authors to patient HJA's condition. Possibly, the observed differences among types of apperceptive agnosia reflect different degrees of impairment in the processing of the elementary visual attributes of objects, without which visual perception simply cannot arise and the formation of an adequate visual percept fails. At the anatomical level, these differences might reflect the degree of impairment of the primary visual areas, where the early stages of visual form processing take place.

In theory, then, apperceptive agnosia in general and visual form agnosia in particular should result from brain lesions with the following two anatomical conditions: first, the lesions should spare the calcarine region; second, they should involve the occipital lobes bilaterally, but they should be located more caudally than are lesions involved in associative agnosia. Both the fact that, in Mr S's case and in several similar cases, no visual field defect could be detected using standard testing and the fact that the main elementary visual functions were preserved, argue in favor of a lesion site located downstream to the primary visual cortex itself. This prediction could not be verified in the case of Mr S, where no precise localization of the lesion could be made—as is often the case with carbon monoxide poisoning, which usually produces lesions spread over large cortical and subcortical zones. In three more recent cases, however, a bilateral occipital localization of the lesion was observed. In the case of HJA, described by Humphreys and Riddoch (1987), a bilateral lesion of the anterior and ventral part of the two occipital lobes was found. The fact that, in addition to his object agnosia, the patient also exhibited a loss of color perception 'can be taken as indicating a lesion to the prestriate cortex in the region of the lower pathway leading to the temporal lobe' (Humphrey and Riddoch 1987: 31). The second case is that of patient DF, reported by Milner *et al.* (1991), which will be fully described below. DF's lesion occupies the occipital region bilaterally; it spares the calcarine area and lays 'on the lower aspects of the lateral occipital cortex and at the polar convexity, extending into the parasagittal occipitoparietal region' (Milner *et al.* 1991: 407–8). Finally, patient SB, described by Lê *et al.* (2002), also to be described below, sustained a bilateral destruction of the occipito-temporal junction sparing the calcarine sulcus. Thus, lesion of this intermediate area, which corresponds to area V4 in the monkey brain, produces, in Zeki's (1993: 313) words, a 'breakdown in early levels of integration' of visual perception.

3.3 The discovery of preserved visuomotor capacities in apperceptive agnosic patients

In the two previous sections, we have reviewed the deep perceptual deficits involved in associative agnosic patients and especially in apperceptive agnosic patients. In the

1990s, it was discovered that lesions responsible for apperceptive agnosia could leave a number of visuomotor functions intact. From what is known about the organization of the visual pathways in the monkey brain (about which see the previous chapter), we can infer with reasonable confidence that the lesions responsible for apperceptive agnosia in humans should have bilaterally disconnected the inferotemporal areas from visual inputs, hence accounting for the impairment in shape perception and recognition. They should, however, have left other more dorsal parts of the visual system intact. In other words, visual areas in the posterior parietal lobe should still be connected to visual input. Interestingly, this obvious possibility was not considered until recently, in spite of the fact that the blindsight phenomenon (investigated in the mid 1970s) had revealed the possibility that visuomotor functions be preserved while other visual abilities—in particular, full visual awareness of objects—were lost. It is true that 'pure' cases of apperceptive agnosia are extremely rare and that the 'two cortical visual systems' hypothesis was not fully popularized until Ungerleider and Mishkin's (1982) seminal paper. More generally, it is also true that the cortical visual system (by contrast with subcortical visual processing) was thought for a long time by many neuropsychologists to be primarily involved in perceptual and cognitive visual processing, i.e. in the visual processing responsible for a subject's conscious visual experience of the world. Other more automatic visual functions, such as the visuomotor transformation involved in the visual guidance of actions directed towards objects, were not recognized as an integral part of human visual processing and consequently as anatomically based upon the human cortical visual system until quite recently (i.e. in the late 1980s and early 1990s). Thus, although knowledge of blindsight patients did pave the way, it came as a genuine surprise when the experimental investigation of a few apperceptive agnosic patients revealed the preservation of remarkable visuomotor capacities.

3.3.1 Patient DF

The main novelty of the neuropsychological description of patient DF's condition—first examined by David Milner and his colleagues—lies in the fact that Milner *et al.* (1991) did not focus exclusively on what DF could *not* do as a result of her lesion. Rather, they investigated in depth what she was still able to do.

Patient DF suffered, as a consequence of carbon monoxide poisoning, a large bilateral occipital lesion destroying the ventral prestriate cortex and disconnecting the inferior temporal lobes from visual inputs (see above). In many respects, her clinical status matches that of Mr S—the patient described by Benson and Greenberg (1969). Careful sensory testing revealed subnormal performance for color perception and for visual acuity with high spatial frequencies, though detection of low spatial frequencies was impaired. Motion perception was poor. DF's shape and pattern perception was tested using the above Efron test (Efron 1969): naming of simple forms (e.g. squares, rectangles) and her same/different form detection were at chance for the 'difficult' trials (i.e. for trials where the difference between the two shapes was small) and did not exceed 80% correct for the 'easy' trials. A similar result was obtained in a size-detection task: DF was unable to indicate the size of an object by matching it by the appropriate distance between the index finger and the thumb of her right hand. Her line orientation detection (revealed by either verbal report or by turning a hand-held card until it matched the orientation presented) was highly variable: although she was above chance for large angular orientation differences between two objects, she fell at chance level for smaller angles. It is therefore not surprising that DF was unable to recognize objects.

Note that DF's visual imagery was preserved, as she was tested with some of the tasks used for patient LH above (Servos and Goodale 1995). For example, although she could hardly draw copies of seen objects, she could draw copies of objects from memory—which she then could hardly later recognize. This is indeed congruent with the fact that the lesion in apperceptive agnosia lies at the occipito-temporal junction, i.e. in a relatively caudal portion of the occipital lobe, whereas the resources for image formation (e.g. long-term semantic memory) are located in a more anterior portion of the temporal lobe. Indeed, patients with posterior occipital lesions, including lesion of the primary visual areas in the calcarine sulcus, who present the typical picture of cortical blindness, spontaneously report vivid visual images and sometimes even deny being blind (e.g. Goldenberg *et al.* 1995). At this point, we can only briefly mention that these clinical data are in direct conflict with the neuro-imaging finding showing that, in normal subjects, primary visual areas are part of the image generation network (Kosslyn *et al.* 1993).

By contrast with her impairment in object recognition, DF was normally accurate when object orientation or size had to be processed, not in view of a perceptual judgment, but in the context of a goal-directed hand movement. During reaching and grasping between her index finger and her thumb, she performed accurate prehension movements with the very same objects that she could not recognize, with the maximum amplitude of her finger-grip normally correlated with object size (Fig. 3.5). Similarly,

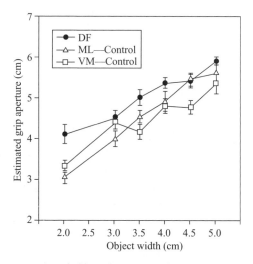

Fig. 3.5 Correct grasping of objects in apperceptive agnosic patient DF. The grip aperture prior to grasping the object (maximum grip aperture, see text) correlates with object width. Compare data from DF (*dark symbols*) with those of two normal controls (*open symbols*). (From Milner *et al.* 1991 permission sought.)

while transporting a hand-held card towards a slot as part of the process of inserting the former into the latter, she could normally orient her hand through the slit at different orientations (Goodale *et al.* 1991; Carey *et al.* 1996).

When DF's visuomotor abilities were tested with everyday familiar implements (instead of neutral shapes), she was not always able to grasp the implement by positing her fingers at the appropriate places: her initial grasp was always guided by visual information about axis orientation and the size of the object, but not by her knowledge of its function. Other experimental results with DF indicate that her visuomotor abilities are restricted in at least three respects. First, she turns out to be able to visually process size, orientation and shape required for grasping objects in the context of a reaching and grasping action, but not in the context of a perceptual judgment. Second, in the context of an action, she turns out to be able to visually process simple sizes, shapes and orientations, but she fails to visually process more complex shapes. For example, she can insert a hand-held card into a slot at different orientations, but when asked to insert a T-shaped object (as opposed to a rectangular card) into a T-shaped aperture (as opposed to a simple oriented slit), her performance deteriorated sharply. Inserting a T-shaped object into a T-shaped aperture requires the ability to combine the computations of the orientation of the stem with the orientation of the top of the object together with the computation of the corresponding parts of the aperture. There are good reasons to think that, unlike the quick visuomotor processing of simple shapes, sizes and orientations, the computations of complex contours, sizes and orientations require the contribution of visual perceptual processes performed by the ventral stream—which, we know, has been severely damaged in DF. Third, the contours of an object can and often are computed by a process of extraction from differences in colors and luminance cues, but normal humans can also extract the contours or boundaries of an object from other cues—such as differences in brightness, texture, shades and complex principles of Gestalt grouping and organization of similarity and good form. Now, when asked to insert a hand-held card into a slot defined by Gestalt principles of good form or by textural information, DF failed.

3.3.2 Patient SB

The second case of an apperceptive agnosic patient is that of SB, a 30-year-old man, who suffered from a meningo-encephalitis at the age of 3 years. SB was educated in an institution for young blinds, although he always refused to be considered a blind person. Twenty-five years after his brain damage, he retains a severe agnosia for objects, letters and faces, although he immediately identifies objects by the tactile channel. His intelligence is normal and he reads and writes braille fluently.

Extensive testing of SB's visual function (Lê *et al.* 2002) revealed a poor visual acuity (4/10 without correction). Contrast-sensitivity was poor—especially at high spatial frequencies—as were color perception, line orientation discrimination and texture discrimination. SB could, though with great effort, recognize some real objects, by using guessing heuristics based on the use of specific features of these objects, such as brightness. However, he could not recognize objects in pictures, nor could he recognize faces and facial expressions. He failed to perceive illusory contours. He did not perceive geometrical visual illusions (Müller-Lyer, Titchener, Ponzo illusions, etc.). Despite these deficits in form recognition, SB was good at using visual imagery (e.g. mentally rotating block letters) and he could draw some common objects from memory.

SB's poor visual perception of objects and forms contrasted with a remarkable preservation of motion perception and visuomotor abilities. In normal life, he runs a motorbike and is able to practice several sport activities, including ping-pong. Formal testing revealed that his perception of coherent motion and of gratings drifting at different velocities was normal. In grasping rectangular objects, he correctly adjusted his maximum grip aperture to object size and he could orient his wrist to pass his hand through slits at different orientations.

As already stated, SB's lesion includes the occipito-temporal junction on both sides. In both hemispheres, the cortical areas corresponding to V1 and V2 are largely spared, whereas areas V3, V4 and areas at the occipito-temporal junction are severely damaged. In addition, on the right side, the lesion extends to the dorsal system where the right inferior parietal lobule is damaged. In summary, SB was left with a bilateral damage of his ventral system and a lesion of his right dorsal system. His residual visual abilities, particularly in the domain of motion perception and visuomotor function, are thus likely to represent the function of the only intact part of his visual brain, his left dorsal system.

3.3.3 Comparing DF and SB

Patients DF and SB exemplify interesting differences. Unlike DF, SB offers the unique opportunity to evaluate what it is like to see with the dorsal system, i.e. with a visual system largely dominated by the magnocellular afferents. The magnocellular pathway is highly competent for detection of motion and brightness and for the detection of low rather than high frequencies, whereas it is poor at detecting static visual cues and color. Thus, Lê et al. (2002) make the point that their patient behaves like a 'nocturnal' animal. On the contrary, DF has no motion perception. Thus, one cannot exclude the possibility that DF's residual abilities are carried out, at least in part, by surviving parts of her ventral system—she had good color vision and retains the ability to detect high spatial frequencies—or by areas upstream to the separation between the two systems. Another difference is that, unlike DF, SB's brain damage took place during his infancy. So, SB came to learn to use cues available to his dorsal system in order to develop some crude conscious shape perception, which made his everyday behavior so strikingly well-adapted. It is likely that DF was only able to use some of the same cues in a more automatic mode and she began to develop the ability to consciously access them only quite recently (see Dijkerman and Milner 1997).

4 Impairments in visually guided behavior following lesion of the dorsal system

The effects of lesions in the parietal lobes were first described by R. Balint and G. Holmes. The two authors, however, offered different interpretations of the symptoms observed in their patients. Whereas Holmes (1918) emphasized the 'visuospatial' nature of his patients' difficulty, Balint (1909), by contrast, discussed the failures of his patient in terms of visuomotor, orienting and attentional functions. As expressed by Harvey and Milner (1995: 262), this difference of interpretation 'is particularly clear in relation to the phenomenon of faulty reaching for targets in visual space, which they both described in their patients. Whereas Balint concluded from his experiments that this disorder was visuomotor in nature, Holmes concluded that it was due to a disorder in localizing objects in space. Balint called it 'optic ataxia', whereas Holmes subsumed it as a 'disturbance of visual orientation'. In the following sections, we will describe impairments in visual function which may fulfill both interpretations.

4.1 Optic ataxia, a specific disorder of the visuomotor transformation

Following the lead of Balint's initial description, optic ataxia is now considered as a specific deficit caused by posterior parietal lesions. Optic ataxia can be characterized as a deep alteration of reaching movements directed towards a visual target, in the absence of any motor impairment. First, the kinematics of the movements are altered: movements have a lower peak velocity and the duration of their deceleration phase is increased. Such a deficit cannot have a motor origin, since the same movements can be executed with a normal kinematic profile in non-visual conditions. Second, the movements are not properly directed towards the target—their directional coding is impaired—and large pointing and reaching errors are observed. This misreaching is more marked when the visual targets are presented outside the fixation point and it tends to increase as the distance between target and the fixation point increases (e.g. Milner *et al.* 1999). Third, alteration of the movements is not limited to the reaching phase. Distal aspects of the movements are affected as well. During the action of grasping an object, the finger grip aperture is increased and the usual correlation between maximum grip aperture (MGA) and object size is lost (Jeannerod 1986b) (Figs 3.6 and 3.7). Similarly, optic ataxic patients fail to orient their hand properly when they have to insert an object through an oriented slit (Perenin and Vighetto 1988).

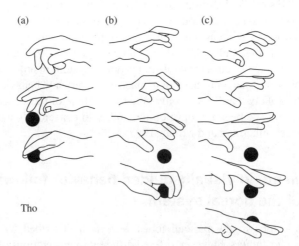

(a)   (b)   (c)

Tho

Fig. 3.6 Impairment of grasping in a patient with optic ataxia following a lesion of the right parietal lobe. (a) Prehension of a sphere with the normal, right hand. Drawings made from successive film frames. Note the normal pattern of opening/closure of the finger grip prior to contact with the object. (b) Abnormal prehension of the same object with full visual control of the hand movement. (c) Lack of hand preshaping during prehension in the absence of visual control. Note absence of grip formation and misreaching of the object. (From Jeannerod 1986b with permission from the author.)

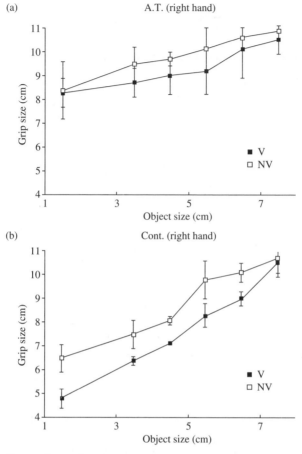

Fig. 3.7 Abnormal grasping of objects in optic ataxic patient AT. (a) Patient AT. The maximum grip aperture prior to contact correlates very poorly with object size. Note exaggerated aperture for the smaller objects. (b) A normal control subject. *Dark symbols*: prehension under normal visual control (V). *Open symbols*: prehension in the absence of visual control of the movement. (From Jeannerod *et al.* 1994 with permission from the author.)

The lesion responsible for optic ataxia was localized by different authors at the convexity of the posterior parietal cortex in a region centered on the superior parietal lobule (see Perenin and Vighetto 1988) (Fig. 3.8). When the lesion is limited to one hemisphere, only the contralateral hand is affected. Lesions are usually relatively large and they affect both reaching and grasping movements. The question arises, however, whether the reaching component and the grasping component can be selectively affected by more limited lesions. In a selected series of patients presenting a deficit limited to the grasping phase, Binkofski *et al.* (1998) were able to circumscribe the responsible area to the anterior part of the intraparietal sulcus on the side contralateral to the impaired hand. Patients with lesions sparing the intraparietal sulcus showed intact grasping. The same authors (Binkofski *et al.* 1999) confirmed this localization in an

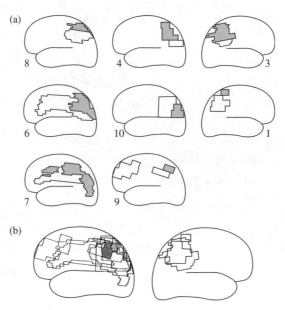

Fig. 3.8 Reconstruction of lesions in optic ataxia patients. Unilateral lesions in eight patients have been reconstructed from CT scans (a) and superimposed (b). Note overlap of lesions in the superior part of posterior parietal lobe. (From Perenin and Vighetto 1988 permission sought.)

fMRI analysis of prehension movements in normal subjects. The activated area was limited to the lateral bank of the anterior part of the intraparietal sulcus. This area had also been found to be specifically activated during grasping tasks in a PET study by Faillenot *et al.* (1997). A similar, though less accurate localization was found with transcranial magnetic stimulation (TMS): according to Desmurget *et al.* (1999), a single electrical shock applied to the region of the intraparietal sulcus disrupts reaching movements directed to a visual target. It is noteworthy that this exquisite localization of brain areas involved in grasping movements is also found to be activated by mere observation of grasping performed by another agent (Iacoboni *et al.* 1999) and even by observation of graspable objects (Chao and Martin 2000).

4.2 Patient AT: a visuomotor impairment with normal object recognition

Optic ataxia appears to be a disorder limited to transforming visual properties of objects into motor commands for a hand action directed towards these objects. It is not due to misperception of the shape, orientation or size of the objects. This point was clearly established in patient AT, first examined by F. Michel and his colleagues (personal communication). AT's lesion was an infarction of a relatively large occipito-parietal zone on both sides. Areas 18 and 19 were destroyed, as well as parietal areas 7 and 39. At the early stage of her disease, AT had presented a bilateral optic ataxia as part of a typical Balint's syndrome. When she was examined several years later, her reaching accuracy was still grossly impaired in her peripheral visual field although it had became close to normal in her central field of vision (see below). By contrast, she was normal in recognizing, describing and naming visual forms and objects. Finally, AT still presented a severe visuospatial disorder corresponding to what will be described below as 'dorsal simultagnosia'. As a consequence of this disorder, she was hampered in her everyday life for actions like dressing, cooking, ironing, sewing or driving. Incidentally, in everyday life, optic ataxic patients, whose object oriented actions are impaired but whose object recognition is normal, are more deeply handicapped than are agnosic patients, even apperceptive agnosic patients.

AT was tested on two visual tasks similar to those used with patient DF (see above): the reaching and grasping task, and the size matching task (Jeannerod *et al.* 1994). In the reaching and grasping task, she was instructed to reach and grasp with a precision grip target objects (vertical plastic cylinders 1.5–7.5 cm in diameter) with or without visual control of her hand. As these objects all had the same visual aspect, except for their size, they were considered as 'neutral' objects. During reaching for and grasping neutral objects, AT's movements offered a striking dissociation: only a few reaching errors were observed. By contrast, her grasp was systematically incorrect, especially with the smaller objects. The patient ended the trial with the object in contact, not with her fingertips, but with the palmar surface of more proximal phalanxes or even with the palmar surface of her hand itself. This behavior (which was bilateral but more marked with the right hand) resulted in awkward and inaccurate grasps with the thumb and index finger curled around the object. On a few occasions, the grasp was not possible, as the object was pushed down by the palm of the hand. Closer examination revealed an exaggerated aperture of the finger grip, such that the end of the finger closure, which should normally bring the fingertips in contact with the object at the time when the reach stops, was delayed and the reach tended to overshoot target position. Maximum grip aperture (MGA) correlated poorly with object size, due to the fact that grip aperture was grossly exaggerated for the smaller objects, and this correlation was not improved by vision of the hand during the grasp (see Fig. 3.7).

By contrast with the impaired pattern of her grasping movements directed at visual objects, AT's performance appeared to be normal in the size-matching task, i.e. in a task exploring her ability to judge the size of objects. When asked to match with the thumb and index finger of her hidden right hand the size of the same objects as those used for the reaching and grasping task, she gave accurate estimates, which correlated positively with object size (for a very similar case see also Goodale *et al.* 1994).

This dissociation between impaired grasping and normal perceptual judgment on the same objects or shapes (demonstrated with the same motor effector) stands as the mirror image of the reverse dissociation between impaired perceptual judgment and preserved grasping exemplified by the visual form agnosic patient, DF. As such, this double dissociation lends support to the notion that different modalities of object-oriented visual responses are differently distributed in the two cortical visual systems: impaired grasping results from damage to the dorsal system, whereas the intact ventral system still allows normal perceptual judgment for object size. What exactly each system contributes is still a matter of debate. In one of their early papers reporting about patient DF, Goodale *et al.* (1991: 156) stated that the dissociation they had observed between perception and action

[...] suggests that at some level in normal brains, the visual processing underlying 'conscious' perceptual judgments must operate separately from that underlying the 'automatic' visuomotor guidance of skilled actions [...]. Our observations indicate separate processing systems not for different subsets of visual information, but for the different uses to which vision can be put.

One question raised by Goodale *et al.*'s (1991) quoted statements is whether they argue in favor of the view that human visual processing is task-dependent or whether they argue in favor of the view that visual perception is performed by the ventral stream while the visual guidance of hand actions is performed by the dorsal stream. It is not obvious whether the two views are equivalent. Arguably, in normal human subjects, visually guided actions directed towards objects are rarely if ever pure action tasks. They almost always involve perceptual aspects. In normal human subjects, pure action and pure perception can hardly be divorced at any time. Competent actions toward objects by normal human subjects require more than the mere visual encoding of their size and/or their orientation. They cannot be limited to mere mechanical problem solving enabling the efficient use of objects in a manner consistent with their physical properties (see Chapter 7 for further discussion). Instead, as emphasized by Hodges *et al.* (1997: 9447), 'competent conventional use of objects depends on additional conceptual knowledge for which inferotemporal brain structures appear to be critical'.

Indeed, the collaboration of the two systems is clearly suggested by further experiments with AT. Jeannerod *et al.* (1994) observed that AT's grasping performance was improved when familiar objects instead of neutral objects were used as targets. In their experiment, these objects were approximately of the same size and shape as the neutral ones, but they were clearly recognizable (e.g. a lipstick, a reel of thread, etc.). With familiar objects, the correlation between maximum grip size and object size increased up to normal values, indicating that semantic knowledge about these objects was used to calibrate the grip (Fig. 3.9). Finally, and not surprisingly, when AT was tested for her ability to estimate with her fingers the size of the same, imagined familiar objects, her judgments strongly correlated with object size. These striking findings demonstrate that the two visual systems do not work independently from each other. AT's behavior in fact suggests that the dysfunctioning processing of the impaired dorsal system can be supplemented by information processed by the intact ventral system. When semantically identifiable objects are used, the ventral system is activated and the relevant information is transferred to the motor system through a pathway bypassing the impaired parietal cortex. By contrast, when neutral objects are used, correct grasping cannot be achieved because the visual primitives related to object size can no longer be processed by the parietal areas and transferred to the motor system. No other cues can be used, as all objects look alike.

A further example of a substitution of the deficient dorsal pathway by an alternative pathway was observed in patient AT (Milner *et al.* 1999). She was presented with luminous targets appearing in her visual field at locations ranging from midline to 30° on either side. In one set of trials, the target was on for a period of 2 s, after which a tone was presented, indicating that she had to point immediately at the target. In another set of trials, as the tone was presented 5 s after the target was turned off, she had to wait

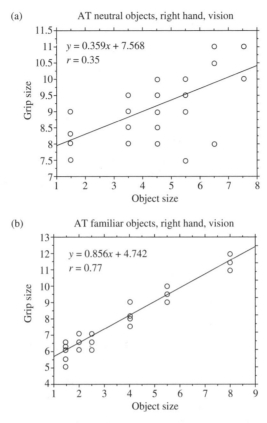

Fig. 3.9 Paradoxical improvement of grasping movements during prehension of familiar objects in optic ataxia patient AT. (a) Poor correlation of maximum grip aperture with object size when AT grasps neutral objects. (b) Good correlation ($r = 0.77$) during prehension of familiar objects of comparable size. (From Jeannerod *et al.* 1994 with permission from the author.)

before pointing at the target location. In the first set of trials, AT made inaccurate pointing responses towards all peripheral targets. In addition, the degree of inaccuracy was a function of the position of the target, i.e. pointing errors increased for more peripheral targets. This is a typical behavior in an optic ataxic patient like AT. The surprising finding was that the pointing accuracy significantly improved in the second set of trials, i.e. when pointing responses were delayed after disappearance of the target (Fig. 3.10). No such effect was found in a group of control subjects: instead, their pointing accuracy significantly decreased in the delayed condition. Milner *et al.* (1999) interpreted these findings by suggesting that the parietal lesion in AT had altered the visuomotor system normally used to reach visual targets, i.e. the system responsible for coding the position of the target in egocentric coordinates. However, the parietal lesion did not damage a distinct system responsible for coding the position of objects in allocentric coordinates—a system that is normally used for localizing objects with respect to each other. This second system (for coding object positions in allocentric

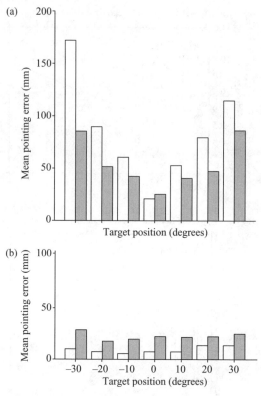

Fig. 3.10 Influence of delaying reaching movements on pointing accuracy in optic ataxia patient AT. (a) Patient AT: targets are presented for 2 s in the central (0°) and peripheral visual field, followed by immediate pointing. Note typical large pointing errors during reaching movements (*white bars*). When pointing to the same target is executed after a delay of 5 s, errors are reduced (*black bars*). (b) Pointing errors in normal control subjects in the same two conditions. (Reproduced with permission from Milner, A. D. *et al.* (1999) A paradoxical improvement of misreaching in optic ataxia: new evidence for two separate neural systems for visual localization. *Proceedings of the Royal Society*, **266**, 2225–9, The Royal Society.)

coordinates) becomes available only after a delay sufficient for the activation of the first, inefficient system to decay. Although in normal conditions, the alternative system is less accurate than the dedicated visuomotor system, as can be verified from the results of the control subjects, in AT, its use allows a paradoxical improvement in pointing accuracy. The problem remains of the exact anatomical location of this system. Because in AT the lesion was restricted to parietal lobes, it is likely that a perceptual pathway (able to allow coding of object positions in allocentric coordinates), making its way through the temporal lobes was activated, which ultimately reached the motor centers without using the parietal route. The problem of the influence of a delay introduced between target presentation and the execution of a movement will be discussed again in the next chapter, using data from normal subjects.

5 Visuospatial disorders following lesions in the parietal lobes

Patients with parietal lesions, with or without optic ataxia, often present visuospatial disorders. As mentioned earlier in this chapter, this fact was first recognized by Holmes (1918), who thought that a general explanation of the impairments observed in these patients could be derived from the specific disturbances in visual orientation. Holmes (1918) classified disturbances of visual orientation into several categories: disorders of absolute localization of objects, disorders of relative object location, inability to compare dimensions of two objects, difficulty of avoiding obstacles while walking, loss of topographical memory, inability to count and group objects, inability to perceive movement in a sagittal plane, defective eye movements. Following Holmes' lead, many authors reported similar observations attesting the existence of disorders of spatial perception or the conscious manipulation of spatial information (once referred to as 'blindness for places' by Kleist 1934) following parietal lesion, more frequently located on the right side. Not only do these disorders include the inability to localize an object in its absolute position in space, but they also include the loss of topographical concepts: patients cannot orient themselves on a map, they are unable to indicate on a map appropriate directions to travel from one point to another. Furthermore, they include the loss of topographical memory: patients cannot evoke an image of familiar places. Nor can they find their way home (for reviews see: Hécaen and Albert 1978; von Cramon and Kerkhoff 1993). We will report below the most common clinical findings related to these spatial disabilities.

5.1 Misperception of the orientation of objects

The processing of the spatial orientation of an object may interfere with the visual recognition and/or identification of that object. Warrington and Taylor (1973) presented right parietal brain-lesioned patients with photographs of common objects (e.g. a basket) taken from a non-conventional (or non-canonical) point of view. The patients failed to recognize these objects, although they had no problem recognizing the same objects when presented in a canonical view. This striking finding might relate to the impairment of parietal patients in spatial imagery tasks involving mental rotation or the mental manipulation of objects.

A related phenomenon, called the rotated drawing phenomenon, which may also reflect a problem with mental rotation at large, has been described in some parietal patients. For example, they may be unable to determine the canonical 2D orientation of objects, letters or faces shown in a drawing, although they can recognize and name them easily (Turnbull *et al.* 1997; Karnath *et al.* 2000).

5.2 Dorsal simultagnosia

Another striking phenomenon observed in these patients is the so-called 'dorsal simultagnosia' (Farah 1995). Simultagnosia is a condition in which a patient accurately perceives the individual elements or details of a complex picture, but cannot appreciate the overall meaning of the picture. Farah (1995) added the term 'dorsal' to refer to the fact that it occurs after bilateral parieto-occipital damage (other types of simultagnosia have also been described following ventral lesion: these syndromes are close to the visual agnosia described earlier in this chapter). Typically, a dorsal simultagnosic patient will recognize most objects but will be unable to see more than one at a time, irrespective of their size. As a consequence of this condition, such patients cannot count objects, their description of complex scenes is slow and fragmentary, they behave like blind people when moving in a visual environment, groping for things and bumping into obstacles. If asked to look for a particular object, they will make random search eye movements. Note that this form of simultagnosia was initially described by Balint (1909) as part of a syndrome, which also included disorganized search with eye movements and optic ataxia. In addition to her optic ataxia, patient AT exemplified a typical picture of dorsal simultagnosia. However, as will be stressed below, the fact that these disorders occasionally occur separately from one another raises the possibility that they pertain to different mechanisms.

Although dorsal simultagnosia may superficially resemble apperceptive agnosia, there are major differences between the two conditions. In apperceptive agnosia, patients may perceive only local cues and still be unable to identify the object, whereas in simultagnosia, they perceive the whole shape and have no identification problem. Thus, dorsal simultagnosia is rather interpreted as a disorder of visual attention. Along with Posner's (1984) hypothesis, Farah (1995) considers the possibility of a specific deficit in disengaging one's visual attention: in order to be able to engage one's visual attention onto a new stimulus, one must first disengage one's visual attention from its prior and/or current location. Parietal lobes would play a critical role in this attentional mechanism. People with a bilateral parietal lesion should thus present a 'sticky' attention on the current object without the possibility to shift to another one. If one assumes that, in an allocentric frame of reference, the location of an object can only be specified relative to another object, simultagnosia, which does not allow seeing more than one object at a time, becomes a highly plausible explanation for most of the disorders in spatial orientation found in parietal patients. The same explanation would also extend to the difficulties met by these patients in drawing tasks. They are frequently unable to copy drawings that they have recognized and their attempts at copying have a characteristic 'exploded' look: the parts of the copied object are not related to each other (the so-called constructional apraxia). According to Farah (1995: 45), 'this can be understood in terms of the necessity, in copying a picture, of drawing a part at a time, which requires patients to shift their attention to the individual parts of the shape and to position the parts with respect to one another'.

The question whether mental imagery is preserved or not in patients with simultagnosia has not been investigated. This is an interesting topic, in view of the notion that there might exist a specific form of 'spatial' imagery. Spatial imagery relates to the ability to manipulate spatial relationships between objects (mental scanning) or to manipulate object orientation (mental rotation) without reference to object identity. Patient LH (Farah *et al.* 1988), who was impaired in visual imagery for objects (see above) retained a normal ability for spatial imagery. Would the reverse dissociation (loss of spatial imagery and preservation of visual imagery) hold for a simultagnosic patient? A study of patient MU with a bilateral parietal lesion (see Wilson *et al.* 1997) allows us to investigate the question. MU did show a loss of spatial imagery (e.g. he failed in a task involving mental rotation of a manikin). He was also impaired in a variety of visuospatial tasks and had visuomotor problems in reaching for objects. However, although he was normal in object recognition and semantic memory, he was not tested for visual imagery.

Another, logical consequence of simultagnosia is the difficulty for the patient to refer different attributes to one and the same object. This problem was described in patient RM who suffered a massive biparietal lesion (Friedman-Hill *et al.* 1995). This patient was asked to report the color of letters or the shape of objects and to judge the relative and absolute locations of letters. When two letters printed in different colors were simultaneously presented to him, RM had great difficulties binding the color to its letter. The same difficulty was observed when two shapes were to be compared for their size. Interestingly, it was easier for him to make this comparison when the letters or shapes were presented sequentially (one after the other), rather than simultaneously: this finding is consistent with the notion that simultagnosics cannot see more than one object at a time and fail when they have to perceive spatial relationships between objects. Indeed, RM was impaired when he had to determine whether a letter was to the right or to the left of the center of the screen he was looking at. He was also impaired when he had to judge which of two letters was to his right or to his left. The authors' conclusion was that access to the explicit spatial information associated with the dorsal pathway is necessary to correctly bind together the different features (color, size, etc.) of an object.

5.3 Unilateral spatial neglect

Another dramatic illustration of the visuospatial disorders produced by parietal lesions is unilateral spatial neglect. Neglect is usually found in patients with right-sided lesions. It, therefore, affects the contralateral left hemispace. Typically, a patient with neglect for the left side of space will ignore visual stimuli presented on that side and will only report items presented on his right. This behavior is illustrated by the well-known 'cancellation' test, in which the patient is instructed to cross out lines of various orientations distributed across a sheet of paper: only the lines on the right side of the sheet are crossed. In copying simple drawings like a house, a clock face or a flower, the patient will copy only the right side of the model.

Neglect is not limited to visual stimuli: acoustic stimuli can be neglected as well. In addition, unilateral spatial neglect can be part of a more severe clinical condition (usually following large right hemisphere lesions extending to the frontal motor areas), which includes motor and somatosensory disorders. When this is the case, neglect extends to tactile and proprioceptive stimuli applied to the left half of the body and affects the representation of the body as a whole: patients may deny ownership of the left side of their body and express delusions with confabulation (somatoparaphrenia) about the nature or the ownership of their arm or leg. Denial of hemiplegia is also part of this syndrome of anosognosia (denial of disease). See Daprati *et al.* (2000) for an illustrative case.

Neglect for the left hemispace affects not only the external sensory world, but also the world as it is mentally represented. Consider a neglect patient imagining that he is standing in front of the Milan cathedral. This patient is asked to verbally describe the surroundings that he can mentally see from his present vantage point. As Bisiach and Luzatti discovered in 1978, he will correctly list the shops and the buildings on the right side of the cathedral, but he will ignore those on the left. If now the patient imagines the same area while he takes the opposite vantage point, he will have a clear mental representation of those buildings he previously ignored, and he will fail to report those that he previously reported. This observation corroborates the notion that one cannot imagine objects in space but from some standpoint or other: there is no imagining 'from nowhere'. This fits with the view that neglect is a spatial attentional disorder or, in other words, a deficit of attention localized to a part of space. Insofar as attention to visual stimuli (and to stimuli in other modalities as well) is a goal-directed process, it is not surprising that a lesion in areas which process visuospatial relationships will result in the inability to direct attention to the corresponding area of space.

A recent experiment by Rushworth *et al.* (2001) in normal subjects provides some insight into this mechanism. Subjects were asked to respond by a key press to the appearance of a target. In most trials, the target was pre-cued, i.e. subjects' attention was directed to the target (valid trials). In some trials, the pre-cue was invalid and the subject had to respond to a non-cued target (invalid trials). In these invalid trials, subjects successfully disengaged their attention from the cue and their reaction time was little affected compared to the valid trials. Rushworth *et al.*'s (2001) experiment involves the application of electrical shocks (via TMS) to different sites of the right and left parietal lobes during the presentation of the visual stimuli. When the shock was applied, during invalid trials, to a site corresponding to the most posterior part of the right angular gyrus, the reaction time increased significantly. The shock produced no effect if applied to another part of the right parietal lobe, nor if applied to the left angular gyrus. The interpretation of this result is that the right angular gyrus is the site responsible for disengaging attention from a visual stimulus: when its activity is disrupted by an intervening electrical shock, disengagement of attention is impaired. The effective site in the right angular gyrus corresponds to the main focus of the lesion observed in neglect patients (see Vallar and Perani 1986). Hence, the possible explanation of unilateral spatial neglect as a deficit in disengaging attention from its current location for directing it to the left side of space.

Highly relevant to the present discussion is the fact that a vast amount of implicit visual processing occurs in the neglected hemispace. A striking experiment by Marshall and Halligan (1994) highlights this fact. In this experiment, the patient was shown drawings of two houses placed on top of each other on a sheet of paper. One of the houses displayed a brightly colored fire on its left side. When asked to compare the two houses, the neglect patient reported no difference. However, when asked a different question: 'In which of these two houses would you rather live?', the patient consistently indicated the intact house. Marshall and Halligan's (1994) finding is supported by several other experiments (see review in Driver and Mattingley 1998): for example, the identification of a word (e.g. the word 'tree') by a neglect patient can be significantly faster if it is preceded by the brief and unnoticed presentation of a relevant object (e.g. an apple) on the left neglected side. This result (McGlinchey-Berroth *et al.* 1993) is evidence that semantic priming takes place in the neglected area of space. Driver and Mattingley (1998) suggested that this residual visual processing is reminiscent of residual visual processing in blindsight patients observed within the 'blind' hemifield following lesions of the primary visual cortex (see above). A major difference between blindsight and neglect, however, is that residual processing is far more extensive in the latter condition than in the former: in neglect patients, residual processing extends to objects' shape and semantic cues, which is not the case for blindsight.

Turning to visuomotor performance, the above results raise the possibility that movements directed to visual targets might be preserved in neglect patients, in spite of the fact that they do not have a correct conscious perception of these targets. As mentioned earlier, lesions responsible for unilateral spatial neglect usually affect the inferior and posterior part of the right parietal lobe, in the opercular region connecting the angular gyrus with the uppermost part of the temporal lobe. This region must be clearly distinguished from the more dorsal part of the parietal lobe, which we have found to be involved in visuomotor functions. Indeed, a recent study by Farné et al. (2003) demonstrates that reaching and grasping movements towards visual objects presented in the left hemispace are not worse in neglect patients than in patients with right brain damage without neglect. In addition, both neglect and non-neglect patients with right brain damage were able to correct the direction of their reach in a situation where the target object was unexpectedly displaced at the onset of their movement.

Another example of this dissociation, following lesions of the parietal lobe, between alteration of visual perceptual processing and preservation of visuomotor processing is provided by a striking phenomenon observed in neglect patients. It has been remarked that objects located in the neglected area, when they happen to be consciously processed, are in fact misperceived: they appear smaller than the same objects placed in the right hemispace. This difference indicates a distortion of space, as if space in the left hemispace would be less extended than on the right side (e.g. Milner et al. 1993). Pritchard et al. (1997) found that this perceptual size underestimation is not paralleled by a corresponding change in grip size during the action of grasping directed to those objects. When patients were to reach and grasp these objects, their finger grip was shaped to the veridical size of the objects, not to their (mis)perceived size.

5.4 Do visuomotor and visuospatial disorders correspond to dissociable functions of the parietal lobes?

The question of whether the visuomotor transformation and the perception of spatial relationships are one and the same thing, or are two separate processes, is a critical one for the validity of the dual model of visual functions. In its radical stronger version, where vision for perception and vision for action pertain to two parallel visual systems, the model predicts that the parietal, dorsal system should subserve a single function ultimately dedicated to acting on the visual world (e.g. Milner and Goodale 1995). On this conception, visuospatial disorders following parietal lesion should reflect the processing of spatial information as a pre-condition for action. This point was made by Bayliss and Bayliss (2001). They report the visual behavior of one patient with Balint syndrome following a bilateral parietal lesion. This patient presented a typical optic ataxia when attempting to reach for targets in visual space with either hand. However, when the location of the same targets was to be named (not reached) by using location descriptors (e.g. 'left', 'right', 'front', etc.), the patient made many more errors than in the reaching task. Furthermore, when the task consisted in first describing the location and then reaching for it immediately afterwards, the errors in describing and in reaching were similar. This difficulty was likely to be related to a problem with visual space processing because, when the blindfolded subject was asked to reach for the same targets on verbal instruction (e.g. 'touch the left target'), errors tended to disappear. Bayliss and Bayliss (2001) take these results to show that their patient's preserved ability to reach is disrupted by his severely degraded visual representation of space. This interpretation, however, is in contradiction with observations reported in other patients (see below).

On the weaker version of the model, the dorsal system subserves both spatial cognition (in Mishkin's sense) and object-oriented actions. On the weaker version, the two sets of disorders should reflect an impairment of two distinct functions. One of these functions would be the visuomotor transformation: a largely automatic process in which the location of a target is coded in egocentric coordinates. The conscious visual perception of the spatial relations between objects would be a distinct perceptual function, which allows the representation of the location of an object in allocentric coordinates. Available neuropsychological data tend to favor the latter weaker version of the model. For example, optic ataxia can be observed in the absence of visuospatial disorders. Also, optic ataxia is limited to one hand when the parietal lesion is unilateral: in this situation, the visuomotor deficit cannot be explained by a disorganized spatial perception. Finally, optic ataxia can be observed following lesion on either side, whereas visuospatial disorders are more likely to be observed after a right-sided lesion.

Neuro-imaging data obtained from normal subjects tend to confirm the view that the visuomotor transformation and visuospatial processing are subserved by separate mechanisms. Using experimental paradigms specifically designed for isolating visuomotor processing from the perception of spatial relationships, we can start to map the functional anatomy of the parietal lobes relevant to each processing (Fig. 3.11). As

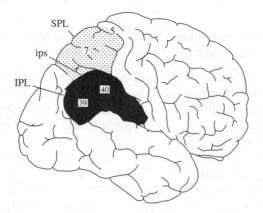

Fig. 3.11 Extent of superior and inferior parietal lobules in the human brain. On a lateral view of a right hemisphere, the superior parietal lobule (SPL), corresponding to Brodman areas 5 and 7, and the inferior parietal lobule (IPL), corresponding to areas 39 and 40, have been outlined. The two lobules are separated by the intraparietal sulcus (ips).

mentioned earlier, the study of the pure visuomotor transformation, involved in a task of grasping objects of varying sizes and shapes, reveals that the brain areas activated are confined to the anterior part of the intraparietal sulcus at the junction between the two parietal lobules (Grafton *et al.* 1992; Faillenot *et al.* 1997; Binkofski *et al.* 1998). In addition, the activation is located contralateral to the hand used in the motor task. The visual perception of spatial relationships was studied with a variety of spatial matching tasks (e.g. comparing displays where the same objects or shapes are arranged in the same or different spatial locations). The results of these studies consistently showed activation of relatively posterior and ventral parietal areas, in the fundus of the intra-parietal sulcus (Haxby *et al.* 1993; Faillenot *et al.* 1999), as well as in the area of the angular gyrus in the inferior parietal lobule (Köhler *et al.* 1995). The crucial point here is that, in all of the above studies, the activation foci were predominantly located within the right parietal lobe. Thus, neuro-imaging findings are generally consistent with the clinical data, which emphasize the role of the right hemisphere in space perception and the separation between visuomotor and visuospatial processes.

This is not to say that there are no functional links between the two kinds of processes. Parietal lobes play a critical role, both in the visuomotor transformation and in the perception of spatial relationships. Arguably, both the visuomotor transformation and the perception of spatial relationships between objects involve the selection and the localization of objects in space. An object can be located in space relative to other visual stimuli or relative to the agent. Thus, the parietal lobes must contribute to the process of selection and localization of objects in the workspace in both perceptual tasks and in goal-directed actions. If so, then according to the context in which visual behavior will take place, the parietal lobes must carry some information about object identity. As long as external objects remain in extrapersonal space, their localization relative to other objects will have to be processed for building a coherent visual representation of the environment, using allocentric coordinates. When objects are to be transferred into intrapersonal space (for manipulation, handling, use, transformation or further identi-fication by tactile cues), then their absolute location has to be determined in egocentric space. Thus, in the context of a visually guided action towards an object, the use of egocentric coordinates is central to the visuomotor transformation.

The crucial point is that the transformation of coordinates is effected in the parietal areas, where not only visual, but also somatosensory cues and eye movement cues are available (see previous chapter). Thus, the parietal areas are involved in tasks as differ-ent as a task of counting objects lying on a table, drawing a copy of objects lying on a table and grasping one of these objects. A normal human subject may switch instanta-neously from a task of either counting objects on a table or drawing a copy of objects on a table to grasping one of them. Thus, in the real life of a normal human subject, the parietal areas must allow for the immediate recoding of the location of an object from one coordinate system to the other: from an allocentric framework to an egocentric framework, and vice-versa.

The above data, along with many others presented in other chapters, can indeed be interpreted within the general framework that has been adopted in this book, namely that several distinct anatomical and functional channels contribute to human visual pro-cessing. However, the simple dualistic view according to which vision-for-perception is performed by the ventral stream and vision-for-action is performed by the dorsal stream of the human visual system turns out to be unable to accommodate the selective contribution of the parietal areas to the visuomotor transformation and to the visual perception of spatial relationships. From an anatomical standpoint, it turns out that the parietal lobe is not a single functional unit onto which to map the dorsal stream. The parietal lobes include, not only mechanisms for the visuomotor transformation, but also mechanisms for the conscious perception of spatial relationships. Furthermore, another set of parietal structures contributes to the perception of biological movements and the recognition of actions. The anatomical regions concerned with these additional properties undergo a much wider development in the human brain than in the monkey brain, due to the extension of the associative cortex in the postero-ventral part of the human parietal cortex. This extension parallels the appearance of hemispheric specialization, which makes any detailed comparison between the two species difficult. The extension of the human right parietal lobe allows for the development of new abilities in the visual perception and the representation of spatial relationships between objects as well as between the agent and the external world. And, as we shall see in Chapter 7, the extension of the left parietal lobe underlies the development of new abilities for representing and imagining actions.

4 The varieties of normal human visual processing

Human visual experience has a special phenomenal character. The human visual system yields subjective experiences of the world that differ from the subjective experiences of the world in modalities other than vision, e.g. touch, olfaction or audition. Seeing can, and often does, make us visually aware of objects, properties and facts in the world. In particular, it makes us visually aware of the size of objects, their shape, texture, color, orientation, spatial position, distance and motion. But it need not make us aware of each and every visual attribute of things in our environment. Often enough, seeing allows us to act efficiently on objects of which we are dimly aware, if at all, while we act. While moving at high speed, experienced drivers are sometimes capable of avoiding an interfering obstacle of whose visual properties they become fully aware afterwards. One may efficiently either catch or avoid being hit by a flying tennis ball without being aware of either its color or texture.

Thus numerous psychophysical experiments have revealed in normal human vision a rich and intriguing set of dissociations between different ways of processing one and the same visual stimulus. Of particular interest are dissociations between *perceptual* and *visuomotor* responses to a given visual stimulus. In the two previous chapters, we focused, respectively, on anatomical and electrophysiological evidence gathered mostly on the brain of macaque monkeys and on neuropsychological research on brain-lesioned human patients. In the present chapter, we shall focus on psychological evidence gathered on normal human adults. Primates in general, and humans in particular, are unique among animals in being able to grasp and manipulate objects in their environment using their arms and the dexterity of their hands. Thus, many relevant visuomotor tasks involve visually guided actions constituted by arm and hand movements directed towards objects, such as pointing, reaching and grasping. In this chapter, we will try to highlight the major differences between the visual computations underlying perceptual and visuomotor responses in normal subjects. In Sections 1 to 3, two main properties will be relevant to the comparison between perceptual and visuomotor analyses of visual stimuli: temporal properties and subjects' awareness of the stimulus. In the subsequent sections, we shall emphasize the fact that the control of visually guided actions requires the computations of the absolute size and/or distance of a target, whereas perceptual judgments arise from the computation of the relative distances and sizes of constituents of a visual array.

1 Pointing to an unperceived target

Consider what is called 'saccadic suppression'. We all know theoretically and practically that we move our eyes when we visually explore our environment. In fact, our eyes move constantly in their orbits. Saccades are rapid eye movements directed towards stationary or moving objects. By moving our eyes saccadically, we glimpse at stationary or moving things in our environment of which we become visually aware. Interestingly, however, although the movement of our eyes makes us visually aware of external objects, we are not visually aware of all the visual properties of objects during a saccade. Nor are we visually aware of the movement of our eyes in their orbits. If you look at yourself in a mirror and if you turn your eyes in any direction, you will fail to see your eyes move. From seeing one of your eyes in one position at time t and seeing it in a different position at $t + 1$, you may come to believe that it occupies a new position in its orbit and therefore that it has moved (Ditchburn 1955). You may thus conclude that it moved, but you did not *see* it move: you did not visually experience your eye movement. Why does one not see the movements of one's eyes? Part of the explanation has to do with perceptual constancy mechanisms: information about eye movement is used in computations that yield constancy of object position (see Chapter 2). Part of the explanation is that the visual threshold for displacements is increased: vision is partly suppressed during eye movements in the sense that sharp, clear images arising from a pair of eye fixations so dominate the blurred image that arises during the saccade itself that the blurred image is suppressed. Yet, in spite of this impaired perception of the change in position of proximal stimuli on my retina, one can accurately guide the movement of one's arm in the direction of a stationary object in one's environment and reach it successfully with one's hand. Thus, although one does not perceive the changing position of the image of the object on the retina, which arises from saccadic eye movements, still one is able to adjust one's visually guided arm movement towards the object.[1] In other words, information about the change of position of a perceived object relative to the eye is available to the visuomotor component, not to the perceptual component of the visual system.

This observation was the origin of a series of experiments performed by Bridgeman and his colleagues. Bridgeman *et al.* (1979) instructed subjects to point to a target that had just been displaced and then extinguished. Sometimes the motion of the target was made unnoticeable by saccadic suppression, i.e. by virtue of coinciding with a saccadic eye movement. Bridgeman *et al.* (1979) found that the accuracy of pointing was independent of the fact that the displacement of the target was actually perceived: surprisingly, failure to perceive the target's displacement (prompted by saccadic suppression) did not decrease the accuracy of pointing. Pointing to a moving target is one thing; perceiving it (let alone noticing it) is something else. This unexpected result strongly suggests that perceiving the motion of a target (*a fortiori* being visually aware that a target is moving) and pointing towards a moving target are two fairly independent processes.

Subsequently, Bridgeman *et al.* (1981) used a version of the phenomenon known as 'induced motion', whereby a stationary visual target appears to be moving during the displacement of a large underlying visual background. Furthermore, the stationary

---

[1]In any case, we see objects by virtue (or by means) of their images projected onto our retina; but what we see are the objects in the environment, not the images on our retina: images are representations by means of which we see objects (see Chapter 1).

target is seen to move in the direction opposite to the actual displacement of the background. Subjects exposed to the visual display were first asked to judge the amplitude of the target's induced motion. Then, in a different series of trials, they were asked to direct a pointer towards the perceived location of the target after each displacement of the background. In spite of their illusory perceptual judgments, subjects pointed in the direction of the actual location of the stationary target as determined in an egocentric frame of reference, not in the direction of its apparent location prompted by the impression of apparent motion. This experiment seems to warrant two complementary conclusions, one of which is that visuomotor (pointing) responses are more immune to the impression of apparent motion than perceptual responses. The other conclusion is that one and the same visual stimulus—a stationary visual target against a moving background—can give rise to two distinct visual analyses: the location of the target can be processed either for the purpose of a visuomotor task of pointing or for the purpose of a perceptual task. Indeed, Bridgeman *et al.* (1981) referred to the 'two visual systems' model (whose anatomical basis we discussed in Chapters 2 and 3) as a conceptual framework for interpreting their data. In the next sections of the present chapter, we shall re-examine in detail further evidence for the thesis that one and the same stimulus can be visually processed in at least two fundamentally different ways.

A similar experiment was performed by Goodale *et al.* (1986). A target jumped by two to four degrees during the ocular saccade directed at the target in its initial position. Although subjects were prevented from noticing the jump by their eye saccade, their pointing hand movement was nonetheless accurately directed at the target's new location. Furthermore, the duration of their hand movement was the same, irrespective of whether the target had jumped or not. In this experiment, the computation of a change in target location by the visuomotor system was thus able to control a change of hand movement in flight without introducing any delay. Goodale *et al.* (1986) reiterated Bridgeman's (1981) conjecture, namely that the neural mechanisms underlying the perception of target position can be dissociated from those underlying visually guided pointing hand movements directed towards that target.

2 Temporal properties of perceptual and visuomotor processings

These findings, together with neuropsychological findings in brain-lesioned patients (already discussed in the previous chapter), constitute an important incentive for further detailed attempts at delineating the distinguishing properties of the perceptual and the visuomotor functions of the human visual system. The relevant questions are: what are the necessary conditions for triggering two distinct (though collaborative) neural systems? Can one provide a precise computational and functional characterization of the differences between the perceptual and the visuomotor subsystems? Can one map functionally distinct visual information-processing systems onto anatomically distinct visual pathways? Along with most researchers in the field, we will confer, in the subsequent discussion, critical importance to such properties as the speed of processing, the degree of subjective awareness (or accessibility to awareness) of levels of processing, the penetrability by (or immunity to) visual illusions.

Typically, the main experimental tool used for measuring the speed of information-processing in visual tasks is reaction time. In the case of a simple perceptual task, such as the identification of a stimulus or the detection of a change in the environment, the response usually consists of a key-press or a vocal utterance. In visuomotor tasks—such as pointing or reach-to-grasp tasks—the response to the stimulus is a visually guided arm and hand movement. In such responses, the relevant parameters of the visuomotor act may be more or less isomorphic with some of the physical dimensions of the stimulus. Unlike visuomotor responses, most responses to perceptual tasks are not so directly related to the physical dimensions of the stimulus. Among visuomotor tasks, however, some responses are more directly related to physical dimensions of the target than others. Consider, e.g. a visuomotor response to a change in target location, such as pointing. Since the response to change in the target location is a visually guided hand movement, the relevant parameter of the motor act is maximally isomorphic with the relevant physical dimension of the stimulus (i.e. its location). Now consider a motor response to a change in the color of the target. Suppose the subject is instructed to point his hand to the target if the latter is red and to stop his hand movement if the target is green. In this case, the motor response is *not* maximally isomorphic with the relevant physical dimension of the stimulus (i.e. its color). The motor act involves (and depends on) a prior preliminary perceptual analysis of the target's color. As it turns out, corrections of hand trajectory in response to changes of target position require 100 ms or less (Paulignan *et al.* 1991). Correction of hand trajectory in response to a change of the color of the target requires a longer time (at least 80 ms more; Pisella *et al.* 2000).[2]

Both the location and the color of a target can change. Arguably, one cannot point to a target unless one processes its location. In a pointing task, however, processing a target's color is optional. For future reference, we shall call the principle involved 'the principle of congruence': the more a visual attribute of a stimulus is critical to the motor response, the faster the response.

Reaction times reflect fundamental computational and architectural constraints that the visuomotor and the visual perceptual systems must satisfy. The output of visual perceptual processing must serve as input to a memory buffer capable of storing visual pictorial information that can be accessed and retrieved over relatively long periods of time by higher cognitive functions. By contrast, the output of visuomotor processing must be at the service of a continuous process of on-line motor corrections. The former must be impervious to abrupt changes of frames of reference. The latter must be flexible enough to serve as input to a system capable of constant adjustments within a process of continuous updating of information about the position and orientation of targets of hand movements. As already mentioned, a change of position of a visual target occurring at the onset of a hand movement can influence its trajectory within 100 ms or less. The high speed of visuomotor processing is correlated with the temporal demands made by the motor system upon the memory storage. Visual information needs to be stored within the motor system no longer than what the motor system requires to run

---

[2] Key-press reaction times involved in the identification of an item in a picture (Thorpe *et al.* 1996) or in semantic comparison (Dehaene *et al.* 1998) are still significantly slower: they are within the range of 500–1000 ms.

a movement at its natural speed and achieve the goal of the action subserved by the movement. Therefore, visual information is likely to be stored in a highly schematic—spatio-motor—form in the motor system and storage is likely to decay rapidly. Thus, if the onset of a movement is delayed for a sufficiently long period of time after visual presentation of a target, then presumably the information relevant for the visuomotor task proper should become unavailable when the movement starts, and motor performance should therefore decline. There is indeed experimental evidence that upon the introduction of a delay between the visual presentation of a target and the onset of a pointing movement towards it, the accuracy of the pointing movement deteriorates after a few seconds (cf. Elliott and Maladena 1987).

In a series of experiments, Wong and Mack (1981) have used a phenomenon very similar to the production of 'induced motion' used by Bridgeman *et al.* (1981). The displacement of a visual background induces the apparent change of location of a stationary target. Whereas in Bridgeman *et al.*'s (1981) experiment, subjects were asked to point their hand towards the location of the target, in Wong and Mack's (1981) experiment, subjects moved their eyes to the spatial location of the target. What Wong and Mack (1981) found was that subjects moved their eyes to the actual position of the target, not to its perceptually displaced (apparent) location. However, if a delay is introduced between the perceptual displacement and the onset of the eye movement, the eye movement must be based on a stored representation of the location of the target; and the eyes use a 'perceptual', not a 'spatial', system of coordinates to code the location of the target. As Wong and Mack (1981: 128) put it, 'saccades to targets whose positions are specified by information stored in memory are programmed in terms of perceptual coordinates whereas otherwise [...] spatial coordinates are used'.

A more recent experiment by Bridgeman *et al.* (1997) provides still a deeper insight into the contrast between the temporal properties of visuomotor and perceptual processing of visual information. This experiment, which is based on a visual illusion called 'the Roelofs effect', is also reminiscent in some respects of Bridgeman's (1981) experiment on induced motion, already discussed. The main difference between the two experiments is that the Roelofs effect merely requires the display of a target against a stationary, not a moving, rectangular frame. Subjects are presented with a visual target that shortly appears against a luminous rectangular frame in an otherwise dark environment. They are asked to judge the position where the target was presented. If the position of the target relative to the rectangular frame coincides with what is in subjects' egocentric frame of reference, the midline of the frame, then subjects' judgments are accurate. If, however, the rectangular frame is displayed off-center with respect to subjects' midline, then subjects systematically misjudge the position of the target: e.g. if the frame is displayed to the left of subjects' midline, then subjects perceive the target further to the right than it actually is—as if subjects' perception of target position was biased towards the center of the rectangular frame. Thus, the Roelofs effect consists of an illusory displacement of the position of a stationary target towards the center of the stationary frame. However, when asked to reach and point towards the visual target, subjects were again able to direct their hand to the true position of the target, not its perceptually biased position. In other words, as already evidenced by Bridgeman *et al.* (1981) and Wong and Mack (1981), in a slightly different experimental context, visually guided pointing is more immune to illusory bias than is pure perception. What is surprising, however, is the fact that when the onset of pointing was delayed by 4 s with respect to the visual presentation of the target, then pointing became indeed subject to the Roelofs effect: in this delay condition, subjects pointed to the same illusory position at which they had misperceived the target to be. In Bridgeman's *et al.* (1997: 468) words, 'if a subject must make motor responses to stimuli no longer present, [the visuomotor] system must take its spatial information from the cognitive representation and brings any cognitively based illusion along with it'. This point will be discussed again later in this chapter.

Another, more direct, way of looking at the effects of delayed response on visuomotor processing is to examine the spatio-temporal characteristics of target-oriented movements executed after a delay. The idea is that a change in the kinematics of the delayed movement compared to the same movement executed without a delay should reveal a difference in the metrics used by the motor system according to whether or not a delay was introduced. Hu *et al.* (1999) compared grasping movements directed at objects of varying width, executed without a delay or with a 5-s delay. In both conditions, the movement was performed without visual access to the hand (in the so-called 'open-loop' condition). In the delay condition, subjects' reaches took longer and achieved peak velocity proportionately earlier than in the no-delay condition. In addition, maximum grip aperture (MGA, a critical parameter of the finger-grip that anticipates contact with the object, which is scaled to object size; see below for further details) was larger than in the no-delay condition. This result suggests that actions performed after a delay, use different transformations and a different metrics than those used during real-time grasping with no-delay. This point was confirmed by a further experiment by Hu and Goodale (2000), in which subjects had to grasp an object flanked by either a smaller or a larger object (Fig. 4.1). In the no-delay condition, grip was scaled to the actual physical size of the object to be grasped, irrespective of the fact that it appeared larger or smaller than the flanking object. By contrast, in the 5-s delay condition, grip size was influenced by the perceived size of the grasped object relative to the size of the flanking object. Thus, in the first no-delay condition, grip size reflected the absolute object's size irrespective of the surrounding context. In the second condition with a delay, grip size reflected the estimated relative size of the object as determined by a comparison with the differently sized neighboring object.

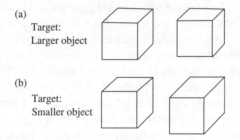

Fig. 4.1 A size-contrast illusion for dissociating perceptual and visuomotor responses. Subjects are instructed to grasp the larger object in the pair displayed in (a) and the smaller object in the pair displayed in (b). In fact, the target objects in both displays are identical in size. (From Hu and Goodale, 2000, *Journal of Cognitive Neuroscience* © MIT Press Journals.)

The above results suggest first that visual information present in the memory buffer for, and used by, the perceptual processing remains available for a longer period of time than visual information stored in the memory buffer for, and used by, the visuomotor processing. Admittedly, although they may overlap to some extent, the visual information selectively exploited by one system differs somewhat from the visual information selectively exploited by the other system. In particular, while the visuomotor system concentrates on the absolute size of an object, the perceptual system irrepressibly makes comparative judgments of the relative size of neighboring objects. The experimental results suggest that the motor system may draw upon the same information as the perceptual processing when its natural temporal profile is upset and when, e.g. the onset of action is delayed.

3   Time and awareness in perceptual and visuomotor tasks

Now, if one wants a clear-cut demonstration of the temporal dissociation between the visuomotor and the perceptual modes of processing, then one ought to design an experiment in which both systems would be simultaneously triggered in response to one and the same visual stimulus. Such an experiment has been designed by Castiello *et al.* (1991). Subjects are presented with three dowels, one of which they are instructed to grasp when it becomes illuminated. In 20% of randomly distributed cases, the light is switched on to a different dowel at the very onset of the hand movement. First, subjects are able to modify the trajectory of their hand movement on line so as to reach successfully for the new target with a slight increase in movement duration. Kinematic analysis revealed that the first correction of the trajectory occurred around 100 ms after target change. Second, in those trials in which the target changed at the onset of movement, subjects were, in addition, instructed to emit the sound 'Tah!' when they became aware of the change. This 'perceptual' response was found to lag the motor response (i.e. the correction of the movement's trajectory) by approximately 300 ms.

This experiment raises a methodological problem, which must be discussed before the temporal differences between the two systems can be taken for granted. This problem is that subjects were required to generate two distinct motor responses—a corrective hand movement and a vocal utterance—more or less at the same time. Since, some people think, this situation is a potential source of interference between the two responses, the two responses cannot be generated concomitantly: hence, they would interfere with each other and would be generated sequentially. In this particular experiment, however, interference was minimized by the fact that the two motor responses were different in nature. Unlike the vocal utterance, the corrective hand movement is part of a goal-directed action: the action of reaching a physical object. In the experimental condition designed by Castiello *et al.* (1991), it is part of an automatic process, involving no conscious awareness of motor preparation on the subjects' part. By contrast, the vocal utterance is a controlled motor signal consciously used to describe a visual event and/or report subjects' conscious awareness of a visual signal. The latter's aim is to warn the experimenter about subjects' conscious awareness of an event, not to act upon a physical object or a target. As reflected by the principle of congruence, unlike the hand movement, the vocal utterance is not isomorphic (or congruent) with the critical parameter of the target, i.e. location. It is known from the literature that interference between automatic and consciously controlled processes is very limited. Controlled processes, which are conscious and effortful, can interfere with one another, because they compete for common attentional resources. But they do not compete with automatic processes for the allocation of attention (cf. Engelkamp 1998). Thus, we should not worry excessively about the risk that Castiello *et al.*'s (1991) results be biased by a potential interference between the two motor responses, since one is automatic and the other one is under the conscious control of attention.

The previous sections were devoted to a systematic comparison between perceptual and visuomotor processing of one and the same visual event. In particular, we tried to assess the differences between the two modes of visual processing along two main axes: their temporal properties and their accessibility to conscious awareness. References to visual illusions (such as induced motion and the Roelofs effect) have been merely incidental to the systematic comparison between the temporal properties and the accessibility to consciousness of the two kinds of visual information-processing. In the subsequent sections, we turn to a detailed analysis of the effects of pictorial illusions on perception and on visually guided action.

4 Frames of reference

Pictorial illusions have fascinated perceptual psychologists because they demonstrate that normal perception is not always veridical. Not only can the eyes of normal observers be fooled by features of a visual display, but even after the trick has been revealed, the illusory percept will persist: knowing that your perception is illusory does not make the illusion go away. In this respect, the visual information-processing that gives rise to pictorial illusions is, in Fodor's (1983) words, 'modular' or 'information-ally encapsulated', i.e. it is immune to (or not penetrable by) general background knowledge. The main issue to be addressed in subsequent sections is whether a visual display that fools the eye also fools visually guided hand movements.

Arguably, as noticed by Milner and Goodale (1995), perception and visually guided actions upon objects impose sharply different computational requirements on the human visual system. Visually based perceptual judgments of distance and size are typically comparative (or relative) judgments: in a perceptual task, one cannot but fail to see some things as smaller (or larger) and closer (or further away) than other neighboring things that are parts of a single visual array. In perceptual tasks, the output of obligatory comparisons of sizes, distances and positions of constituents of a visual array serves as input to perceptual constancy mechanism (some of which were mentioned earlier in this chapter). As a result, of two physically equal objects, if one is perceived as more distant from the observer than the other, the former will be perceived as larger than the latter. By studying errors in perceptual judgments, which arise from illusory pictorial displays, perceptual psychologists have learned a great deal about normal perception. By contrast, visually guided actions directed towards objects are typically based on the computation of the absolute size and location of objects on which to act.

In order to grab successfully a branch or a rung while climbing a ladder, one must presumably compute the distance and metrical properties of the object to be grabbed quite independently of pictorial features of the surrounding visual array. For example, the physical distance of the rung must be computed on the basis of stereopsis and retinal motion. The distance must then enter into a computation of the physical size of the rung. Thus, there are seemingly good evolutionary reasons why, unlike perception, visually guided goal-directed actions such as reaching and prehension could not afford the luxury of being deceived by pictorial illusions. 'There are', as Haffenden and Goodale (1998: 124) put it, 'situations in which the life or death of an organism will depend on the accuracy of a motor output; sensitivity to a visual illusion in the scene could be an enormous liability'. In fact, there is, or so we shall argue, evidence provided, in part by Haffenden and Goodale, that suggests that visually guided actions *can* be selectively fooled by a visual display. However, if and when they are, they are fooled by features of the display that are distinct from the features involved in illusory perceptual judgments.

Thus, one of the major computational differences between the requirements of perception and visually guided actions upon the visual system lies in the different frames of reference in which visual information is coded (or represented). The position and/or distance of a visually presented object must first of all be coded in a frame of reference centered on the subject's retina (a retinocentric frame of reference). Then this information can be transformed into information coded in a frame of reference centered on the subject's head or body axis. Cognitive neuroscience studies systematically the set of such transformations of systems of coordinates for representing visual attributes of objects (see Chapter 2). In this section, we shall emphasize the contrast between two fundamental frames of reference in which the position and/or distance of a visual stimulus can be coded: an egocentric frame of reference and an allocentric frame of reference. Coding the position and/or distance of a visually presented object in an egocentric frame of reference is representing the object's position and/or distance relative to the observer's body. Coding the position an object's position and/or distance in an allocentric frame of reference is representing the object's position and/or distance relative to some other object in the visual display. Because, as we said, visual perceptual judgments of distances and sizes are fundamentally comparative, the visual information they exploit must be coded in an allocentric frame of reference. In order to direct a hand movement towards a target, an agent must determine the size, position and/or distance of a target relative to his or her body position. Therefore, in a visually guided action directed towards an object, visual information must be coded in an egocentric frame of reference.

According to the dualistic model of the human visual system, one and the same visual stimulus can be submitted to two different kinds of processing according to whether the task is a perceptual or a visuomotor task. Now, it is important to realize that the dualistic model presupposes that the visual processing involved in either the perceptual or the visuomotor task occurs in the visual system at some anatomical stage located further ahead in the stream of visual information processing than at the point where the ventral stream and the dorsal stream bifurcate into two separate visual pathways. The illusory effects, which we shall examine, arise from the obligatory comparison between the sizes of components of the visual array. It is highly likely that such comparisons are constrained by mechanisms ensuring the preservation of size and shape constancy across the display and that they are carried by brain areas located higher than the primary visual cortex. If the processing involved in the illusory visual percept took place in the primary visual cortex prior to the division between the ventral pathway and the dorsal pathway, e.g. in areas V1 or V2, then presumably the effect of the size-contrast illusion should affect equally the perceptual judgment and the visuomotor task. If the processing responsible for the illusory percept takes place after the anatomical bifurcation, then the perceptual task and the visuomotor task should be affected differently.

In the sequel, we shall examine several experimental paradigms designed to explore the different computational demands on the visual system made by perceptual judgments and by visually guided actions directed towards objects. These paradigms involve different pictorial size-contrast illusions and exploit different motor tasks.

5   Do size-contrast illusions deceive pointing?

In the Müller–Lyer illusion, two segments of equal length with two opposing wing (or arrow) configurations are displayed. Although the two segments are equal, the segment with two converging arrows seems longer than the segment with two diverging arrows. Even though subjects may know that the two segments are equal, nonetheless they visually experience the two segments as unequal (Fig. 4.2).

In an experiment by Gentilucci *et al.* (1996), subjects sat in front of a table on which three possible stimuli could be displayed: one of two Müller–Lyer segments with opposing arrow configurations, and a control segment without arrows. The index finger of subjects' right hand was positioned on a disk located towards the nearest vertex of the displayed segment. Subjects were asked to execute a pointing gesture: they were asked to move the index finger of their right hand from its starting position to the more distant vertex of the segment. Gentilucci *et al.* (1996) compared four distinct conditions. In all four conditions, subjects could inspect the display for 5 s before the go signal instructed them to move:

(1) in the 'full-vision' condition, subjects could see both their hand and the target during execution of the action;

(2) in the 'non-visual feedback' condition, subjects could see the target but not their hand;

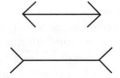

Fig. 4.2 The Müller–Lyer illusion. Two segments of equal size look unequal.

(3) in the 'no-vision 0 delay' condition, subjects could see neither their hand nor the target during the action, hence, action was executed in the dark;

(4) finally, in the 'no-vision 5-s delay' condition, subjects could see neither their hand nor the target during the action and there was a 5-s delay before the go-signal.

What Gentilucci *et al.* (1996) found was an increasing effect of the Müller–Lyer illusion on the pointing movement from the first to the fourth condition. Let us see why. Pointing to a target involves a computation of the distance between the effector and the target. When both target and hand are visible during the movement, the task is a pure visuomotor task. After visual presentation of the display upon the beginning of the action, the location of the target can be coded in an egocentric frame of reference centered on the subject's body. In the first condition, in which both target and hand are visible during the visuomotor task, subjects can keep track of the decreasing distance between the target and their moving hand. Hence, they can continuously update their transitory representation of the position of the target relative to their own body parts. In effect, they can take into account incoming visual information about the changing distance of the position of the target relative to their hand by coding it in a frame of reference centered on their hand. Or perhaps they code the decreasing distance between the target and their moving hand in an egocentric frame of reference centered on the axis of their body. Hence, the movement of the index finger is guided by what may be called a motor representation of the target. Crucially, such a motor representation of the target can ignore all surrounding features of the visual array, such as the arrow configuration surrounding the vertex. For the purpose of guiding the hand motion, the motor representation selects in the visual display the target to be reached and neglects elements that may be relevant to a perceptual representation. In other words, in the motor representation, the target is a landing site for the movement of the index finger. Thus, the motor representation of the position of the target is both quite short-lived and relatively immune to the Müller–Lyer illusion.

When neither the hand nor the stimulus is visible during the action, the motor representation fades away and the task is increasingly driven by perceptual cues, by cognitive and working memory processes. When subjects cannot see either their hand or the target, they cannot code the position of the target in a frame of reference centered on their moving hand. Presumably they cannot either code the continuously changing distance between the target and their moving hand in an egocentric frame of reference centered on the axis of their body. The location of the target must then be coded in an allocentric frame of reference, i.e. as the distance between the two vertices of the segment. So the conversion from an egocentric frame of reference to an allocentric frame of reference prompts a fundamental change in the representational format. When subjects have no visual access to their body parts, they must use a visual representation of the stimulus. Hence, the length of the segment becomes relevant. When the length of the segment is relevant to determining the location of the target—as in the third and especially in the fourth condition—the representation of the distance takes into account the surrounding features of the visual layout, such as the orientation of the arrow configuration surrounding the two vertices. The perceptual representation, which can be stored in memory, is more sensitive to the Müller–Lyer illusion than the short-lived motor representation of the target.

In summary, Gentilucci *et al.*'s (1996) experiment shows that, by varying some of the visual cues available to normal subjects, as well as some of the temporal properties of their action, a purely visuomotor task can be turned progressively into a more perceptual task. In the process, demands made on the visual system change accordingly: the visual system is increasingly required to produce a perceptual judgment. The experiment reveals that normal subjects can make perceptual judgments about the location of a visual stimulus that are in some way at odds with the motor acts that they can direct towards those stimuli. Hence, judgments about an object's location can be dissociated from visuomotor processing about the very same object location.

Another well-known visual illusion is the Titchener circles illusion (also called the Ebbinghaus illusion). The standard version of this illusion consists of the display of two circles of equal diameter, one surrounded by an annulus of circles greater than it, and the other surrounded by an annulus of circles smaller than it. Although the two central circles are equal, the former looks smaller than the latter. On what seems like the most plausible account of the Titchener illusion, the annulus of smaller circles is judged to be more distant than the annulus of larger circles. As a consequence, the central circle surrounded by smaller circles is perceived as more distant than the central circle surrounded by larger circles. Hence, the size of the former is perceived as larger than the size of the latter. A non-standard version of the illusion consists in the display of two circles of unequal diameter: the larger of the two is surrounded by an annulus of circles larger than it, while the smaller of the two is surrounded by an annulus of circles smaller than it, so that the two unequal circles look equal (Fig. 4.3).

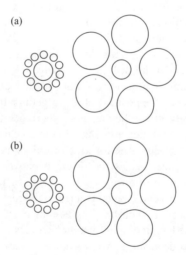

Fig. 4.3 Two varieties of the Titchener illusion. (a) The circle surrounded by a smaller annulus appears larger than an identical circle surrounded by a larger annulus. (b) In order for two unequal circles to appear equal, the circle surrounded by the larger annulus has been enlarged by about 10% with respect to the other one.

In a recent experiment, van Donkelaar (1999) has examined the influence of the Titchener illusion upon the visuomotor task of pointing. Subjects were instructed to point at the center of one of two standard Titchener illusory circles. Accurate pointing gestures are known to obey Fitts' law (a psychophysical law named after Fitts 1954), according to which the duration of a movement directed at a visual target varies as a function of the size of the target, so that a pointing movement aimed at a smaller target will require more time than the same movement aimed at a larger target. In van Donkelaar's (1999) experiment, subjects were operating in an 'open loop' condition, i.e. without visual access to the movement of their hand. What this author found was that pointing movements aimed at the center of the circle surrounded by an annulus of larger circles were slower than pointing movements aimed at the center of the circle surrounded by an annulus of smaller circles. Conversely, no difference in duration was found when subjects were asked to point to the center of two unequal circles that looked equal because the larger of the two circles was surrounded by an annulus of circles larger than it, whereas the smaller circle was surrounded by an annulus of circles smaller than it.

On the face of it, this result suggests that the visuomotor analysis of a stimulus can be influenced by the Titchener illusion. It suggests that a size-contrast illusion can deceive pointing. However, before drawing any general conclusion from this experiment as to the scope of the distinction between perceptual and visuomotor analysis of one and the same stimulus, let us pause to reflect on the ecological validity of the motor response used in the experiment. There are two alternative possibilities well worth exploring. One is that the task of pointing to the center of a Titchener circle is guided by two representations of the target: a motor representation and a perceptual representation. The other is that this result is not so much a counter-example to the distinction between perceptual judgment and visuomotor actions, as an argument for distinguishing two kinds of visuomotor analysis of visual information.

On the one hand, pointing is one example of a broader category of visually guided movements, which includes also reaching-to-grasp movements. These movements are aimed at matching the effectors of the upper limb with the physical attributes of the target. On the other hand, pointing can be part of ostensive communicative behavior as when one demonstrates an object for the purpose of attracting another person's attention towards it. Human infants perform so-called 'proto-imperative' pointing actions directed towards distant objects in order to request adults to bring them the distant objects. Later, they perform so-called 'proto-declarative' pointing actions aimed at monitoring others' visual attention towards objects of potential common interest for thought. Unlike purely visuomotor pointing movements, communicative pointing gestures are controlled by perceptual and attentional visual processes and are designed to monitor the visual attention of others. Pointing movements that exemplify Fitts' law are unlike communicative acts of pointing in that they usually involve a physical contact between the index finger and the object pointed to. Fitts' law applies first and foremost to fast visuomotor actions whose terminal point consists in touching the object (the prototypical example on which Fitts based his findings was reciprocal tapping between two targets). Arguably, in the task used in van Donkelaar's (1999) experiment, pointing was guided by two interacting representations: a purely visuomotor representation of the target of the pointing movement and a perceptual representation of the center of a Titchener circle—since this is where subjects were instructed to point. Presumably, subjects must have formed a perceptual representation of the display and this representation had to include perceptual parameters such as the size of the circle. If so, then the duration of the pointing gesture was affected by both the motor representation and the perceptual representation, not by the motor representation alone. It would be interesting to design an experiment in which subjects would be asked to point their finger to demonstrate the larger circle without touching it. The question to be tested is whether in a task of pure 'ostensive demonstration', the duration of the pointing gesture would reveal a greater influence of the Titchener illusion than the pointing movement ending in contact with the circle.

6   Do size-contrast illusions deceive grasping?

Even though the computation of the size of an object partly relies on an estimation of its distance, the Titchener circles illusion is a size-contrast illusion: it is primarily about the *size*, not the distance of objects. As we said, the standard version of this illusion consists in the display of two circles of equal diameter, one surrounded by an annulus of circles greater than it, and the other surrounded by an annulus of circles smaller than it. Although they are equal, the former looks smaller than the latter. As Haffenden and Goodale (2000: 1598) put it, the perceptual illusion arises from 'the perceptual system's attempt to maintain size constancy across the entire visual array'. On this view, the annulus of smaller circles is judged to be more distant than the annulus of larger circles. Consequently, the central circle surrounded by smaller circles is taken to be more distant than the central circle surrounded by larger circles. Hence, the size of the former is perceived as larger than the size of the latter.

Aglioti *et al.* (1995) designed an experiment in which they replaced the two central circles by two graspable three-dimensional plastic disks, which they displayed within a horizontal plane. Secondly, they exploited the non-standard version of the Titchener circles illusion. In a first row of experiments with pairs of unequal disks whose diameters ranged from 27 mm to 33 mm, they found that on average the disk in the annulus of larger circles had to be 2.5 mm wider than the disk in the annulus of smaller circles in order for both to look equal. These numbers provide a measure of the delicacy of the visual system. Thirdly, Aglioti *et al.* (1995) alternated presentations of physically unequal disks that looked (or were perceptually) equal, and presentations of physically equal disks that seemed (or were perceptually) unequal. Both kinds of trials were presented randomly and so were the left vs. right positions of either kind of annuli. Subjects were instructed to pick up the disk on the left if they thought the two disks to be equal, or to pick up the disk on the right if they judged them to be unequal.

In Aglioti *et al.*'s experiment, the sequence of subjects' choices of the disk on the right or on the left (either when equal disks appeared unequal or when unequal disks appeared equal) provided a measure of the magnitude of the illusion prompted by the comparison between two disks surrounded by two distinct annuli upon perceptual judgments. In the visuomotor task, the measure of grip size was based on the unfolding of the natural grasping movement performed by subjects, while their hand approached the object. During the movement, fingers progressively stretch up to a maximal aperture before they close down until contact with the object. This maximum grip aperture (MGA) takes place at a relatively fixed point in the duration of the movement: it occurs at approximately 60% of the movement (Jeannerod 1981). In non-illusory contexts, MGA has been found to be reliably correlated with the object's physical size. Although much larger, it is directly proportional to the object's physical size. Due to this remarkable property, MGA can thus be held to be a faithful index of the computation of an object's size made and used by the visuomotor system in a grasping task. Aglioti *et al.* measured MGA in flight using optoelectronic recording. That MGA does not depend on a conscious visual comparison between the size of the object and the hand during the movement is corroborated by the fact that the correlation with the object's size turns out to be reliable in open-loop condition, with no visual access to the hand (cf. Jeannerod 1984). Hence, MGA must result from an anticipatory automatic non-conscious visual process of calibration.

Thus, Aglioti *et al.* compared two kinds of responses to the display of two kinds of Titchener disks surrounded by two different annuli. In one kind of display, subjects were presented with two equal disks that looked unequal. In the other kind of display, subjects were presented with unequal disks that looked equal. One kind of response consisted in making a comparative judgment that was revealed by selecting either the disk on the left or the disk on the right (according to whether they appeared equal or unequal). The other response consisted in grasping the selected disk.

What Aglioti *et al.* found was that, unlike comparative perceptual judgments as non-verbally expressed by the sequence of choices of either the disk on the left or the disk on the right, the grip was not significantly affected by the illusion. Thus, the influence of the illusion was significantly stronger on the perceptual judgment than on the grasping task. The latter turned out to be more reliably correlated with the physical size of the disks than the former. Taken at face value, this experiment suggests that the size of one and the same physical object can give rise to two different kinds of visual representations according to the task: one task consists in comparing the size of two disks; the other task consists in grasping one of the two disks.

This experiment raises a number of methodological problems, one of which is that Aglioti *et al.* relied on two different methods for measuring the influence of the illusions upon the two tasks. They used a continuous measure of MGA for grasping, namely the distance between thumb and index finger, but they used a binary or discrete measure for the perceptual comparison, namely the choice between the disk on the left and the disk on the right. Traditionally, in perceptual tasks, several psychophysical methods have been used to measure the influence of the illusory display on perceptual judgments, such as asking subjects to report verbally which of the two disks looks larger. An alternative method, which provides a continuous measure of perceptual judgment, is to ask subjects to match object size by the distance between thumb and index finger—a method that, incidentally, uses the same effector as the motor grasping task. In response to this problem, Haffenden and Goodale (1998) reproduced Aglioti *et al.*'s (1995) experiment, but they designed one more task: in addition to instructing subjects to pick up the disk on the left if they judged the two disks equal in size or to pick up the disk on the right if they judged them to be unequal, they required subjects to manually estimate (between thumb and index finger) the size of the disk on the left if they judged the disks to be equal in size and the size of the disk on the right if they judged them to be unequal (Fig. 4.4).

(a)   Grasp

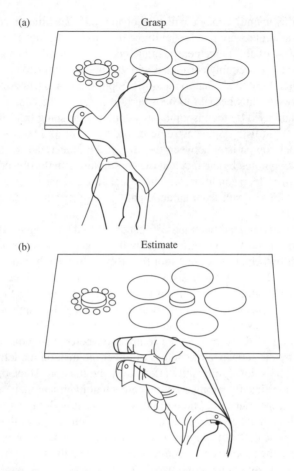

(b)   Estimate

Fig. 4.4 Method for comparing the influence of the Titchener illusion in the grasping and the matching tasks. (a) The size of the finger-grip reaches its maximum aperture as the hand approaches the target disk. (b) The subject manually demonstrates (or estimates) the size of the target disk without reaching towards it. Note the sensors attached to the index and thumb for measuring finger position. (From Haffenden and Goodale 1998, *Journal of Cognitive Neuroscience* © MIT Press Journals, courtesy of Professor Melvyn Goodale.)

What Haffenden and Goodale (1998) found was that when subjects were presented with two physically unequal disks surrounded by two distinct annuli, and after they had indicated by their illusory choice that they thought that the disks were equal, manual estimate confirmed the illusory comparative judgment; but MGA did not. The latter, unlike the former, remained reliably correlated with the physical size of the disk. When subjects were presented with two physically equal disks surrounded by two distinct annuli, and after they had indicated by their illusory choice that they thought that the disks were unequal, again their manual estimate confirmed their illusory comparative judgments; but, again, MGA did not.

7 Disentangling the pictorial from the motoric role of annuli

Taken together, these experiments strongly suggest that the same stimulus can be subjected to two kinds of visual analyses according to whether the task is perceptual or visuomotor. Furthermore, in Haffenden and Goodale's (1998) experiment, it is quite striking that the illusion has different effects on two distinct tasks involving the same effector: namely, distancing one's index finger from one's thumb as a function of object's size. However, Pavani *et al.* (1999) and especially Franz *et al.* (2000) have argued that the results of Aglioti *et al.*'s (1995) experiment might arise from an unnoticed asymmetry between the two tasks (the perceptual judgment and the grasping task). Whereas in the perceptual task, subjects are asked to compare two distinct disks with two different annuli, by contrast in the visuomotor task, only one disk is relevant to grasping and subjects can focus their attention on a single disk, i.e. the disk they are about to grasp. The dissociation between estimation and grasping might be an artifact of this asymmetry. Franz *et al.* (2000) argue that if the two tasks are carefully matched, then the illusion might affect perception and action in strikingly similar ways. In support of the view that one and the same representation might guide both a perceptual and a motor task, they ran three kinds of experiments: in the first experiment, they compared a perceptual task and a motor task that were designed to be perfectly symmetrical. The other two experiments compared two perceptual tasks (Fig. 4.5).

First, in what they called a 'single context' experiment, Franz *et al.* displayed a single disk surrounded either by an annulus of circles larger than it or by an annulus of circles smaller than it. In the grasping task, subjects were asked to grasp the disk. In the perceptual condition, subjects had to match the perceived size of the central disk with a comparison circle devoid of annulus, which was displayed on the monitor of a computer, and whose size they could adjust. In this 'single-context' experiment, Franz *et al.* found no significant dissociation between the two tasks and they found that the level of influence of the illusion prompted by a single disk surrounded by an illusory annulus was comparable to the influence on grasping found by Aglioti *et al.* (1995). This finding, which confirmed that obtained by Pavani *et al.* (1999), raises the question of whether, in these experiments, one and the same visual representation of the stimulus is used in both tasks.

Second, Franz *et al.* (2000) compared the effects of the above perceptual task in a 'single context' with the effects of Aglioti *et al.*'s (1995) 'direct comparison' between two equal disks with two distinct illusory annuli.

Finally, they compared the effects of a 'direct comparison' with what they called 'separate comparison' in which subjects are presented with two equal disks surrounded by two distinct illusory annuli and asked to match the size of (only) one of them by adjusting the size of a separate circle without an annulus. They found that 'direct comparison' gives rise to what they call a 'super-additive effect', namely that the illusion prompted by the comparison between two disks with two distinct illusory annuli is greater than the result of the sum of either two 'single context' experiments or two 'separate comparisons' experiments.

Interestingly, Daprati and Gentilucci (1997) report similar findings using the Müller–Lyer illusion. Subjects were presented with a wooden bar of varying lengths

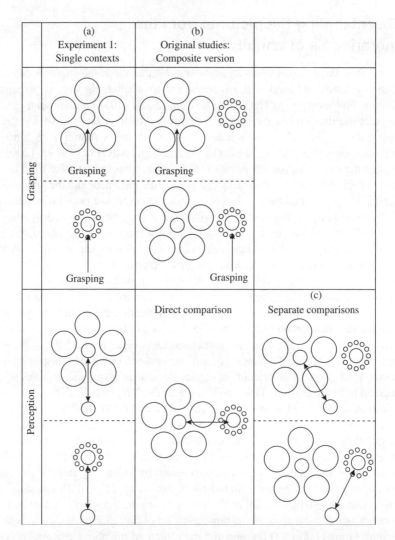

Fig. 4.5 Experiments for testing the influence of the Titchener illusion on grasping and perception. For explanation see text. (From Franz *et al.* 2000. Grasping visual illusions: no evidence for a dissociation between perception and action. *Psychological Science*, Blackwell Publishing Ltd.)

(5 cm, 6 cm, and 7 cm, respectively) superimposed upon one of three possible line segments (of length equal to the bar): one with converging arrows, one with diverging arrows and one without. Daprati and Gentilucci compared three tasks: a drawing task, a grasping task and a finger-matching task. Importantly, stimuli were always presented one at a time. First of all, they found that a bar with converging arrows yields larger estimates than a bar with diverging arrows. Second, they found that, in both the finger-matching and the drawing tasks, when stimuli are presented one at a time, the perceived difference between two distinct bars superimposed on segments with different arrows

was smaller than the difference between two segments with two different arrows presented simultaneously in other experiments. Third, with bars presented separately, there was a small dissociation between the grasping task and the perceptual task.

At this point, although it is probably premature to provide a final assessment of the experimental situation (see below), we do want to ask the question whether, altogether, these experiments on size-contrast illusions support the view that one and the same visual stimulus can be submitted to two distinct visual analyses. We will presently argue that in fact they do.

First of all, let us ask whether, as argued by Pavani *et al.* (1999) and Franz *et al.* (2000), the asymmetry between the perceptual task and the visuomotor task can explain the different effects of the size-contrast illusion upon the two tasks first found by Aglioti *et al.* (1995). One way to examine this question is to ask: what is the significance of what Franz *et al.* (2000) call the 'super-additivity' of 'direct comparison'? We believe that the finding that 'direct comparison' of two disks surrounded by two distinct illusory annuli involves a 'super-additive' effect is an interesting finding—a finding corroborated, as we said, by Daprati and Gentilucci (1997) with a different illusory display. However, for two complementary reasons, we do not think that, in and of itself, this finding is sufficient to refute the dualistic hypothesis according to which visual perceptual processing differs from visuomotor processing of the same display.

In their first paradigmatic experiment on 'single contexts', Pavani *et al.* (1999) and Franz *et al.* (2000) did compare grasping and manual estimation of the size of one disk surrounded by an illusory annulus presented one at a time. They did find that the level of influence of the display in both tasks is roughly the same as that obtained by Aglioti *et al.* (1995) on grasping. This level of influence of the illusion on perception is weaker than that found by Aglioti *et al.* (1995) and Haffenden and Goodale (1998). This raises the key question: what is the main difference between 'single-context' experiments and the paradigm used by Aglioti *et al.*'s (1995) and by Haffenden and Goodale's (1998)? The main difference is that, in the former, unlike in the latter, there is no prior comparative judgment on two disks surrounded by two distinct illusory annuli.

Now, let us ask to what extent Haffenden and Goodale's (1998) results might arise from an unnoticed asymmetry between the perceptual and the motor tasks. It is true that Aglioti *et al.* (1995) relied on a contrast between two asymmetrical tasks, only one of which involved an explicit comparative judgment between two disks and the other of which focused upon a single disk. In Haffenden and Goodale's (1998) experiment, however, subjects always start by providing a comparative judgment between two (physically equal or unequal) disks, which issues in a choice of either the disk on the left or the disk on the right. Then, the second step consists either in grasping or in the manual estimation of the selected disk. In other words, whether the next task is perceptual judgment or grasping, subjects are first required to provide a comparative judgment. The motor task and the perceptual task are thus perfectly matched.

So, although it is interesting to have experimental data showing that in purely perceptual tasks, the size-contrast illusion is far stronger when two disks with two illusory annuli are displayed than when a single disk with an illusory annulus is displayed, this discovery, in and of itself, does not argue against the dissociation between a motor task and a perceptual task, for the simple reason that it does not arise from a comparison between a perceptual task and a motor task. Rather, it arises from a comparison between different perceptual tasks. From the contrast between 'single-context' experiments and 'direct-comparison' experiments, what follows is not that there is no dissociation between perceptual processing and visuomotor processing. What follows rather is that the motor task is more immune than the perceptual task to the result of the prior comparative judgment used by Aglioti *et al.* (1995) and Haffenden and Goodale (1998). So far as the perceptual tasks are concerned, we can order the situation in the following way from the strongest to the weakest effect of the illusion on perception:

(1) comparison between two disks surrounded by two distinct illusory annuli;

(2) indirect estimation of the size of one disk with an illusory annulus after comparison of two disks with two distinct illusory annuli;

(3) direct estimation of the size of a disk with an illusory annulus (which is roughly equivalent to the influence of the illusion upon grasping).

Thus, we do not believe that, altogether, the experiments on size-contrast illusions, which we have reviewed so far, are inconsistent with the dualistic hypothesis according to which visuomotor processing differs from perceptual processing of one and the same stimulus. Furthermore, in our view, the preliminary results of an investigation by Haffenden and Goodale (1998) of the potential motoric effects of the presence of an annulus upon grasping, reinforce the dualistic picture of visual information-processing.

The crucial contrast in this investigation is the contrast between two displays: in one display, disks were presented on their own or against a blank background (without any annulus). In the other display, disks were presented with an annulus of circles of equal size mid-way between the larger circles and the smaller circles involved in the contrasting pair of illusory annuli. Haffenden and Goodale (1998) found that when a pair of physically different disks were presented against either a blank background or a pair of annuli made of equal-sized circles, both grip scaling and manual estimates reflected the physical difference in size between the disks. When physically equal disks were displayed against either kind of background, Haffenden and Goodale (1998) found no significant difference between grasping and manual estimate. However, they found the interesting following dissociation between grasping and manual estimate. When physically equal disks were presented with a middle-sized annulus, they found that the overall MGA was smaller than when physically equal disks were presented against a blank background. In other words, the presence of an annulus of middle-sized circles prompted a smaller MGA than a blank background. Conversely, overall manual estimate was larger when physically equal disks were presented against a background with a middle-sized annulus than when they were presented against a blank background. The illusory effect of the middle-size annulus presumably arises from the fact that the circles composing the annulus are slightly larger than the equal disks. Thus, whereas the presence of a middle-sized annulus contributes to increasing manual estimation, it contributes to decreasing grip scaling. This dissociation shows that an annulus may have conflicting effects on perceptual estimate and grip aperture.

Subsequently, Haffenden and Goodale (2000) have gone one step further in the investigation of conflicting effects of 'flanking elements' upon visuomotor processing and perceptual processing. Subjects were presented with one of two physically unequal disks (of 30 mm and 32 mm) surrounded by two flanking equal and parallel rectangles of 63×22 mm. The orientation of rectangular flankers was either vertical or horizontal with respect to the central disk. The distance between the disks and the proximal edge of flanking rectangles was 3, 11, 21 or 31 mm. The display in which the flanking rectangles were 3 mm away from the disks matched the distance between the disks and the annulus of smaller circles (in the Titchener illusion). The display in which the flanking rectangles were 11 mm away from the disks matched the distance between the disk and the annulus of larger circles (in the Titchener illusion). Subjects were instructed either to grasp the disk or to manually estimate its size by matching it by the distance between thumb and index finger.

What Haffenden and Goodale (2000) found was that manual estimation of disk size decreased as the distance between target and flankers increased, regardless of flankers' orientation. Hence, estimated disk size was significantly smaller when the gap between it and flankers was 11 mm than when it was 3 mm. But importantly, the orientation of flankers was irrelevant. According to Haffenden and Goodale's (2000) speculation, this perceptual effect arises from an 'assimilation' or 'attraction' illusion, whereby the edges of the central element of a display are perceptually drawn towards the edges of the neighboring elements. On average, MGA did not reflect the large effect of flankers on the perceptual task. Grip scaling, however, followed an interestingly different pattern: the orientation of flankers played a crucial role at 11 mm. When the orientation of flankers was horizontal, grip aperture was smaller when the gap between target and flankers was 11 mm than when it was 3 mm. Hence, for horizontal orientation of flankers, grip scaling decreased as space between target and flankers increased. Furthermore, for the 11-mm gap between target and flankers, grip scaling was significantly smaller when flankers' orientation was horizontal than it was when flankers' orientation was vertical. If the influence of the presence of flankers resulted from a perceptual change—i.e. a change in the perceived size of the disk—then grip scaling should presumably decrease for both flanker orientations at 11 mm distance.

Thus, this experiment shows that only distance of neighboring elements influences the estimated size of a disk. By contrast, not only does distance of neighboring elements on average affect less grip scaling than size estimation, but grip scaling is selectively affected by two specific parameters. Flankers' orientation plays a role at a distance of 11 mm, not 3 mm. It is thus tempting to hypothesize with Haffenden and Goodale (2000) that flankers act on the visuomotor system as 'obstacles' that must be avoided. First of all, when vertically oriented, flankers do not interfere with the positioning of subjects' fingers on opposing points of the target. By contrast, when horizontally oriented, they do interfere. Second, when the gap between flankers and target is only 3 mm, the gap is too small to allow subjects to plan the positioning of their fingers in between the target and the flankers. An 11-mm gap, however, does allow such a motor plan and therefore encourages subjects to scale down their grip to fit in the gap. Although in the study of the Titchener circles' illusion, surrounding annuli of circles of different sizes, unlike flankers, are 2D pictures—not physical obstacles—they might be treated by the visuomotor system as potential (or virtual) obstacles. We know from Haffenden and Goodale (1998) that the mere presence of an annulus of circles mid-way in size between the larger circles and the smaller circles has opposite effects on perception and grasping: disks surrounded by an annulus were judged larger than disks without. But grip scaling was smaller for the former than the latter. This finding does suggest that the a 2D annulus of circles may act as a potential obstacle on the visuo-motor processing of information.

In both Aglioti *et al.*'s (1995) and Haffenden and Goodale's (1998) studies of the Titchener circles' illusions, the distance between a disk and an annulus of either smaller or larger circles was, respectively, 3 mm and 11 mm. Thus, it is tempting to conjecture that the effects of the presence of an annulus on grasping may sometimes coincide and sometimes diverge from its effects on perception. Orientation of flankers affects grip scaling but not size estimation of a disk. On the assumption that a 2D annulus of circles can indeed be treated by the visuomotor system as an obstacle in a grasping task accord-ing to its distance from the target, then the presence of an annulus of larger circles surrounding a disk might contribute to decreasing both manual estimation of the size of the disk and grip scaling for independent though converging reasons. It contributes to decreasing manual estimation because the perceptual processing is influenced by the illusion. It may contribute to decreasing grip scaling because the visuomotor processing treats the annulus as an obstacle.

Finally, one more recent experiment corroborates the view that, unlike perceptual judgment, grasping is selectively affected by the distance between target and potential obstacles. Haffenden *et al.* (2001) presented subjects with three distinct Titchener disk displays one at a time, two of which are the traditional Titchener central disks sur-rounded by an annulus of circles either smaller than it or larger than it. In the former case, the gap between the edge of the disk and the annulus was 3 mm. In the latter case, the gap was 11 mm. In the third display, the distance between the edge of the disk and the annulus was manipulated: the annulus was made of small circles (the size of the cir-cles in the annulus of the first display) but the gap between it and the disk was 11 mm, like in the second display with the annulus of larger circles. What Haffenden *et al.* (2001) found was the following dissociation: estimate was far more sensitive to the size of the circles in the illusory annulus than to the distance between target and annulus. For both distances between annulus and target, the disk surrounded by smaller circles was judged significantly larger than the disk surrounded by larger circles. Grasping, however, was far more sensitive to the distance between target and annulus than it was to the size of the circles in the illusory annulus. Grip scaling was significantly smaller when the distance between target and annulus was 11 mm than it was when the distance was 3 mm, irrespective of the size of the circles in the surrounding annulus (Fig. 4.6).

Although the above analysis is somewhat speculative, if it is on the right track, then what follows is not that the visuomotor control of grasping differs from perceptual judg-ment in that, unlike the latter, the former is immune to illusions or that it cannot be fooled by a visual display. What follows rather is that they are selectively fooled by different features of the visual display. The effect of size-contrast illusions on perceptual judgment arises mostly from a size-constancy mechanism: the disk surrounded by smaller circles is perceived as more distant and hence larger than the disk surrounded by larger circles because smaller circles are perceived as more distant than larger circles. Whereas the perceptual processing yields comparative or relative computations of sizes based on the estimation of relative distances, grip scaling is calibrated on the basis of the computation of the absolute non-relative size of the target. The perceptual processing thus yields a perceptual representation of relative distances and sizes of constituents of the visual

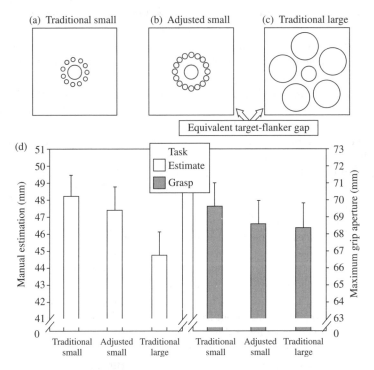

Fig. 4.6 Influence of the distance between the annulus and the central disk on the grasping and matching tasks. (a) Traditional display of disk surrounded by small annulus at a small distance. (b) Display of adjusted disk surrounded by small annulus at a large distance, i.e., same distance as traditional large display. (c) Traditional large display of disk surrounded by large annulus at a large distance. (d) The perception (as measured by manual estimation, *white bars*) of adjusted disk is very similar to the perception of traditional small disk. By contrast, maximum grip aperture for adjusted disk is very similar to maximum grip aperture for traditional large disk (*black bars*). (From Haffenden *et al.* 2001 permission sought.)

array within an allocentric frame of reference. The visuomotor processing yields a motor representation of the absolute distance and size of the target in an egocentric frame of reference. The visuomotor control of grasping, however, is sensitive to the distance between the edge of the target and its immediate environment. So much so that it can be led to process two-dimensional cues as if they were 3D obstacles.

8 The interplay between perceptual judgment and visuomotor processing

We started this chapter by emphasizing the contrast between two broad kinds of visual processing of one and the same stimulus by normal humans: the contrast between perceptual judgment and visually guided actions directed towards objects. Although it is plausible to assume at the outset—as Milner and Goodale (1995), Goodale (1995) and Haffenden and Goodale (1998) do—that, unlike perceptual judgment, visually guided actions cannot afford the luxury of being fooled by a visual display, we have reviewed psychophysical experiments that reveal that visuomotor representations of a target can indeed be fooled after all. In particular, evidence provided by Haffenden and Goodale (1998) and by Haffenden *et al.* (2001) suggests that visuomotor representations can misrepresent aspects of the visual display. Thus, whatever the fate of the dualistic model of normal human visual processing, the relevant contrast is not between fallible visual percepts and infallible visuomotor representations. Both kinds of representations can be illusory, but when they are, they are selectively fooled by different aspects of the display. We do think that the evidence, as it stands, is compatible with the dualistic model of normal human visual processing. But in these concluding remarks, we would like first to examine a potential objection to Haffenden *et al.*'s (2001) argument in favor of the dissociation between perceptual and visuomotor processing. Second, we would like to examine some evidence that could be appealed to against the dualistic model.

Haffenden *et al.* (2001) have compared three conditions involving a combination of two relevant parameters: a disk can be surrounded by an annulus of either smaller or larger circles than it. The annulus can be located nearer to or further away from the disk. They find the following dissociation: the presentation of a disk surrounded by smaller circles located further from the disk (condition 3) prompts a perceptual response similar to the perceptual response prompted by the presentation of a disk surrounded by smaller circles located near the disk (condition 1). But the presentation of a disk surrounded by smaller circles located further from the disk prompts a motor response similar to the presentation of a disk surrounded by larger circles located further from the disk (condition 2). Haffenden *et al.* (2001) conclude that the comparison between the diameter of the disk and the diameter of the circles in the annulus matters to perceptual processing and the distance between the disk and the annulus matters to the visuomotor processing. So far so good.

However, the following question arises. Haffenden *et al.* (2001) consider two parameters: the size of the diameter of the circles in the annulus and the distance between the disk and the annulus. But they consider only three conditions, not four, as they should, since the full combination of the two parameters can only be fully tested in four distinct conditions. In other words, they have omitted one relevant condition, i.e. the presentation of a disk surrounded by larger circles located near the disk (condition 4). The question is: what should the dualistic model of normal human visual processing predict in the fourth condition? In particular, is the dualistic model committed to the prediction that the motor response in condition 4 should stand to the motor response in condition 2, as the motor response in condition 1 stands to the motor response in condition 3? Should the change in distance between the disk and the annulus prompt one and the same motor contrast whether the circles in the annulus are smaller or larger? If the dualistic model was so committed and if the empirical evidence showed that the motor contrast between conditions 4 and 2 did not mirror the motor contrast between conditions 1 and 3, then presumably the dualistic model would be refuted.

In the absence of known empirical evidence about the motor response in condition 4, we want to argue that the dualistic model is not committed to the above prediction. First of all, it may seem paradoxical that, given smaller circles in the annulus, MGA decreases as space increases between the disk and the annulus. According to the dualistic interpretation sketched by Haffenden *et al.* (2001), as the gap increases between the target and the illusory obstacle constituted by the annulus, the visuomotor processing plans the positioning of the thumb and index finger around the target. Conversely, when the gap is too small for inserting the fingers between the target and the illusory obstacle, the visuomotor processing plans a different action: it prepares the grasping of the whole display (including the central disk and the annulus). As a result of the switch from grasping the disk to grasping the full display, MGA increases. Thus, the dualistic model offers an explanation of the surprising finding that MGA decreases as the distance between the disk and the annulus increases.

No hypothesis, however, can be tested unless it is combined with auxiliary assumptions. Any hypothesis about the visual processing of a Titchener circles' display must accommodate the following fundamental asymmetry. In conditions 1 and 3, the diameter of the central disk is 30 mm, the diameter of smaller circles is 10 mm, the diameter of larger circles is 55 mm. In condition 1, the small gap between the disk and the annulus is 3 mm. In condition 3, the large gap between the disk and the annulus is 10 mm. So, in condition 1, in which the disk is surrounded by smaller circles located near the disk, according to the dualistic model, the visuomotor processing is expected to plan the grasp of a display whose overall diameter is 56 mm (i.e. the sum of the diameter of the central disk, the small gap between the disk and the annulus and the sum of the diameters of two surrounding circles). But now consider the contrast between condition 2 (disk surrounded by larger circles located far) and condition 4 (disk surrounded by larger circles located near). In condition 2, the diameter of the full display is 160 mm. In condition 4, the diameter of the full display is 146 mm. The size of the display in condition 4 is almost three times the size of the display in condition 1: one cannot prepare the grasping between thumb and index finger of a display of 146 mm the way one prepares the grasping between thumb and index finger of a display of 56 mm. The point of the dualistic model is that there may be circumstances in which the motor response will parallel the perceptual response, although they are produced by distinct mechanisms. But whatever the empirical findings, the dualistic model is certainly not committed to the claim that the motor response in condition 4 should stand to the motor response in condition 2 as the motor response in condition 1 stands to the motor response in condition 3.

We now turn our attention to some findings based on the study of size-contrast illusions that seem to be counterexamples to the dualistic model. We earlier discussed evidence from an experiment by Van Donkelaar (1999) based on a pointing task. Although pointing to a target shares a good deal of motor organization with the reaching phase of a reach-to-grasp task, the evidence suggests that the visuomotor representations guiding one's movement in a pointing task might not be identical with those involved in a reach-to-grasp task. Whereas the evidence suggests that grip aperture is more sensitive to the gap between the disk and the illusory annulus than to the comparison between the diameter of the disk and the diameter of the surrounding circles, the data gathered by Van Donkelaar (1999) does suggest that an illusory estimate of the size of a Titchener disk can affect the duration of a pointing movement. The temporal profile of a pointing gesture would seem to be affected by the very feature that plays a role in perceptual illusions: the duration of pointing is sensitive to the computation of the relative sizes of the ingredients of the visual display. Hence, a temporal property of the motor representation of the target is affected by factors relevant to computations otherwise involved in delivering a perceptual representation of the stimulus.

Our previous discussion of grasping Titchener disks reveals that computations underlying calibration of grip scale might be sensitive to factors other than those involved in computations leading to perceptual judgements. Recent studies of yet another size-contrast illusion—the Ponzo illusion—still reveal a further contrast. The standard version of the Ponzo illusion consists of the display of two horizontal segments of equal length surrounded by two converging lines. In this context, the two equal horizontal segments are perceived as unequal: the upper segment is perceived as longer than the lower one. According to a standard interpretation of the illusion, the converging lines are assumed by the visual system to be two parallel lines receding in the distance (much like the rails of railroad tracks). The horizontal segments are assumed to lie in the plane of the two parallel and receding rails (holding them together). The upper horizontal segment is thus expected to connect the rails at a further distance away from the observer than the lower horizontal segment (Fig. 4.7). Hence, once again the visual illusion arises from the attempt on the part of the perceptual system to maintain size constancy across the entire visual array.

In the standard version of the Ponzo illusion, two objects of equal size are compared in the context of two surrounding converging lines. In another version of the same illusion, a single object can be displayed against a background of several converging lines at different locations on the array. The object seems larger when displayed near the converging point than when displayed further away from it. Using this version of the Ponzo illusion, Brenner and Smeets (1996) designed two closely related visuomotor tasks that revealed a very interesting dissociation. Subjects were facing a black disk that could be located either near or far away from the converging point of an array of Ponzo converging lines. The visual display was in a horizontal plane. Subjects were instructed to pick up the black disk and move it to their left. The diameter of the movable disk varied from 6.3 cm to 7.7 cm; its weight varied from 0.79 kg to 1.17 kg; its thickness was constant. Brenner and Smeets (1996) measured subjects' grip scale and they measured

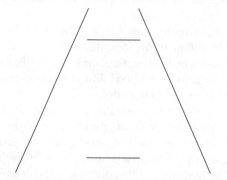

Fig. 4.7 The Ponzo illusion. Although they are equal, the upper segment looks larger than the lower segment.

the time interval between the instant the disk was grasped and the instant it started to move. This time interval provides a measure of the force the subject is prepared to use to lift the disk: the heavier a disk is estimated, the faster it is lifted (or the earlier it starts moving). Conversely, the lighter a disk is estimated, the slower it starts moving (the later it is lifted). What Brenner and Smeets (1996) found was that while grip scale was not affected by the illusory estimate of the size of the disk, the force used for lifting it was indeed affected by the illusory estimate of the size of the disk.

This result was confirmed by several related experiments. On the one hand, Ellis *et al.* (1999) found that, if a metal bar is placed at different locations against an array of Ponzo converging lines, then the illusory estimate of the bar's size does influence the computation of the respective positions of the fingers on either side of the bar. Because of the Ponzo array, the bar was judged to be larger and hence heavier on one side than on the other, and subjects positioned their fingers so as to compensate for the estimated asymmetry. On the other hand, the dissociation found by Brenner and Smeets (1996) was confirmed by experiments performed by Jackson and Shaw (2000) and by Westwood *et al.* (2000) using again the Ponzo illusion. Subjects grasped the bar with an exaggerated force, following the illusion of a relative increase in size, although they calibrated maximum grip size to the absolute size of the bar.

The apparently contradictory effects produced by the Ponzo illusion, e.g. reflect differences between the types of actions upon the bar. Obviously, calibrating the force of the grip to lift the bar depends in part on a perceptual estimate of the weight of the bar. This process is influenced by the size-contrast illusion. On the contrary, calibrating the maximum grip aperture for grasping the bar involves the computation of the absolute size of the bar. It does not involve computing its apparent size. Thus, information about the size of an object relevant to a motor task can be processed differently according to whether this information is used for making a precise grasp, for hitting the object as quickly as possible or for calibrating grip strength to its weight, which in turn depends on a perceptual estimate. These are differences between motor tasks.

9   Concluding remarks

Franz *et al.* (2001: 1126) draw a tripartite distinction between what they call the 'strong separate representation model', the 'weak' version of the separate representation model and the 'common representation model'. According to the first model, 'two different representations of object size' are at work 'for the purposes of perception and action'. According to the weaker version of the separate representation model, 'some cross talk between the two representations' can take place. According to the common representation model, which they favor, a single representation of object size 'is influenced by the visual illusion and is used to generate the percept of size as well as to guide grasping'. In our view, the dividing line is between either version of the separate representation model and the common representation model. According to either version of the dualistic model, there are relevant differences between some visuomotor processing and perceptual processing. But we take it that the dualist model is not committed to the view that one and the same visuomotor representation should be involved in all motor tasks. Nor do we think that no motor task should involve a combination of visuomotor processing together with perceptual processing. The very idea that both types of processing may collaborate in some tasks presupposes the distinction between two basic kinds of processing.

The present book is an argument in favor of the dualistic model of human visual processing. Thus, we adopt what Franz *et al.* (2001) call the 'weak version of the separate representation model'. We would like to make three qualifying remarks to end the present chapter. First of all, the kind of visuomotor processing that can be dissociated from perceptual processing in normal human subjects and that is exemplified by apperceptive agnosic patients (studied in Chapter 3 and to which we go back in Chapter 6) is low-level elementary visuomotor processing. It should be distinguished from the kind of higher level 'pragmatic' processing involved in, e.g. the skilled use and manipulation of tools. In the everyday life of normal human subjects, outside the psychophysical lab, it is hardly at work all by itself. Our claim here is that such low-level visuomotor processing is being instantiated in calibrating the grip between thumb and index fingers in tasks of grasping. Second, in so far as the dual visual processing reflects the anatomical duality between the dorsal and the ventral stream of the human visual system, there is likely to be collaboration between the two modes of processing as there is likely to be cross-talk between the streams. By this admission, our view is an instance of what Franz *et al.* (2001) call the weak version of the dual model. Finally and importantly, we think that the anti-dualist common representation model (defended by Franz *et al.* 2000, 2001), is committed to an implausible anatomical assumption. According to the common representation model, a single representation of size of an object can give both rise to an illusory size-contrast illusory percept and guide grasping. This means that the common representation must have been formed prior to the bifurcation between the two pathways. According to the common representation model, the single representation involved in both perceptual judgment and grasping is sensitive to the size-contrast illusion. But, as we pointed out, it is implausible on neurophysiological grounds to suppose that there are mechanisms responsible for size-contrast illusions in the primary visual cortex prior to the separation between the dorsal and the ventral pathway. Thus, we think that the dual model of human visual processing in normal human subjects stands.

Part III

Perceiving objects and grasping them

5   Visual perception

1   Introduction

As empirical evidence reviewed in previous chapters suggests, vision is not a unitary psychological ability. Not all human vision has been designed to allow visual perception. Many experiments on normal human subjects and on brain-lesioned human subjects along the years have shown that the human visual system can build different representations according to the task. Much of the human visual system, like non-human vision, is geared towards the control of action—particularly, the control of visually guided hand movements directed towards objects. One crucial function of human vision, however, is visual perception, to which the present chapter will be devoted. Like many psychological words, 'perception' can be used to refer both to a process and to its product: the resulting experience. In this chapter, we shall examine both what can be perceived and how what can be perceived is perceived. As we have said above (in both the Introduction and Chapter 1), we do not subscribe to Clark's (2001) EBC assumption, i.e. the view that the non-conceptual content of visual perception is geared towards the monitoring of fine-tuned bodily movements. But we do subscribe to what he calls the 'assumption of experience-based selection', i.e. the view that visual percepts do serve to select particular goals of hand actions. For example, the rich texture of a visual percept is not involved in guiding the automatic reach of one's hand movements and the calibration of one's finger-grip, but is involved in the selection of, e.g. a red apple from a basket of fruits of various shapes, textures and colors.

There are at least two sides to perception—visual or otherwise: there is an objective side and a subjective side. On the objective side, visual perception is a fundamental source of knowledge about the world. Visual perception is a paradigmatic perceptual process by means of which human beings gather knowledge about objects, events and facts in their environment. Not only does it interact with other perceptual processes, but it also interacts with memory, reasoning and communication. Hence, visual perception has always been of paramount importance for epistemology (i.e. the area of philosophy devoted to the study of knowledge and related topics), as it now is for cognitive science. On the subjective side, vision in the perceptual mode yields a peculiar kind of awareness: namely, sight. Sight has a special kind of phenomenal character. The puzzles of visual phenomenology and visual awareness have been central to both philosophy of mind and cognitive neuroscience. The phenomenology of human visual experience is unlike the phenomenology of human experiences in modalities other than vision, e.g. touch, olfaction or audition.

The main issue to be addressed in this chapter is the puzzle of how something eminently subjective—a visual experience or, as philosophers like to call it, a visual *quale*—could be a reliable source of information about the world. How do human beings come to know as much as they do about their environment by virtue of enjoying visual experiences? Indeed, as we shall argue, much of the scope and limits of visual knowledge arises from some of the very facts that determine the phenomenology of visual perception. First, we shall ask the question: how can visual perception provide knowledge at all? Since knowledge of the world acquired by perception depends on the identification and the recognition of objects, we shall first examine problems raised by visual recognition. Second, we shall examine the question of how human vision interacts with the rest of human cognition: how is knowledge gained by visual perception integrated with knowledge gained by other means? Third, we shall examine the scope and limits of purely visual knowledge. Fourth, we shall ask the question: how intelligent are perceptual processes? Fifth, we shall ask whether all of one's visual experiences ought to be treated as beliefs or judgments. Finally, we shall re-examine the puzzles of the phenomenology of human visual experience in the light of the problem of binding.

2 Visual perception, identification and recognition

2.1 The reliability of visual perception

As a matter of psychological fact, human beings make reliable judgments about visually presented facts and they take their visually based judgments about the world to be reliable. People make such visual judgments on the basis of how things look to them, i.e. on the basis of the phenomenal appearances of visually presented objects. In making reliable perceptual judgments, humans achieve a certain amount of visual knowledge about the world. No doubt, not all of a human being's knowledge about the world derives from his or her visual perceptual judgments, but a significant portion does. Normal visual perception is a reliable process because it allows a human being to get properly connected to facts in his environment. Normal visual perceptual judgment is not 100% reliable since, as the previous chapter has established at length, it can be fooled by illusory displays. But it can be reliable. When it is, as it often is, we do want to understand how it can be. By virtue of opening her eyes, letting the information flow from objects and events in the world and hit her retina and exploring her environment by using her gaze, eye-movements and head-movements, an intact human being allows herself to achieve visual knowledge of some parts of the world. Two broad sets of conditions must be met for visual perception to yield knowledge of the world. On the one hand, visual processing must be reliable. On the other hand, a person's visual system must be properly hooked to her other cognitive functions, i.e. her conceptual system, her memory system. In the words of O'Regan and Noë (2001a: 943), a sensory modality is a peculiar 'mode of exploration' of the world 'mediated by distinctive sensorimotor contingencies'. In other words, a person's visual system must also be properly hooked up to her motor system.

As emphasized in Chapter 1, the human visual perceptual subsystem, unlike the human visuomotor subsystem, paves the way for the human cognitive system of categorization, reasoning and memory. As Goodale and Humphrey (1998: 185) put it, 'these systems, which generate our perception of the world, are [...] linked [...] to cognitive systems involving memory, semantics, spatial reasoning, planning and communication'.

For human visual perception to be reliable, several conditions must be met—some of which are internal, some external to a person's cognitive equipment: the person's visual system must be in good working conditions, the lighting conditions must be appropriate, the person must be at a suitable distance from the perceptual object and so on. When these auxiliary (or enabling) conditions are met, then visual perception is reliable in the following sense. Suppose a person sees a red triangle in front of her under the right enabling conditions. Suppose that as a result she recognizes what she is presented with as a red triangle and comes therefore to believe that there is a red triangle in front of her. Of course, she could not come to believe this unless she had such concepts as the concepts of red and triangle. But if she does, then her belief that the object in front of her is a red triangle counts as a piece of visual knowledge, if the conditions under which she saw the red triangle are such that the object would not look to her the way it does—i.e. the way red triangles distinctively look, namely triangular and red—unless it were a red triangle. So in the above circumstances, she saw that the object in front of her was a red triangle and the distinctive way the object looked to her is her grounds for justifiably believing and hence knowing that it is a red triangle. Now, to start understanding how such an accomplishment is possible—how knowledge (reliable belief) can depend upon visual phenomenology—it is worth paying attention to some elementary facts about visual perception.

2.2 Visual attributes and visual modes of perception

In Nagel's (1974) famous phrase, 'there is something [unique] it is like' to enjoy human visual experiences. As we emphasized in the first chapter, one basic reason why the human visual system yields subjective experiences of the world different from the subjective experiences of the world in other sensory modalities, is that humans do not experience the same basic (or elementary) properties of objects in each of the different sense-modalities. Vision makes us directly aware of the size of objects, their shape, orientation, contours, internal structure, texture, color, spatial position, distance and motion. Audition makes us directly aware of sounds, tones, pitch and intensity. Olfaction makes us directly aware of smells and odors. Touch makes us directly aware of pressure and temperature. Colors, e.g. can be seen, not heard, smelled or touched. Sounds can be heard, not seen, smelled or touched. Odors can be smelled, not seen, heard or touched. Temperature can be experienced through touch. It cannot be seen, heard or smelled. So a normally sighted person cannot see directly an object's temperature, the pitch of a sound or the perfume of a rose by seeing the objects that exemplify these properties. These are not properties that the human visual system has been designed to respond to. The function of each of the different human sensory modalities is to respond to a distinct set of basic properties: critical to the phenomenology of visual perception is the processing of specifically visual attributes. When one and the same property of an object, e.g. shape, can be perceived in more than one modality, e.g. vision and touch, then it is perceived under two distinct modes of presentation. When an object is seen in normal illumination conditions, one cannot visually perceive the shape of an object unless one perceives its color. One can, however, touch the shape of an object without perceiving its color. Thus, in visual perception, the mode of perception of the shape of an object is uniquely combined with the representation of color.

As previous chapters have documented, different basic 'visual' attributes of an object are processed by different areas of the human visual system and selective lesions in the human visual system can deprive a person from the ability to visually experience some of the properties of objects which the human visual system has been designed to respond to. Apperceptive agnosics discussed in Chapter 3, e.g. cannot recognize the shape of objects. Achromatopsic patients cannot perceive the color of objects. Akinetopsic patients cannot perceive the motion of objects. As we discussed in Chapter 1, some properties of objects can be experienced in different sense-modalities. One and the same object (or event) may exemplify many different properties (or attributes)—some visual, others non-visual. If so, then each experience will be different from the other. For example, one can both see and hear Ann-Sophie Mutter play the violin. Although one can both see and hear her play at the same time, seeing her play and hearing her play are, however, very different subjective experiences. The visual and the auditory modes of perception of one and the same event are thus different. The condition of an associative agnosic patient examined by Rubens and Benson (1971) and discussed in Chapter 3, supports the claim that perceiving one and the same object in different modalities gives rise to different subjective experiences. Rubens and Benson's (1971) associative agnosic could not identify and name objects visually presented, but he could very well identify and name objects presented in either the auditory or the tactile modality. Hence, experiences in either the olfactory and/or auditive modality could lead the associative agnosic to identify objects that he failed to identify in the visual modality.

No doubt, the shape of an object can be seen; and so can its motion. Can they also be touched? The question is reminiscent of Molyneux's. Suppose they can. If so, then the phenomenal character associated with touching the shape and motion of an object will nonetheless be quite different from the phenomenal character associated with seeing them. In seeing, e.g. a red square, a normally sighted person will see both the object's shape and its color. In seeing a blue ball moving to her left, she will see the motion, shape and color of the ball. If a blind person (or a blindfolded normally sighted person) touches a blue moving ball, she may feel its shape and motion, but not its color. In fact, the condition of an akinetopsic patient examined by Zihl *et al.* (1983) and discussed by Zeki (1993: 82, 280–1) illustrates the claim that if one and the same property of an object, e.g. motion, is processed in different modalities, then the resulting subjective experience is bound to be different in each modality. Zihl *et al.*'s (1983) patient had suffered a bilateral cerebral lesion involving area V5 of her visual cortex. As a result, she could not visually detect the flow and rise of a liquid from a teapot into a cup. Nor could she accurately judge the position of moving cars while she was crossing a street; and she had difficulties seeing the lip movements of speakers' mouths. However, 'this was not a defect in the appreciation of movement as such because the perception of movement elicited by auditory or tactile stimulation was unaffected' (Zeki 1993: 82). Again, this is evidence that we need to distinguish a property (such as the shape or the motion of an object) and what Peacocke (2001) calls a 'way of perceiving' or a mode of perceptual presentation of that property.

Since individual objects are so important for human categorization, reasoning and memory, one task of the human visual perceptual system is to achieve a segregation of the visual scene into visual objects.[1] On the one hand, it is part and parcel of the visual experience of objects in normally sighted persons that several elementary visual attributes of an object (such as its shape, color, orientation, internal structure, texture, spatial position, distance, motion) are 'bound' together in a single visual percept. On the other hand, an ordinary visual scene will contain several distinct objects or items. In order for various attributes of an object to be referred to a single object, the visual scene must first be parsed into distinct objects so that the proper attributes be linked to their appropriate bearers. In the section on apperceptive agnosia in Chapter 3, we described an 'integrative' agnosic patient, HJA: although he was able to process very local aspects of shapes, he failed to segment such features adequately and, as a result, was unable to integrate these features into a perceptual whole.

Consider the complexity of the perceptual task performed by the visual system. The fundamental role of the visual perception of objects is to enable the identification and recognition of objects. If, as Biederman (1995: 121) puts it, 'object recognition is the activation in memory of a representation of a stimulus class', then understanding the job of human visual perception requires an appreciation of the link between visual processing and memory and it requires an elucidation of what a 'stimulus class' could be. The starting point for the perception of a visual scene are photons reflected by objects in a visual array hitting a human retina. Unlike a mere optical scanner that is provided with invariant inputs, the human visual system is never provided with the same retinal images twice, even from a single visual array. The lighting and the luminance conditions are never exactly the same. An observer never occupies exactly the same spatial position relative to a visual arrray. A 3D display will never occupy exactly the same depth orientation twice. The surface of an item in a visual scene may occlude the surface of another. As Spelke *et al.* (1995a: 299–300) put it:

[...] objects are not fully visible from anyone point of observation: the back of every opaque object is hidden, and the front surface of many objects are partly occluded as well [...]. Moreover, the connections and separations among adjacent surfaces in a scene are not themselves visible [...]. Finally, objects are frequently obscured from view by movements—the perceiver's, the object's itself, or those of other objects. In these cases, perceivers have no direct information about what might have occurred while objects were occluded and must decide, from highly incomplete information, whether something seen now is the same object as something seen in the past.

The task of visual perceptual processing nonetheless is to help the perceiver achieve recognition of objects. And the visual system is highly successful in the task.

Very early on in the course of development, normal human beings manage to visually recognize a great variety of things: people, cows, horses, cats, tigers, daffodils, roses, tomatoes, strawberries, apples, sofas, chairs, telephones, TV sets, cameras, and so on and so forth. On the basis of ever-changing retinal inputs, human beings manage to visually recognize and classify an enormous variety of objects. To recognize an object is to assign it to a 'stimulus class', i.e. to subsume it under some concept or other.

---

[1]As showed by the work of, e.g. Spelke (1988), human infants parse the world into objects very early on.

For the purpose of recognizing the identity of an object, especially for the purpose of identifying the function of an artifact, visual information about it needs to be compared with data stored in long-term memory.[2]

This operation requires the matching between visual information and conceptual processing. But in order for visual information to reach the conceptual level relevant to thought and memory, the visual system must solve a number of problems, ambiguities and indeterminacies that arise from surface occlusions, the processing of shadow information, reflections, luminance edges, gradients due to lighting, various motions and movements, which jointly contribute to the segmentation of the visual array into separate objects and make the perceptual task complex. Consider, e.g. shadow information: it is useful for the detection of such visual attributes of objects as their size, orientation, texture, relative distance and motion. Shadow information, however, must be processed pre-attentively, since we are not visually aware of the shadow cast by an object in the process whereby we become visually aware of the object that casts it. Only through the effort of spatial exploration and attention do we become aware of shadows that are useful in the recognition of the objects that cast them. Once a scene has been segmented into different objects, each object is perceived as exhibiting several visual attributes all at once.

No doubt, the notion of an 'object of perception' is itself of considerable complexity. As Marr (1982: 270) insightfully wrote:

What [...] is an object, and what makes it so special that it should be recoverable as a region in an image? Is a nose an object? Is a head one? Is it still one if it is attached to a body? What about a man on horseback? These questions show that the difficulties in trying to formulate what should be recovered as a region from an image are so great as to amount to philosophical problems. There really is no answer to them—all these things can be an object if you want to think of them that way or they can be part of larger objects.

The import of Marr's remarks lies in the fact that, although visual parsing of an array imposes some limits on what counts as an object of perception, the notion of an object must satisfy both perceptual and conceptual constraints, since visual perception terminates in recognition and recognition involves the matching of visual information with concepts.

2.3 Recognitional concepts and prototypes

Now, objects that are visually processed can be classified and conceptualized at several levels of abstraction using many different sortals—some subordinate, others superordinate. Something can be classified as, e.g. Ralph, a mustang, a horse, a mammal, an animal, a living thing or a physical object. For classification or categorization to take place, visually presented information must interact with information stored in memory: visual information must be conceptually processed. Interestingly, cognitive psychologists have found that the best match between visual information and conceptual processing occurs at a privileged conceptual level called the *basic level* (see Rosch and Mervis 1975; Rosch *et al.* 1976; Smith and Medin 1981). For such things as horses, the basic level is

---

[2]In order to form what we called in Chapter 3, a 'semantic representation' of an object.

the concept *horse*, not *mustang*, not *animal*, not *mammal*. Roughly speaking, the basic level is the level that offers the best trading relation between the amount of inter-category distinctiveness and the amount of intra-category informativeness. When you ascend from the basic level (horse) towards more superordinate concepts (e.g. animal), you sacrifice much informativeness without gaining enough distinctiveness. When you descend from the basic level towards more subordinate concepts (e.g. mustang), you gain little informativeness at the cost of much distinctiveness. Thus, the basic conceptual level is easiest to recall in memory. It provides for fastest identification and categorization of visually presented objects. It is associated with prototypical information: sparrows and robins, for instance, are judged to be better prototypes (or representatives) of the class of birds than are either ducks or penguins. Apples and oranges are judged to be better prototypes of fruits than tomatoes and avocados. Conversely, there is evidence that pictures of non-typical birds, such as ducks and penguins, are more easily classified, respectively, as ducks and penguins, than as birds (see Biederman 1995: 123).

At the basic conceptual level then, pictorial information provided by visual processing of retinal inputs is converted into conceptual information. In the section on cognitive dynamics in Chapter 1, we discussed this process. As we emphasized there, unlike visual percepts, thoughts and conceptual representations are both systematic and productive. Hence, it must be a property of concepts that simpler conceptual units may, by means of various logical operators, be combined and recombined in ever larger more complex units. For example, one may entertain the concept of a unicorn, even though one cannot visually perceive any. One can visually perceive horses, horns and pictures of unicorns; but one cannot visually perceive a unicorn. Nonetheless, one can think of a unicorn. In so doing, one presumably uses a complex concept involving the simpler concepts *horse* and *horn*. In light of the role of basic concepts and the importance of prototypicality in visual recognition tasks, it may be worth reflecting on the fact that perhaps no single account of the nature of concepts is to be offered. On the one hand, visual concepts must interface with visual percepts in tasks of object identification and recognition. On the other hand, concepts must have combinatorial properties such that complex ones must be compositionally derivable from simpler ones.[3]

Thus, visual concepts must play two pivotal roles in human cognition: they must allow thoughts to be compositional (and/or productive) and they must allow visual recognition to take place. As emphasized by Fodor (1998a, 1998b), however, the two desiderata pull in two different directions. Consider, e.g. the concept of a pet fish. It is the result of combining the simpler concept of a fish and the simpler concept of a pet. Now, the prototypical instance of a pet fish is the goldfish. As Fodor (1998a: 43) writes:

[...] compositionality can tell you that the instances of PET FISH are all and only the pet fish; but it can't tell you that the *good* instances of a pet fish are the goldfish; which is, all the same, the information that pet fish *recognition* (as opposed to mere PET FISH *instantiation*) is likely to depend on. How could you expect semantics to know what kind of fish people keep for pets?.

---

[3]It is important to distinguish the property of a concept of being basic from that of being simple or primitive. A concept is said to be simple or primitive if its content cannot be exhaustively defined in terms of other concepts. Being basic, a concept stands in the relation of subordinate and superordinate, respectively, to concepts that are less abstract and more abstract than it. Being basic, not being simple, is what facilitates visual identification and recognition. Being primitive is a compositional, not a recognitional property of a concept.

Concept application is a classificatory matter: something does or does not instantiate a concept. Typicality is comparative, not classificatory: some instances are better prototypes of a concept than others. That the prototype of a pet fish is a goldfish is not something that could be deduced compositionally from combining the prototype of a pet (e.g. a domestic cat) together with the prototype of a fish (e.g. a tuna). Fodor assumes that compositionality is, as he puts it, a 'non-negotiable' condition on concepts. Thus, his inclination is to conclude that concepts cannot be prototypes or that concepts cannot have prototypical structure. Prototypes might matter to recognition, but as Fodor (1998a: 61) says, 'there are no recognitional concepts, not even RED'. One might be an expert both at the visual recognition of typical pets (e.g. cats) and of typical fish (e.g. tunas) and still fail to be an expert at recognizing typical pet fishes, namely goldfishes.

Given the tension between compositionality and prototypicality and/or recognition, perhaps what one should conclude is not that 'there are no recognitional concepts', but that there is no algorithmic mechanism for generating a prototypical instance of a complex concept out of the prototypical instances of each of its constituent simpler concepts. Many simple or primitive concepts have prototypical instances (e.g. *fish* and *pet*)—not all do, e.g. the concept of an integer does not have a prototypical instance (see Armstrong *et al.* 1983). Any integer is as good an instance of the concept of an integer as any other. Concepts with prototypical instances (e.g. visual concepts) are 'recognitional' concepts. For recognitional concepts, the recognition routine, as well as the existence of prototypical instances, do matter. In our view, from the fact that a complex concept is composed of simpler concepts each with its own recognition procedure, it does not follow that the recognition procedure for the complex concept—if there is one—can be compositionally formed by combining the recognition procedures of its constituents.[4]

In order for one to possess the concept of a pet fish, one must possess the concept *fish* and the concept *pet* and be able to put them together coherently. Now, in order to possess the concept of a fish, it is possible that one must be able to tell a fish from other things. If there are prototypical fish, then being able to recognize a prototypical fish is part of the possession conditions for having the concept *fish*. Similarly for possessing the concept *pet*. But from the fact that there are prototypical instances of the concept fish and prototypical instances of the concept pet, it does not follow that one can construct a prototypical instance of the concept pet fish by combining a prototype of the concept fish and a prototype of the concept pet. Nor does it follow that the procedure for recognizing pet fish should be constructed out of the procedures for recognizing respectively a fish and a pet.

The importance of the issue lies in the fact that for many visual concepts (e.g. color concepts), it seems important to require that, unless a person could recognize (visually or otherwise) its instances, the person should not be ascribed mastery or possession of the concept. Unless a person could recognize instances of red things and tell red things from non-red things, she should not be ascribed mastery of the concept red. It matters that one knows that red is a color, and it also matters that one can recognize instances of red. Arguably, in order to possess the concept of an apple, one must *inter alia* be able

---

[4] It is a property of concepts that a complex concept with no prototypical structure can result from the combination of two simpler concepts, one of which has prototypical structure. For example, robin is a protypical bird. But there is no protypical three-legged robin.

to recognize apples from non-apples and presumably know what fruits are. However, in order to possess the concept of a red apple, it is enough that one possesses the concept of red, the concept of an apple, and that one be able to combine them coherently into a complex concept. So if what it takes to possess the concept of red is to recognize instances of red things, then one could not possess the concept of a red apple unless one could recognize red things from non-red things. But it does not follow that an expert recognition procedure for red apples could be built by combining an expert recognition procedure for red things and an expert recognition procedure for apples. Clearly, what counts as red in the context of a red apple differs from what counts as red in the context of blood or red wine. For example, an apple does not have to be red all over, the way a sample of red blood looks, in order to count as a red apple. A red car does not need to have red wheels, red windows and red seats in order to count as red. Nor does red wine look red the way blood does.

Thus, we think that one should not sacrifice the contribution of recognition procedures and/or prototypical structure to an account of visual concepts. Nor do we think that proper acknowledgment of the contribution of recognition procedures and of prototypicality in visual recognition tasks stands in contradiction with the importance of compositionality and productivity for conceptual structure. Concepts may have recognition procedures and they may combine, even though the recognition procedures of concepts do not combine. Simpler concepts cohere into complex ones by combinatorial procedures. The possession conditions of simpler concepts may involve the ability to recognize their typical instances. As Fodor (1998a, 1998b) insists, the possession conditions of a complex concept must involve the ability to combine its constituent concepts. In addition (and contrary to what Fodor acknowledges), the possession conditions of a complex concept may also involve the ability to recognize its typical instances. But if, and when, they do, the ability to recognize the typical instances of a complex concept is not derivable compositionally from the ability to recognize the typical instances of each of its constituents. The possession conditions of a complex concept with prototypical instances then, may involve both the ability to combine its constituents and the ability to recognize its typical instances.

Not all human knowledge is visual knowledge. In so far as visual perception generates visual knowledge, it is important to understand how visual knowledge—knowledge generated by visual perception—interacts with the rest of an individual's knowledge. We presently turn our attention to the interaction between visual and non-visual knowledge.

3 The interaction of visual and non-visual knowledge

3.1 Seeing and knowing

Although (as we have said) a normally sighted person cannot see the temperature, touch is not the only way available to her for determining the temperature of, e.g. a liquid. Exploiting her conceptual resources, a normally sighted person can use a reliable mercury thermometer to see what the temperature is. She can immerse the thermometer into the liquid and then she can tell the temperature of the liquid by looking at the height of the column of mercury. Notice that seeing what the temperature is, is not the same thing as seeing the temperature—something we claim one cannot do. What one is visu-ally attending to when one sees what the temperature is, is the thermometer's column of mercury, not the liquid (e.g. the tea) whose temperature one is trying to figure out. One is focusing onto the immersed thermometer by seeing through the liquid. One learns or comes to know that the temperature of the liquid is so and so by seeing the thermometer. In so doing, one does not sense the temperature directly. The tempera-ture of the liquid is detected by the thermometer, not by the exercise of one's visual sys-tem. What happens in this case is that one uses vision to extract the information carried by an artifact whose function is to detect a property that vision itself cannot detect, namely temperature. This simple example reveals the hierarchical structure of knowledge in general and visual knowledge in particular.

Traditional epistemology has focused on the problem of sorting out genuine instances of knowledge from cases of mere opinion or guessing. According to epistemologists, what one knows are facts (or propositions). Propositional knowledge must be distinguished from what Russell (1911) called 'knowledge by acquaintance' (or knowledge of individual objects), from the kind of tacit knowledge illustrated by a native speaker's implicit knowledge of the grammatical rules of her language and from procedural knowledge or what Ryle (1949) called 'knowing how' (illustrated by know-ledge of how to ride a bicycle or knowledge of how to swim).

In the propositional sense, one cannot know a fact unless one believes that the cor-responding proposition is true, one's belief is indeed true, and the belief was not formed by mere fantasy. On the one hand, one cannot know that a cup contains coffee, unless one believes it; one cannot have this belief unless one knows what a cup is and what coffee is. On the other hand, one cannot know what is not the case: one can falsely believe that the cup contains coffee. But one cannot know it, unless a designated cup does indeed contain some coffee. True belief, however, is not sufficient for knowledge. If a true belief happens to be a mere guess or whim, then it will not qualify as know-ledge. What else must be added to true belief to turn it into knowledge? Broadly speak-ing, epistemologists divide into two groups. According to externalists, a true belief counts as knowledge if it results from a reliable process, i.e. a process that generates counter-factually supporting connections between states of a believer and facts in her environment. According to internalists, for a true belief to count as knowledge, it must be justified and the believer must in addition justifiably believe that her first-order belief is justified. We already embraced an externalist reliabilist view of perceptual knowledge by claiming that, in appropriate conditions, the way a red triangle visually looks to a person having the relevant concepts, and being located at a suitable distance from it, provides grounds for the person to know that the object in front of her is a red triangle.

Although the issue is controversial and is by no means settled in the philosophical literature, externalist intuitions suit our purposes better than internalist intuitions. Arguably, one thing is to be justified or to have a reason for believing something. Another thing is to use a reason in order to offer a justification for one's beliefs. Arguably, if a perceptual process (e.g. visual) is reliable, then the visual appearances of things may constitute a reason for forming a belief. However, one cannot use a reason unless one can explicitly engage in a reasoning process of justification, i.e. unless one can distinguish one's premises from one's conclusion. Presumably, a creature with perceptual abilities and relevant conceptual resources can have reasons and form justified beliefs, even if she lacks the concept of reason or justification. However, she could not use her reasons and provide justifications unless she had language, the concept of justification (and reason) and meta-representational resources. Internalism derives most of its appeal from reflection on instances of mathematical and scientific knowledge that result from the conscious application of explicit principles of inquiry by teams of individuals in the context of special institutions. In such special settings, it can be safely assumed that the justification of a believer's higher-order beliefs do indeed contribute to the formation and reliability of his or her first-order beliefs. Externalism fits perceptual knowledge better than internalism and, unlike internalism, it does not rule out the possibility of crediting non-human animals and human infants with knowledge of the world—a possibility made more and more vivid by the development of cognitive science.

What one knows are facts. Visual knowledge is no exception. In the relevant sense of 'knowledge' (i.e. propositional knowledge), one can only know facts, not objects. One can be 'acquainted' with objects (e.g. by seeing them), but in the propositional sense relevant to epistemology, only facts can be known. Although one can only know facts (visually or otherwise), one can nonetheless see a great variety of things: one can see physical objects, events (e.g. John's opening the door, Mary's painting the wall or the landing of the plane), substances (gold or beer), gases (bubbles), shadows, clouds, flames, smoke, pictures, movies, and so on. Arguably, events, substances, shadows, clouds, flames, smoke and movies are not garden variety ordinary physical objects in some narrow sense, but they are not facts either. Since they can be seen and they are not facts, let us say that they are objects in a broad sense. In a strict sense, only facts can be known. In some broad sense, facts can also be seen. One can, e.g. see the fact that the triangle is red by seeing the red triangle. Finally, objects in a broad sense can be seen, e.g. a red triangle. Interestingly, as the previous chapter has shown, the objects of visual perception turn out to be slightly different from the targets of visually guided hand movements. For example, one can perceive but one cannot grasp or manipulate clouds, flames, holes and shadows.

3.2 Primary and secondary epistemic seeing

As we said, human visual perceptual abilities are at the service of thought and conceptualization. At the most elementary level, by seeing an object, one can see a fact involving that object, if one has the concept of the property instantiated by the object. By seeing one's neighbor's car in her driveway, one can see the fact that one's neighbor's car is parked in her driveway. One thereby comes to believe that one's neighbor's car is parked in her driveway. This belief, which is a conceptually loaded mental state, is arrived at by visual perception. If one's visual system is—as we have claimed it is—reliable, then by seeing one's neighbor's car in her driveway, one thereby comes to know that one's neighbor's car is parked in her driveway. Hence, one comes to know a fact involving an object that one actually sees. This is a fundamental epistemic situation, which Dretske (1969: 78 sq.) labels 'primary epistemic seeing': one's visual ability allows one to know a fact about an object that one perceives. However, if one's neighbor's car happens to be parked in her driveway if and only if she is at home (and one knows this), then one can come to know a different fact: one can come to know that one's neighbor is at home. Seeing that one's neighbor is at home by seeing that her car is parked in her driveway is something different from seeing one's neighbor at home (e.g. seeing her in her living-room). Certainly, one can come to know that one's neighbor is at home by seeing her car parked in her driveway, i.e. without seeing her. Perhaps, one could even say that one can *see* that one's neighbor is at home by seeing that her car is parked in her driveway. Perhaps, one can. And if so, then this is precisely what Dretske (1969, *ibid.*) calls 'secondary epistemic seeing'.[5]

This transition from seeing one fact to seeing another displays what we called the hierarchical structure of visual knowledge. In primary epistemic seeing, one sees a fact involving a perceived object. But in moving from primary epistemic seeing to secondary epistemic seeing, one moves from a fact involving a perceived car to a fact involving one's unperceived neighbor (who happens to own the perceived car). One thereby moves from a fact involving a perceived object to a fact involving an unperceived object. This epistemological hierarchical structure is expressed by the 'by' relation: one sees that y is G *by* seeing that x is F where $x \neq y$. Although it may be more or less natural to say that one 'sees' a fact involving an unperceived object by seeing a different fact involving a perceived object, the hierarchical structure that gives rise to this possibility is ubiquitous in human visual knowledge.

One can see that a horse has walked on the snow by seeing hoof prints in the snow. One sees the hoof prints, not the horse. But if hoof prints would not be visible in the snow at time t unless a horse had walked on that very snow at time $t - 1$, then one can see that a horse has walked on the snow just by seeing hoof prints in the snow. One can see that a tennis player has just hit an ace at Flushing Meadows by seeing her hit an ace on a television screen located in Paris. Now, does one really see the tennis player hit an ace at Flushing Meadows while sitting in Paris and watching television? Does one see a person on a television screen? Or does one see an electronic image of a person relayed by a television? Whether one sees a tennis player or her image on a television screen, it is quite natural to say that one 'sees' that a tennis player hit an ace by seeing her (or her image) do it on a television screen. Even though, strictly speaking, one perhaps did not see her do it—one merely saw pictures of her doing it—nonetheless seeing the pictures comes quite close to seeing the real thing. One can see that the gas-tank in one's car is half-full by seeing, not the tank itself, but the dial of the gas-gauge on the dashboard of the car. If one is sitting by the steering wheel inside one's car so that one can comfortably see the gas-gauge, then one cannot see the gas-tank. Nonetheless, if the gauge is reliable and properly connected to the gas-tank, then one can (perhaps in some loose sense) 'see' what the condition of the gas-tank is by seeing the dial of the gauge.[6]

One could wonder whether secondary epistemic seeing is really seeing at all. Suppose that one learns that Mount Saint Helens (an active volcano in Washington

---

[5]For further discussion of the distinction between primary and secondary epistemic seeing, see Jackson (1977, ch. 7).

[6]Some of these issues have been subtly discussed by Evans (1982: 144) who writes: 'We speak of seeing someone on the television, or hearing him on the radio. We speak of seeing someone in a mirror as well as seeing his reflection—but only of seeing someone's shadow, not of seeing him in a shadow. We speak without qualification of seeing stars, despite the long delay that the channel involves; but we could not speak without qualification of hearing Caruso when we listen to a record'. We are not quite sure whether we agree with Evans' last statement. But since it deals with auditory cognition, we will not discuss it here.

state, USA) erupted on July 1 1998, by reading about it a year later in a French newspaper in Paris. One could not see Mount Saint Helens—let alone its eruption—from Paris. What one sees when one reads a newspaper are letters printed in black ink on a white sheet of paper. But if the French newspaper would not report the eruption of Mount Saint Helens unless Mount Saint Helens had indeed erupted, then one can come to know that Mount Saint Helens has erupted by reading about it in a French newspaper. There is a significant difference between seeing that Mount Saint Helens has erupted by seeing it happen on a television screen and by reading about it in a newspaper. Even if seeing an electronic picture of Mount Saint Helens is not seeing Mount Saint Helens itself, still the visual experience of seeing an electronic picture of it and the visual experience of seeing it have a lot in common. The pictorial content of the experience of seeing an electronically produced color-picture of a volcano's eruption is very similar to the pictorial content of the experience of seeing it. Unlike a picture, however, a verbal description of an event has conceptual content, not pictorial content. The visual experience of reading an article reporting the eruption of Mount Saint Helens in a French newspaper is very different from the experience of seeing it erupt. This is the reason why it may be a little awkward to say that one 'saw' that Mount Saint Helens erupted if one read about it in a French newspaper in Paris as opposed to seeing it happen on a television screen.

Certainly, ordinary usage of the English verb 'to see' is not sacrosanct. We say that we 'see' a number of things in circumstances in which what we do owes little—if anything—to our visual abilities. 'I see what you mean', 'I see what the problem is' or 'I finally saw the solution' report achievements quite independent of visual perception. Such uses of the verb 'to see' are loose uses. Such loose uses do not report epistemic accomplishments that depend significantly on one's visual endowments. By contrast, cases of what Dretske (1969) calls secondary epistemic seeing are epistemic achievements that do depend on one's visual endowments. True, in cases of secondary epistemic seeing, one comes to know a fact without seeing some of its constituent elements. True, one could not come to learn that one's neighbor is at home by seeing her car parked in her driveway unless one knew that her car is indeed parked in her driveway when and only when she is at home. Nor could one see that the gas-tank in one's car is half-full by seeing the dial of the gas-gauge unless one knew that the latter is reliably correlated with the former. So secondary epistemic seeing could not possibly arise in a creature that lacked knowledge of reliable correlations or that lacked the cognitive resources required to come to know them altogether.

Nonetheless secondary epistemic seeing has indeed a crucial visual component in the sense that visual perception plays a critical role in the context of justifying such an epistemic claim. When one claims to be able to see that one's neighbor is at home by seeing her car parked in her driveway, or when one claims to be able to see that the gas-tank in one's car is almost empty by seeing the gas-gauge, one relies on one's visual powers in order to ground one's state of knowledge. The fact that one claims to know, is not seen. But the grounds upon which the knowledge is claimed to rest are visual grounds: the justification for knowing an unseen fact is seeing another fact correlated with the former. Of course, in explaining how one can come to know a fact about one thing by knowing a different fact about a different thing, one cannot hope to meet the philosophical challenge of scepticism. From the standpoint of scepticism, the explanation may seem to beg the question since it takes for granted one's knowledge of one fact in order to explain one's knowledge of another fact (see Stroud 1989). But the important thing for present purposes is that—scepticism notwithstanding—one offers a perfectly good explanation of how one comes to know a fact about an object one does not perceive by knowing a different fact about an object one does perceive. The point is that much—if not all—of the burden of the explanation lies in visual perception: seeing one's neighbor's car is the crucial step in justifying one's belief that one's neighbor is at home. Seeing the gas-gauge is the crucial step in justifying one's belief that one's tank is almost empty. The reliability of visual perception is thus critically involved in the justification of one's knowledge claim.

Thus, secondary epistemic seeing lies at the interface between an individual's directly formed visual knowledge and the rest of her knowledge. In moving from primary epistemic knowledge to secondary epistemic knowledge, an individual exploits her knowledge of regular connections. Although it is true that, unless one knows the relevant correlation, one could not come to know the fact that the gas-tank in one's car is empty by seeing the gas-gauge, nonetheless one does not consciously or explicitly reason from the perceptually accessible premiss that one's neighbor's car is parked in her driveway together with the premiss that one's neighbor's car is parked in her driveway when and only when one's neighbor is at home to the conclusion that one's neighbor is at home. Arguably, the process from primary to secondary epistemic seeing is inferential. But if it is, then the inference is unconscious and it takes place at the 'sub-personal' level.

What our discussion of secondary epistemic seeing so far reveals is that the very description and understanding of the hierarchical structure of visual knowledge and its integration with non-visual knowledge requires an epistemological and/or psychological distinction between seeing objects and seeing facts or between non-epistemic seeing and epistemic seeing—a point much emphasized in both Dretske's and Shoemaker's writings on the subject.[7]

The neurophysiology of human vision is such that some objects are simply not accessible to human vision. They may be too small or too remote in space and time for a normally sighted person to see them. For more mundane reasons, a human being may be temporarily so positioned as not to be able to see one object—be it her neighbor or the gas-tank in her car. Given the correlations between facts, by seeing a perceptible object, one can get crucial information about a different unseen object. Given the epistemic importance of visual perception in the hierarchical structure of human knowledge, it is important to understand how by seeing one object, one can provide decisive reasons for knowing facts about objects one does not see.

4 The scope and limits of visual knowledge

4.1 The justificatory role of vision in secondary epistemic seeing

We now turn our attention again from what Dretske calls secondary epistemic seeing, i.e. visually based knowledge of facts about objects one does not perceive, back to what he calls primary epistemic seeing, i.e. visual knowledge of facts about objects one does

---

[7]See Dretske (1969, 1978; 1990b, 1995a) and Shoemaker (1994).

perceive. When one purports to ground one's claim to know that one's neighbor is at home by mentioning the fact that one can see that her car is parked in her driveway, clearly one is claiming to be able to see a car, not one's neighbor herself. Now, let us concentrate on the scope of knowledge claims in primary epistemic seeing, i.e. knowledge about facts involving a perceived object. Let us suppose that someone claims to be able to see that the apple on the table is green. Let us suppose that the person's visual system is working properly, the table and what is lying on it are visible from where the person stands, and the lighting is suitable for the person to see them from where she stands. In other words, there is a distinctive way the green apple on the table looks to the person who sees it. Presumably, areas V1 to V3 and V4 of her visual system are busily processing visual information about the shapes, colors and texture of the stimulus displaying the apple on the table. Under those circumstances, when the person claims that she can see that the apple on the table is green, what are the scope and limits of her epistemic claims?

Presumably, in so doing, she is claiming that she knows that there is an apple on the table in front of her and that she knows that this apple is green. If she knows both of these things, then presumably she also knows that there is a table under the apple in front of her, she knows that there is a fruit on the table. Hence, she knows what the fruit on the table is (or what is on the table), she knows where the apple is, she knows the color of the apple, and so on. Arguably, the person would then be in a position to make all such claims in response to the following various queries: is there anything on the table? What is on the table? What kind of fruit is on the table? Where is the green apple? What color is the apple on the table? If the person can see that the apple on the table is green, then presumably she is in a position to know all these facts.

However, when she claims that she can see that the apple on the table is green, she is not thereby claiming that she can see that all of these facts obtain. What she is claiming is more restricted and specific than that: she is claiming that she knows that there is an apple on the table and that the apple in question is green. Furthermore, she is claiming that she learned the latter fact—the fact about the apple's color—through visual perception: if someone claims that she can see that the apple on the table is green, then she is claiming that she has achieved her knowledge of the apple's color by visual means, and not otherwise. But she is not claiming that her knowledge of the location of the apple or her knowledge of what is on the table have been acquired by the very perceptual act (or the very perceptual process) that gave rise to her knowledge of the apple's color. Of course, the alleged epistemic achievement does not rule out the possibility that the person came to know that what is on the table is an apple by seeing it earlier. But if she did, this is not part of the claim that she can see that the apple on the table is green. It is consistent with this claim that the person came to know that what is on the table is an apple by being told, by tasting it or by smelling it. All she is claiming and all we are entitled to conclude from her claim is that the way she learned about the apple's color is by visual perception.

4.2 Is visual knowledge closed under deduction?

Why do we make such a fuss about the scope and limits of knowledge claims in primary epistemic seeing? Why should one bother about sorting out what one claims to know by visual perception alone from what one does not so claim to know by visual perception? Our response to this question will mostly interest our philosophically minded readers.[8]

The investigation into the scope and limits of primary visual knowledge is relevant to the challenge of scepticism. As we pointed out above, our discussion of visual knowledge does not purport to meet the full challenge of scepticism. In discussing secondary epistemic seeing, we noticed that in explaining how one comes to know a fact about an unperceived object by seeing a different fact involving a perceived object, one takes for granted the possibility of knowing the latter fact by perceiving one of its constituent objects. Presumably, in so doing, one cannot hope to meet the full challenge of scepticism that would question the very possibility of coming to know anything by perception. We now turn to the sceptical challenge to which claims of primary epistemic seeing are exposed. By scrutinizing the scope and limits of claims of primary visual knowledge, we shall examine briefly the extent to which such claims are indeed vulnerable to the sceptical challenge. Claims of primary visual knowledge are vulnerable to sceptical queries that can be directed backwards and forwards. They are directed backwards when they apply to background knowledge, i.e. knowledge presupposed by a claim of primary visual knowledge. They are directed forward when they apply to consequences of a claim of primary visual knowledge. We turn to the former first.

Suppose a sceptic were to challenge a person's commonsensical claim that she can see (and hence know by perception) that the apple on the table in front of her is green by questioning her grounds for knowing that what is on the table is an apple. The sceptic might point out that, given the limits of human visual acuity and given the distance of the apple, the person could not distinguish by visual means alone a genuine green apple—a green fruit—from a fake green apple (e.g. a wax or a plastic copy of a green apple). Perhaps the person is hallucinating an apple when there is in fact nothing at all on the table. If one cannot visually discriminate a genuine apple from a fake apple, then, it seems, one is not entitled to claim that one can see that the apple on the table is green. Nor is one entitled to claim that one can see that the apple on the table is green if one cannot make sure by visual perception that one is not undergoing an hallucination. Thus, the sceptical challenge is the following: if visual perception itself cannot rule out a number of alternative possibilities to one's epistemic claim, then the epistemic claim cannot be sustained.

The proper response to the sceptical challenge here is precisely to appeal to the distinction between claims of visual knowledge and other epistemic claims. When the person claims that she can see that the apple on the table is green, she is claiming that she learned something new by visual perception: she is claiming that she just gained new knowledge by visual means. This new perceptually based knowledge is about the apple's color. The perceiver's new knowledge—her epistemic 'increment', as Dretske (1969: 97–8) calls it—must be pitched against what he calls her 'proto-knowledge', i.e. what the person knew about the perceived object prior to her perceptual experience. The reason it is important to distinguish between a person's prior knowledge and her knowledge gained by visual perception is that primary epistemic seeing (or primary visual knowledge) is a dynamic process. In order to determine the scope and limits of what

---

[8]Non-philosophically minded readers can skip the end of the present section and go straight to the next section.

has been achieved in a perceptual process, we ought to determine a person's initial epistemic stage (the person's prior knowledge about an object) and her final epistemic stage (what the person learned by perception about the object). Thus, the question raised by the sceptical challenge (directed backwards) is a question in cognitive dynamics: how much new knowledge could a person's visual resources yield, given her prior knowledge? How much has been learned by visual perception, i.e. in an act of visual perception? What new information has been gained by visual perception?[9]

So when the person claims that she can see that the apple on the table is green, she no doubt reports that she knows both that there is an apple on the table and that it is green. She commits herself to a number of epistemic claims: she knows what is on the table, she knows that there is a fruit on the table, she knows where the apple is, and so on. But she merely reports one increment of knowledge: she merely claims that she has just learned by visual perception that the apple is green. She is not thereby reporting how she acquired the rest of her knowledge about the object, e.g. that it is an apple and that it is on the table. She claims that she can see of the apple that it is green, not that what is green is an apple, nor that what is on the table is an apple. The claim of primary visual knowledge bears on the object's color, not on some of its other properties (e.g. its being an apple, a fruit or its location). All her epistemic claim entails is that, prior to her perceptual experience, she assumed—as part of her 'proto-knowledge' in Dretske's (1969: 96–8) sense—that there was a apple on the table and then she discovered by visual perception that the apple was green.[10]

Let us now turn our attention to the sceptical challenge directed forward—towards the consequences of one's claims of visual knowledge. The sceptic is right to point out that the person who claims to be able to see the color of an apple is not thereby in a position to see that the object whose color she is seeing is a genuine apple—a fruit—and not a wax apple. Nor is the person able to see that she is not hallucinating. However, since she is neither claiming that she is able to see of the green object that it is an apple nor that she is not hallucinating an apple, it follows that the sceptical challenge cannot hope to defeat the person's perceptual claim that she can see what she claims that she can see, namely that the apple is green. On the externalist picture of perceptual knowledge that we are accepting, a person knows a fact when and only when she is appropriately connected to the fact. Visual perception provides a paradigmatic case of such a connection. Hence, visual knowledge arises from regular correlations between states of the visual system and environmental facts. Given the intricate relationship between a person's visual knowledge and her higher cognitive functions, she will be able to draw many inferences from her visual knowledge. If a person knows that the apple in front of her is green, then she may infer that there is a colored fruit on the table in front of her. Given that fruits are physical objects, she may further infer that there are at least some

---

[9]We are assuming that the person's dynamical report that she acquired knowledge of the color of the apple by visual means (by contrast with her 'proto-knowledge' of its being an apple that she is seeing) is part of the proposition expressed by her knowledge claim, not a Gricean implicature. For a more general discussion of cognitive dynamics, see Section 4 of Chapter 1.

[10]We do not presuppose by any means that, unlike the knowledge of other visual attributes of objects, the knowledge of color is immune to sceptical doubts. We are merely imagining an example in which one is claiming to have acquired knowledge of the color of an apple by visual perception, not that what has the color is an apple. Of course, the apple might look green without being green by virtue of, e.g. the peculiarities of the lighting conditions.

physical objects. Again, the sceptic may direct his challenge forward: the person claims to know by visual means that the apple in front of her is green. But what she claims she knows entails that there are physical objects. Now, the sceptic argues, a person cannot know by visual perception alone that there are physical objects—she cannot see that there are. According to the sceptic then, failure to see that there are physical objects entails failure to see that the apple on the table is green.

A person claims that she can know proposition p by visual perception. Logically, proposition p entails proposition q. There could not be a green apple on the table unless there exists at least one physical object. Hence, the proposition that the apple on the table is green could not be true unless there were physical objects. According to the sceptic, a person could not know the former without knowing the latter. Now the sceptic offers grounds for questioning the claim that the person knows proposition q at all— let alone by visual perception. Since it is dubious that she does know the latter, then, according to scepticism, she fails to know the former. Along with Dretske (1969: 126–39) and Nozick (1981), we think that the sceptic relies on the questionable assumption that visual knowledge is deductively closed. From the fact that a person has perceptual grounds for knowing p, it does not follow that she has the same grounds for knowing q, even if q logically follows from p. If visual perception allows one to get connected in the right way to the fact corresponding to proposition p, it does not follow that visual perception *ipso facto* allows one to get connected in the same way to the different fact corresponding to proposition q even if q follows logically from p.

A person comes to know a fact by visual perception. What she learns by visual perception implies a number of propositions (such as that there are physical objects). Although such propositions are logically implied by what the person learned by visual perception, she does not come to know by visual perception all the consequences of what she learned by visual perception. Seeing a green apple in front of one has a distinctive visual phenomenology. Seeing that the apple in front of one is green too has a distinctive visual phenomenology. By seeing a green apple, the person comes to know that there is a green apple. There is something distinctively visual about what it is like for one to see that the apple in front of one is green. If an apple is green, then it is colored. Hence a person who has learned by visual perception that there is a green apple can come to know that there is a colored apple. However, it is dubious that she learned this latter fact by visual perception alone, for it is dubious whether there is a visual phenomenology to thinking of the apple in front of one that it is colored. A person who knows that there is a colored apple in front of her can come to know that there is a colored fruit in front of her. From that last piece of knowledge, she can infer that there is at least one physical object, hence that there are physical objects. But if she does, then she does not know by visual perception that there are physical objects—if she knows it at all. Hence, contrary to what the sceptic assumes, we want to claim that visual knowledge is not deductively closed.

5 How intelligent are perceptual processes?

One can see objects and one can see facts—or so we claimed above. Our claim has been that one cannot make sense of the hierarchical structure of visual knowledge unless one recognizes an epistemological difference between seeing an object and seeing a fact. We argued that, in some circumstances, seeing some facts may have an epistemological priority over seeing other facts, in that the former contributes to explaining the latter, and seeing an object played a distinctive role in the explanation.

As we said earlier in this chapter, like so many psychological words, the word 'perception' can be used to refer either to a (perceptual) process or to its product: the resulting experience. Whether one can see facts and/or objects is a question about what is perceived—what the resulting experience is about. Questions about perceptual processes are questions about how perceptual experiences arise. Thus, we can ask questions about perceptual processes such as: are perceptual processes intelligent processes? If so, how intelligent are they? How similar to thought processes are they? How similar to belief-forming mechanisms are they? How much are they like reasoning processes? How much are they like deductive and inductive inferential processes?

Such questions have been central to much psychological and philosophical theorizing about perception. As pointed out by Norman (2001), there have been two broad responses to such questions about perceptual processes: an older 'constructivist' tradition and a more recent 'ecological' tradition.[11]

The similarity between perceptual processes and intelligent, thought-like, belief-forming mechanisms, such as problem solving, have been emphasized by the former tradition and de-emphasized by the latter tradition. If the distinction between seeing objects and seeing facts has psychological validity, then presumably there are two kinds of perceptual products. If so, then presumably seeing facts must be more like believing (or judging) than seeing objects. If this is the case, then distinct psychological processes might give rise to two distinct perceptual outcomes. In which case, it is tempting to argue that the ecological tradition and the constructivist tradition might each be correct in their own perceptual domains. Indeed, the two traditions have generally focused upon different empirical phenomena. In fact, in these few paragraphs, we shall not adjudicate between the two views. Indeed, on our view, as we shall argue in the next chapter in more details, some of the insights of the ecological tradition are best interpreted as contributions to the analysis of visually guided actions, not visual perception in a narrow sense.[12]

5.1 Filling-in and constructivism

Central to the thinking of most constructivists have been phenomena of perceptual completion or 'filling-in'. Such perceptual processes consist mostly in adding information to the incoming visual input, so that there is more information in the perceptual outcome than is available in the stimulus. As Ramachandran and Blakeslee (1998: 88) put it, 'a glimpse of your cat's tail sticking out from underneath the sofa evokes the image of the whole cat; you certainly don't see a disembodied tail, gasp and panic or like Lewis Carroll's Alice, wonder where the rest of the cat is'. It is worth noticing that many phenomena of perceptual 'filling-in' were noticed by perceptual psychologists

---

[11]Gregory (1978) and Rock (1983) are two leading contemporary representatives of constructivism. Gibson (1979) is the leading representative of the ecological tradition. See Palmer (1999) for extensive discussion.

who wanted to emphasize the top-down effects of fairly high-level cognitive representations upon the analysis of the visual stimulus. Early on, Fodor (1983: 65–80) argued that the linguistic phenomenon of 'phoneme restoration' noticed by Warren (1970)—a non-visual psycholinguistic instance of 'filling-in' whereby a hearer mentally supplies a missing phoneme—is consistent with the modularity thesis according to which the information filled in by the language module 'counts as top-down flow within the language module' (Fodor 1983: 77). As we shall argue, not all modular processes have to be bottom-up: although 'filling-in' is indeed a top-down psychological process, such a process may nonetheless be modular, i.e. 'informationally encapsulated' in Fodor's (1983) sense.

Hence, constructivists like to concentrate upon displays that give rise to Gestalt switches (such as the bird/rabbit example) or upon ambiguous stimuli such as the Necker cube (Fig. 5.1). In spite of the fact that no change occurs within the display itself, sudden changes occur in the perceptual experience. Given that the information in the stimulus has not changed, the change must come from the brain: the informational gap must have been filled in by the brain. The famous Kanizsa triangle offers another piece of evidence in favor of the constructivist view that the fundamental perceptual process consists in filling-in information missing from the stimulus: although no actual lines are present in some parts of the display, the brain fills them in so as to produce an impression of subjective or 'illusory' contours (Fig. 5.2). It is possible not only to produce the visual impression of subjective contours of straight triangles but also of curved triangles. Interestingly, a visual agnosia prompted by a lesion in area V2 has been described by Wapner et al. (1978) in which the patient (a visual artist) is deprived of the experience of subjective contours when seeing a Kanizsa triangle (see Zeki 1993: 316–7). The phenomenon of apparent motion—the so-called 'phi phenomenon'—supplies yet another such piece of evidence (see Kolers 1972; Goodman 1978; Marr 1982; Dennett 1991). If a spot of light is flashed against a uniform background and a similar spot is flashed 10 to 45 ms after the first spot a short distance away (within a visual angle of some 4 degrees), then one sees a single spot moving from one position to the next. If the two spots differ in color, then the visual impression of apparent motion persists: the spot is seen to be moving and to suddenly change color without any transition (i.e. without exemplifying any intermediate color). Arguably, the most compelling evidence in favor of the constructivist standpoint comes from the famous phenomenon of filling-in the blind spot on one's retina. The optic disk on the retina, which is the area of the retina to which the optic nerve is connected, is a blind spot: it is a natural scotoma that does not respond to incoming light. Since subjects do not experience any discontinuity in their visual field when visual information falls on their blind spot, the brain is said to 'fill in' the missing information. All sorts of visual attributes can be filled in by the brain: the missing color, the missing shape, the missing texture, the missing orientation.[13]

---

[12]Thus, in our view, levels of visual perception should not be confused with visuomotor representations. For example, non-epistemic visual perception is different from visuomotor representation, as its function is to serve as an intermediary level in the perceptual processing of a stimulus.

[13]Interestingly, in the context of an explanation of the concept of informational encapsulation, Fodor (1983: 65) refers to filling in the blind spot on one's retina.

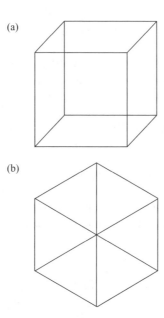

Fig. 5.1 Perceiving a cube. (a) In seeing a Necker cube, you perceive at once a cube and you can flip from seeing one of the two squares as being in front of the other. (b) Although this Kopfermann cube is a possible view of a cube, it takes some time to see it as a 3D cube.

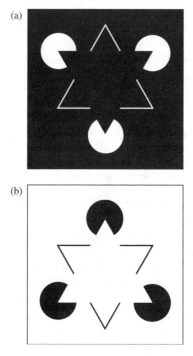

Fig. 5.2 Perceptual experience of subjective contours in Kanizsa triangles. Although the black triangle (a) and the white triangle (b) have no physical contours, they have subjective contours.

With Dennett (1991, 1992), one might wonder how seriously one should take the view that in these various perceptual experiences, the brain really 'fills in' missing information. Dennett's point really is that the phenomena generally labeled 'filling-in' do not result from the brain adding anything, but from the brain neglecting the fact that it is not receiving any information. By presupposing that the brain is adding something, according to Dennett, the 'filling-in' metaphor surreptitiously encourages a misplaced search for determinacy in the information supplied. As he (1992) puts it, 'it suggests that the brain is *providing* something when in fact the brain is ignoring something; it mistakes the omission of a representation for the representation of presence'.

First, consider for example the way the philosopher Nelson Goodman (1978: 85) describes the phenomenon of apparent motion produced by the flashing of two spots of different colors: 'each of the intervening places along the path between the two flashes [must be] filled in [...] with one of the flashed colors rather than with successive intermediate colors'. Goodman (1978: 73) is thus led to ask the question: 'How are we able [...] to fill in from the first to the second flash before the second flash occurs?'. According to Dennett (1991), this is a wrong metaphysical question to ask for it wrongly presupposes that it has a determinate answer. Asking this question, it may seem as if one is faced with a choice between two rival views, which Dennett (1991: 123) labels, respectively, 'Stalinesque' and 'Orwellian'. According to the former, the brain would fill in 'on the upward, pre-experiential path'. According to the latter, the brain would produce a retrospective 'memory revision [...] on the downward post-experiential path'. Now, according to Dennett's (1991) rather extreme 'verificationist' view, there is no fact of the matter between these two hypotheses because no empirical evidence will ever allow adjudication.

Second, it misleads one into thinking that the brain literally uses something like a 'cerebral paintbrush' for filling-in colors or a 'cerebral pen' for filling-in shapes and so on. Going back to blind spots, according to Dennett (1992):

[...] the brain does not have to fill in for the blind spot [since the brain is not receiving any information from that region] and not getting any evidence from the blind spot region is not the same as getting contradictory evidence [...]. The area is simply neglected. In other words, all normally sighted people suffer from tiny bits of anosognosia—we are (normally) unaware that we are receiving no visual information from our blind spots.

In response to Dennett's interesting challenge, Ramachandran and Blakeslee (1998) distinguish various forms of filling-in: not only do they argue in favor of a distinction between 'perceptual' and 'conceptual' forms of filling-in, but perceptual filling-in or completion can have various degrees of determinacy. They report several ingenious experiments performed with patients who lost a portion of their visual cortex and who have, as a result, a large scotoma in their visual field. For example, in Ramachandran and Blakeslee (1998: 101), they report an experiment in which they presented numerals 1, 2 and 3 above the patient's scotoma and numerals 7, 8 and 9 below his scotoma. They used numerals of both size and relative distance from one another such that they could be treated by the visual system as textural information. The question was: how would the patient's brain fill in the middle of the sequence, i.e. the part of the sequence that fell upon the patient's scotoma? The result of the experiment was that in the middle area, the patient saw 'numberlike stuff in this region' but could not identify any particular numeral. Ramachandran and Blakeslee (1998: 102–3) link the condition of this patient to a form of 'temporary dyslexia': 'those middle numbers did not exist, were not flashed before his eyes, yet his brain was making up the textural attributes of the number string and completing it'. Hence, the brain filled in numeral textural information, not specific individual numerals. If so, then the completion of textural (and color) information ought to be distinguished from completion of individual numerals, i.e. objects. Hence, the proper response to Dennett's reminder might be that there are different degrees of determinacy according to which information is relevant to the perceptual task. Missing objects, e.g. might be more difficult for the brain to fill in than missing colors or missing textures.[14]

5.2   The ecological tradition and the modularity of perception

Let us now turn to what we called the 'ecological' approach to visual processes. The ecological approach arose mainly as a reaction to some of the claims made by constructivists on behalf of the similarity between visual perception and conceptual thought. There are at least three separable strands in the ecological approach. One fundamental strand has been forcefully expounded by Gibson in a number of works (e.g. Gibson 1979). Gibson has emphasized the fact that there is far more information in what he calls the 'optic array' than many constructivists were willing to recognize. If the optic array fully determines the nature of the distal stimulus, then perceptual processes do not consist of filling-in or completing gaps. Rather their task is simply to extract the information present in the proximal stimulus. According to this stimulus-driven strand of the ecological approach then, perceptual processes do not resemble anything like thought or reasoning processes. On this view, there is no room left for genuinely inferential processes, either inductive or deductive, in visual perception. This is why the ecological approach has often been dubbed the direct theory of visual perception: if perceptual processes are not inferential, then they directly pick up the relevant information. The second strand in Gibson's ecological approach to visual perception lies in his dual emphasis on affordances and the role of action and movement in capturing the visual information contained in the optic array. According to Gibson, visual perception is not the passive registration of the incoming optic flow by a stationary observer: it involves eye-movement, head-movement and body-movement on the part of the perceiver. Nor are these movements directed to neutral physical objects. They are directed to what Gibson calls 'affordances', i.e. to objects insofar as these afford various possibilities for action to perceiving organisms. In effect, one and the same object may afford different kinds of action to differently built organisms. Although these are no doubt very important insights, they are, or so we shall argue in the next chapter, best recast, not so much as proposals for understanding visual perception properly so-called, but rather as proposals for analyzing visually guided actions or vision-for-action, to use Milner and Goodale's (1995) felicitous phrase.

---

[14]Incidentally, Ramachandran's experiment adds an interesting twist to Marr's insightful reflection (quoted in Section 1) about the notion of a perceptual object: missing numerals in a sequence can be filled in by the brain as completing textural information, not as objects.

Relevant to the debate between constructivists and advocates of the direct ecological approach to the nature of perceptual processes, is Fodor's (1983) claim that visual perception is a modular process. An information-processing (or computational) subsystem is modular, according to Fodor, if it is 'informationally encapsulated', i.e. if not all of the information that is available to the overall cognitive system is used by the subsystem. We have alluded already to the fact that a perceptual process may be both top-down and informationally encapsulated. Thus, the visual perceptual processing of an illusory display, such as the Müller–Lyer illusion, the Ponzo illusion or the Titchener illusion, is typically modular or informationally encapsulated. For although one knows that the two segments of the Müller–Lyer illusion are equal, still they look unequal: the segment whose arrows are converging looks longer than the segment whose arrows are diverging. Conversely, how things look may differ from how things are: even though the two segments look unequal, one's considered judgment is that they are equal, not unequal. Unlike input systems, what Fodor (1983) calls 'central' thought processes are not modular: they are, in his own words, 'Quinean' and 'isotropic'. The output of the processing of an informationally encapsulated input system is only one factor on the basis of which central thought processes reach their verdict. Not only may all of the information available to the overall cognitive system be relevant to central processes, but they are also sensitive to factors such as simplicity and conservatism. The modularity of visual perceptual processes ought to be distinguished from a closely related property that Fodor (1983) calls 'domain-specificity': visual perception is domain-specific in the sense that it depends on the visual system and the visual system processes only visual stimuli, not auditory, olfactory or tactile stimuli. Unlike visual perception, conceptual thought can integrate inputs coming from many different input systems (or various sensory modalities).

It is tempting—and it has tempted Dretske (1995b: 343)—to link the modularity of perceptual processes to the Gibsonian emphasis on the directness of visual perception along the following line: if visual perception is modular, then perceptual processes do not exploit all of the information otherwise available to the overall cognitive system. Hence, if visual perception is modular, it is not an intelligent inductive reasoning process. Hence, the modularity of visual perception would seem to lead naturally to the view that visual perception is 'direct', i.e. to the Gibsonian view that the task of visual perception is merely to extract the information available in the optic array. But it is a mistake. The reason it is a mistake is that, as we said above, the paradigm of a modular perceptual process is the visual processing of an illusory display. Now, when confronted with the Müller–Lyer display, one sees the segment with converging arrows as longer than the segment with diverging arrows. So it is not the case that the perceptual process responsible for the illusory judgment merely extracts the information that is contained in the optic array. Since the two segments are equal, the information present in the optic array is that the two segments are equal, not that they are unequal. The underlying process is modular precisely because although one knows that the two segments are equal, one keeps seeing them as unequal. Modular processes may be dumb insofar as they neglect information relevant for knowledge or true belief. But nonetheless they do not merely extract information contained in the optic array.

6 Is seeing believing?

6.1 Seeing, seeing that and seeing as

Epistemic seeing is seeing facts. Hence, epistemic seeing is (visual) knowledge. Following Dretske (1969), we distinguished primary epistemic seeing from secondary epistemic seeing on epistemological grounds. In Sections 2 and 3 of the present chapter, we examined the intricate relationships between primary and secondary epistemic seeing. Primary epistemic seeing is seeing a fact involving a perceived object. Secondary epistemic seeing is seeing a fact involving an unperceived object. Seeing a fact involving a perceived object may have epistemic priority over seeing a fact involving an unperceived object because the former may contribute to the explanation and the justification of the latter—or so we argued. Now one cannot know a fact unless one believes the corresponding proposition. One cannot know that the object in front of one is a purple triangle unless one believes and/or one judges that it is. One cannot believe that the object is a purple triangle unless one knows what a triangle is and what purple is—unless one possesses the concept of purple and the concept of a triangle. In the present section, we shall discard secondary epistemic seeing and concentrate upon primary epistemic seeing. The questions we want to ask are: is visual perception entirely the same as believing or judging? Are all cases of visual experience instances of epistemic seeing? Must one know (hence, believe) that the object in front of one is a purple triangle in order to be visually aware of a purple triangle? Must one possess the concept of purple and the concept of a triangle in order to visually experience a purple triangle? If the epistemological distinction between seeing facts and seeing objects makes sense, then is it a psychologically relevant distinction?

As a first clue to the distinction between epistemic and non-epistemic perceptual states, let us examine how one makes linguistic reports of visual experiences. When one reports one's own visual experience or when one tries to describe the visual experiences of others in English, one uses a sentence containing the verb 'to see'. Now, as a matter of syntax, there is a basic distinction between two possible uses of the English verb 'to see'. One can 'see a purple triangle' and one can 'see that the triangle is purple'. In other words, it is a syntactic fact about the English verb 'to see' that its complement can either be a noun phrase or a 'that' clause. This syntactic distinction seems to mirror the distinction between seeing objects and seeing facts.

When the complement of the verb 'to see' is a noun phrase, there is in addition another distinction to be noticed between 'seeing a purple triangle' and 'seeing something *as* a purple triangle' or perhaps 'seeing something *to be* a purple triangle'. Presumably, a person can be said to see a purple triangle even though she would not report her visual experience using words such as 'purple' and 'triangle'—either because she does not know the words and/or the concepts that these words express or because she did not pay attention at the time. However, a person could not be said to see that something is a purple triangle unless she was ready to say so, and unless she possessed the relevant concepts and had paid attention to the fact that what she was seeing is a purple triangle. Now, the conditions in which it would be true and felicitous to say of a person that she saw an object as (or to be) a purple triangle seem to be different from both the conditions in which it is true to say of her that she saw a purple triangle and that she saw that the triangle is purple. First of all, one can see a purple triangle and it may not register. But for a person to see something to be (or as) a purple triangle, it is necessary that some visual modes of perceiving both the color and the shape of the object were deployed in the person's visual experience. Unlike seeing that something is a purple triangle, however, it is not clear that for seeing something as a purple triangle, the perceiver must have deployed her concept of a triangle and her concept of purple. Nor does it seem necessary for someone to see something as a purple triangle that there is one to be seen. But in order for someone truly to see that something is a purple triangle, it is required that there is one to be seen. On the assumption that seeing the fact that a triangle is purple is the paradigm example of (strong) epistemic perception, then seeing an object as (or to be) a purple triangle can be said to be an instance of weak epistemic perception.

With respect to 'loose uses' of the verb 'to see' in which the reported achievements owe nothing to visual cognition, we said above that ordinary usage is not sacrosanct. So we should not rush from the syntactic distinction between two or more uses of the verb 'to see' to the conclusion that there are two or more psychological kinds of visual achievements: epistemic seeing (corresponding to reports in which the complement of the verb is a 'that' clause) and non-epistemic seeing (corresponding to reports in which the complement of the verb is a noun phrase). The distinction between epistemic and non-epistemic seeing, however, can be supported by a number of converging arguments.

6.2   First-person and third-person perceptual reports

Further reflection on the difference between perceptual experience and perceptual reports corroborates the distinction between epistemic and non-epistemic seeing. Obviously, unlike non-linguistic creatures, linguistic creatures can report their perceptual experiences. But clearly, the perceptual experiences of linguistic creatures should not be confused with their perceptual reports. When a linguistic creature reports her perceptual experience, she engages in a highly cognitive intentional task, namely verbal communication with a conspecific. So what is true of a perceptual report is not *ipso facto* true of a perceptual experience. First-person perceptual reports may seem, on the face of it, to count against the distinction between epistemic and non-epistemic seeing. Arguably, a person would not say that she saw a kangaroo unless she intended her audience to believe that she did see a kangaroo. Nor would she, in normal circumstances, say so unless she believed that she did. Presumably, she would not believe that she saw a kangaroo unless she identified what she saw as a kangaroo. Hence, first-person perceptual reports seem to lend support to the view that perceiving is indeed believing.

However, a famous paradox first discussed by the early twentieth century philosopher G. E. Moore—Moore's (1942) paradox—tells us that first-person belief reports interestingly differ from third-person belief reports. One may non-paradoxically say: 'It is raining but Sam does not believe it'. But one may not similarly say: 'It is raining but I do not believe it'. The reason why the latter is odd is that by uttering the sentence 'It is raining', the speaker is expressing (or indirectly communicating) her belief that it is raining. Then, by adding 'I do not believe it', she is undermining something implied by what she just said. There is nothing paradoxical in the fact that someone—anyone— fails to believe that it is raining when it is raining (or conversely to believe that it is raining when it is not). A pragmatic paradox arises, however, from the utterance of the complex first-personal belief report: 'It is raining but I do not believe it'.

A similar asymmetry between first- and third-person reports arises in the case of perceptual reports. One cannot truly say that one saw a kangaroo unless one believes it, i.e. unless one believes that what one saw was a kangaroo. In other words, one cannot truly say that one saw a kangaroo without having identified what one saw as a kangaroo. But, as noticed by Dretske (1969: 22–3), following Grice (1961), if one says that Sam saw a kangaroo, it does not follow that Sam believes that what he saw was a kangaroo. Saying that Sam saw a kangaroo pragmatically suggests—in Grice's (1961, 1975) terms, it carries the implicature—that Sam identified what he saw as a kangaroo. But the implication is not fool-proof. In Grice's (1975, 1989) view, one cannot conclude that what was said—the proposition expressed—is false from the falsehood of one of its implicatures. Normally, if a person, e.g. Sam, is said by a speaker to have seen a kangaroo, the hearer can assume that the person identified what he saw as a kangaroo and believed that the object standing in front of him was a kangaroo. Normally, the person will share a number of collateral beliefs about kangaroos, such as that females carry their babies in pouches, that they are tremendous jumpers, that they mostly live in Australia, and so on. If, however, Sam turns out to be a six-month-old baby comfortably sitting in his pram at the zoo, then the implicature loses much of its plausibility as Sam is not likely to share any of these beliefs. If Sam's visual system is in good working condition, if Sam was at the right distance from the kangaroo, if the lighting was good enough and if Sam was not asleep, then it may be perfectly true that Sam indeed saw a kangaroo even though it is false that he thought or believed that he did.

Examination of third-person perceptual reports shows that one is not always an authority about what one sees. One may or not be an authority about what one believes, but one is not always authoritative about what it is that one sees. As noticed by Dretske (1978) and Von Wright (1998: 47), one may see something and not notice it. One may see an object and not notice some of its visual properties. Nonetheless, it may well be true that one saw either the object or the property. One may see a tachometer and have no idea what one is seeing. One may then learn from another person that what one saw was a tachometer. One saw a tachometer, but one does not believe that one did. Thus, examination of third-person perceptual reports corroborates the view that visual experiences should not be confused with beliefs. In other words, non-epistemic seeing should not be confused with epistemic seeing.[15]

6.3 What must one believe and/or notice in order to perceive?

Further support for this conclusion can be adduced from the possibility of perceptual mistakes, i.e. the possibility of misidentifying (or misrecognizing) a perceived object. One may, e.g. believe that the horse in the distance is black upon seeing a black donkey in the distance. The question is: if one misperceives a donkey as a horse, what is it that one sees? One's visual experience will have triggered one's concept of a horse and one will come to think or believe that what one is seeing is a horse. But what one is seeing

---

[15]Nor should, in our view, non-epistemic visual perception be confused with low-level visuomotor representations (about which see Chapter 6).

is a donkey, not a horse, for there is no horse to be seen. The person is not seeing the fact that the object in front of her is a donkey, since she believes that it is a horse. But she is nonetheless seeing a donkey. Otherwise how else could one describe the perceptual situation? In this case, misperception involves the misapplication of a concept of an animal. One may also see a star at night that one takes to be a plane. Misperception can involve more radical category mistakes, as when one mistakenly believes that a human hand is dangling at night when one sees a branch dangling at night. One believes that the dangling branch that one is seeing at night is a human hand. One then mistakes a branch for a human hand. Although the person is not seeing that the object in front of her is a branch, since she believes that it is a human hand, nonetheless what she is seeing is a branch, not a human hand, for there is no human hand to be seen there. Again, unless one assumes that the object seen is a branch, how could one describe the perceptual situation?

In such cases of misperception, one believes of an object that it is something different from what it is. Although one is seriously mistaken about what one sees, one is not thereby deprived of visual experience. There is something it is like to see a black donkey that one takes to be a horse. There is something it is like to see a star that one takes to be a plane. There is something it is like to see a dangling branch that one takes to be a human hand. Clearly then one may visually perceive an object and have drastically wrong beliefs about what one sees. However, the question is: can one see an object without having any true belief of it at all? Can one see an object without identifying it— or correctly conceptualizing it—at some level? There are two broad responses in the philosophy of perception to this difficult question. 'Cognitivists' about visual experience (or 'judgmentalists' such as Descartes, Armstrong, Dennett, McDowell) say: No. Anti-judgmentalists (such as Dretske, Evans, Peacocke) say: Yes.

Philosophers we call 'judgmentalists' hold an intellectualist theory of visual perception. When in the course of the *Second Meditation*, looking out of the window and seeing 'men crossing the square', Descartes (1644) wonders whether he can really see 'any more than hats and coats which could conceal automatons' and he argues that he in fact '*judges* that they are men', he counts as a judgmentalist. So does Armstrong (1968) who brilliantly defends the view that perception is the acquisition of 'potential' beliefs, i.e. the inclination to form beliefs. Although Dennett (1991, 1994) wants explicitly to divorce his own 'micro-judgments' and/or 'micro-cognitions' pitched at the 'sub-personal' level from Armstrong's 'personal' level beliefs and judgments, for our purposes, Dennett too counts as a judgmentalist. And so does McDowell (1994), who bases his argument for the view that all content is conceptual content on the claim that indexical and demonstrative concepts can capture the pictorial content of visual experience (about which see Chapter 1, Section 3.2).

By contrast, philosophers we label 'anti-judgmentalists' hold the anti-intellectualist view that the quality of a visual experience cannot be properly captured by conceiving of it as a belief and/or a conceptual judgment. Dretske (1969, 1978, 1981, 1990b, 1995a) over the years has been a leading advocate of the anti-intellectualist representationalist approach to the puzzles of visual experience. And so have Evans (1982), Peacocke (1983, 1992, 1998) and Tye (1995), who have provided detailed arguments for the view that not all representations have conceptual content, hence for the existence of non-conceptual content (see the first chapter). As Evans (1982: 122–4) puts it:

[...] when a person perceives something, he receives (or, better, gathers) information about the world [...]. The subject's *being* in an informational state is independent of whether or not he believes that the state is veridical [...]. The operations of the informational system are more primitive [than the operations of the belief system].

As we see it, the controversy is about whether, within visual perceptual processing, there is a level of processing that deserves to be called 'visual experience' that takes place before the uptake of judgment, recognition or identification of the visual stimulus. Assuming that visual perceptual processing culminates in the identification of the stimulus, the question is whether what Dretske (1969) calls non-epistemic perception provides an elementary level of visual experience.[16] Of course, as we are quite ready to acknowledge, it is much easier to say what is wrong with either view than to provide a conclusive response to the question: Is seeing believing? We shall nonetheless examine two crucial points related to the controversy.

The first point is that it may well be that for a creature—any creature—to enjoy visual experiences, not only must her visual system be in good working condition, but it must also be properly connected to the rest of her cognitive system, i.e. her concept-forming capacities and her memory system. In other words, processing visual information might not be a sufficient condition: the creature must also have non-visual cognitive and/or conceptual capacities. This is not in dispute between intellectualists and anti-intellectualists (see, e.g. Dretske (1978) and Evans (1982)). What is in question is whether, in order to be visually aware of an object, one must form some true beliefs and deploy some definite concepts about the perceived object.[17]

When the issue is so formulated, intellectualists are quick to point out that, although one may have drastically wrong beliefs about what one sees, nonetheless presumably one cannot see a black donkey that one wrongly takes to be a horse without believing correctly that it is a mammal, let alone without believing correctly that it is an animal. One cannot see a dangling branch that one wrongly takes to be human hand without believing that it is a physical object. One cannot see a star that one wrongly takes to be a plane without believing that it is a physical object of some sort. Hence, according to intellectualists, some correct identification of the stimulus is required for visual experience to take place.

Anti-intellectualists will grant that, as a matter of fact, most of the time, adult human beings cannot be visually aware of some object without forming some correct belief about what they are seeing. What they will question, however, is whether it is constitutive of visual experiences—whether it is conceptually necessary for visual experience to occur—that some correct identification of the stimulus takes place. Must human infants and non-human animals possess the concept of a triangle for them to visually experience a purple triangle? Will a human infant have no distinctive visual experience upon seeing a purple triangle unless she knows the definition of a triangle? If so, then there

---

[16]As we shall argue in Chapter 6, Section 5, both developmental work on the perceptual capacities of human infants and work on multiple tracking experiments by human adults show that in low-level perceptual tasks, perceptual proto-objects are individuated by location, not by featural information. We take such experimental work to corroborate the existence of non-epistemic visual perception of proto-objects.

[17]As we observed in the Introduction, lack of belief does not preclude non-epistemic seeing. Nor does possession of belief preclude it.

would be nothing it would be like for a creature to visually experience a purple triangle, unless she knew that a triangle has three sides and three angles whose sum equals 180°. Unless she knew what triangles are (unless perhaps she had a word for triangles), she would not experience something different upon seeing a purple triangle and upon seeing a purple square or a purple circle. This intellectualist consequence does not sound right. How could concept acquisition take place at all if there was nothing it was like to visually experience a purple triangle unless one already knew what a triangle was and how to categorize its color? On the assumption that some sensory experience may be required to play a triggering role in the acquisition of geometrical concepts, how could a human infant come to acquire the concept of a triangle unless she could experience triangles in a distinctive way—visually or otherwise—before mastering the concept? According to anti-intellectualists, not to know something—to lack a piece of knowledge—is not the same thing as being blind. Conversely, there is a sense in which seeing something differs from knowing a fact.

As emphasized by Dretske (1969, 1978), seeing is like touching. According to him, it is even like stepping on something. By touching it, one may become tactually aware of something even if one does not form much of a belief about what it is that one touches. Like touching, seeing is a process. It may take time to become visually aware of some of the details of a visual array. If so, then it seems as if, by distinguishing non-epistemic seeing from epistemic seeing, anti-intellectualists are in a better position than intellectualists to offer a general account of sensory experience applicable to sensory modalities other than vision. Furthermore, as anti-intellectualists (e.g. Dretske 1978) point out, one may presumably see an object and wrongly believe oneself to be having a visual hallucination. If so, then while seeing an object, one would not even correctly believe that one is seeing a physical object. At this point, intellectualists are likely to deny that seeing something is at all like stepping on it. One can presumably step on something, e.g. an ant, and not be aware of it at all. If so, then the sense in which seeing is like stepping on something does not count as an instance of being visually aware of what one saw. Along the same lines, Dennett (1994) has objected that, unless some 'cognitive (or conceptual) uptake' occurs, it will be hard to distinguish non-epistermic seeing from 'what happens on the inert wall of a unoccupied camera obscura'. Perhaps so. Perhaps some conceptual uptake is necessary for visual experience to occur. But if so, the question still arises: the uptake of which concept is necessary?

On behalf of intellectualists, Dennett (1994) has argued that early experiments on change blindness could decisively refute the anti-judgmentalist assumption that visual experience could occur in the absence of conceptual uptake. Although we certainly do not want to claim that the dispute over non-epistemic vision is settled, we do want to point out that we do not think that experiments on change blindness could be decisive—let alone that they could conclusively disprove the anti-intellectualist point of view. In experiments on change blindness, subjects are presented with visual displays of natural scenes. Their task is to detect cyclically repeated changes in the display, such as changes of shape, color or orientation of a prominent object or the contrast between the presence and the absence of a large object in the scene. The method used in the experiments consists of superimposing on the image, at the very instant of the change, a flicker every 250 ms that remains on for 150 ms. As a result, subjects have great difficulty seeing changes 'even though the changes are very large, and occur in full view

[and] are perfectly visible to someone who knows what they are' (O'Regan and Noe 2001a: 954). Inattentional blindness is a related phenomenon exemplified by e.g. a film showing a basketball game (reported in Noë and O'Regan 2000). Subjects are asked to count the number of times one team takes hold of the ball. Now, in the middle of the basketball game, a person dressed in a gorilla suit strolls in the middle of the players, faces the audience, moves around and then disappears. The surprising fact is that subjects who see the film, engaged as they are in counting the number of times each team takes possession of the ball, fail to notice the gorilla.

No doubt, the intellectualist can argue that the results of experiments on blindness-change and on inattentional blindness show that one cannot see something unless some basic recognition or identification of the stimulus—some basic conceptual uptake—has occurred. But the reason why these experiments cannot settle the issue is that it is wide open to the anti-intellectualist to take these results as corroborating his view that not all seeing is noticing—let alone knowing. After all, it is natural to describe the result of these experiments by saying that subjects fail to notice something visible. Nor is it as if in the experiments on change-blindness and on inattentional blindness, subjects were blind and did not see anything. They do see things, but they do not notice some major changes. Arguably, one can see a thing that is F without seeing it as F, let alone without seeing that it is F. Changes (or events) should be no exception: one can see a change witout either seeing it as a change or seeing that a change has taken place.

7 The phenomenology of visual experience

7.1 Phenomenal realism and the explanatory gap

As we said at the beginning of this chapter, the puzzle raised by visual perception is: how a visual experience—something eminently subjective—could yield knowledge of the world—a reliable piece of objective information. It is time to go back to the phenomenology of visual awareness. In the last section of this chapter, we want to examine the question of visual *qualia* in the context of philosophical discussions of phenomenal consciousness. Block (1995) has argued that 'the concept of consciousness is a hybrid or better, a mongrel concept'. His rather radical claim is that the ordinary noun 'consciousness' and the ordinary adjective 'conscious' can be used to express two distinct concepts: access-consciousness (A-consciousness) and phenomenal consciousness (P-consciousness). A-consciousness is a matter of cognitive architecture: a state is said to be A-conscious if 'it is poised for free use in reasoning and for direct 'rational' control of action and speech'. As Block (1995) puts it, 'P-conscious properties are experiential properties. P-conscious states are experiential states, that is, a state is P-conscious if it has experiential properties. The totality of the experiential properties of a state are 'what it is like' to have it'. Furthermore, 'it is of course P-consciousness rather than access-consciousness [...] that has seemed such a scientific mystery'.

Several philosophers are prone to endorse the claim that phenomenal consciousness is not so much a scientific problem as a major mystery that is likely to remain beyond the boundaries of scientific understanding. One such line of thought has been developed by Nagel (1974) according to whom:

[...] consciousness is what makes the mind-body problem really intractable [...]. Without consciousness the mind-body problem would be much less interesting. With consciousness it seems hopeless [...]. Fundamentally an organism has conscious mental states if there is something it is like to *be* that organism—something it is like *for* the organism [...]. Call this the subjective character of experience [...]. Every subjective phenomenon is essentially connected with a single point of view, and it seems inevitable that an objective, physical theory will abandon that point of view.

Clearly, Nagel's claim that phenomenal consciousness constitutes a mystery derives from his attempt at creating what Levine (1983, 1993) has called an 'explanatory gap' between the first-person perspective inherent to subjective experience and the third-person perspective inherent to the scientific enterprise.

Levine's (1993) idea of the explanatory gap can be put thus: the whole scientific enterprise provides convincing reasons to assume that human conscious subjective experience—like so many other phenomena—is a physical phenomenon with physical, chemical and biological properties. But if so, then this very statement has not yet been given any intelligible sense: if human consciousness is physical, then we are presently at a loss to explain it or to understand how it can be so. Science provides us with a great many examples whereby some facts have been unexpectedly explained by some other underlying facts. For example, science has provided a physical explanation of the fragility of glass by appealing to its underlying molecular structure and to fundamental laws of nature. Science has provided a chemical explanation of the transparency and liquidity of water by appealing to its molecular structure and to fundamental laws of nature. Scientific explanation in this sense provides understanding because knowledge of the underlying physical or chemical facts and the relevant laws of nature enables one to derive the facts to be explained (e.g. the fragility of the glass or the transparency and liquidity of water). Levine's (1983, 1993) basic observation is that we are presently unable to derive the characteristic properties of human conscious phenomenal experience from our knowledge of underlying neurobiological facts about the functioning of the human brain. Hence, on his view, when we believe that human conscious experience is physical, we are presently in the situation of believing something that might well be true but which we do not really understand. As it will turn out, we believe that this claim is too strong.

Thus, the idea of the explanatory gap is closely associated to the idea of the gap between the first-person perspective and the third-person perspective. Presumably, if phenomenal consciousness derives its mystery from the gap between the first-person and the third-person perspectives, then no matter how much objective science may change its conceptions in the future, it is not likely ever to bridge the gap. If so, then phenomenal consciousness is bound to remain a mystery by fiat. Nagel's recipe for creating an explanatory gap has recently been forcefully revived by Chalmers (1996) who calls the mystery 'the hard problem':

Why should there be something it is like to be [...] an experiencer? Present-day scientific theories hardly touch the really difficult questions about consciousness. We do not just lack a detailed theory; we are entirely in the dark about how consciousness fits into the natural order [...]. How does the brain process environmental stimulation? How does it integrate information? [...]. These are important questions, but to answer them is not to solve the hard problem: Why is all this processing accompanied by an experienced inner life?

Block (1996) has recently drawn attention to a more tractable version of the 'hard problem', i.e. the problem that the phenomenal mind raises for anyone who subscribes to 'phenomenal realism':

> The greatest chasm in the philosophy of mind [...] separates two perspectives on consciousness. [It is about] whether there is anything in the phenomenal character of conscious experience that goes beyond the intentional, the cognitive and the functional [...]. Those who think that the phenomenal character of conscious experience goes beyond the intentional, the cognitive and the functional are said to believe in qualitative properties of conscious experience, or *qualia* for short. The debates about *qualia* have recently focused on the notion of representation [...]. All can agree that there are representational contents of thoughts, for example, the representational content *that virtue is its own reward*. And friends of *qualia* can agree that experiences at least sometimes have representational content too, e.g. *that something red and round occludes something blue and square*. The recent focus of disagreement is on whether the phenomenal character of experience is exhausted by such representational contents. I say no [...]. What I insist on is that the phenomenal character [of sensations] outruns their representational contents.

Phenomenal realism is thus the view that the phenomenal character of an experience— what it is like to have the experience—is not identical with any other property of the experience. If the experience is a mental representation, then according to phenomenal realism, the phenomenal character of the experience is not identical with any of its cognitive, functional or even intentional properties. In particular, the phenomenal character of the experience 'outruns' its representational content—if any.

Phenomenal realists claim that not all features of a conscious phenomenal experience are representational features or that conscious phenomenal experience has non-representational properties. One such claim was made by, e.g. Peacocke (1983: 12), who considers a pair of trees standing on a road, one a hundred yards, the other two hundred yards, from an observer. He supposes that the observer's visual experience represents the two trees 'as being of the same height'. Yet, at the same time, 'the nearer tree occupies more of [her] visual field than the more distant tree'. Peacocke then points out that no single 'veridical representation can represent one tree as larger than another and also as the same size as the other'. He thus embraces the phenomenal realist conclusion that the 'visual field property' or the property of the retinal images of having different sizes must be what he calls a 'sensational' property, i.e. a non-representational property of the experience.

Now, it seems clear that the representation of the two trees as being of the same height is part of the non-conceptual content of the visual experience. By means of her visual experience, the observer would see, and thus would come to believe, that the trees are equal in height. Arguably, the non-conceptual content of the observer's visual experience may be said to justify her visually acquired belief that the two trees are equal in height. The content of her visual experience provides her with reasons for her belief. It is also clear that the retinal image of one tree is not equal to the retinal image of the other tree. But it is not clear that the inequality of the sizes of the retinal images should itself be part of the visual experience. Not everything that happens in the course of visual processing is part of the final visual experience. Nor does the inequality of the sizes of the retinal images provide any reason for believing that the trees are of equal height. What is being represented by the visual experience is the relative sizes of the trees. The size of each tree is represented by means of a retinal image of the tree. Whereas each visually represented size is a property of the tree, the size of each retinal image is a property of the vehicle of the representation, not of what the experience represents. One and the same size property (of a pair of trees) can be visually represented by means of two retinal images with two different sizes.

7.2 Dismissing the explanatory gap

As Block's (1995) distinction between P-consciousness and A-consciousness testifies, not all philosophers assume that there is a single concept of consciousness. Block (1995) offers his own distinction as part of an argument for the phenomenal realist view that not all the phenomenal features of a conscious experience derive from its representational properties. Rosenthal (1986, 1993), who develops the view that the phenomenal character of a conscious experience is constituted by the subject's ability to form what he calls a 'HOT' or a 'higher-order thought' about her experience, draws a different distinction, i.e. between 'creature consciousness' and 'state consciousness'. A creature can be either transitively or intransitively conscious. A creature can be transitively conscious *of* things, properties and relations in her environment. In a slightly different sense, she is thereby intransitively conscious, if she is awake and is normally responsive to ongoing stimuli. Intransitive creature-consciousness is a property a creature can lose and then regain. A creature can lose it by falling asleep, by being knocked out in various ways, by being drugged, by being comatose. Mental states (e.g. beliefs and experiences) too can be conscious or unconscious. If conscious, a mental state can only be intransitively conscious. According to the HOT theory, a creature's state is conscious if the creature is conscious of being in that state by virtue of having formed a HOT about the state in question. Clearly, phenomenality in the sense of Block's P-consciousness is a feature of state consciousness, not of creature consciousness.

It is, however, an assumption shared by phenomenal realists and by their opponents that phenomenality—whatever it is—is a single property that can be instantiated by mental states of many different kinds. It is widely assumed that phenomenality can be exemplified by visual, auditory, olfactory or tactile experiences, as well as by conceptual thoughts. Curiously, as we shall see, philosophers hostile to phenomenal realism and impatient with the idea of the explanatory gap have rarely questioned this assumption.

Unlike phenomenal realists, representationalists claim that all the phenomenal features of a visual experience can be explained in terms of some representational properties or other of the experience. Representationalists roughly divide into three camps. According to HOT theorists (such as Rosenthal 1986, 1993), the phenomenal quality of a visual experience is constituted by the subject's ability to form a higher-order thought (or HOT) about her visual experience and reflect about it. Other representationalists, who deny the distinction between the conceptual content of thought and the nonconceptual content of experience, tend to reduce the mysteries of phenomenal consciousness to the ability to form conceptual judgments. One version of the conceptualist response to the explanatory gap, currently being explored by several psychologists and neuroscientists, is the view that for a representation to have a phenomenal character, is, as Baars (1988: 42) puts it, for its content to be 'broadcast' to the rest of the cognitive system. On this conceptualist view, no state of a system can give rise to a conscious visual experience with a phenomenal character unless the system to which it belongs is equipped with a working memory or with what Baars (1988) and Dehaene and Naccache (2001) call a 'global workspace' capable of receiving and relaying broadcast signals. States of isolated, encapsulated, modular information processing systems compete for attention. A happy few win the competition and temporarily manage to attract the attention of the community by having their content widely circulated. As a result, they are endowed with phenomenal character. Finally, 'intentionalists' such as Dretske (1995b), Tye (1995) and the authors of the present book argue that the phenomenal features of visual experiences depend on the perceptual non-conceptual content of representations produced by the visual system. According to visual intentionalism, a visual experience cannot represent an object as exemplifying the same set of attributes under the same modes of presentation as sensory experiences in other modalities, let alone as conceptual thoughts. Thus, unlike both HOT theorists and conceptualists, visual intentionalists are less inclined to assume that phenomenality might be a single quality shared by experiences in different modalities and by conceptual thoughts, since on the one hand, they accept the conceptual/non-conceptual content distinction and on the other hand they claim that the content of a sensory experience depends on the particular intentional properties that the experience represents objects as having.

Over the years, the most consistently dismissive reaction to the various versions of the view that phenomenal consciousness is an ineffable mystery has been expressed by Dennett (1991, 2001a, 2001b), who belongs to the third category of conceptualist representationalists. Although Dennett (1991) has famously denounced the idea of the 'Cartesian theater', i.e. the view that there is a single place in the brain where conscious experience takes place, he nonetheless accepts the view that, whatever it is, phenomenality is a property that may be exemplified by states of many different categories. Unlike some phenomenal realists, Dennett (1991) sees no hope of building up a scientific understanding of conscious experience that would abandon the objectivity of the third-personal stance. The purpose of what he (*ibid.*, ch. 4) calls 'heterophenomenology' is to take into account subjects' reports of (i.e. beliefs about) their subjective experiences. As he points out, how could one better honor the first-person point of view than by including in one's data subjects' reports of subjective experiences?

Now, it is one thing to agree with Dennett (2001b) when he argues that the project of 'first-person science' is a 'fantasy' and that advocates of the explanatory gap cannot seriously recommend that we abandon the only standpoint available for doing science, i.e. the third-person perspective. It is another thing to accept his (2001a) suggestion that phenomenal consciousness is 'cerebral celebrity, fame in the brain [...] or political influence. When processes compete for ongoing control of the body, the one with the greatest clout dominates the scene until a process with even greater clout displaces it'. As Dennett (2001a: 225) recognizes:

[...] of course, consciousness couldn't be *fame*, exactly, in the brain, since to be famous is to be a shared intentional object in the conscious minds of many folk, and although the brain is usefully seen as composed of hordes of demons (or homunculi), if we were to imagine them to be au courant in the ways they would need to be to elevate some of their brethren to cerebral celebrity, we would be endowing these subhuman components with too much human psychology—and, of course, installing a patent infinite regress in the model as a theory of consciousness. The looming infinite regress can be stopped the way such threats are often happily stopped, not by abandoning the basic idea but by softening it. As long as your homunculi are more stupid and ignorant than the intelligent agent they compose, the nesting of homunculi within homunculi can be finite, bottoming out, eventually, with agents so unimpressive that they can be replaced by machines.

From our point of view, assuming with Dennett that the 'looming regress' can be stopped, what is objectionable about the view that phenomenal consciousness is 'political influence' is not its metaphorical character. Rather, what is objectionable is that, in line with Dennett's own judgmentalist proclivities, it tries to capture the phenomenal character of experience in judgmental terms. Being famous, being influential or having a clout are extrinsic, not intrinsic, properties of whatever exemplifies them. More precisely, for anything x, x would not be 'famous' or 'influential' unless there existed other things y able to form beliefs (or to enter belief-like states) and/or pass judgments about x. But it was the burden of the previous section of this chapter to argue that the phenomenal character of visual experiences is not to be identified with the beliefs and/or judgments of the creature who is having the experience—let alone with the beliefs and/or judgments of some other creatures. The phenomenal character of one's visual experience does not depend on one's beliefs. It does not depend on the beliefs of anyone else either. Of course, on the view under discussion, the beliefs and judgments on which fame depends are not personal states, i.e. states of a person. Rather they are sub-personal states of a person's brain. Nonetheless, according to the view under discussion, being belief-like or judgment-like states, such sub-personal states have conceptual content. They do not have non-conceptual content. But the whole point of the distinction between the conceptual content of thought and the non-conceptual content of experience is precisely that the latter is independent of the former.

Another view that is closely related to Dennett's judgmentalist or conceptualist response to the mysteries of phenomenal realism is the so-called 'skill' theory of visual conscious experience, also called the 'enactive view', especially the version of this view based on the perceiver's 'knowledge of sensorimotor contingencies' advocated in a series of important papers by O'Regan and Noë (2001a, 2001b) and Noë (2002). The basic contention of the 'skill' theory of visual experience is that the content of a creature's visual experience is constituted by her implicit (or practical) knowledge (or mastery) of 'sensorimotor contingencies'. In most of the formulations of the view, there is an oscillation between two quite distinct theses. According to one thesis, the phenomenal character of a visual experience—what it is like to have the experience—is a matter of doing something or acting. For example, O'Regan and Noë (2001a: 960) write that 'experiences are not states. They are ways of acting. They are things we do'. Elsewhere (2001b), they write that visual experiences are not things 'that happen to our brains', they are things 'we do'. According to a distinct thesis, the phenomenal character of a visual experience is a matter of knowing something—having some implicit knowledge. These two theses are importantly different. Whereas the former thesis is reminiscent of a behavioristic approach to the content of visual experiences, the latter suggests a cognitive approach to the puzzle of visual experiences. We shall examine the first thesis first.

According to the first thesis, what matters to visual experiences are the sensorimotor contingencies themselves. This thesis raises at least three problems. First of all, it is one thing to recognize, as we did at the beginning of this chapter, that in one good sense of the term, 'perception' denotes a process. But it does not follow that human visual experiences are not states of the human visual system. Nor does it follow that visual experiences are not things that happen to a perceiver. After all, if perception is a process, it may result in, or give rise to, visual experiences. Also it is one thing to emphasize—following Gibson—that unless one's eyes can move in their orbits and unless one can move one's head, numerous visual experiences will simply not take place. It does not, however, follow that the ability to move one's eyes in one's orbit and the ability to move one's head are constitutive of the phenomenal character of one's visual experience.

Second, it is not always clear whether what matters to the first thesis are sensorimotor contingencies or correlations between environmental parameters that owe nothing to the perceiver's bodily movements. For example, O'Regan and Noë (2001a, 2001b) stress the importance of being able to move around an object in their account of the content of the visual experience of an occluded object or of an object only parts of which are visible. Indeed, we do visually experience an occluded object as having parts that we do not currently see. However, Myin and O'Regan (2001) write that 'red objects have their characteristic way of behaving-under-motion with respect to light sources, and importantly, changes in light sources'. Clearly, the covariation between changes in the redness of red objects and changes in light sources is not a sensorimotor contingency.

Third, we know from the neuropsychological study of brain-lesion human patients that optic ataxia results from a brain lesion in the superior parietal lobe. In optic ataxic patients, the visuomotor transformation is impaired, but the patients are still able to recognize, perceive and visually experience the shape, size and orientation of objects. Conversely, apperceptive agnosic patients with a lesion in the inferotemporal cortex are deprived of the visual experience of the shapes of objects. But they can still efficiently perform visually guided actions on objects (see Chapter 3). Thus, it does not seem as if the sensorimotor ability to reach and grasp manually an object is constitutive of the content of a visual experience. From our perspective, the first thesis is a version of Clark's (2001) EBC assumption, which is, as we already said, inconsistent with the dual approach to human vision that we endorse.

Unlike the first thesis, the second thesis does not link the content of one's visual experience directly to one's bodily movements but rather to one's *knowledge* of sensorimotor contingencies, where the knowledge in question is not supposed to be propositional knowledge but practical knowledge, i.e. a skill. Again, this thesis raises at least three problems. First of all, one's knowledge of sensorimotor contingencies seems better suited as an account of the conceptual contents of one's visually based-thoughts (or of the possession of one's visually based observational concepts), than as an account of the non-conceptual content of visual experience. At least, prima facie, the appeal to one's knowledge of sensorimotor contingencies does not seem to be compatible with our distinction between the non-conceptual content of visual experience and the conceptual content of thoughts.

Second, if all visual experiences were constituted by one's knowledge of sensori-motor contingencies, how to explain the fact that one may be surprised by the content of one's visual experience? Presumably, if the phenomenal character of one's experience were determined by one's implicit knowledge of the sensorimotor contingencies between one's movements and properties of objects in one's environment, how could the content of one's visual experience ever be unexpected?

Third, consider one's normal visual experience of an illusory display. As we made clear in Chapter 4, the content of one's visual experience may be dissociated from both one's knowledge and from one's visuomotor response. A subject may experience as unequal two Titchener circles of equal diameters, one surrounded by an annulus of circles larger than it and the other surrounded by circles smaller than it. She may experience the two circles as unequal, even though she knows that they are equal. Furthermore, measure of the grip between thumb and index finger reveals that her visuomotor representation is less subject to the illusion than her visual experience. Arguably, a subject's explicit knowledge that the two circles are equal is not what the skill theorist of conscious experience calls her implicit knowledge of sensorimotor contingencies. However, it is certainly tempting to identify the subject's implicit knowledge of sensorimotor contingencies with her capacity for forming a visuomotor representation of the target of prehension. But according to our interpretation of the psychophysical evidence, the dissociations between perceptual and visuomotor responses precisely call into question the very idea that the content of one's visual experience should be identified with one's implicit knowledge of sensorimotor contingencies. If one's capacity for reaching and grasping does not appropriately capture one's implicit knowledge of sensorimotor contingencies in the case of the Titchener illusion, which sensorimotor capacities will do the job?

Our disagreement with both Dennett's judgmental approach and the 'skill theory' approach to the phenomenology of visual experience does not mean that we embrace Block's phenomenal realism or Peacocke's distinction between the representational and the sensational properties of visual experience. As we tried to make clear in Chapter 1, we do subscribe to a representational view of the mind. But, as we argued in Chapter 1, the version of visual intentionalism that we endorse does not commit us to a sense-data theory. Accordingly, we assume that the phenomenal character of visual experiences derives from the representational powers of the visual system. What we take to be crucial to the phenomenal character of visual percepts is, first of all, that it is the function of the visual system to respond to the visible properties of objects. As we pointed out at the beginning of this chapter, we can see the shape, orientation, color, texture, motion, distance of objects. Some other properties of objects, we can hear, smell or touch, but we cannot see. Arguably, some properties we may both see and touch (e.g. shape). But seeing and touching an object's shape will be very different phenomenal experiences because one can touch an object's shape—if at all—without touching its color, but (if one's visual system is working properly), one cannot see an object's shape unless one sees its color. Arguably, one can feel the triangularity of a red triangle without feeling its redness. But one cannot see a red triangle unless one sees a triangle and one sees a red object. Hence, in a visual percept, an object's visual attributes are bound in a unique fashion. Thus, visual perception yields distinctive modes of perception of an object's properties (e.g. its shape or size).

7.3 Visual experience and binding

As evidence from Chapter 3 has shown, in the visual experience of brain-lesion patients, some of these attributes can be 'unbound': an agnosic patient, such as DF, e.g. is likely to lack the visual experience of the spherical shape of a blue moving ball. An achromatopsic patient will not perceive its color. Nor will an akinetopsic patient visually experience its motion. Blindsight patients are deprived of visual experience altogether. This is what Zeki (1993: 309) calls 'the disintegration of cerebral integration'. The view that the binding of an object's visual attributes is a fundamental source of the phenomenology of visual experience is, of course, compatible with the anti-judgmentalist view that perceiving is not believing or that non-epistemic vision should not be confused with epistemic vision. A creature's visual experience depends, not only on her motor resources and conceptual resources, but foremost on the functioning of the diverse areas of her visual cortex whose proper function is to process various properties of an object.

As we said above, one could not perceive an object in a visual scene unless the scene was parsed and segregated into constituent units. When we perceive an object—however complex—we subjectively group together several of its attributes. For example, we group its local shapes into contours, which are parts of one unit. Furthermore, we experience the color, the contours, the texture, the orientation, the surfaces and the motion (if any) of an object as properties jointly exemplified by the perceived object. 'Binding' is the name of this process whereby the different visual properties of an object are experienced as instantiated together in a visual percept. Now, in the cognitive science of visual perception, there are two closely related uses of the concept of binding.

Cognitive psychologists working on the role of attention in visual perception (e.g. Treisman and Gelade 1980) have hypothezised that the visual system starts by processing elementary 'separable' visual features (such as colors, simple shapes, textures and orientations of objects). According to Treisman's (1993: 5) 'feature-integration' theory:

[...] simple features are registered in parallel across the visual field, in a number of specialized subsystems. Information from the resulting feature maps is localized and recombined to specify objects through the use of focused attention, scanning serially through a master map of locations and giving access to the features currently occupying the attended location.

Thus, on this view, early preattentive visual processes consist in the detection of simple separable features (which are particular values of dimensions of visual targets such as color, orientation, texture, brightness). One criterion for individuating such separable features is that, in Treisman's (1993) terminology, they 'pop out' of their surroundings. So a red bar may pop out of a surrounding background of green bars. A horizontal bar may pop out of a surrounding background of vertical bars, and so on. At the preattentive level, separable features are registered in parallel across the visual field and information about them is coded within feature maps. Roughly speaking, by this view, focal attention works serially to conjoin or combine the information about separable features into unitary objects providing for what Treisman (1993) calls a 'master map' of the locations of objects possessing the combined features. In other words, by this view, visual attention binds or provides the 'glue' that combines the features of one and the same object together.

Much of the empirical support for the 'feature-integration' theory of attention comes from the difference in reaction time between the visual search of, respectively, 1D targets among a set of distractors and conjunctive targets among a set of distractors. A pink target will pop out among brown and green distractors. So will an 'O' among 'N' and 'T' distractors. The visual search of such separable targets, which proceeds in parallel, is to be contrasted with the visual search for conjunctive targets such as a pink 'O' among a set of green 'O' and pink 'T' distractors, which requires attention and proceeds serially. Empirical support for the 'feature-integration' theory also comes from the study of illusory conjunctions of features. For example, Treisman (1993) reports that subjects have been exposed to an array with two black digits on the extreme left and the extreme right and three colored letters in between: a green X, a blue O and a red T. Subjects are required to distribute their attention over the whole array so as to be able to identify the digits. When asked to report the colors of the letters, they assigned the wrong color to the wrong letter, e.g. they reported seeing a red X and a green O.

A slightly different use of the concept of binding is illustrated by the following quote from Crick (1994: 208):

It seems probable that, at any moment, any particular object in the visual field is represented by the firing of a *set* of neurons. Because any object will have different characteristics (form, color, motion, etc.) that are processed in several different visual areas, it is reasonable to assume that seeing one object involves neurons in many different visual areas. The problem of how these neurons temporarily become active as a unit is often described as 'the binding problem' [...]. Our experience of perceptual unity thus suggests that the brain in some way binds together, in a mutually coherent way, all those neurons actively responding to different aspects of a perceived object.

Here, binding the different attributes of a single object is presented as a requirement for experiencing a unified visual percept of that object. Different areas of the visual system specialize for the processing of different attributes of a single object. The brain must put together these activities by some process of binding, so that the color of a given object be associated with the right shape.

In fact, there are several distinct levels at which the binding process must operate for the unified percept to emerge. First, at the macro-level, the problem is to bind together different visual attributes, which are processed in different brain areas. Color and shape, e.g. are known to be processed in different areas of the visual cortex: color is predominantly processed in area V4, whereas contour, length and orientation, which are cues for object shapes, are assembled in areas V1 and V2. In so far as these areas are both coded in retinotopic space, however, they should automatically refer the object attributes they respectively process to the same retinal locus. Attributes that arise from the same locus in space should belong to the same object, provided that they are processed at the same time (or at least within a short temporal window). When one of these areas is affected by a lesion, the patient will miss perceiving the corresponding object attribute: in the case of a lesion in, e.g. the color area, color will not be perceived. This reasoning implies that coordinate transformations, e.g. transferring the representation of the location of a visual stimulus from retinotopic to egocentric space, should occur at a level of processing where the percept is being formed. It is only under this condition that the object attributes that are to be used in object-oriented actions (such as size and orientation), can be matched with attributes of the same object that matter to a different (e.g. perceptual) task, such as color. If this condition were not satisfied, then an object's color could be perceived as being instantiated at one place and its shape at another place. Instances of such dissociations may be found in pathological conditions due to brain lesions (e.g. simultagnosia, see Chapter 3).

At a more fine-grained or more micro-level, the problem is to bind together parts that belong to the same object. Houses have windows and chimneys. Cars have wheels and windows. Faces have eyes, a mouth and a nose. How can these parts, which impinge upon distinct retinal areas, be linked together in a single percept? Tanaka *et al.* (1991) suggest that the analysis of visual stimuli effected by single inferotemporal neurons is not complex enough to specify a complex biological object on the basis of a single-cell discharge (see Chapter 2). Incidentally, this claim stands in contradiction with the alleged existence of so-called 'grandmother cells' whose single activity were supposed to specify a full object. Thus, Tanaka *et al.*'s (1991) work suggests that the activities of a whole group of cells specified for different critical features are required in order to code a particular complex biological object. Cells with overlapping but slightly different selectivities tend to cluster in modules of roughly 500 μm by 500 μm on average. Complex stimuli can thus be detected via the coordinated activities of several cells with overlapping retinotopic projection and organized in such modules. The contribution of several modules may be necessary for forming the whole image of a single object. Because, however, TE receptive fields are too large to discriminate different objects according to their retinal projections, the problem arises of disentangling the activities of several modules involved in the perception respectively of a single object and of different objects.

One solution to this problem could be that activities of different and sometimes distant modules relating to a single object would in some way be temporally synchronized with one another, as emphasized by Engel *et al.* (1992) and Singer *et al.* (1997). By contrast, activities arising from different objects would remain asynchronous (Tanaka 1993). The cue for synchronization could be constituted by the fact that the parts of the same object move together when the eyes make microsaccades or drift during visual fixation. Thus, agnosic patients may see object parts without relating them to a single object (see Chapter 3). If so, then they will fail to recognize it. It has been suggested that the temporal synchronization of firing patterns of neurons with distinct feature-detection properties but with overlapping receptive fields, might constitute a signal for binding different properties together. Furthermore, several writers (e.g. Milner and Goodale 1995: 200) emphasize the unique role of processing in the ventral stream for conscious visual experience. Although we do not accept the claim that processing in the dorsal stream plays no role in conscious visual experience, it is worth emphasizing, as Block (2001: 202) recognizes, that such a claim on the neural basis of visual consciousness is not consistent with the assumption that phenomenality is a single property that can be exemplified by experiences in different modalities, let alone by conceptual thoughts.[18]

Finally, there are reasons to believe that the temporal synchronization of the activities of cells firing in response to the same retinal locus could be best achieved by what is called 'retropropagation' of information from higher level brain areas onto lower level areas, not purely sequential bottom up processing of information from lower to

---

[18]See the end of the Epilogue for why we cannot accept the claim that only processing in the ventral stream can support visual conscious experience.

higher levels. Lower level areas processing information from the same object converge on higher level areas, whose output is 'retroprojected' back onto lower level areas.

Thus, in this section, we have tried to examine some of the third-personal neuroscientific and psychological attempts at explaining the facts of first-personal human visual subjective experience. The neuroscientific and psychological project starts with the observation that the basic phenomenon of human visual phenomenal experience is that in a visual percept, different elementary visual attributes are referred to a single object or that different visual attributes are experienced as co-exemplified by a single object. Some psychologists credit visual attention with the power to combine these separable features into a complex percept. Neuroscientists have discovered that different brain areas are responsible for the processing of different elementary visual attributes. They hypothesize that the binding of the different elementary attributes of a single object is achieved by a temporal synchronization of the firing of neurons in the different relevant brain areas. Whether the hypothetical mechanism of temporal synchronization of the activities of neurons located in separate brain areas leaves some 'explanatory gap' unfilled is an open question.

In the name of phenomenal realism, Nagel (1974), Levine (1993), Block (1995) or Chalmers (1996) have claimed that the physicalist assumption that human phenomenal conscious experience is physical, though possibly true, is unintelligible. In our view, this intriguing and paradoxical assessment is not really justified by the scientific situation. If true, the claim that human visual consciousness is a matter of binding, which in turn is achieved by the synchronized activity of cells in the visual cortex, raises new scientific problems of their own. But it is not in and of itself a baffling metaphysical mystery. Clearly, if binding by the synchronized activity of distant cells in the visual cortex turns out to play the same role in unconscious visual processing as in conscious visual experience, then the hypothesis will be refuted. What is, on our view, a source of baffling metaphysical mystery, is the claim that human phenomenal experience has a single character, whether it arises from vision, audition, olfaction, touch or conceptual thought. Because they have meta-representational abilities, humans can introspectively reflect about any of their first-order mental states. The supposition that phenomenality is a single property shared by so many different mental states might be an illusion nourished by introspection.

6 Visuomotor representations

1 Introduction

In the present chapter, we consider both conceptual reasons and empirical evidence in favor of the dualistic model of the human visual system applied to the vision of objects. In Chapter 5, we examined in some detail the contribution made by visual perception and visual phenomenal experience to human knowledge. Indeed, we argued that something as eminently subjective as a human visual perceptual experience can be a source of objective knowledge of the world, on the assumption that the human visual system is reliable. In the present chapter, we shall examine the contribution of the visual system to a restricted class of human actions, i.e. reaching, grasping and manipulating objects in one's vicinity. Our argument will be that one and the same visual stimulus can undergo perceptual processing or motor processing. In this chapter, we shall try to characterize the major differences between these two kinds of processing of visual inputs, which Jeannerod (1994, 1997) calls, respectively, 'semantic' and 'pragmatic' processing. In Chapter 5, we argued that, unlike thoughts, visual percepts are informationally encapsulated. In the present chapter, we shall examine the respects in which the output of the motor processing of visual stimuli is 'motorically' encapsulated, in a way in which visual percepts are not. Visual percepts, we argued in Chapters 1 and 5, are informationally encapsulated in a way thoughts are not; but visuomotor representations have a distinctive motor encapsulation.

In this chapter, we make the bold claim that a new kind of non-conceptual content has been discovered by the cognitive neuroscientific study of the visual system, i.e. visuomotor content. As we discussed in Chapter 1, most of the arguments from philosophers of mind in favor of the distinction between the conceptual content of thoughts and the non-conceptual content of perceptual representations depend on the phenomenology of perceptual experiences—particularly, visual perceptual experiences. In essence, these arguments have relied on the fact that the conceptual content of thought is no match for the informational richness and the fine-grainedness of the content of perceptual representations. The latter outruns the former. Thus, in the present chapter, we make our own contribution to the distinction between conceptual and non-conceptual content by drawing a further distinction within the category of non-conceptual content: the distinction between perceptual and visuomotor content. Since visuomotor content is informationally poorer, not richer, than perceptual content, it follows that the argument for the bifurcation between perceptual non-conceptual content and visuomotor non-conceptual content is quite different from the argument for the distinction between conceptual content and perceptual non-conceptual content. The arguments for the distinction between visuomotor non-conceptual content and perceptual non-conceptual content do *not* appeal to a distinctive kind of visual phenomenology since, unlike perceptual content, visuomotor content generally does not reach subject's conscious awareness. They do not, for principled reasons: the postulation of visual representations with non-conceptual visuomotor content is forced on us by empirical results from both the detailed neuropsychological examination of brain-lesioned human patients and from psychophysical experiments in normal human subjects, which reveal visuomotor processing of visual information without much phenomenology (if any). The relevant brain-lesioned human patients are deep apperceptive visual-form agnosics whose visuomotor capacities are surprisingly well-preserved. However, they lack visual phenomenological awareness of many visual attributes of objects that normal subjects experience. The psychophysical results provide in turn numerous instances of dissociations in normal human subjects between accurate visuomotor responses and full phenomenological awareness of the visual stimulus. As it will turn out in Section 5 of the present chapter, the main argument for postulating representations with a pure visuomotor content will rely on the fact that very often subjects' visuomotor responses turn out to be responses to what we shall call 'non-local' properties of the stimulus. Succinctly put, the argument for the existence of visuomotor representations has the form of a dilemma: either visuomotor responses are mere reflexive responses to stimuli or they are genuine actions. Only if the latter is true are visuomotor responses caused by genuine representations. We argue that they are actions. Thus, our argument for the distinction between the visuomotor and the perceptual content of visual representations will appeal to the role of visuomotor representations in the explanation of behavior, not to the phenomenology of subjective visual experience.

No doubt, the dualistic model of the human visual system faces a major challenge. Any purported distinction between perceptual and motor processing of visual stimuli is far beyond the boundaries of human introspective awareness. First of all, normally sighted human beings keep switching back and forth between the motor processing and the perceptual processing of visual inputs. In real life, there is no discontinuity between actions performed on visual targets and the enjoyment of the phenomenal experience of the perceptual processing of their color, orientation, texture, shape and internal structure. Second, most actions directed towards visual targets of prehension performed by normally sighted human beings depend upon the collaboration between both kinds of processing. Rarely if ever outside the psychophysical lab, do normally sighted human beings grasp or point to simple geometrical targets. One does not grasp in the same way a book, a glass, a cup, a hammer, a bottle, a cork-opener, a knife, a fork, a screw-driver, a tennis ball or a pen. In forming the appropriate finger-grip in each of these cases, one relies not only on one's visual perception of the relations among the relevant parts of the object, but also on one's stored knowledge of the function of the different artifacts.

In this respect, it is important to emphasize the fact that in this chapter, we concentrate on the contrast between perceptual processing and visuomotor processing of one and the same visual stimulus. Such a low-level 'pragmatic' processing, as Jeannerod (1994; 1997) calls it, gives rise to elementary visuomotor representations of the visual targets of such hand actions directed upon objects as grasping a disk, a cup or a glass. In Chapter 7, we shall ascend to a higher level of pragmatic processing of visual objects, which allows a normal human being, not only to reach for and/or grasp an object but, to perform skilled actions such as the manipulation and use of complex tools. We shall argue that this higher level pragmatic processing of artifacts may include the retrieval of a stored script for the manipulation of tools. In our view, this higher level pragmatic processing of tools stands to the lower level pragmatic processing of visual targets of action, as epistemic visual perception stands to non-epistemic visual perception. And as we shall see in Chapter 7, the lower level and the higher level pragmatic processings of objects can be selectively damaged by parietal brain lesions.

Only careful experimental investigation based upon strenuous idealizations can provide evidence for the dissociation between pure low-level motor processing and pure perceptual processing of visual stimuli. Not surprisingly, in this chapter we assemble selective empirical evidence drawn from Part II. Thus, in Section 2, we extract from Chapter 2 the contrast between the perceptual responses and the visuomotor responses of neurons found, respectively, in the inferotemporal cortex and in the posterior parietal cortex of macaque monkeys. We argue that this contrast is corroborated by psychophysical evidence extracted from Chapter 4. Sections 3–5 of the present chapter play a pivotal role in our argument. In Section 3, we review the visual capacities of what we take to be a pure case of low-level motor processing of visual inputs: namely, the visuomotor responses of the apperceptive visual-form agnosic patient, DF, first examined by Milner and collaborators. In Section 4, we discuss what seem to us to be two pure cases of elementary perceptual processing of visual inputs: we consider the individuation of visual proto-objects by 10-month-old human infants using locational information alone and we consider the ability of human adults to track several distinct proto-objects simultaneously. On the basis of the contrast between DF's visuomotor capacities and the elementary perceptual processing that goes on both in human babies and in a task of multiple object-tracking, we argue in Section 5 that visuomotor representations have a distinctive kind of informational encapsulation, not exemplified by perceptual representations. In Section 6, we face a new challenge: we ask the question whether the output of the motor processing of visual stimuli deserves to be called 'representation' at all. Not surprisingly, our response to this question is that, indeed it does. Our argument here turns on a re-analysis of some of the psychophysical experiments on the Titchener circles' illusions and the asymmetry between motor responses and perceptual responses discussed in Chapter 4.

Finally, in Section 7, we take a different perspective altogether and examine the functional role of visuomotor representations within the human cognitive architecture. Here we pick up the thread of Chapter 1 (Section 5). First we argue that, by virtue of their motoric encapsulation, visuomotor representations are appropriate inputs to motor intentions. Here, we draw an important contrast between the function of visual percepts and the function of visuomotor representations. The function of the former is to provide input for further conceptual processing, whose output will ultimately be stored in what we call the 'belief box'. The function of the latter is to provide visual information to motor intentions, which control and monitor one's actions directed towards objects. It is important to our argument that motor intentions have non-conceptual content and that they have a peculiar commitment to action, which they derive from their world-to-mind direction of fit and from their mind-to-world direction of causation. Second, we argue that, unlike visual percepts, visuomotor representations are best categorized by causally indexical concepts, which, unlike other indexical concepts, have a crucial action-guiding role.

2 Seeing affordances

In our view, one major impetus for the proper appreciation of the distinction between motor processing and perceptual processing of one and the same visual stimulus came from Gibson's (1979) ecological approach to vision. Gibson himself took his ecological framework to contribute, not merely to the understanding of visually guided actions but, to the puzzles of visual perception as well. We think it is best interpreted more narrowly as a major contribution to the study of visually guided actions. Gibson's ecological approach relies on three major views, the first of which is that vision is seeing *affordances*. Gibson's second insight is his emphasis on the role of active exploration in visual processing. Gibson's third thesis is that affordances can be directly picked up in the optic array. In our view, Gibson's first two ecological insights are important contributions to our current understanding of the motor processing of visual stimuli. As it will turn out, we do not accept Gibson's third thesis that affordances can be directly picked up. Nor do we think that it follows from his two other insights, as we shall presently explain.

According to Gibson (1979), objects and surfaces in a creature's environment afford different visual possibilities for action. Different objects or surfaces offer different visual opportunities to one and the same organism. One and the same object or surface may offer different visual opportunities to differently built organisms. Affordances are both dispositional and relational properties. As Gibson (1979: 127) puts it, 'the affordances of the environment are what it offers the animal, what it provides or furnishes, either for good or for ill'. In his view (1979: 134), it would be a mistake to assume that 'objects are composed of their qualities [...] what we perceive when we look at objects are their affordances, not their qualities'.

To take one of Gibson's (1979) favorite examples, a rigid horizontal surface differs from a non-rigid surface (such as the surface of a lake). Unlike the latter, the former affords support to a variety of animals: it affords different possible bodily postures to mammals, reptiles, birds and insects. It affords different possibilities for locomotion such as walking, running, galloping, crawling or landing. Water surface, by contrast, affords support and locomotion to water bugs and to such birds as ducks and swans. If and when the visual detection of an affordance matches an agent's motor intention, then no concept of either the action or of its goal seems required for the agent to perform the afforded action. Seeing an affordance in Gibson's sense results from the fast visuomotor processing of the target of an action. The agent, it seems, needs no conceptual representation of the goal of its action. Nor does it need a perceptual representation of the target of its action. In many human actions directed towards objects in one's vicinity and executed with the movements of one's arm and hand, the visual processing of the target consists in seeing an affordance. Providing one's motor intention with the visual information appropriate for reaching and grasping a glass is a very different visual task from, for example, perceiving the glass as being to the left of the bottle. Similarly, providing one's motor intention with the visual information for picking up a coin lying on a table is a very different visual task from counting a set of coins lying on a table. As we are about to argue, however, it does not follow that seeing an affordance requires no visual representation at all of the target of one's action.

For the purpose of reaching and grasping a glass, what the agent needs to represent is the position of the glass relative to the axis of her body. Hence, in a visuomotor task, the visual system must code the position of the glass in an egocentric frame of reference. Seeing the glass as a target of one's action of grasping is seeing an affordance. As Norman (2001) puts it on behalf of Gibson, 'to be graspable, an object must have opposite surfaces separated by a distance less than the span of the hand. A five-inch cube can be grasped, but a ten-inch cube cannot. A large object needs a "handle" to afford grasping. Note that the size of an object that constitutes a graspable size is specified in the optic array'.[1]

By contrast, in order to deliver a perceptual representation of the glass to the left of the bottle, the visual system must code the position of the glass relative to the position of the bottle in an allocentric frame of reference. Hence, the position of one and the same object can be visually coded in two radically different representational formats and/or frames of reference. Visually perceiving a glass to the left of the bottle is not *ipso facto* seeing an affordance. Conversely, seeing a glass as an affordance is not *ipso facto* forming a visual percept of a glass. Similarly, when the visual perceptual system selects a red apple in preparation for grasping it, it first forms a percept in which the various attributes of the apple (its color, texture, size, orientation) are part of a representation of its location within a allocentric frame of reference. In such a visual percept, the position of the red apple is represented relative to other fruits in the basket. Once the perceptual selection by the semantic processing is achieved, the low-level pragmatic system takes overt and yields a visuomotor representation of relevant visual attributes of the target of prehension in which its location is coded within an egocentric frame of reference.

It is an important contention of Gibson that affordances can be picked up directly. As he (1979: 143) puts it, 'the basic affordances of the environment are perceivable and usually perceivable directly, without an excessive amount of learning'. In his (1979: 160) view, certain invariant ratios, such as size constancy, are directly perceived in the ambient array: they are 'not cues but information for direct size perception'. What Gibson objects to is the 'old (constructivist) view' that the visual perception of size is the conclusion of an inference starting from premises about retinal information.[2]

Although Gibson's notion of an affordance and his insistence on the role of action for vision are important insights, nonetheless we do not accept his third view according to which affordances can be directly picked up. According to Gibson (1979), visual perception consists of the manipulation of information contained in the optic array, which in turn is an objective commodity present in an agent's environment. It contains, and makes available to the agent, all the visual information about the environment necessary for the agent's survival. According to Gibson, the agent's task is merely to extract the information from the optic array and it requires no computation. Nor does it require the construction of mental representations. We disagree for two reasons.

First of all, Gibson remained unaware of the rationale for a dualistic model of the human visual system, so he misconstrued his own contribution to the study of motor processing of visual information as an account of visual perception. Not all of vision, however, consists in seeing affordances.[3]

---

[1] For corroborating psychophysical remarks made for the purpose of defending the dualistic model, in the context of experiments on illusory stimuli, see Section 8, Chapter 4. For a critical assessment of the last sentence of Norman's (2001) quote, see the end of Section 7 of the present chapter.

[2] For a penetrating criticism of Gibson's view that visual information can be directly picked up, from the standpoint of cognitive perceptual psychology, see Fodor and Pylyshyn (1981).

[3] See Chapter 5.

The motor processing of visual targets is seeing affordances, but much visual perception is not. Furthermore, much visuomotor processing, as Gibson (1979) emphasized, involves the agent's movements: it involves eye-movements, head-movements and locomotion. However, as noticed by Spelke *et al.* (1995a), both an agent's movements and the motions of surrounding objects may also interfere with the goal of visual perception, namely object-identification. In a task of identification and/or recognition, a perceiver may lack direct information about some object partly occluded, either by her own movements or by the motion of some neighboring object, and she may have to make a decision, in a state of incomplete perceptual information, based on working memory.[4] Arguably, some of the very movements that might serve the purpose of a visually guided actions might interfere with the task of perceptual identification of an object.

Second, Gibson failed to recognize the computational complexity of the task faced by the motor processing of the human visual system—even when the task is a low-level visuomotor one. When an agent is involved in a visually guided task—such as grasping a glass—the visual system must represent the location of the object to be grasped in an egocentric frame of reference centered on the axis of the agent's body. Visual stimuli, however, first hit the retina so that the location of an object is first coded by the visual system in retinocentric coordinates. As argued at length in Chapter 2, a moving agent will not reach an object unless it combines the retinocentric representation of the location of the object with signals carrying information about the position of the eye in its orbit and the position of the head relative to the rest of the body, in order to instruct the arm and hand to move towards a location coded in egocentric coordinates.

3 Evidence for dual visual processing in primates

3.1 Electrophysiological evidence for dual visual processing

Not only is Gibson's concept of an affordance an important ancestor to what we presently call a visuomotor representation of the target of an action, but so is his view that seeing is an action. Gibson's emphasis on the role of the agent's own movement and action in seeing affordances has been, or so we shall presently argue, corroborated by electrophysiological studies of cells in the visual system of macaque monkeys. Starting with the pioneering work of Mountcastle and colleagues (1975), it has been found that, unlike cells in the inferotemporal cortex, the responses of neurons in the posterior parietal cortex covary to a great extent with many aspects of the animal's visual behavior. The activity of cells in the posterior parietal cortex is involved in visual fixation, in the monitoring of saccadic eye movements, in guiding reaching towards, and the manipulation of, objects. As the recording of individual neurons in the posterior parietal cortex of anesthetized animals reveals, little or no coherent activity will show up unless the animal can move its eyes, its head and its hands relative to visual stimuli.[5]

By contrast, cells in the temporal cortex of anesthetized animals keep responding to retinal inputs. We take the contrast between the responses of posterior parietal cells and

---

[4]See Chapter 5, section 2.2 for quotation of Spelke *et al.* (1995a).
[5]Even though neurons in the posterior parietal cortex of anesthetized animals receive visual inputs.

the responses of cells in the temporal cortex of anesthetized animals as evidence for both Gibson's view that the visual system detects affordances in his sense and for his insistence that the visual detection of affordances depends on the animal's movements.

One major electrophysiological piece of evidence relevant to the duality between motor processing and perceptual processing of visual stimuli comes from the observed differences in the responses of neurons found in the anterior intraparietal area (AIP) by Sakata *et al.* (1995) and in the inferotemporal cortex (TE) by Tanaka (1993) and Tanaka *et al.* (1991) (see Chapter 2 for review). The comparison between the visual stimuli, which elicit distinctive responses of AIP neurons and TE neurons, is especially important because they constitute a minimal pair: as it will turn out, from a chromatic point of view, both involve a mere contrast between black and white surfaces and both involve static geometric shapes. The difference is that Sakata *et al.* (1995) used 3D objects with clear-cut geometrical shapes. Tanaka *et al.* (1991) used more complex stimuli such as a picture of an animal's head. AIP neurons visually detect affordances: they respond to the motoric properties of 3D targets of prehension. By contrast, TE neurons are perceptual cells: they respond to the pictorial content conveyed by complex 2D geometric patterns, which do not afford any particular hand manipulation. As noticed in Chapter 2, some cells in the inferotemporal cortex of monkeys too have been found to be sensitive to 3D shapes; but if so, they were sensitive to the complex contours of 3D shapes, not to their motoric properties.

Sakata *et al.* (1995) used 3D objects with distinct clear-cut geometrical properties, such as a plate, a ring, a cube, a cylinder, a cone and a sphere. The objects were all white in color and they were displayed against a black background. The experimenters compared four different tasks: a 'hand-manipulation task', an 'object-fixation task', a 'delayed hand-manipulation task' and a 'light-interrupted object-fixation task'. On the basis of these four distinct experimental conditions, AIP neurons were divided into three groups: the visual dominant, the motor dominant and the visual-and-motor dominant neurons. The visual dominant neurons fired in the 'hand-manipulation task', i.e. when the animal manipulated the object in the light, not in the dark. The motor dominant neurons fired both when the animal manipulated the object either in the light or in the dark. The visual-and-dominant neurons were more active when the animal manipulated the object in the light than in the dark. Then, according to whether or not they responded to the mere sight of a geometrically well-defined object, the visual dominant and the visual-and-motor neurons were further divided into object and non-object types (see Fig. 2.9). Hence, AIP neurons respond primarily to the geometric shapes relevant for grasping and manipulating visible objects.

Inferotemporal neurons, which are located in the ventral stream and which have a much larger receptive field than parietal neurons, have been studied by Tanaka *et al.* (1991). They recorded the responses of TE neurons to the presentation of black and white pictures of such complex biological stimuli as the head of a tiger seen from above. By a process of successive reduction of the complexity of the visual stimulus, Tanaka (1993) and Tanaka *et al.* (1991) found that an individual TE cell responds to the presentation of a white rectangle flanked by a pair of two symmetrical black rectangles partially overlapping with the white rectangle, which can be thought of as the schematic pictorial representation of the tiger's head from above. The individual TE neuron fails to respond to either the white rectangle alone or the pair of disjoint black rectangles (see Fig. 2.4).

TE cells have a columnar organization and, according to Tanaka (1993), the visual response to complex stimuli (such as the full image of a tiger's head from above) depends on the coordinated activity of cells in different columns. The selective responses of cells in different columns are bound together. One possible binding mechanism involved in such a coordination across different columns is the synchronization of the firings of the cells from different columns. As a result of this synchronization, the firing of cells from different columns has what Tanaka (1993) calls 'pictorial' content (see Chapter 5, Section 6). The pictorial content of visual representations produced in the inferotemporal cortex contrasts with the visuomotor content of representations produced in the posterior parietal cortex in the following way: the visual responses of the hand-manipulation task-related neurons in AIP are sensitive to the spatial characteristics of 3D objects relevant for hand manipulation, where these spatial properties are coded in a body-centered frame of reference. By contrast, at the most elementary level, individual TE neurons either respond to the display of bidimensional shapes or to the complex contours of 3D shapes, whose relevant spatial relationships must be coded in an allocentric frame of reference. Furthermore, they contribute to the pictorial depiction of more complex spatial relationships among shapes by synchronizing the pattern of their discharge with the pattern of firing of cells from neighboring columns.

3.2 Psychophysical evidence for dual visual processing

The contrast between the behavior of AIP neurons and TE neurons in the monkey is consistent with recent psychophysical results obtained in normal human subjects (many of which were reviewed at length in Chapter 4), which show that the visual processing yielding a subject's conscious visual awareness of an object differs from the motor processing allowing a subject to point her finger towards the target when the object is the target. For example, Bridgeman *et al.* (1979) and Goodale *et al.* (1986) found that subjects can point accurately to a target whose motion they do not notice because it coincides with a saccadic eye movement. Motor processing is faster than perceptual processing. Thus, Castiello *et al.* (1991) found that subjects are able to correct the trajectory of their hand movement directed towards a moving target some 300 ms before they become conscious of the target's change of location.

Pisella *et al.* (2000) and Rossetti and Pisella (2000) performed experiments involving a pointing task, which strongly corroborate the temporal asymmetry between visuomotor and perceptual processing of visual inputs. Normal subjects were presented with a green target towards which they were requested to point their index finger. Some subjects were instructed to stop their pointing movement towards the target when, and only when, it changed location by jumping either to the left or to the right. The authors found a significant percentage of fast unwilled correction movements. In an optic ataxic patient with a posterior parietal lesion (see Chapter 3, Section 4 for discussion), the automatic corrections for location were missing. The authors conclude that the fast corrections of hand movements in normal subjects are produced by what they call an 'automatic pilot' located in the posterior parietal cortex and involved in fast visuomotor processing of the location of a target coded in egocentric coordinates.

In a second experiment, normal subjects were presented with pairs of a green and a red target. They were instructed to point to the green target, but the color of the two targets could be interchanged unexpectedly at movement onset. Some subjects were requested to stop their movement in response to the color change. Unlike a change of target location, a change of color did not elicit fast unwilled corrective movements. The authors are inclined to conclude that, unlike the fast visuomotor processing of the location of a target in egocentric coordinates, the visual processing of the color of an object is performed by the ventral stream which is slower than the dorsal stream.

We take the electrophysiological and the psychophysical results as evidence for the dissociation in human and non-human primates between fast motor processing and slower perceptual processing. The visuomotor representation of a target, generated by the motor processing, consists in the visual detection of an affordance. Not all of the visual attributes of the object seem relevant to the motor processing of a target of an action. As we argued in Chapter 4, in a pointing task, the location of a target *must* be computed, while the computation of its color is optional. Experiments like Pisella *et al.*'s (2000) suggest that different visual attributes of an object can be selectively processed: the color and the location of a target, for example, can be processed along distinct channels with different temporal properties and coded in separate representations.

4   What is it like to see with a dorsal pathway?

In the present section, we shall argue that the residual 'pure' visuomotor capacities of an apperceptive visual-shape agnosic patient reveal the peculiar encapsulation of low-level visuomotor representations. On the basis of these elementary visuomotor capacities, we shall draw a systematic contrast between the visual output of motor processing and of perceptual processing. In fact, we shall draw a contrast between the visuomotor processing of the agnosic patient and the elementary perceptual capacities at work in 10-month-old human infants, and in the perceptual representations involved in multiple-tracking tasks in human adults.

The basic contrast found at the electrophysiological level between the responses of neurons located in the posterior parietal cortex and in the inferotemporal cortex of the macaque monkey brain has been refined and extended by the detailed neuropsychological study of two complementary visual disorders in human brain-lesioned patients, namely: visual-form apperceptive agnosia and optic ataxia (reviewed at length in Chapter 3). Much recent neuropsychological research has been devoted to the analytic comparison between these two remarkably complementary disorders in the human visual system. Whereas visual-form agnosics lack the perceptual ability visually to recognize and identify the shapes of objects, optic-ataxic patients have visuomotor disabilities. In this section, we shall concentrate on DF, a patient poisoned by carbon monoxide and examined by Goodale *et al.* (1991), who became an apperceptive visual-form agnosic with a major perceptual deficit in the ability to recognize the shape of visually presented objects. The impairment of apperceptive visual-form agnosics results from an interruption of the flow of visual information in the ventral pathway of the human visual system. As illustrated by AT, a patient examined by Jeannerod *et al.* (1994), optic ataxia consists of a visuomotor deficit in the ability to reach and grasp objects with the fingers of one's hand. It results from a lesion located in the dorsal pathway of the human visual system.

As we pointed out in Section 3.3.3 of Chapter 3, unlike patient SB, patient DF has good color perception and poor motion perception. Arguably, this is evidence that some of DF's residual visual abilities may be carried out by surviving parts of her ventral system. If so, then patient SB, who has excellent motion perception and poor color perception, better exemplifies than patient DF what it is like to see with a dorsal system alone. Nonetheless, the asymmetry between some of DF's deep perceptual deficit and her striking residual visuomotor abilities, which has been studied in depth, reveals one crucial feature of visuomotor representations.

First of all, when asked to locate a source of light without a delay, DF's performance was normal (cf. Milner *et al.* 1991; Milner and Goodale 1995). Conversely, AT's performance was very poor when tested on immediate pointing, but it improved dramatically when tested after a 5-s delay (cf. Milner *et al.* 1999). These results show that in a visual-form agnosic patient whose ventral pathway has been damaged, her intact dorsal pathway is better at faster than slower processing, whereas in an optic-ataxic patient whose dorsal pathway has been damaged, her intact ventral pathway is better at slower than faster processing. These results fit with the selective psychophysical results summarized earlier. As described in Chapter 2, whereas the dorsal stream receives mostly inputs from magnocellular fibers, the ventral stream receives inputs from both magnocellular and parvocellular fibers. The former is designed for simpler and cruder visuomotor processing. The latter is designed for perceiving more complex attributes of objects.

Second, like other apperceptive agnosics, DF can draw good copies of objects from memory, but her deep perceptual deficit prevents her from drawing copies of visually presented objects. In spite of her deep perceptual deficit in the visual recognition and identification of the shapes of objects, DF has kept remarkable visuomotor abilities (e.g. Goodale 1995; Milner and Goodale 1995). Although she cannot recognize the shape of a visually presented object, nonetheless she can reach an object and shape accurately her finger-grip in order to grasp it efficiently. Presumably, although she cannot recognize the shape and size of a particular object, she can perceive the presence of some object or other against a background, so that when instructed, she can reach and grasp it. When, however, a 2-s delay is introduced between the presentation of the object and the onset of reaching, DF fails to calibrate a grip scale to the size of the object (see Milner and Goodale 1995: 136–7).

This striking dissociation between her poor perceptual visual abilities and her accurate visuomotor abilities was tested on a variety of tasks. She was shown a slot in which to insert a card. The slot could have many different orientations around the clock. When asked to match the orientation of the slot by merely rotating a hand-held card without inserting the card in the slot, she failed. However, when asked to introduce the card into the slot in any number of orientations, her performance was virtually normal (Fig. 6.1). When shown a pair of objects selected from twelve objects of different shapes for same/different judgment, she failed. When asked to grasp them using a 'precision grip' between thumb and index finger, she succeeded. And the analysis of the grasp points she selected on the objects to ensure the stability of her grasp are remarkably similar to those selected by neurologically intact subjects. When presented with a pair of

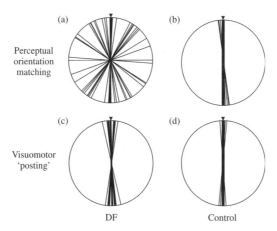

Fig. 6.1 Poor perceptual abilities and accurate visuomotor abilities in apperceptive agnosic patient DF. (a)–(b) Matching hand orientation to the orientation of a slot over successive trials: (a) patient DF's performance; (b) performance of control subjects. (c)–(d) Posting the hand through the slot. Note almost equivalent performance for (c) patient DF and (d) normal control subjects. (From Goodale 1995, in D. Osherson (ed.) *An invitation to cognitive science, Vol. 2, Visual cognition*, published by MIT Press, with permission.)

rectangular blocks that could either be of the same or of different dimensions, and asked whether they were the same or different, she failed. When she was asked to reach out and pick up a block, the measure of her grip aperture between thumb and index finger revealed that her grip was calibrated to the physical size of the object, like that of normal subjects (Fig. 3.5).

Conversely, optic-ataxic patients show the reversed pattern of dissociation. While they can recognize and identify the shape of visually presented objects, they have very serious visuomotor deficits: either their reach is misdirected or their finger-grip is improperly adjusted to the size and shape of the target of their movement. Optic-ataxic patient AT, for example, is able to provide a manual estimate of the size of an object by matching it to the distance between her thumb and index finger, but she is unable to grasp the very same object by scaling her grip between her thumb and index finger to the size of the object (Jeannerod et al. 1994). Notice that the same effector is being used in both the perceptual-matching task and the visuomotor task, namely scaling the distance between thumb and index finger to the size of an object. Thus, close examination of both visual-form agnosics and optic-ataxic patients has revealed two remarkable double dissociations (see Jeannerod 1997 for review).

The fundamental questions raised for us by the neuropsychological discovery of such double dissociations are: What is the structure and content of visuomotor representations? What is it like—if anything—to have the ability to submit visual stimuli to motor processing alone? What is it like to see with an intact dorsal pathway and a damaged ventral pathway? Which visual attributes of objects can be processed by the dorsal pathway alone? Which visual attributes of an object can be coded in a visuomotor representation of the target of an object? Unless DF was capable of visually computing the location of an object in egocentric coordinates, she could not reach it. Unless she could visually process the orientation of a visual stimulus, she could not successfully insert a card into an oriented slot. As described by Goodale (1995) and Milner and Goodale (1995), however, DF's ability to visually process orientations has two limits: she is limited in the complexity of the oriented stimulus and she can only process orientation defined by luminance cues. This is the sense in which in DF, the pragmatic processing of objects is a low-level one.

When asked to insert a T-shaped object (as opposed to a rectangular card) into a T-shaped aperture (as opposed to a simple slot), she had trouble combining the orientation of the stem and the orientation of the top. As Goodale (1995: 197) noticed:[6]

[...] in fact the transformations underlying the rotation of the wrist appear to be sensitive to only one axis of the goal object at a time. From an evolutionary perspective, this makes good sense. Rotating the wrist so that the extended hand can fit into an aperture or grab a branch quickly would have been a common event in the lives of our primate ancestors and, therefore, might be expected to utilize relatively hard-wired, dedicated systems (presumably located in the dorsal stream) that can compute a single optimal orientation quickly and with some precision. Such a dedicated system would be of little use when an observer is required to rotate the hand to match the axes of a complex hand-held object with those of an equivalent pattern. In that sense, it might make more sense to coopt more flexible perceptual systems (perhaps in the ventral stream) that have evolved to analyze such objects for other reasons.

As noted by Milner and Goodale (1995: 139), in perceptual tasks, the contours or boundaries of an object can be extracted from several different visual cues. They can be defined by differences in brightness, in texture, by shades or by complex Gestalt principles of grouping and organization of similarity and good form. Similarity itself may depend upon the intensity, color, size, shape and orientation of constituents of a visual array. Milner and Goodale (1995: 139–40) report that DF's visuomotor responses to an oriented slot were disturbed when the contours of the slot were defined, not by luminance cues, but by more complex principles of organization. For example, when she was asked to insert a card into a 'virtual' slot defined by a missing rectangle on a background of parallel lines, she generally failed. However, she was significantly better when the orientation of the lines matched that of the target missing rectangle than when their orientation was orthogonal to that of the missing rectangle, especially when the background consisted of high-contrast stripes. When the target rectangle was defined by the textural similarity of items in a background, she also failed (Fig. 6.2). Presumably, the extraction of contours from such cues is a genuine perceptual achievement. If so, then the success in such tasks requires the collaboration between pure visuomotor and perceptual processing of the stimulus—a collaboration that is compromised in DF by the disruption of her ventral pathway. In other words, she successfully inserted a card into an oriented slot only when the orientation of the slot was defined by luminance-difference cues.

Nonetheless, limited as they are, DF's visuomotor capacities require an explanation. Unless DF could visually process the size and contour or shape of a simple 3D object, she could not grasp objects as successfully as she does. However, being an apperceptive

---

[6]See the end of the Epilogue for the expression of our doubts about the exclusive role of the ventral stream in conscious visual processing.

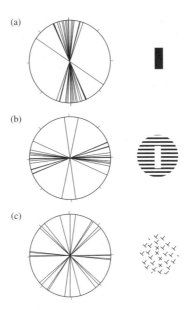

Fig. 6.2 Poor ability to extract contour information about a slot from other cues than luminance cues in apperceptive agnosic patient DF. Patient DF's performances in a task of posting a hand-held card into a 'virtual' slot, where the slot is defined in top row (a) by luminance cues, in middle row (b) by a missing rectangle on an orthogonal background of high contrast stripes, and in lower row (c) by the similarity of patterned items. Note that the only slot DF can deal with is (a) defined by luminance cues. (From Goodale 1995, in D. Osherson (ed.) *An invitation to cognitive science, Vol. 2, Visual cognition*, published by MIT Press, with permission.)

visual-form agnosic, DF could not process the shape of an object in a task of perceptual identification or judgment. The experimental demonstration of the dissociation between two tasks using the same effector is striking. But of course it raises the question: what is the key difference between a visuomotor task of grasping an object and a task of perceptual judgment using one and the same effector?

The response is quite simple: unlike the perceptual task, the motor task is an object-oriented action and it includes a reaching phase. In the motor task, the scaling of the grip is part of a broader action involving a movement of the arm towards the target. In the perceptual task, there is no reaching phase and the arm does not move the hand towards the object. In fact, in the perceptual task, the scaling of the grip is not at the service of the action of grasping at all: it is used to report a visual analysis of the size and shape of the object. In the perceptual task, the subject uses her finger scale to report her visual perceptual experience. She is not acting on the target. She could have been asked to report her visual experience otherwise than by scaling her finger-grip: she might have been asked to provide a verbal response or to draw a copy of the object. In the perceptual task, the subject is asked to 'pantomime' part of her action on the object, without performing it. DF's success in visuomotor tasks—subject to the limitations discussed above—shows her remarkable sensitivity to such visual attributes of an object as its orientation, size and shape in a visuomotor representation that also contains visual information about the object's location coded in egocentric coordinates. When the task requires that the visual information about orientation, size and shape of the object be detached from a visuomotor representation of the target's location coded in an egocentric frame of reference, DF fails.

In his discussion of object-oriented behavior, Jeannerod (1997: 79–81) makes a distinction between two kinds of visuomotor processing involved, respectively, in reaching and grasping. Reaching involves an abduction movement of the arm and a movement of flexion–extension of the forearm. While the former is guided by the visuomotor processing of the direction of the target, the latter is guided by the visuomotor processing of the distance of the target. Both the direction and the distance of the target are coded in egocentric coordinates. Grasping must take into account grip size and the number of fingers needed for the grasp. While the former involves computations based on size cues, the latter involves computations based on depth cues.

Following Jeannerod's (1997) model of reaching and grasping in normal human subjects, we want to claim that in DF, the computation of the size, shape and orientation of a target in object-centered coordinates is tied to a visuomotor representation of the location of the target coded in an egocentric frame of reference. Unlike DF, normal human subjects are able to recode the information about the location of a target from an egocentric to an allocentric frame of reference. This conversion of the representation of the location of an object from an egocentric to an allocentric frame of reference allows normal subjects to compute the relative sizes of two distinct objects. The transformation from one coordinates system to another for coding the location of an object is the source of perceptual comparative judgments about orientations, sizes and shapes of objects in normal subjects. Unlike normal subjects, DF cannot switch from one coordinates system to another for coding the location of a target. Thus, she can only compute the absolute size of an object, whose location is coded in egocentric coordinates. Perhaps in a task of perceptual judgment, when a normal subject uses the scaling of his finger-grip to estimate the size of an object, he imagines the whole action of grasping: he imagines himself reaching towards the object. If so, then presumably he must inhibit the execution of the reaching phase of the action. In any case, the very fact that a normal subject can correctly assess the correct size of an object without reaching for it shows that, as Jeannerod (1997) hypothesizes, his ability to code the size of an object is not tied to his representation of its location in an egocentric frame of reference. This is precisely what DF cannot do because her representation of the shape, size and orientation of an object operates only as part of her representation of the location of the target of her reaching action within egocentric coordinates.

Here we reach, or so we think, a crucial distinction between the pure low-level motor processing and the perceptual processing of a visual stimulus. In order to highlight this distinction, we want to contrast DF's visuomotor capacities with the elementary visual perceptual processing performed by 10-month-old human infants and by human adults in perceptual tasks of so-called multiple tracking experiments. We shall argue that there is a subtle difference between visual form agnosics and human infants.

5   The perceptual individuation of visual objects by location

There are both conceptual reasons and empirical evidence for thinking that the visual system cannot represent an object at all unless the representation contains visual information about one of the object's visual attributes, namely its spatial location. Seeing an object perceptually or otherwise involves seeing it somewhere or other. Although they are not in space, one can think about numbers, but one cannot see them. What one can see are not numbers but numerals. One can think of a dog without representing the location of any particular dog. But one cannot see a dog unless one's representation contains information about the location of the dog that one sees. Seeing something is representing it and localizing it in space (see Chapter 1, Section 3).

Drawing on the work of Spelke (1988), using a habituation/dishabituation paradigm, Wynn (1992a, 1992b) has showed that 4.5-month old human babies (whose coordination between eye and hand movements is still immature) can distinguish between two objects on the basis of spatial and locational evidence and that, on this basis, they can track small numerosities. Such babies saw a human hand bring one Mickey Mouse onto a stage— the puppet was hidden behind a screen and the babies saw the empty hand leave the stage. Then, the babies saw the hand bring a second puppet onto the stage. As before, the second puppet was hidden behind the screen and the babies saw the empty hand leave the stage for the second time. Then, the screen was removed and the babies saw either two puppets or one. By measuring the babies' looking time, Wynn (1992a, 1992b) found that they look longer at one than two puppets. Hence, their visual attentional behavior shows that they are more surprised to find only one object rather than two.

In a further set of experiments by Carey (1995) and Xu and Carey (1996), 10-month old human babies were shown alternatively a red metal car and a brown teddy bear. The babies saw the red metal car appear from, and disappear behind, the left side of a screen. They saw the brown teddy bear appear from, and disappear behind, the right side of the screen. The infants were never shown the two objects simultaneously. When the screen was removed, as in Wynn's (1992a, 1992b) experiment, the infant could see either two or only one object. Measuring the infants' looking time, it turned out that 10-month-old babies were no more surprised to see only one object rather than two. Carey (1995) and Xu and Carey (1996) argue from this experiment that, in the absence of visual spatial locational information, 10-month old infants fail to conclude that they are being presented with two distinct objects. In this experiment, featural information alone about the color, texture and shape of pairs of objects presented separately does not seem sufficient to warrant in 10-month-old human infants the judgment that they are presented with two distinct objects.[7]

Based on the developmental work described above, Leslie et al. (1998) argue that visual objects can be visually 'indexed' by two separate distinct 'indexing' mechanisms: one mechanism—object-individuation—uses locational information. According to Leslie et al. (1998), Ungerleider and Mishkin's (1982) anatomically defined 'where' system contributes to the process of object-individuation by locational information.[8]

---

[7]Recent experiments by Bonatti et al. (2002) suggest that 10-month old infants might make use of visual featural information to individuate and/or identify objects if the stimuli are human faces or human face-like.

[8]For discussion of Ungerleider and Mishkin's (1982) distinction, see Chapter 2.

The other mechanism—object-identification—uses featural information (such as orientation, color, shape or texture). According to Leslie *et al.* (1998), Ungerleider and Mishkin's (1982) 'what' system contributes to the process of object-identification by featural information. In their view 10-month-old infants only use the former object-individuation mechanism, not the latter object-identification mechanism. They use locational information, not featural information for distinguishing objects.

Pylyshyn (2000a, 2000b) reports relevant experiments on so-called 'multiple object-tracking' in normal human adults. Subjects were shown eight identical circles at rest on a screen, four of which flickered briefly. Then, the eight circles were shown moving randomly on the screen for about 10 s. Subjects were requested to keep track of the four circles that initially flickered. The human adult visual ability to track the motions and positions of identical objects extends up to four-to-five distinct objects. Pylyshyn reports that, in such multiple object-tracking experiments, changes in the color and shape of visual objects go unnoticed.[9]

Presumably, just like human infants in Wynn's (1992a, 1992b), Carey's (1995) and Xu and Carey's (1996) experiments, human adults in Pylyshyn's multiple object-tracking experiments use locational information, not featural information, to individuate and keep track of four-to-five randomly moving circles. Arguably, the result (or output) of the indexing by locational information falls considerably short of the concept of an object. Pylyshyn (2000a, 2000b) aptly calls 'proto-objects' such purely visual preconceptual objects.

Our present discussion of experimental results in both infant cognition and in multiple object-tracking in human adults is highly relevant to the important question discussed in both Chapters 2 and 3 about the duality between space perception and the visuomotor transformation. Individuation of proto-objects by locational information depends upon the representation of the location of a visual object in allocentric coordinates, i.e. the perception of spatial relationships between objects. Babies aged 10 months, according to Carey's (1995) and Xu and Carey's (1996) results, are restricted in their ability to use non-locational featural information to make further perceptual identification of visual objects. Human adults engaged in multiple object-tracking cannot, according to Pylyshyn's (2000a, 2000b) results, notice changes in the color and shape of the proto-objects that they are tracking. So these results present us with a modular encapsulated perceptual system whose proprietary input is locational information coded in allocentric coordinates. We claim that we are presented with a 'pure' spatial perceptual module that is best contrasted with the 'pure' visuomotor module at work in DF, whose task is to process visual information about the location of a target in egocentric coordinates. Both modules might depend upon an intact posterior parietal cortex, but they are clearly distinct modules, as we further argue in the next section. Thus, this is developmental and psychophysical evidence for the dual view of the role of the parietal lobes (argued for at the end of Chapter 3), according to which they must be involved in both the visuomotor transformation and in the perception of spatial relationships among objects.[10]

---

[9]It is important to notice the difference beetween Pylyshyn's (2000a, 2000b) multiple-tracking task and Pisella *et al.*'s (2000) and Rossetti and Pisella's (2000) pointing task. The former is a perceptual task: it requires coding of objects' locations in allocentric coordinates. The latter is a visuomotor task: it requires coding of the target's location in egocentric coordinates.

[10]For further elaboration on the dual role of the parietal lobes, see the Epilogue.

6 The motoric encapsulation of visuomotor representations

Although 10-month-old human infants do not exploit featural information alone to distinguish pairs of visual proto-objects, nonetheless they are not apperceptive visual-form agnosics. Nor is a human adult engaged in a task of multiple object-tracking, even if she cannot pay attention to changes in shape and/or color of the four or five visual targets that she is currently tracking. We shall presently argue that an apperceptive visual-form agnosic patient such as DF could not successfully track four among eight moving identical circles on a screen.

In his seminal work on the dynamics of perception, Evans (1982) has emphasized the crucial role of recognition and re-identification in the human visual perceptual capacity to keep track of objects in space and time. In the course of a single perceptual episode, a normally sighted human being is able to monitor the movements of her eyes in her orbit, the movement of her head relative to the rest of her body and the movement of her body in order, not to reach-and-grasp an object, but to attend to and follow its evolution in space and time.[11]

The perceptual processing of a visual stimulus allows one to open an object 'file' or to index an object by featural information in Pylyshyn's (2000a, 2000b) and Leslie *et al.*'s (1998) sense. One thereby fills the object file with visual information about, e.g. the object's color, shape, orientation and texture. Furthermore, the human episodic memory system allows one to re-identify one and the same object at different instants by re-opening stable object files. We shall assume that visual representations produced by perceptual processing of a stimulus typically satisfy what, following Dokic (2002), we shall call the constraint of contrastive identification:

Unless a creature has the resources to make contrastive identifications and/or comparisons among different instantiations of one and the same visual attribute or property, she will not be able to recognize or re-identify the property or attribute in question.

According to the constraint of contrastive identification, recognition or re-identification of property *F* (e.g. the property of being cylindrical in shape) requires the ability to contrast and compare different instantiations of property *F*, either by different objects or items at the same time or by the same object at different times. Notice first of all that of two distinct representations of one and the same property (e.g. shape), one might satisfy the constraint of contrastive identification and the other not. Second, notice that the constraint of contrastive identification, which applies to visual percepts (or to the non-conceptual content of visual experiences), is very much in line with Clark's (2001) EBS assumption: the function of visual percepts in the human cognitive architecture is to select objects either for thought or as possible goals for action; it is not to monitor detailed bodily movements *per se*. So, forming a visual percept of, for example, the size, shape, orientation, texture and color of an apple, might serve to select an object as a goal for prehension. On the basis of this perceptual selection, the visuomotor transformation launches the ballistic movements of reaching, the automatic preshaping of

---

[11]Clearly, the processing and monitoring of information about eye-movement and head-movement occurs at a sub-personal level.

the fingers and finally the grasping of the object involving the appropriate automatic rotation of the wrist. Although the size, shape and orientation of the object are coded in the visuomotor representation of the target of prehension, only their perceptual representation appropriate for the selection of the object meets the constraint of contrastive identification.[12]

As we argued in the previous section, 10-month-old human babies can use locational information, not featural information. When they do so, they are engaged in a task of object-individuation, which is typically a low-level perceptual task. For the purpose of performing such a task, their visual system builds an elementary perceptual representation of the respective locations of two proto-objects. Similarly, when a human adult successfully tracks, for example, the movements and positions of four among eight distinct circles on a screen, her visual system builds a low-level perceptual representation of the respective locations of four proto-objects. Arguably 10-month-old infants do not use information about the shape, color, texture and orientation of objects for object-identification. Nor do adults engaged in a task of multiple object tracking. Hence, their visual representation of the size, shape, color, texture and orientation of objects might not satisfy the constraint of contrastive identification. However, their elementary perceptual representation of the locations of proto-objects does satisfy the constraint of contrastive identification. In other words, they have information about the locations of or the spatial relationships among at least two objects in a visual array available for perceptual processing.

As we said above, no object can be visually represented at all unless the representation contains information about its location. In an elementary perceptual representation of two or more proto-objects (in either a human infant or in an adult performing a task of multiple object-tracking), their relative locations must be coded in an allocentric frame of reference: only an allocentric frame of reference allows the representation of the relative locations of two or more (proto)-objects. Only an allocentric frame of reference can underlie a perceptual judgment to the effect that, e.g. one object lies to the left of another. Thus, the infant's visual representation of the relative locations of two objects and the adult visual representation of the relative locations of four circles satisfy the constraint of contrastive identification as it applies to the visual representation of locations.

We claim that the visual representation of a target whose localization is coded in egocentric coordinates does not satisfy the constraint of contrastive identification. The early twentieth-century French mathematical physicist Henri Poincaré (1902–68: 82) considered the question: What do we mean when we say that we localize an object in space? His own answer was that localizing an object in space is representing to oneself the movements necessary to reach it. He further added that to represent these movements consists in representing the muscular sensations that accompany the movements. According to Poincaré (1905–58: 47):

[...] to localize an object simply means to represent to oneself the movements that would be necessary to reach it. It is not a question of representing the movements themselves in space, but solely of representing to oneself the muscular sensations which accompany these movements and which do not presuppose the existence of space.

---

[12]In other words, the constraint of contrastive identification is satisfied by perceptual modes of presentation of such properties as size and shape, not by visuomotor modes of presentation of the same properties.

In these few sentences, Poincaré insightfully anticipates contemporary psychophysical research into motor imagery. However, Poincaré's remarks apply to the localization of a target in egocentric coordinates, not to the localization of an object in allocentric coordinates, which is necessary, on our view, for the uptake of perceptual identification.

We shall now argue that DF's visuomotor representation of the visual attributes of an object relevant to grasping it fails to satisfy the constraint of contrastive identification altogether. DF has a residual dorsal visual system that allows her to reach and grasp accurately targets of prehension. In order to guide the action of reaching towards an object, the visual system must code the location of the object in egocentric coordinates. DF's visuomotor ability to match the orientation of a slot by the orientation of her wrist, as well as her ability to scale her finger-grip to the orientation, size and shape of objects in an object-oriented action, shows that her visual system processes the orientation, size and shape of objects in the context of such a task. Our argument, however, is that DF's visual sensitivity to the orientation, size and shape of objects is tied and limited to the visual representation of the object's location in egocentric coordinates. DF can code the orientation, the size and the shape of an object within a visuomotor representation that guides her full action consisting of a reaching phase and a grasping phase, but this visual information is tied to a visuomotor representation of the location of her target coded in egocentric coordinates.

In order for such visual attributes of an object as its orientation, size and shape to be available for perceptual judgment and/or experience, it must be available for comparison. What is distinctive of the perceptual representation (as opposed to the motor representation) of the orientation, size and shape of an object is that it satisfies the constraint of contrastive identification. To make such a comparative judgment is to be able to represent simultaneously the orientation, size and shape of at least two distinct items in a visual array: No comparison between orientations, sizes and shapes can be performed unless the orientations, sizes and shapes of at least two distinct items are being represented. In order for the orientations, sizes and shapes of at least two distinct items to be represented, their relative locations—or their spatial relationships—must be visually represented. Thus, unless the visual system represents the relative locations of at least two distinct objects, such a comparative judgment between visual attributes can simply not arise. It follows that unless the visual system codes the relative locations of at least two distinct objects in an allocentric frame of reference, no perceptual comparison is possible. But unless the information about the orientation, size and shape is available for comparison, the orientation, size and shape of an object will not be visually perceived. Unless they are part of a representation of the relative locations of at least two objects in an allocentric frame of reference, the orientation, size and shape of an object will not be available to conscious visual perception.

DF, we submit, can only compute the absolute size and shape of an object. She cannot compute the relative sizes and shapes of two or more objects. She cannot make perceptual comparisons between the sizes and shapes of two distinct objects. In DF, the visual information about the absolute value of the size and shape of a target of her reaching-and-grasping movements remains encapsulated within the visuomotor representation of the location of the target in egocentric coordinates. The visual information about the orientation, size and shape of an object cannot be recoded from a visuomotor representation of the location of an object coded in egocentric coordinates into a perceptual representation of the relative positions of two objects coded in an allocentric frame of reference. The visual information about the orientation, size and shape of an object cannot be transferred at all to a visual representation of the spatial relationships between two or more objects for recoding into an allocentric frame of reference. If so, then in DF, the visual information about the absolute orientation, size and shape of an object is bound to remain trapped in the encapsulated visuomotor representation of the location of the object coded in egocentric coordinates. It can be passed on to the motor intention, but since it cannot satisfy the constraint of contrastive identification, this information is unsuited for perceptual representation and it therefore cannot reach what we called in Chapter 1 the 'belief box'.

Thus, our claim that, in DF the visual information about the orientation, size and shape of a target for action is trapped in a visuomotor representation of the location of a target in egocentric coordinates, leads to the following conditional testable prediction. Let us suppose that an apperceptive visual-form agnosic patient like DF is able to reach and grasp simultaneously two distinct objects, e.g. a pen with her left hand and its cap with her right hand. Then we predict that DF could not match the size, shape and orientation of the cap onto those of the pen. She could not put them together to form a new complex object. We suppose that DF's visual system could give rise to two separate visuomotor representations respectively of the pen and of the cap. If so, then DF could grasp simultaneously the pen with one hand and the cap with the other hand. But we predict that DF could not merge the two egocentric maps of each object and construct a single visual representation of the relative positions of the cap and the pen in allocentric coordinates.

In our view then, there is a gap between the way the visual information about the orientation, size and shape of an object is contained, respectively, in a visuomotor representation and in a perceptual representation. Unless the visual information can be recoded from an egocentric coordinate system into an allocentric coordinate system, it cannot satisfy the constraint of contrastive identification: it cannot be available for perceptual processing and give rise to perceptual judgment. The contrast between DF's remarkable visuomotor capacities and her deep perceptual impairment is empirical confirmation of the need to distinguish between such properties of an object as its shape, size and orientation and non-conceptual modes of presentation of these properties (emphasized in Chapter 1). DF's visual system can represent the shape of an object in a visuomotor mode of presentation, i.e. coded within a representation of its position in egocentric coordinates, not in a perceptual mode of presentation, i.e. coded within a representation of its relative position in allocentric coordinates.

As we argued in Chapter 5, visual percepts are informationally encapsulated, relative to concepts. Conceptual thought allows us to transcend the limitations of perceptual representations. The output of the pure motor processing of a visual stimulus is informationally encapsulated, relative to the output of the perceptual processing of the same stimulus. As we already pointed out in Chapters 1 and 5, there is more information in a visual percept than there is in a concept: the former is both informationally richer and more fine-grained than the latter. The transition from a visual percept to a conceptual representation applying to one and the same state of affairs requires a change of processing: whereas a visual percept results from processing by a mechanism with the function to encode information coded in analogical form, a conceptual representation results from processing by a mechanism with the function to encode information in digital form. Thus, the transition from a more informationally encapsulated percept to a concept involves a selective loss of information, as the following example will remind us.

Consider a visual perceptual representation of a mug to the left of a telephone. In the visual percept, the location of the mug relative to the location of the telephone is coded in allocentric coordinates. The percept has an iconic or pictorial content that is both informationally richer and more fine-grained than any conceptual representation of the same state of affairs. For example, it cannot depict the mug as being to the left of the telephone without depicting how far the former is from the latter. Nor can it depict the relative distance of the mug from the telephone without depicting the orientation, shape, texture, size and content (if any) of the mug, the orientation, shape size, and color of the telephone.

In a sense, the iconic or pictorial representation of the location of the mug relative to the telephone matches the conceptual content expressible, as it might be, by the English two-place relation 'left of'. Thus, conceptual processing of the pictorial content of the visual representation can yield a representation whose conceptual content can be expressed by the English sentence: 'The mug is to the left of the telephone'. An utterance of this sentence, however, conveys only part of the pictorial content conveyed by the visual percept, since the utterance is mute about any visual attribute of the pair of objects other than their relative locations, and it is mute about the relative distance between the mug and the telephone.

Further conceptual processing of the conceptual content conveyed by the utterance could yield a more complex representation involving, not just a two-place relation, but a three-place relation, also expressible by the English 'left of'. Thus, one can think that the mug is to the left of the telephone for someone standing in front of the window, not for someone sitting at the opposite side of the table. Although one can form the thought involving the ternary relation 'left of', one cannot see one's own egocentric perspective. Hence, the visual system cannot deliver a perceptual representation whose iconic or pictorial content matches the concept of the ternary relation 'left of'. This is the sense in which the perceptual representation is informationally encapsulated. Whereas the pictorial non-conceptual content of a visual percept is richer and more fine-grained than the conceptual content of a thought, the latter is hierarchically more complex in the sense that thoughts satisfy the constraint of detachment, which allows the increase of the arity of a predicate (see Chapter 1, Section 4.1). Arguably, only by satisfying the detachment constraint, can a thought rise above the limitations of a visual percept. The selective elimination of pictorial information is a necessary condition for increasing the arity (or the logical complexity) of a spatial predicate (e.g. 'left of'). Finally, unlike visual percepts, thoughts are not limited to representing objects in space since one can think about, e.g. numbers, which are not in space at all.[13]

We presently claim that a pure visuomotor representation of a target is informationally encapsulated, relative to a perceptual representation of the same stimulus. But if so, then its informational encapsulation differs interestingly from that of a visual percept, relative to a concept: the motoric encapsulation differs from the perceptual encapsulation. The content of a visuomotor representation is not informationally richer than the content of a perceptual representation. Quite the contrary: the latter is informationally richer than

---

[13]See Chapter 1 for elaboration.

Table 6.1

	Detachment constraint	Constraint of contrastive identification	Localization of object in allocentric coordinates	Localization of object in egocentric coordinates
Visuomotor representation	−	−	−	+
Percept	−	+	+	−
Thought	+	+	−	−

the former. The crucial parameter responsible for the informational encapsulation of a visuomotor representation of a target is that the location of the target is coded in egocentric coordinates. When the location of a target is coded in egocentric coordinates, not in allocentric coordinates, the representation of visual attributes of an object (such as its size, shape and orientation) cannot satisfy the constraint of contrastive identification. This is why a visuomotor representation can only represent the absolute orientation, size and shape of the target. The transition to a perceptual representation of the stimulus consists in a transformation from egocentric coordinates into allocentric coordinates.

To sum up, conceptual thoughts, which are productive and systematic, satisfy the detachment constraint. Because they are productive and systematic, they can rise above the spatial limitations inherent to perception. Only thoughts can represent entities not in space at all. Because they code the relative positions of objects in allocentric coordinates, visual percepts satisfy the constraint of contrastive identification. Because they code the absolute position of an object in egocentric coordinates, visuomotor representations fail to satisfy the constraint of constrastive identification. The situation can be represented as in Table 6.1.

7   Are there visuomotor representations at all?

The question now arises: Are there visuomotor representations at all? Are visuomotor representations really genuine representations? Are visually guided actions real actions? Are they not mere behavioral non-intentional responses? Is not the detection of an affordance the direct extraction of information in the optic array in Gibson's sense? Do we need to postulate mental representations at all in order to explain visually guided actions directed towards objects? As we put it earlier, we ought to face the following dilemma: either visuomotor responses are mere reflexive responses to visual stimuli or they are not. If they are not, then they are genuine actions. If so, then when a subject produces a visuomotor response to a visual stimulus, her behavior is guided by a mental representation of the stimulus.

In the previous section, we argued that the information about the orientation, size and shape of an object contained in the output of the motor processing of visual inputs is locked into a visuomotor representation of the location of the object coded in egocentric coordinates. It was a surprising neuropsychological finding to discover that an apperceptive visual-form agnosic patient like DF can indeed process such visual information. The evidence for this surprising claim was that she succeeds in various visuomotor tasks: she can successfully insert a hand-held card into a slot at different orientations around the clock. She can successfully grasp an object between her thumb and index finger. But if so, then the question arises whether we do really need to postulate visual representations at all to explain DF's visuomotor performances. Perhaps DF's visuomotor responses can be explained without the need for intermediary mental representations of the stimulus. Behavioral failures, not successes, are generally thought to provide evidence in favor of intermediary mental representations. Perhaps nomic correlations between the physical properties of the distal stimulus and DF's visuomotor responses are all we need to explain her visuomotor capacities. Perhaps, the motor processing of visual stimuli differs from the perceptual processing of the same stimuli in that the latter, unlike the former, yields direct responses, not mediated by visual representations at all. This is a perfectly reasonable challenge and we ought to face it.

As we pointed out earlier in this chapter, as well as in Chapter 1, the paradigmatic arguments in favor of the distinction between conceptual and non-conceptual content has relied on the distinctive phenomenology of visual perceptual experience. Since visual percepts exemplify both an informational richness and a degree of fine-grainedness that exceeds a subjects's conceptual repertoire, the conclusion is that visual percepts are representations with a non-conceptual content. The argument for the distinction between non-conceptual visuomotor content and non-conceptual perceptual content cannot rely on the same strategy. In preceding sections, we have made a case for the distinction between the output of motor processing and the output of perceptual processing of visual stimuli by exhibiting responses to visual stimuli in conditions in which subjects are typically unaware of most of the stimuli's visual attributes. This was true of DF and of most of the dissociations obtained in the psychophysical literature in normal subjects. So we ought to appeal to a different strategy here. And such a strategy is indeed available. In arguing in favor of positing an intermediate level of mental representations between the input and the behavioral output in the perceptual processing of a visual stimulus, philosophers and psychologists (e.g. Pylyshyn 1984; Fodor 1986, 1987; Dretske 1988) have typically appealed to two conspiring lines of thought: misperception and the sensitivity to non-local properties of the stimulus. We shall first briefly explain why and then we shall argue that the same considerations do apply to the motor processing of visual stimuli. So we propose to meet the challenge of the above dilemma and argue that visuomotor responses are actions, not reflexes. Thus, the methodological considerations we shall offer have to do with the causal explanation of behavior, not with the phenomenology of visual experience.

If a normal subject perceives two equal line segments as unequal (as in the Müller–Lyer illusion) or two circles of equal diameter as unequal (as in the Titchener circles' illusion), then this provides good evidence for the assumption that the visual perceptual system builds a representation of the stimulus that results in a misascription of a property not instantiated by the stimulus. In Chapter 4, we have examined many psychophysical experiments that do show that the perceptual processing of visual inputs involves misrepresentation and hence a representation of the stimulus. As Chomsky (1965) noticed long ago, speakers of natural languages are sensitive to grammatical properties of linguistic signals, such as being a noun phrase or being a grammatical sentence. Since such grammatical properties cannot be directly transduced from the speech signal, they are best construed as non-local properties of sequences of words of natural languages. As Loewer and Rey (1991: xiv) and Rey (1997: 126) note, human beings respond to many non-local properties instantiated by non-linguistic stimuli, such as being a Rembrandt portrait, being granny's favorite wine glass, being a crumpled shirt, being a survivor of the battle of Waterloo, being a collapsed star, timidity, pomposity, being an American citizen, a marriage proposal, and so on. Presumably, only creatures with conceptual abilities could respond to such non-local properties. Perceptual visual illusions too, can be thought of as perceptual responses to non-local properties of visual stimuli. Responses to non-local properties in general are evidence for the construction of mental representations—whether the representations have conceptual or perceptual non-conceptual content. This is why we presently go back to the psychophysical study of visual illusions reviewed in Chapter 4.

In the discussion of their experimental work designed to get evidence for dissociations between perceptual processing and visuomotor processing of illusory displays in normal subjects, Haffenden and Goodale (1998: 124) have argued, on evolutionary grounds, that there are good reasons to think that, unlike 'pure' perceptual judgment, the motor processing of visual stimuli could not afford the luxury of being fooled. However plausible the reasoning, we have argued in Chapter 4, and shall presently argue again, that it is not supported by the psychophysical evidence adduced precisely by Haffenden and Goodale (1998, 2000) and Haffenden *et al.* (2001), based on the Titchener circles' illusions, to which we now go back.

According to Haffenden and Goodale (1998), there is a dissociation between the visuomotor response and the perceptual response to the presentation of a pair of disks surrounded by an annulus of circles whose diameters are equal to the diameter of the disks. When physically equal disks are presented with an annulus of circles of the same diameter, normal subjects respond by a larger manual estimate (or perceptual judgment) than they do when the same disks are presented against a blank background. However, normal subjects produce a smaller motor response to the first than to the second display. Haffenden and Goodale (2000) found a further dissociation between perceptual processing and motor processing. Normal subjects were presented with disks surrounded by rectangular flankers whose orientation relative to, and distance from, the disk could vary. Haffenden and Goodale (2000) found that manual estimation (i.e. perceptual judgment) decreases as the distance between the disk and flankers increases, regardless of flankers' orientation. By contrast, grip scaling (the motor response) is influenced jointly by the distance from, and the orientation of, flankers relative to the disk. Finally, in a crucial experiment, Haffenden *et al.* (2001) compared the motor response and the perceptual response to one and the same stimulus in three distinct conditions. In traditional displays of the Titchener circles' illusion, the gap between the disk and the surrounding smaller circles is significantly smaller than the gap between the disk and the larger circles. So Haffenden *et al.* (2001) presented subjects with three distinct displays one at a time, two of which were the traditional display of the central disk surrounded by an annulus of smaller circles with a smaller gap and the traditional display of the central disk surrounded by an annulus of larger circles with a larger gap. In addition, they presented a third display in which the central disk was surrounded by an annulus of smaller circles with a gap as large as the gap betweeen the disk and the larger circles. They found the following dissociation between the motor response and the perceptual response: the perceptual response treated the third display—smaller surrounding circles with a large gap—like the first display—smaller surrounding circles with a small gap. The motor response, however, treated the third display like the second display—larger surrounding circles with a large gap. Hence, whereas the perceptual response was sensitive to the size of the circles in the annulus, the motor response was sensitive to the distance between the target and the annulus.

These results provide evidence that the motor processing of visual inputs produces visuomotor representations of the target that differ from the output of the perceptual processing. In fact, it provides strong evidence that the motor processing of visual inputs does yield representations with some of the constitutive features of representations. These results suggest that the reason the motor processing is sensitive to the gap between the target disk and the surrounding annulus is that it treats an annulus of 2D circles *as if* it were a 3D obstacle for positioning the fingers on the target. So these results show that the motor processing of visual inputs can be fooled by selective features of a visual display. Or, equivalently, they show that the output of the motor processing of visual inputs does respond to non-local properties of the stimulus. Thus, the visuomotor representation of a target for reaching and grasping involves a response to a non-local property of a visual display. Contrary to Norman's (2001) claim on the behalf of Gibson that 'the size of an object that constitutes a graspable size is specified in the optic array', we claim that seeing an object as affording an action of grasping between index and thumb is being sensitive to a non-local property of an object. Hence, seeing an affordance is representing: it involves entertaining a visuomotor representation of a target. Again, the dissociation between visuomotor and perceptual processing of an illusory display in normal human adults is empirical confirmation of the need to distinguish between two kinds of non-conceptual modes of presentation of one and the same property of an object, e.g. the size of a Titchener disk.

8 The role of visuomotor representations in the human cognitive architecture

Reaching and grasping objects are visually guided actions directed towards objects. As we argued at length in the first chapter, all actions are caused by intentions. As argued by O'Shaughnessy (1980), some bodily movements—moving one's tongue in one's mouth as one reads or tapping one's foot to the rhythm as one is listening to a piece of music—might not be caused by one's intention. However, such bodily movements, which belong to what O'Shaughnessy calls 'sub-intentional acts', are not part of visually guided actions directed towards objects. Visually guided hand movements directed towards objects are always, or so we claim, caused by the agent's intentions. Intentions are psychological states with a distinctive intentionality. Unlike beliefs and perceptions, and like desires, intentions have a world-to-mind direction of fit. They do not match the world or represent facts: they represent goals, i.e. possible non-actual states of affairs. Unlike the contents of desires, the contents of intentions cannot represent actions performed by others: one can only intend to perform one's own actions.[14]

---

[14]An intention cannot represent an action performed by another even if, as we shall argue in Chapter 7, the visual perception of an action performed by another can trigger in the observer an action plan isomorphic to the plan of the action whose execution is being perceived.

Unlike a desire, an intention cannot represent a state of affairs that the agent knows to be impossible. Intentions are causally self-referential in the sense that the state of affairs represented by the intention must be causally produced by the intention itself. Intentions have both a world-to-mind direction of fit and a mind-to-world direction of causation. Whereas a perceptual experience is caused by the state of affairs that it represents, an intention causes the state of affairs that it represents. Thus, intentions derive their peculiar commitment to action from the combination of their distinctive world-to-mind direction of fit and their mind-to-world direction of causation. In this section, we shall argue that pure visuomotor representations have a dual function in the human cognitive architecture: they serve as inputs to motor intentions and they serve as input to a special class of indexical concepts, the 'causally indexical' concepts.

8.1 Visuomotor representations serve as inputs to motor intentions

As we argued in the first chapter, not all actions are caused by what Searle (1983, 2001) calls prior intentions, but all are caused by what he calls intentions in action. Pacherie (2000b) has persuasively argued that what Searle (1983, 2001) calls intentions in action are what Jeannerod (1994) calls motor intentions. Unlike prior intentions, motor intentions are directed towards immediately accessible goals. Hence, they play a crucial role in the execution, the monitoring and the control of the ongoing action. Arguably, prior intentions may have conceptual content. Motor intentions do not. For example, one intends to climb a visually perceptible mountain. The content of this prior intention involves the action concept of climbing and a visual percept of the distance, shape and color of the mountain. In order to climb the mountain, however, one must intentionally perform an enormous variety of postural and limb movements in response to the slant, orientation and the shape of the surface of the slope. Human beings automatically assume the right postures and perform the required flexions and extensions of their feet and legs. Since they do not possess concepts matching each and every such movements, their non-deliberate intentional behavioral responses to the slant, orientation and shape of the surface of slope is monitored by the non-conceptual non-perceptual content of motor intentions.

Not any visual representation can match the peculiar commitment to action of motor intentions; visuomotor representations can. Percepts are informationally richer and more fine-grained than are either concepts or visuomotor representations. As we argued in Chapter 1, visual percepts have the same mind-to-world direction of fit as beliefs. This is why visual percepts are suitable inputs to a process of selective elimination of information, whose ultimate output can be stored in the belief box. We shall presently argue that visuomotor representations have an entirely different function: they provide the relevant visual information about the properties of a target to an agent's motor intentions. As we argued in Section 5 of the present chapter, unlike visual percepts, visuomotor representations fail to satisfy the constraint of contrastive identification: they fail to satisfy the constraint that must be satisfied by any representation for it to undergo further conceptual processing whose output will ultimately end up in the 'belief box'. But this failure in turn makes visuomotor representations an appropriate input to motor intentions. Whereas visual percepts must be stripped of much of their informational richness to be conceptualized, visuomotor representations can directly provide relevant visual information about the target of an action to motor intentions. Their 'motoric' informational encapsulation makes them suitable for this role. The non-conceptual non-perceptual content of a visuomotor representation matches that of a motor intention.

According to Jeannerod (1994: 197), motor intentions are representations of action and as such they have a dual structure: on the one hand they involve 'the parameters and constraints dictated by the execution [of the action] by the motor system'. On the other hand, they involve 'the goal of the action', where the latter is analyzed in turn as an 'internal representation of both the external object toward which it is directed and the final state of the organism when that object has been reached'. The representations of the agent's bodily constraints are in turn decomposed into a representation of the expected duration of the action, a representation of the expected force and effort to be invested in the action and a representation of what Jeannerod (1994: 196) calls the 'motor rules'. The latter are decomposed into representations respectively of kinematic regularities and biomechanical constraints on the agent's bodily movements. To put it crudely, the content of motor intentions has two sides: a subjective side (i.e. the representation of the agent's body in action) and an objective side (i.e. the representation of the target of the action).

Jeannerod (1994, 1997) provides much psychophysical and neurophysiological evidence for the view that motor imagery is a fundamental source of the various levels of the agent's representations of the constraints that have to be met by her bodily movements.[15] Experiments by Decety *et al.* (1989) show that an actually performed action involves the same duration as its imagined or implicit counterpart. This is true in the domain of actions involving natural or unlearned movements, as well as in the domain of skilled or learned movements. Walking to a designated target requires the same time as imagining walking towards the same target. Overt and mental recitation of the alphabet take the same time; and so do writing a letter and imagining writing one. In an experiment by Georgopoulos and Massey (1987), subjects were shown a fixed visual stimulus on a screen. They were requested to move a lever towards a location different from the location of the visual stimulus. By measuring the reaction time necessary for adjusting the direction of the lever, the authors found that the reaction time increased as a function of the size of the angle between the visual stimulus and the target of the movement of the lever. According to Georgopoulos and Massey (1987), subjects were mentally rotating the movement vector until it reached the desired angle. By application of Fitts's law, the larger the angle, the longer the rotation, hence the longer the movement.

On the one hand, the fact that motor imagery is involved in both overt actions and imagined actions shows that motor preparation differs from action mainly, if not only, in that in the former case, unlike the latter, execution is inhibited. On the other hand, if motor imagery is involved in motor preparation, then motor imagery must be the internal source of the component of the content of motor intentions devoted to the representation of 'the parameters and constraints dictated by the execution [of the action] by the motor system'. If so, then the non-conceptual content of motor imagery constitutes one major component of the content of motor intentions: it fills the 'subjective' slot of

---

[15] As we noted above, Poincaré (1902/1968, 1905/1958) insightfully anticipates empirical psychophysical work on motor imagery when he wrote, e.g. that one can represent one's own movements by representing the muscular sensations necessary to execute them.

the content of motor intentions. We submit that the visuomotor representation of the target of an action fills the 'objective' slot of the content of motor intentions.

Thus, in order for the visual information about a target of an action carried by visuo-motor representations to be suitable for motor intentions, visuomotor representations must share the world-to-mind direction of fit of motor intentions. Like visual percepts, visuomotor representations, however, are effects, not causes, of what they represent. Visuomotor representations cannot, therefore, share the mind-to-world direction of causation of motor intentions. On our view, then, a visuomotor representation of a target for action is a hybrid mental representation with a dual direction of fit.

The existence of such hybrid representations with a dual direction of fit has been anticipated in an important paper by Millikan (1996), who calls them 'pushmi-pullyu' representations (or PPRs). As Millikan (1996) observes, 'it is important to see that PPRs are not merely conjunctions of a descriptive plus a directive representation'. Arguably, purely descriptive and purely directive representations require more complex computa-tional capacities than hybrid representations such as Millikan's PPRs. A purely descriptive representation of a fact will not yield any practical decision on the basis of which to act, unless it is combined with a purely directive representation of a goal. Nor will a purely directive representation yield a practical decision either, unless it is com-bined with a purely descriptive representation. Furthermore, an organism will not be able to combine pairs of purely descriptive and purely directive representations in order to produce a decision, unless it has the computational capacity to make practical inferences. As Millikan (1996) notices, because PPRs have a hybrid direction of fit, they represent at once parts of a fact and parts of a goal. As she speculates, PPRs might well be more primitive and phylogenetically more ancient than both purely descriptive representations of facts and purely directive representations of goals.

Millikan's (1996) characterization of PPRs fits very well with our notion of a visuo-motor representation of a target for action. Unlike her, however, we do not think that human intentions are PPRs with a hybrid direction of fit. Unlike Millikan (1996), we do not believe that there is room for a distinction between intending to achieve a goal, which would involve 'describing one's future', and making 'plans' on this basis. Intending *is* planning. In our view, intentions are, just like desires, purely directive mental representations of goals or possible states of affairs with a world-to-mind direction of fit. Like desires, they represent possible states of affairs that may obtain in the future. But they no more 'describe' such possible states of affairs than desires do. Only beliefs can describe actual and possible states of affairs. It is not obvious that, as she points out, 'a person cannot sincerely intend to do a thing without believing she will do it'. It might well be that a person cannot sincerely intend to do a thing if she believes or knows that she will fail. Clearly this is something that distinguishes intentions from desires, for one can desire that a state of affairs obtain even though one knows it cannot obtain. But it may be sufficient for someone to sincerely intend to do something if she believes that she can do it or if she believes that she will try to do it. Even if it were true that one could not intend to do something unless one believed that one will succeed, this would hardly show that the belief is part of the intention or that like beliefs, intentions have also a mind-to-world descriptive direction of fit. The fact that an intention brings about a belief—if it does—is compatible with the fact that, unlike beliefs, intentions are purely directive representations of goals with a world-to-mind direction of fit.

8.2 Visuomotor representations serve as inputs to causal indexicals

Borrowing from the study of language processing, Jeannerod (1994, 1997) has drawn a distinction between the semantic and the pragmatic processing of visual stimuli. As he (1997: 77) writes:

> [...] at variance with the [...] semantic processing, the representation involved in sensorimotor transformation has a predominantly 'pragmatic' function, in that it relates to the object as a goal for action, not as a member of a perceptual category. The object attributes are represented therein to the extent that they trigger specific motor patterns for the hand to achieve the proper grasp.

Thus, the crucial feature of the pragmatic processing of visual information is that its output is a suitable input to the non-conceptual content of motor intentions. We shall now argue that what underlies the contrast between the pragmatic and the semantic processing of visual information is that, whereas the output of the latter is designed to serve as input to further conceptual processing with a mind-to-world direction of fit, the output of the former is designed to match the non-conceptual content of motor intentions with a world-to-mind direction of fit and a mind-to-world direction of causation. The special features of the non-conceptual contents of visuomotor representations can be inferred from the pure behavioral motor responses which they underlie, as in patient DF. They can also be deduced from the structure and content of elementary action concepts with the help of which they can be categorized.

We shall consider a subset of elementary action concepts, which, following Campbell (1994), we shall call 'causally indexical' concepts. Indexical concepts are, as we argued in Chapter 1, shallow but indispensable concepts, whose references change as the perceptual context changes and whose function is to encode temporary information. Indexical concepts respectively expressed by 'I', 'today' and 'here' are personal, temporal and spatial indexicals. Arguably, their highly contextual content cannot be replaced by pure definite descriptions without loss. Campbell (1994: 41–51) recognizes the existence of causally indexical concepts whose references may vary according to the causal powers of the agent who uses them. Such concepts are involved in judgments having, as Campbell (1994: 43) puts it, 'immediate implications for [the agent's] action'. Concepts such as 'too heavy', 'out of reach', 'within my reach', 'too large', 'fit for grasping between index and thumb' are causally indexical concepts in Campbell's sense. As Pacherie (2000b: 412) observes:

> Campbell's notion of causal indexicality fits nicely with Jeannerod's idea of a pragmatic mode of representation of objects and I think it would not be betraying Jeannerod's position to say that pragmatic representations of objects are causally indexical representations, where object attributes are treated in terms of their immediate implications for action, that is to the extent to which they afford specific motor patterns.

Surely, Campbell's idea of causal indexicality does capture a kind of judgment that is characteristically based upon the output of the pragmatic (or motor) processing of visual stimuli in Jeannerod's (1994, 1997) sense. One qualification, however, is required. Unlike the content of the direct output of the pragmatic processing of visual stimuli or that of motor intentions, the contents of judgments involving causal indexicals is conceptual. Judgments involving causally indexical concepts have low conceptual content, but they have conceptual content nonetheless. The non-conceptual contents of either visuomotor representations or motor intentions is better compared with that of an affordance in Gibson's sense.

Causally indexical concepts differ in one crucial respect from other indexical concepts, i.e. personal, temporal and spatial indexical concepts. Thoughts involving personal, temporal and spatial indexical concepts are 'egocentric' thoughts in the sense that they are perception-based thoughts. This is obvious enough for thoughts expressible with either the first-person pronoun 'I' or 'you'. To refer to a location as 'here' or 'there' and to refer to a day as 'today', 'yesterday' or 'tomorrow' is to refer, respectively, to a spatial and a temporal region from within some egocentric perspective: a location can only be referred to as 'here' or 'there' from some particular spatial egocentric perspective. A temporal region can only be referred to by 'today', 'yesterday' or 'tomorrow' from some particular temporal egocentric perspective. In this sense, personal, temporal and spatial indexical concepts are egocentric concepts.[16] As we argued in Chapter 1, egocentric indexicals lie at the interface between visual percepts and an individual's conceptual repertoire about objects, times and locations.

Many philosophers (e.g. Kaplan 1989; Perry 1993) have argued that personal, temporal and spatial indexical and/or demonstrative concepts play a special 'essential' and ineliminable role in the explanation of action; and so they do. As Perry (1993: 33) insightfully writes:

I once followed a trail of sugar on a supermarket floor, pushing my cart down the aisle on one side of a tall counter and back the aisle on the other, seeking the shopper with the torn sack to tell him he was making a mess. With each trip around the counter, the trail became thicker. But I seemed unable to catch up. Finally it dawned on me. I was the shopper I was trying to catch.

To believe that the shopper with a torn sack is making a mess is one thing. To believe that oneself is making a mess is something else. Only upon forming the thought expressible by 'I am making a mess' is it at all likely that one may take appropriate measures to change one's course of action. It is one thing to believe that the meeting starts at 10:00 a.m., it is another thing to believe that the meeting starts now, even if now is 10:00 a.m.; not until one thinks that the meeting starts now will one get up and run. Consider someone standing still at an intersection, lost in a foreign city. One thing is for that person to intend to go to her hotel. Something else is to intend to go this way, not that way. Only after she has formed the latter intention with a demonstrative locational content, will she get up and walk.

Thus, such egocentric concepts as personal, temporal and spatial indexicals and or demonstratives derive their ineliminable role in the explanation of action from the fact that their recognitional role cannot be played by any purely descriptive concept. Indexicals and demonstratives are mental pointers that can be used to refer to objects, places and times. Personal indexicals are involved in the recognition of persons. Temporal indexicals are involved in the recognition of temporal regions or instants. Spatial indexicals are involved in the recognition of locations. To say that they are involved in recognition is of course to acknowledge that they satisfy the constraint of contrastive identification at the conceptual level. To recognize oneself as the reference

---

[16] The egocentricity of indexical concepts should not be confused with the egocentricity of an egocentric frame of reference in which the visual system codes the location of a target. The former is a property of concepts. The latter is a property of visual representations.

of 'I' is to make a contrast between oneself identified as the speaker and another person one addresses in verbal communication as 'you'. To identify a day as 'today' is to contrast it with other days that might be identified as 'yesterday', 'the day before yesterday', 'tomorrow', etc. To identify a place as 'here' is to contrast it with other places referred to as 'there'.

The important point here is that indexicals and demonstratives satisfy the constraint of contrastive identification because they are concepts and all concepts do. Nonetheless they have non-descriptive conceptual content. The conceptual system needs such indexical concepts because it lacks the resources to supply a purely descriptive symbol, i.e. a symbol that could uniquely identify a person, a time or a place. A purely descriptive concept would be a concept that a unique object, a unique person, a unique time or a unique place would satisfy in virtue of uniquely exemplifying each and every of its constituent features. We cannot specify the references of our concepts all the way down by using uniquely identifying descriptions on pain of circularity. If, as Pylyshyn (2000b: 129) points out, concepts need to be 'grounded', then on pain of circularity, 'the grounding [must] begin at the point where something is picked out directly by a mechanism that works like a demonstrative' (or an indexical). If concepts are to be hooked to, or locked onto, objects, times and places, then on pain of circularity, definite descriptions will not supply the locking mechanism.

Personal, temporal and spatial indexicals owe their special explanatory role to the fact that they cannot be replaced by purely descriptive concepts. Causally indexical concepts, however, play a different role altogether. Unlike personal, temporal and spatial indexical concepts, causally indexical concepts have a distinctive quasi-deontic or quasi-evaluative content. To categorize a target as 'too heavy', 'within reach' or 'fit for grasping between index and thumb' is to judge or evaluate the parameters of the target as conducive to a successful action upon the target. Unlike the contents of other indexicals, the content of a causally indexical concept results from the combination of an action predicate and an evaluative operator. What makes it indexical is that the result of the application of the latter onto the former is relative to the agent who makes the application. Thus, the job of causally indexical concepts is not just to match the world but to play an action guiding role. If it is, then presumably, like Millikan's (1996) PPRs (or 'pushmi-pullyu' representations), causally indexical concepts have a world-to-mind direction of fit or at best a hybrid direction of fit, not a pure mind-to-world direction of fit.

Since Chapter 1, we have assumed a dichotomy between mental representations with a mind-to-world direction of fit—beliefs and perceptions—and mental representations with a world-to-mind direction fit—desires and intentions. We have assumed that the visual information contained in visual percepts is designed to undergo further conceptual processing whose output is stored in the belief box. In the previous section, we have argued that, unlike visual percepts, visuomotor representations present visual information to motor intentions, which have non-conceptual content, a world-to-mind direction of fit and a mind-to-world direction of causation. We are presently arguing that the visual information of visuomotor representations can also serve as input to causally indexical concepts, which are elementary contextually dependent action concepts. Judgments involving causally indexical concepts have at best a hybrid direction of fit. When an agent makes such a judgment, he is not merely stating a fact: he is not thereby coming to know a fact that holds independently of his causal powers. Rather, he is settling, accepting or making his mind on an elementary action plan. The function of causally indexical concepts is precisely to allow an agent to make elementary action plans. Whereas personal, temporal and spatial indexicals lie at the interface between visual percepts and an individual's conceptual repertoire about objects, times and places, causally indexical concepts lie at the interface between visuomotor representations, motor intentions and what Searle calls prior intentions. Prior intentions have conceptual content: they involve action concepts. Thus, after conceptual processing via the channel of causally indexical concepts, the visual information contained in visuomotor representations can be stored in a conceptual format adapted to the content of prior intentions. Hence, the output of the motor processing of visual inputs can serve as input to further conceptual processing whose output will be stored in the 'intention box'.

Part IV

The perception of action

7　Seeing humans act

1　Introduction

In previous chapters, we have argued for a dual model of the visual processing of objects. We have argued that in the presence of one and the same stimulus, the human visual system can build two sorts of representations: a visual percept and a visuomotor representation. We have argued that many of the relevant differences between visual percepts and visuomotor representations flow from the fact that they have a different role in the human cognitive architecture. In Chapter 2, we reviewed electrophysiological evidence from registration of single cells in the brain of macaque monkeys that shows the contrast between two kinds of responses. We compared the responses of intraparietal neurons to the visual presentation of geometric stimuli that are affordances for prehension and the responses of inferotemporal neurons to the visual presentation of such complex stimuli as a picture of a tiger's head seen from above. In Chapter 3, we discussed a number of neuropsychological deficits in brain-lesioned human patients. In particular, we examined the contrast between visual agnosia and optic ataxia. Visual agnosic patients are impaired in their ability to recognize and identify the shapes of objects, but in many cases, their visuomotor capacity to reach and grasp objects are preserved. Conversely, in optic ataxic patients, the visuomotor transformation is impaired, but the perceptual processing of objects is preserved. In Chapter 4, we discussed psychophysical evidence showing that one and the same visual display can undergo perceptual or visuomotor processing in normal human subjects according to the task.

In a nutshell, our argument has been that, whereas visual percepts offer food for thought, visuomotor representations present visual information to motor intentions. In the course of our systematic comparison between the perceptual (or semantic) processing and the visuomotor (or pragmatic) processing of objects, we have so far concentrated on actions directed towards objects such as pointing to, reaching and grasping, neighboring objects. In many such actions, the target of the action may seem to play the role of a Gibsonian affordance. In Chapter 6, however, we have argued that pointing, reaching and grasping are not reflexive behaviors: they are genuine actions involving bodily movements produced by motor intentions. Even though a motor intention can be prompted by the possibilities for action afforded by a target, nonetheless no such non-deliberate action can unfold in the absence of a motor intention. It has been part of our argument that the motor intention in turn exploits the content of a visuomotor representation of the target.

As we argued in Chapter 6, both visual percepts and visuomotor representations of objects have non-conceptual content. But we claim that the non-conceptual content of visuomotor representations ought to be distinguished from the non-conceptual content of visual percepts. As we emphasized above, the structure of the argument for the distinction between the non-conceptual content of visuomotor representations and the non-conceptual content of visual percepts is very different from the structure of the argument for the distinction between the conceptual content of thoughts and the non-conceptual content of visual percepts. Unlike the latter, the former cannot appeal to the phenomenology of visual experience. Whereas the non-conceptual content of visual percepts must be legible to conceptual processes involved in the formation of thoughts, the non-conceptual content of visuomotor representations must be legible to motor intentions that initiate and monitor object-oriented actions. Whereas the non-conceptual content of visual percepts outstrips the conceptual content of thoughts, the non-conceptual content of visuomotor representations is far poorer than the non-conceptual content of visual percepts.

In the present chapter, we shall examine how the human visual system responds to human actions. Now, in seeing a human action, one sees a number of different things at once. First of all, since an action is an event, in seeing a human action, one sees an event; but one also sees a human individual act. Hence, one sees a human body move. If and when an action is directed towards an object, one sees the object that is the target of the action. When the action is directed towards an animal or a conspecific, one sees the animal or the other human being. Because social interactions matter so much to human beings, it is likely that evolution has wired in specific visual responses to the perception of human individuals. Thus, human individuals are peculiar sorts of visual objects whose perception can trigger powerful emotions in the perceiver. They are complex visual objects made up of many important distinct parts, which are themselves peculiar visual objects, whose visual perception can trigger various kinds of emotions. Thus seeing human actions involves processing visual objects with peculiar visual attributes: human bodies, human bodily parts and in particular human faces.

The visual perception of the distinct bodily parts of human bodies provides quite specific information to a conspecific. Given the anatomical, neurophysiological and psychophysical importance of the visual control of hand actions directed towards objects in the human visual system, it is likely that the visual perception of the movements of another individual's arm and hand towards objects must be in turn an important source of information. It may be an important source of information about his goals and intentions. But given that human culture has given rise to an evolutionarily unprecedented development of tools and artifacts, observing another's arm and hand movements involved in the complex manipulation of a tool must be a very significant source of information in learning skills. Think for instance of the importance of observing others' actions in the process of learning to use such different artifacts as a screwdriver, a saw, a microscope, a compass or a violin.

The visual perception of the shape, orientation and movements of others' bodily parts plays a crucial role in the process of understanding social interactions. When one sees a conspecific walk in the distance, the perception of the orientation, shape and movements of her upper and especially her lower limbs is a fundamental cue to determining some of her intentions, such as the spatial goal of her locomotion. Seeing the orientation and movements of individual A's torso and upper limbs in relation to individual B may provide crucial cues as to the significance of the interactions between the two individuals (such as whether A greets B or A fights B). Now, seeing the orientation and movements of an individual's upper and lower limbs in relation to oneself provides a crucial information relevant to the contents of one's own intentions, decisions and further actions.

Arguably, however, no other bodily part can convey as much and as important social information as a human face. As we shall argue, the neural basis for face processing is at the center of the circuit for social perception. While the perception of invariant features of a human face allows us to recognize the identity of a conspecific, the perception of changing aspects of a face plays a large role in social communication. Within the face, perceiving the mouth and the movements of the lips contributes to determining the content of others' speech and communicative intentions as well as their emotions. The eyes of course play a particularly significant role. Perceiving another's gaze direction provides fundamental evidence about her attention and intention. It is a source of information about others' social and non-social attention and intentions. Eyes provide peculiar information about others' emotional states and the perception of either a direct or an averted gaze is of course of crucial relevance for determining one's own reactions towards the person whose gaze one is perceiving.

In the first section of the present chapter, we shall start with the examination of what we shall call the human 'praxic' system, i.e. a high-level visual pragmatic processing of artifacts as tools. In the next section, we shall examine what seems to be the primary level of the visual analysis of human action, namely the perception of biological motion. Thus, we shall pick up the thread of Chapter 6 on visuomotor representations of objects. But we shall ascend from a fairly low-level to a higher level system of pragmatic processing of inanimate objects. In the second section, we shall move on to the primary level of visual analysis of human actions that delivers elementary judgments of animacy and/or agency. We shall start with data on the parameters of so-called 'biological motion'. As we shall see, evidence from cognitive psychology strongly suggests that the human brain has been prepared by evolution to detect the parameters of biological motion, even as exemplified by the motions of geometrical stimuli. It will turn out that seeing the motions of things as devoid of human visual features as circles, squares and triangles, may suffice to trigger judgments of goal-directedness.

In Sections 3 and 4, we shall ascend from the primary level to higher levels of the visual analysis of human actions. We shall argue that the human visual system has two complementary specialized neural circuits for processing human actions. On the one hand, in Section 3, we shall claim that what has come to be called, since the work of Di Pellegrino *et al.* (1992) and Rizzolatti *et al.* (1995), 'mirror neurons' (or the 'mirror system') form a cortical circuit whose task is to match the observation and the execution of motor actions directed towards objects. Because this system is triggered both by one's execution of object-oriented actions and by one's observation of object-oriented actions performed by others, we shall argue that it is a maximally engaged system for the visual recognition of object-oriented actions and intentions. We shall argue that this system is at work in the retrieval of non-social intentions and is the basis for mimicry, out of which may have evolved the human capacity to imitate, which in turn plays a pivotal role in the acquisition of technical skills. On the other hand, in Section 4, we shall examine evidence in favor of the view that a distinct neural circuit is specialized for the visual analysis of social intentions. Our distinction between non-social motor intentions and social intentions is meant to reflect the difference between an intention to grasp an object and an intention to affect a conspecific's behavior, which, in the

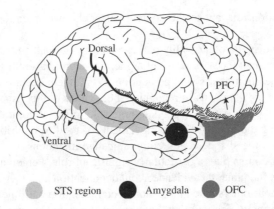

Fig. 7.1 Schematic representation of brain areas involved in social perception. The region of the superior temporal sulcus (STS, *shaded area*), the amygdala (*dark circle*) and the orbito-frontal cortex (OFC, *dark area*) are shown on a lateral view of a right hemisphere. Note putative reciprocal connections between the dorsal pathway and the STS region, and between the amygdala and both the STS and OFC areas. (Adapted from *Trends in Cognitive Science*, **4**, Allison, T., Puce, A. and McCarthy, G., Social perception from visual cues: role of the STS region, 267–78 (2000), with permission from Elsevier.)

human case, may involve the intention to cause a new mental state or representation, e.g. fear or a belief, in a conspecific on the basis of visual cues.

We shall call 'social perception network' the brain circuit devoted to the visual analysis of human actions directed towards conspecifics. To put it in a simplified way, the mirror system detects motor intentions, i.e. intentions directed towards inanimate objects. The social perception system detects social intentions, i.e. intentions directed towards conspecifics. The outputs of both 'the mirror system'—non-social motor intentions—and the 'social perception' system—social intentions—serve as inputs to the 'mindreading' system, i.e. to the cognitive system in the human brain whose job is to ascribe mental states to one's conspecifics as well as to oneself. Broadly speaking, the cortical system underlying social perception mainly involves three brain areas: the superior temporal sulcus (STS), the amygdala and the orbito-frontal cortex (Fig. 7.1).[1]

Electrophysiological evidence from the brains of macaque monkeys and brain imagery in humans strongly suggest that the visual perception of bodily movements, movements of the hand, mouth and the eyes activates neurons in the STS. So does the perception of static images of human faces and bodies. Neurons in the amygdala are active during gaze monitoring and the detection of gaze direction. The perception of both biological motion and gaze direction has been found to be impaired following amygdalotomy. Cells in the amygdala are activated by the perception of others' emotional states. Finally, there is evidence that the orbito-frontal cortex is involved in mindreading tasks.

---

[1]Since the orbito-frontal cortex is not really part of visual cognition, we will not talk about it anymore.

2 From grasping objects to manipulating tools

2.1 The praxic system: a high-level visual pragmatic processing of objects

As we argued in earlier chapters, pointing, reaching and grasping are actions; they are not merely reflexive behaviors. Rather, they are basic actions in two senses of 'basic'. First, the chain leading from the motor intention to the execution of the action is paradigmatically short. Second, however accurate such object-oriented actions turn out to be, the visual processing of the goal is sharply restricted. The motor intention requires elementary visual information about the target that can be provided by low-level visuomotor processing.[2]

Clearly, humans may plan actions at many different levels of conceptual sophistication. At the lowest level of conceptual sophistication, seeing the affordance of an object may trigger a motor plan immediately executable. At the highest levels of conceptual sophistication, humans may plan actions whose goal is not visible. Many human actions are so complex that their unfolding requires social cooperation within a legal and institutional setting. Intending to act in such a complex social and cultural setting requires verbal communication, understanding and knowledge of the relevant institutions. Satisfying a distant unobservable goal (e.g. getting married, getting divorced, writing a book, applying for a job or running for a political office) may involve the ability to entertain both complex instrumental beliefs and a hierarchy of several intermediary goals. The more the goal of an action is remote in space and time, the longer the chain leading from the representation of the goal to the execution of the action. The longer the chain, the greater the degree of freedom in selecting from among competing motor schemata. The greater the degree of freedom, the more the representation of the goal needs to be conceptualized and the more the ability to achieve the goal will rest on memory. A highly conceptualized goal is likely to require that the agent design a large number of intermediary steps. The planning and even the execution of actions with such highly conceptualized goals as getting married owes little if anything to the human visual endowment. In between immediately executable actions (such as grasping an object) and actions with a remote goal (such as getting married), lies a variety of actions of intermediate complexity such as e.g. getting dressed (or getting undressed), going to work (or going home) and preparing a meal. The planning and execution of actions of such intermediate complexity depend for a large part on the human visual system.

In the present section, we shall stick to visually guided actions in which the goal is visually accessible to the agent in the course of the execution of her bodily movements. We shall examine skilled actions that include, but do not reduce to, reaching towards and grasping objects, i.e. actions that consist in the use and the skilled manipulation of tools. Arguably, pointing and reaching towards a target involve the primary level of pragmatic processing of the visual attributes of a stimulus: at bottom, the visual information most relevant to pointing or reaching towards a stimulus is the representation of its location in an egocentric frame of reference. Grasping an object involves the scaling of

---

[2]Arguably, there is a trade-off between the accuracy of a visually guided action and the richness of the content of the visual representation of the target. The poverty of visuomotor representations might promote the accuracy of the action.

the grip: it involves processing its size, shape and orientation in object-centered coordinates, in addition to representing its location in egocentric coordinates (see Chapter 6). Tools, however, are complex cultural and/or technical objects. Their manipulation includes but does not reduce to mere grasping. On the one hand, one does not grasp a hammer, a screwdriver or a violin and a bow in a single fashion: knowing how to use them contributes to grasping them. On the other hand, grasping an artifact is merely an elementary step in the process of using it. Thus, the manipulation of tools includes a higher level of pragmatic processing of the visual attributes of an object than either pointing or reaching. Grasping is necessary but it is not sufficient for the correct use and skilled manipulation of a tool. It is not sufficient because one cannot use a tool (e.g. a hammer, a pencil, a screwdriver let alone a microscope or a cello) unless one has learned to use it, i.e. unless one can retrieve an internal representation of a recipe (a schema) for the manipulation of the object.

The visual processing involved in the use and the manipulation of tools is more complex than the visual processing involved in grasping objects since the latter is only a component of the former. What must be added to grasping an object is the ability to retrieve an internal representation of a schema for manipulation stored in memory. Presumably, no representation can be retrieved from memory unless it has antecedently been stored there. Arguably, one cannot store in memory a representation of a schema for the manipulation of a tool, unless one has seen repeated instances of such a schema, i.e. unless one has regularly observed other humans manipulate the tool according to the schema. The 'praxic' system, as we shall call it, which includes the retrieval of a stored script for the manipulation of a tool, is part of the pragmatic visual processing of cultural objects. We think of it as the higher level pragmatic processing of objects that allows normal subjects to see an object not merely as an affordance but as a tool, i.e. an artifact that can be used for the performance of skilled actions. On the one hand, it relates the visuomotor analysis of the visual attributes of the object relevant to prehension to the selection of an appropriate motor schema that will guide the skilled manipulation of the object. On the other hand, it lies at the interface between seeing objects and seeing actions. There is evidence that the parietal lobe is involved in this higher level pragmatic processing required by the manipulation of tools.

2.2 Neuropsychological evidence: apraxia

The neuropsychological examination of patients with parietal lesions, who are impaired in their ability to perform skilled actions with tools, has contributed significantly to our understanding of the neural basis of the system that underlies the generation of competent skilled actions in normal subjects. In normal subjects, what we call the 'praxic system' is a complex system that involves the preparation and execution of skilled actions at different levels, including the representation of the goal of the action, the control of its execution, the visual recognition of the action performed by another and the ability to imitate it. Close examination of pathological alterations of this system prompted by lesions in the parietal lobe shows that this higher pragmatic level of processing, which can be selectively impaired, ought to be distinguished from the lower-level visuomotor transformation involved in automatic object-directed actions, whose functioning can survive lesions affecting the praxic system.

The idea that one's movements involved in skilled actions directed towards artifacts are guided by internal representations (or motor schemas) has been entertained for a long time in neuropsychology by, e.g. Liepmann (1900) and Heilman (1979), who assumed respectively that so-called apraxic patients had lost 'movement formulas' or 'motor engrams', which are normally stored in the parietal cortex. If apraxia arises from the disruption of the normal mechanisms for action representations, then an apraxic patient should be impaired in her ability, not merely to use a tool or an object, but especially in her ability to pantomime the use of a tool when the tool is absent. Indeed, examination of apraxic patients' ability to pantomime the use of a tool also can help solve a methodological problem raised by the fact that more automatic visuomotor capacities may be triggered by the visual and especially tactile processing of the affordances offered by the tool.

Thus, Clark *et al.* (1994) tested apraxic patients' movements involved in their pantomime of an action of slicing bread (in the absence of both bread and knife). They found that the kinematics and spatial trajectories of patients' movements in their pantomime of an action of slicing an imaginary piece of bread with an imaginary knife were incorrect: patients improperly oriented their movement, and the spatiotemporal coordination of their joints was defective. Ochipa *et al.* (1997) made similar observations upon patient GW, who suffered from a bilateral parietal atrophy. When asked to demonstrate the use of 15 common household tools, GW failed in all cases. She failed using both hands and she failed in a variety of conditions: when she was verbally instructed, when the tool was visible but not used, and when she was asked to imitate the action of an actor. She committed mostly spatial errors: e.g. the direction of her movements was generally incorrect. Handling the object did not help GW very much: her success rate increased from 0/15 to 3/15. Despite her deep impairment in pantomime, GW's detached knowledge of the function of objects was preserved: she could correctly distinguish objects according to their function and she could verbally describe the sequence of an action. Finally, intertwined with her pantomime deficit, GW was also impaired in motor imagery; for example, she could not answer questions about the specific positions of her hands while performing a given action.

We argued that the praxic system is not restricted to the preparation and execution of skilled actions. Not only does it involve the ability to pantomime actions in the absence of the relevant tool, but it also involves the ability to see and recognize actions either executed or pantomimed by others. If so, then apraxic patients with a parietal lesion should also fail to recognize actions performed or pantomimed by others. This is exactly what Sirigu *et al.* (1995) found in patient LL with a bilateral parietal lesion. LL was impaired in positioning her fingers upon an object in order to grasp it for manipulation, such as a spoon in an action of eating soup. Furthermore, when asked to sort out correct from incorrect visual displays of another's hand postures, she consistently failed. Finally, she was unable to describe verbally hand postures related to specific object uses.

Action representation, as we understand it, involves the storage of engrams (schemas) that guide the generation of actions and the mechanisms for activating and retrieving these schemas. The activation of a schema can be triggered endogenously and exogenously. It is triggered endogenously when an individual forms an intention to act. It is triggered exogenously when an individual perceives a token of the same action performed by another agent. Importantly, the activation of the engram (or schema) for an action may or not result in the overt execution of the action. On this model of action representation, one can capture a subtle difference between apraxic patients GW and LL. GW was clearly impaired in her ability to activate endogenously an action schema: she was impaired in the execution of action, in pantomime and in motor imagery. However, GW was still able to tell the function of objects and to recognize actions. Hence, presumably, some internal action representation was preserved and it could be triggered exogenously by the perception of tools and the observation of actions. By contrast, in patient LL, all access to the representations of hand actions seems to have been damaged as neither endogenous nor exogenous triggering was efficacious. As a caveat, it should be noted that the full validation of this hypothetical explanation of the deficits of apraxic patients would require that all the relevant aspects of action representations be tested in one and the same patient—something that is yet to be done.

Previously discussed apraxic patients have parietal lesions. The role of the parietal lobe in the representation of action can be inferred from further neuropsychological evidence. In a recent paper, Sirigu and Duhamel (2001) compare the impairment of two patients in tasks of imagery: one with a parietal lesion, the other with an inferotemporal lesion. The patient with a parietal lesion was impaired in tasks of motor imagery and normal in tasks of visual imagery. Conversely, the patient with an inferotemporal lesion was impaired in tasks of visual imagery and normal in tasks of motor imagery. The double dissociation revealed by the neuropsychological examination of brain-lesioned patients is consistent with evidence obtained by brain imaging techniques on normal human subjects. PET experiments on tasks of motor imagery consistently show the involvement of the posterior parietal cortex (see Decety *et al.* 1994; Grafton *et al.* 1996). Conversely, tasks of visual imagery (discussed in Chapter 3) involve the inferior temporal cortex.

A complete picture, however, of the visual processing of human skilled actions involving the use of tools cannot be restricted to mechanisms located in the parietal lobe. The contribution of other areas of the visual brain, including the ventral stream, can be inferred from two main investigations. On the one hand, a PET study by Decety *et al.* (1997) revealed that seeing meaningful actions activated areas 20–21 in the inferotemporal cortex. On the other hand, some temporal lesions can indeed affect the recognition of pantomimed actions. Rothi *et al.* (1986) described two patients, who exhibited what they called 'pantomime agnosia' upon a left temporal lesion. Both patients could execute pantomimes upon verbal request and they could imitate gestures of others. However, they were impaired in naming the gestures performed by the examiner, in gesture discrimination and in gesture comprehension. Patients with ventral lesions (examined by Rothi *et al.* 1986) have the ability to retrieve action schemas when they are prompted both endogenously and exogenously, since these patients can execute pantomimes and imitate others' gestures. They fail, however, to 'extract the meaning' of the gestures that they see others perform.

So the following picture of apraxic deficits emerges. First of all, patients with a ventral lesion, who are impaired in action recognition and tool recognition, can still accurately use tools and perform skilled actions involving tools and even perform pantomimes of such actions. Their deficit stands in contrast with the deficit of apraxic patients with a posterior parietal lesion, who are impaired in the correct use of tools and in the ability to pantomime skilled actions. Second, the deficit of patients with a ventral lesion, who are impaired in the recognition of actions and tools, is reminiscent of the perceptual deficit of associative agnosic patients (discussed in Chapter 3), who are impaired in the visual recognition and identification of objects, but who can still grasp and use them. Finally, apraxic patients with a parietal lesion seem to stand to optic ataxic patients the way associative agnosic patients stand to apperceptive agnosic patients. Both apraxia and optic ataxia result from parietal lesions. Both sorts of agnosias result from ventral lesions. Each kind of agnosia results in an impairment of the semantic processing of objects: apperceptive agnosia is a deeper impairment than associative agnosia. Both optic ataxia and apraxia result in an impairment of the pragmatic processing of objects.

One of the reasons why the 'praxic' system lies at the interface between seeing objects and seeing actions is that it contributes to the selection of engrams (or schemas) necessary for the skilled manipulation of tools. And the storage of such schemas requires in turn the conscious observation of the manipulation of tools by others. We presently turn our attention from seeing objects to seeing humans act.

3   The primary level of the visual processing of actions

As we emphasized in Chapters 1 and 6, humans and non-human animals can be agents. Human actions are bodily movements caused by intentions. All actions are caused by 'motor intentions'. Some are caused in addition by what Searle (1983, 2001) calls 'prior intentions'. Human actions can be directed either towards inanimate objects or animate objects. The animate target of a human action can either be a member of a different biological species or a conspecific.

Thus, human beings can see conspecifics act either towards inanimate targets or towards animate targets. In the preceding section, we argued that observing skilled human actions directed towards artifacts plays an important role in the acquisition, the learning and the storage of schemas for the manipulation of tools. Arguably, human actions differ along their social dimension: human actions directed towards a conspecific have a stronger social dimension than human actions directed towards an inanimate object. Human actions directed towards non-human animals fall somewhere in between: on the one hand, they may involve the skilled use of tools (e.g. artifacts used for hunting, for skinning and for preparing food). On the other hand, they may involve social coordination and cooperation among conspecifics (e.g. in tracking and catching preys). Therefore, intentions at work in human actions differ along their social dimensions too. Human intentions at work in actions directed towards inanimate objects (including cultural artifacts used as tools) have a weaker social content than human intentions involved in actions directed towards conspecifics. Human intentions involved in actions directed towards non-human animals fall in between. There is much psychological evidence that humans are expert at detecting and understanding others' social and non-social intentions. This expertise is part of a cognitive capacity called 'mind-reading'. In this section, we shall examine what we call the 'primary level' of the visual processing of human actions, i.e. the responses of the visual system to the perception of basic movements that can provide cues of either non-social or social intentions.

The primary level of visual processing of human actions has given rise to two sorts of empirical investigations. On the one hand, the perception of so-called 'biological motion' has been investigated in human adults using the tools of psychophysics and cognitive neuroscience. On the other hand, developmental psychologists have investigated the visual responses of human infants to two sorts of visual cues of goal-directedness: patterns of self-propulsion embodied in motions of a variety of stimuli, and the perception of human hand movements directed towards a target. The primary level of visual processing of patterns of motion converts visual cues of actions into elementary judgments of animacy and/or agency. It is close to what Baron-Cohen (1995) calls 'ID' (for intentionality detector, where 'intentionality' means 'goal-directedness'). As Baron-Cohen (1995) notes, the inputs to ID may include the motions of a person, a butterfly, a billiard ball, a cat, a cloud or a unicorn. Thus, ID may be triggered by the motion of things whose shapes might be as diverse as that of an amoeba, a giraffe, an elephant or a stick insect. ID might overshoot and produce false-positives. As Baron-Cohen (1995: 35) notes, 'in evolutionary terms, it is better to spot a potential agent [. . .] than to ignore it'. We now start with the perception of biological motion.

3.1 Seeing biological motion

Arguably, the ability to detect the differences between the movements of animals and the motions of inanimate objects must have adaptive value, especially in animals with a well-developed visual system. The survival of an animal may certainly depend on its visual sensitivity to the differences between the locomotory movements of a predator, a prey and a mate. In highly social animals such as human beings, the visual detection of the locomotory movements of conspecifics may be highly adaptive. Indeed, there is psychophysical evidence that the human visual system has the ability to detect the loco-motion of conspecifics from very subtle cues.

Johansson (1973) devised an elegant psychophysical paradigm for the study of pure biological motion, in which subjects can perceive the motions produced by a walking human individual independently of their detection of any other visual attributes of the perceived agents (such as their shapes, textures and colors). He attached light sources to an agent's main joints and he recorded the agent's movements in a dark environment. The mere display of light sources attached to the joints of a walking individual sufficed to prompt in subjects the visual recognition of a walking person. By contrast, the display of light sources attached to the joints of a non-moving individual failed to produce the visual experience of anything significant, and the displayed motions of a mechanical dummy equipped with light sources in the dark were perceived as artificial non-biological motions.

Using the same paradigm as Johansson (1973), Dittrich (1993) has shown that the mere display of light sources attached to the joints of a moving individual suffices to trigger the visual recognition of a variety of 'locomotory' actions, such as walking, going upstairs or downstairs, jumping or dancing. It also suffices to trigger the visual recognition of 'instrumental' actions, such as hammering, stirring or ironing, and of 'social' actions, such as greeting and boxing. Of these actions, locomotory actions are recognized best and fastest. Koslowski and Cutting (1978) have shown that the mere display of light sources attached to the joints of a moving individual suffices to trigger the visual recognition of the sex (or gender) of the agent and Dittrich *et al.* (1996) have shown that it suffices to trigger the visual recognition of the personality traits and emotions of the agent. Evidence from Fox *et al.* (1982), Dasser *et al.* (1989) and Bertenthal (1993) shows that human infants as young as 3 months old are visually sensitive to the difference between the 'biological motion' of dots produced by a walking person and the random, artificially produced, non-biological motions of similar dots.

Further psychophysical experiments provide evidence that the so-called 'perception of biological motion' discovered by Johansson (1973) is really an elementary perceptual process. The mere detection of a few moving light-points located on the joints of a moving human body can trigger the visual recognition of the form of a human agent, as if the shape of a human agent could be extracted from the detection of a pattern of moving dots. According to Bertenthal and Pinto's (1994) evidence, the perception of the biological motion of a human agent walking upright is hardly impaired by the addition of light-points located randomly (i.e. attached not to the agent's joints but to his inter-joint segments). However, adding such randomly located light-points onto the display of a human agent walking upside down does impair the recognition of biological motion. Thus, biological motion is recognized better and faster in a normal orientation than upside down.

The perception of biological motion has also been studied using the paradigm of apparent motion. As we discussed in Chapter 5, at its simplest, the phenomenon of apparent motion, sometimes called 'phi phenomenon', consists in the fact that if a spot of light is flashed against a uniform background and a similar spot is flashed 10 to 45 ms after the first spot a short distance away (within a visual angle of some 4 degrees), then one sees a single spot moving from one position to the next. When subjects are presented with a pair of static images representing an inanimate object in two different positions at an appropriate time interval, the object is perceived as moving along the shortest or most direct path. Furthermore, the object is perceived to move in a direct path even if it requires the inanimate object to pass through another physical object. Thus, as Blakemore and Decety (2001: 562) put it, 'the visual system, therefore, seems to be biased towards selecting the simplest interpretation of the image when it involves inanimate objects'. Not so, however, when the images represent human bodily postures.

First of all, using fMRI, Kourtzi and Kanwisher (2000) have shown that there is a clear contrast between brain areas activated by the presentation of pairs of static images of human bodily postures according to whether they convey dynamic information or not: unlike seeing pairs of static images of a person sitting in an armchair, seeing pairs of static images of an athlete in the posture of throwing a ball activated areas MT/V5 and MST. Second, Shiffrar and Freyd (1990, 1993) have shown that pairs of images of the human body that can trigger the perception of apparent human bodily movement, can give rise either to the perception of biomechanically possible or of biomechanically impossible apparent motion, depending on the time interval between the two images. The trajectories of biological movements obey biomechanical constraints. Consider two pictures of a person, one with her left arm on the left side of her left knee and the other one with her left arm on the right of her left knee. When such a pair of static images of human bodily postures is sequentially presented and the time interval between the two displays is within 550–750 ms, then an observer sees the biomechanically possible apparent motion of the person's left arm move *around* her knee. When the same pair of static images is presented with a time interval of 150–350 ms, an observer sees the bio-mechanically impossible apparent motion of the person's arm move *through* her knee. Using PET, Stevens *et al.* (2000) have investigated the brain activities involved, respectively, in seeing a biomechanically possible and in seeing a biomechanically impossible apparent motion. They found that the primary motor cortex, the premotor and the inferior parietal cortex were involved only in the former. By contrast, the perception of biomechanically impossible apparent motion prompted bilateral activation of the medial orbito-frontal cortex.

3.2 The kinetic cues of animacy

We now turn to the psychological and psychophysical investigation of the visual cues of elementary animacy and agency. In the first half of the twentieth century, the Belgian psychologist Albert Michotte launched the investigation of the visual perception of causality and animacy. He was interested in the visual conditions necessary and sufficient for triggering judgments of causal relations. He designed numerous experiments (reported in his 1946/1963 *The Perception of Causality*), in which adult subjects see a 2D white circle A on a screen move in a straight line, from left to right, with a uniform velocity towards a black circle B, which stands still. As soon as A comes into contact with B, A stops moving and B starts moving in a straight line in the same direction as A with a uniform velocity. Upon seeing such a display, subjects report the visual experience as of a causal relation: they judge that the motion of the white circle causes the motion of the black circle. In other words, subjects see the transfer of motion from one circle to the next. Since there is no physical interaction between the 2D circles on a screen, Michotte called 'phenomenal causality' the perceptual phenomenon he discovered. Others have called it the perceptual illusion of causality.

What Michotte called the 'launching effect' is the phenomenon described in the above paragraph in which one perceives two distinct items (e.g. two circles of two distinct colors) and a single motion that is being transferred from one to the other. Michotte (1946–63) argued that the launching effect is a high-level perceptual effect, whereby what is perceived (causation) is to be found neither in the physical stimulus nor in its retinal projection. According to Scholl and Tremoulet (2000), the perceptual mechanism at work in the illusion of causality is very much like the 'kinetic depth effect' that allows extraction of structure from the perception of motion, i.e. an assumption hard-wired in the visual perceptual system. Michotte also discovered the 'entraining effect', which consists of the following sequence: after contacting circle B, circle A continues to move along and in contact with B. Subjects then report the experience of A's carrying B along (the former pushing the latter). Michotte discovered that the launching effect can be cancelled by introducing either a temporal or a spatial gap in between A's stopping its own motion upon contacting B, and the subsequent initiation of B's motion. In the case of a spatial gap, A stops moving without coming into contact with B, and the lack of collision between A and B precludes the illusion of causality. Finally, he discovered what he called 'the tool effect' involving now three circles: A's motion launches the motion of an intermediary gray circle C, which in turn launches the ultimate motion of B. In this complex sequence, in which a single motion seems transferred from A to B via C, C is perceived as a 'tool' whereby A moves B (Fig. 7.2).

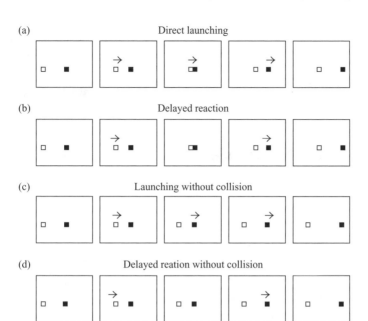

Fig. 7.2 Examples of Michotte's demonstrations of the perception of causality. (a) The launching effect, whereby the motion of the white object is seen to cause the motion of the black object. (b) The launching effect is attenuated if there is a temporal gap between the collision and the beginning of the motion of the black object. (c) The launching effect is also attenuated if there is no collision. (d) The launching effect is still more attenuated if there is a temporal gap and no collision. (From Leslie 1988, who showed that 6-month-old infants look longer in all conditions in which the launching effect is attenuated for adults, than in the launching condition.)

Subsequently, White and Milne (1997) have reported a number of new related findings on the perception of animacy involving more complex displays than Michotte. For example, they presented subjects with a vertical column of five aligned squares. At first, the middle square alone starts moving forward. Then the second and fourth squares start moving at the same speed in the same direction as the middle square following it. Finally the first and fifth squares follow suit. This display gives rise to the perception as of the central square 'pulling' the other four (as if in a military parade). In two other conditions, subjects saw one object move towards a non-moving collection of objects exhibiting some order and upon contacting the collection, the items within the ordered collection start moving in various directions at various speeds. In one condition, a circle moves towards a square composed of lines and columns of nine small squares. In the other condition, a segment moves towards an annulus of eight circles. In both conditions, subsequent to the contact between the moving object and the collection, either the squares or the circles start moving with various speeds in various directions. Subjects experience 'enforced disintegration and bursting' of the initial ordered collections (Fig. 7.3).

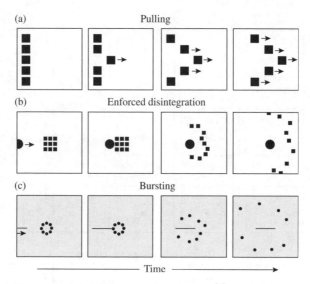

Fig. 7.3 Extensions of Michotte's findings on the perception of causality. (a) Instances of dynamic pattern giving rise to the perception of pulling (the middle square is seen as pulling the others). (b) and (c) Instances of dynamic patterns giving rise to perception of disintegration: (b) of regular group of squares by motion of circle; (c) of annulus of circles by motion of segment. (Adapted from *Trends in Cognitive Science*, **4**, Scholl, B. J. and Tremoulet, P. D., Perceptual causality and animacy, 299–309 (2000), with permission from Elsevier.)

Leslie (1988) reports evidence showing that 6-month-old human infants undergo the illusion of causality. Furthermore, Leslie (1988) and Spelke *et al.* (1995) have devised experiments based on preferential looking time showing that 6–8-month-old infants are more puzzled if the black circle B starts its motion in the absence of a collision between the circles A and B, e.g. if B starts moving after A stopped moving without contacting B (the 'spatial gap' condition). Spelke (1988, 1995) interprets such findings as showing that human infants expect causal interactions between inanimate objects to conform to what she calls 'the principle of contact' (or 'collision').

At roughly the same time as Michotte (1946/1963), Heider and Simmel (1944) showed human adults an animation on a screen involving three geometric objects: a small circle, a small triangle and a large triangle moving in the vicinity of a very large non-moving square (Fig. 7.4). Subjects saw the circle move erratically on the screen followed by the large triangle. They could see the circle locked in one of the angles of the square, while one of the apexes of the large triangle kept moving back and forth in the direction of the circle. Alternatively, they could see the small triangle slowly approach the circle and the two move while staying close to each other. Unlike the perception of static displays of the three geometric objects, the perception of the kinetic structure of the patterns of motion of the objects conveyed psychological and even social information about the objects. Subjects used highly intentional verbs to describe the behavior of the triangles such as they *chased, cornered, attacked, caressed* or *comforted* the circle. Subjects were even inclined to attribute personality traits (such as

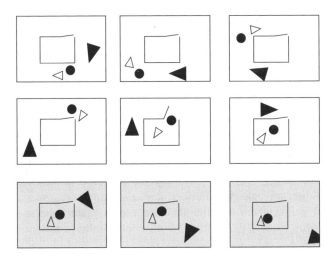

Fig. 7.4 Heider and Simmel's (1944) demonstration of perceived agency. Upon perceiving their motions, normal adults ascribe goals and emotions to geometrical stimuli. (Adapted from *Trends in Cognitive Science*, **4**, Scholl, B. J. and Tremoulet, P. D., Perceptual causality and animacy, 299–309 (2000), with permission from Elsevier.)

shyness or bulliness) and emotions (anger or frustration) to the geometrical objects. Berry and Springer (1993) report that 3- and 4-year-old children also attribute mental states and emotions to geometric shapes upon perceiving Heider and Simmel's animations. It is significant that the visual perception of patterns of motions of geometrical stimuli with no faces and/or human (or animal) bodily appearances at all, can cause in the perceiver the attribution of emotions to such objects. Clearly, seeing a triangle *as* threatening or a circle *as* scared arises from epistemic visual perception.

Building on Michotte's and Heider and Simmel's work, Premack (1990) and Premack and Premack (1995) hypothesize that the human mind is tuned to the visual detection of the motion of what they call 'self-propelled' objects, i.e. objects whose motion appears to be internally caused. In their view, visual cues of self-propulsion involve the spontaneous transition from rest to motion, patterns of acceleration, deceleration and sudden changes of direction (that are reminiscent of patterns of biological motion). According to Premack (1990), very early on human infants are prepared to distinguish the pattern of motion of self-propelled objects from that of objects whose motion has been externally caused. The visual contrast between the pattern of motion of a self-propelled object and that of an object whose motion is externally caused is a primitive source of elementary judgments of agency. In his view, the perception of the motion of a self-propelled object automatically triggers the attribution of a goal (if not an intention) to the self-propelled object.

Gergely *et al.* (1995) and Csibra *et al.* (1999) presented 1-year-old, 9-month-old and 6-month-old human infants with a video sequence in which a blue rectangle stands up on its smaller side midway between a large red circle (to its left) and a smaller yellow circle (to its right). Then, the infants see the small yellow circle move in a parabolic trajectory above the blue rectangle and land next to the large red circle. Once infants were habituated to this sequence, they were presented with one of the two following sequences in which the blue rectangle had been removed. In one of them, they saw the small yellow circle move in the same parabolic leftward trajectory and land next to the large red circle. In the other sequence, they saw the small yellow circle move in a straight line until it reached the large red circle. Although the latter sequence was new and infants had already seen the small yellow circle move in a parabolic trajectory in the presence of the blue rectangle, they looked longer at the former sequence than at the latter. Once the blue rectangle has been removed, infants were more surprised when they saw the small yellow circle land next to the large red circle via a parabolic trajectory than via an available rectilinear trajectory. Gergely *et al.* (1995) and Csibra *et al.* (1999) conclude that the parabolic trajectory of the small yellow circle in the presence of the blue rectangle is processed by 6-month-old and older human infants as a visual cue of a goal-directed behavior. Furthermore, the experiment was replicated with 10–11-year-old chimpanzees and the same pattern of preferences as Gergely *et al.* (1995) and Csibra *et al.* (1999) found with human infants was observed in adult chimpanzees.

The importance of the findings reported in this section lies in the fact that they show that the visual experience of causation, goal-directedness, animacy and agency can be triggered by the perception of patterns of self-propelled motions of geometrical stimuli, which bear no visual resemblance to human beings. Human infants as young as 6 months old can, it seems, experience the visual illusion of goal-directedness if not of agency. Very subtle and fragmentary visual cues contained in patterns of self-propulsion of geometrical stimuli suffice to trigger the response of the human cognitive subsystem that delivers judgments of agency at a very early age. If this is correct, then it implies that the system that computes judgments of agency from meagre visual cues contained in patterns of self-propulsion would seem to be 'encapsulated' in Fodor's (1983) sense discussed in Chapter 5.

4 Seeing object-oriented actions

Some of the findings on the perception of biological motion, which we reviewed above, raise the intriguing question of the inseparability between action and perception, or more precisely between the perception and the preparation of some actions. The biological movements produced by animals have a number of kinematic and dynamical properties that distinguish them from the mechanical motions of non-biological physical objects and artifacts. On the one hand, the ballistic motions of non-biological projectiles have a symmetrical kinematic profile. By contrast, the goal-directed movements of animals have an asymmetrical kinematic profile, in which a fast acceleration is followed by a much longer deceleration, as exemplified by a human reaching movement or by a human running race. On the other hand, as first recognized by Lacquaniti *et al.* (1983), the tangential velocity of the moving limb of an animal varies with the radius of the curvature of the movement. A normal subject cannot depart from this relation between the geometry and the kinematics of his movement. When tracking a target, whatever its trajectory, an agent's movements cannot but conform to such biomechanical constraint as decelerating rather than accelerating in a curved trajectory. According to Viviani (1990), when tracking a target, the agent's movements 'bear the imprint of the general principles of organization of spontaneous movements, even though this is in contrast with the specifications of the target'. Interestingly, the same trade-off between acceleration and curvature applies to a subject's perceptual estimate of a target's trajectory. Whereas a target moving at a uniform velocity along an elliptical path will not be perceived as moving at a uniform velocity, a target whose motion is consistent with the trade-off relation between acceleration and curvature will be perceived as moving with a uniform velocity.

According to Viviani and Stucchi's (1992) view, this finding is evidence that the observer's perception of biological motion is guided and/or biased by his or her implicit knowledge of the biomechanical constraints that apply to the execution of his or her own movements. Presumably, if this tacit knowledge is involved in the execution of action, then it must be stored in the observer's motor system. Thus, in their view, the perceptual representation of biological motion delivered by the visual system is biased by representations of biomechanically possible movements stored in the motor system. It is a short step to the conclusion that the perception of biological motion automatically triggers, in the observer, the formation of a motor plan to perform the observed movement. Perceiving and executing biological motions would thus share the common representational resources involved in motor imagery and/or motor preparation. Forming a motor plan, of course, is part of, but is distinct from, executing a movement. This view fits well with the contrast (mentioned above) between the perception of biomechanically possible apparent motion and the perception of biomechanically impossible apparent motion: unlike the perception of a biomechanically possible apparent motion, the perception of a biomechanically impossible apparent motion would not trigger in the observer a motor plan to perform the perceived motion.

There is, as we mentioned in Chapter 6, much psychophysical evidence in favor of the view that motor imagery is at work in both object-oriented actions and in the observation of object-oriented actions performed by others. While motor imagery is crucially involved in motor preparation, motor preparation is of course a part of the execution of one's actions and it turns out to be prompted by one's observations of the actions of others. Thus, motor imagery lies at the interface between the planning of movements and the observation of others' movements. Arguably, in humans, the capacity for motor imagery may have a unique adaptive value, since the observation of others' bodily movements is a crucial source for the learning of skilled gestures by imitation.

With Jeannerod (1994: 189):

[...] consider a pupil learning a motor skill such as playing a musical instrument. The pupil watches the teacher demonstrate an action that he must imitate and reproduce later. Although the pupil remains immobile during the teacher's demonstration, he must form an image in his mind of the teacher's action. Conversely, when the teacher watches the pupil's repetition, though not performing the action himself, he will experience a strong feeling of what should be done and how.

As Jeannerod further notes, sport addicts watching sport on television are reported to mentally perform the actions that they are observing without executing them. Psychophysical measurement has revealed that an actually or overtly performed action involves the same duration as its mental or implicit counterpart. This is true in the domain of learned skills, where comparison has been made between overt and mental recitation of the alphabet or in comparing an actual writing task to its mental counterpart. And it is true of natural motions: walking to a specified target requires the same time as imagining walking to the same target. Sport psychologists have reported that mental practice facilitates future performance. Increase in muscular strength consequent upon actual training (i.e. undergoing actual muscle contraction) has been compared with increase in muscular strength consequent upon mental training. In mental training, the subject imagines muscle contraction while the muscle is quiescent. It has been found that muscular strength increased by 30% upon actual training, while it increased by 22% upon mental training. In both, actually performed and simulated physical exercises, heart rate and respiration rates were measured and found to increase (see Jeannerod 1997).

4.1 The discovery of mirror neurons in the brain of macaque monkeys

In the 1990s, a group of neuroscientists from Parma (Di Pellegrino *et al.* 1992 and Rizzolatti *et al.* 1995) discovered neurons in area F5 of the brain of macaque monkeys that discharge, not only when the monkey performs specific object-oriented actions such as grasping or manipulating objects but also, when the monkey observes another monkey or a human experimenter perform the same action. Area F5, which occupies the most rostral part of inferior area 6, has reciprocal connections with the inferior parietal lobule, in particular with area AIP (examined in Chapters 2 and 6). As we discussed there, neurons in area AIP, which have been studied by Sakata and collaborators (e.g. Murata *et al.* 2000), provide a visuomotor analysis of the shape, orientation and size required for the grasping of such objects as a plate, a ring, a cube, a cylinder, a cone or a sphere. Arguably, neurons in AIP send the result of their visuomotor analysis of targets of prehension to neurons in F5, where schemas for object-oriented actions are stored. As Rizzolatti *et al.* (1995) put it, 'AIP and F5 form a cortical circuit which transforms visual information on the intrinsic properties of objects into hand movements that allow the animal to interact appropriately with the objects. Motor information is then transferred to F1 to which F5 is directly connected' (see also Arbib 2000). As we are about to see, the significance of the discovery of mirror neurons lies in the fact they are sensory-motor neurons.

Rizzolatti *et al.* (1995) registered single cells in area F5. They found two sorts of neurons: 'canonical' neurons and 'mirror' neurons. While the former discharge only during the execution of hand actions directed towards objects (and are thus purely motor neurons), the latter discharge both during execution and during observation of object-oriented actions. This is why mirror neurons are sensory-motor neurons. The activity of mirror neurons is correlated with specific hand and mouth movements: they have been classified as 'grasping neurons', 'holding neurons', 'tearing neurons', 'manipulation neurons'. Their activity has been described by Rizzolatti *et al.* (1995) as a 'motor vocabulary' of actions of prehension. Typically, a grasping neuron, for example, will discharge when the monkey grasps a small piece of food presented on a tray. It discharges also when the monkey sees the experimenter grasp the piece of food on the tray. Thus, grasping an object between thumb and index finger with precision grip and seeing an object being grasped between thumb and index finger with precision grip will trigger the response of a grasping mirror neuron. The simple presentation of an object, however, will fail to activate such neurons. Also, mimicking the action in the absence of a target object or performing the action with the use of a tool fails to prompt the neuronal response. In one-third of the recorded mirror neurons, the response of the neurons depended on a strict 'congruence' between the movements performed by the monkey and the movements produced by the experimenters and observed by the monkey. For example, a highly congruent mirror neuron will discharge when the monkey produces a wrist rotation to take away food from the experimenter's hand. It will also discharge when the experimenter rotates his hands around a raisin in opposite directions (as if for breaking it). But it will discharge neither when the monkey grasps, nor when the monkey observes grasping by the experimenter. In the other two-thirds of the recorded mirror neurons, what mattered was the goal of the action, not the details of its motor execution (Fig. 7.5).

Thus, the mirror system in area F5 of the monkey brain has been described by a number of researchers as 'a cortical system that matches observation and execution of motor actions' (Gallese and Goldman 1998: 495). As Rizzolatti *et al.* (1995) put it, 'when the monkey observes a motor action that belongs (or resembles) its movement repertoire, this action is automatically retrieved. The retrieved action is not necessarily executed. It is only represented in the motor system. We speculate that this observation/execution mechanism plays a role in understanding the meaning of motor events'. Arguably, the mirror system in monkeys constitutes a primitive system for the visual recognition of, and the application of proto-concepts of actions to, such object-oriented actions. It is a maximally engaged system for the visual recognition of, and the application of proto-concepts of actions to, object-oriented actions in the two following senses: on the one hand, the same cortical circuit governs the execution and the observation of

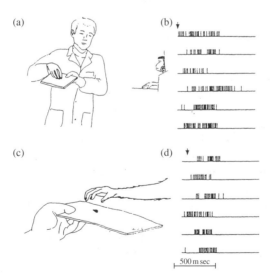

Fig. 7.5 Activity of a mirror neuron in the monkey prefrontal cortex. (a) The monkey watches actions of grasping food pellets by an experimenter. (b) Discharge of mirror neurons during six different trials. *Arrow* indicates onset of experimenter's action. (c) and (d) Activity of the same neuron when the monkey itself grasps the food. (From di Pellegrino *et al.* 1992. Understanding motor events: a neurophysiological study. *Experimental Brain Research*, **91**, 176–80, © Springer Verlag.)

actions; on the other hand, the visual detection of an object-oriented action performed by another automatically triggers in the observer an action plan—the plan to perform an action isomorphic to the observed action. By this view, the mirror system in monkeys is a maximally engaged system for categorizing object-oriented actions because it will not apply a proto-concept of an action unless the monkey's motor system retrieves a motor plan involved in the preparation to act similarly, i.e. unless the monkey's motor system engages in the planning of an action that will not be executed.

Two important complementary features of the mirror system in monkeys are worth emphasizing. On the one hand, as Rizzolatti *et al.* (1995) and Arbib (2000) emphasize, when prompted by the observation of an action performed by another, the discharge of mirror neurons in the monkey brain is not followed by the execution of the action. Furthermore, mirror neurons are not activated as a piece of food is moved closer towards the animal and thus becomes easily available to him. The activity of mirror neurons, therefore, does not seem related to food expectancy. Nor is it part of a system of automatic response to food affordances. The mirror system is indeed a 'matching system' for the observation/execution of motor actions. The first point, however, is that its conceptual resources are sharply limited by the high degree of its engagement in action preparation: 'the understanding of the meaning of motor events' provided by such a matching system is precisely limited by its inability to disengage, i.e. by its inability to apply action concepts when the application is detached from motor preparation. On the other hand, the object-oriented actions that prompt the discharge of mirror neurons in the monkey brain are not social actions directed towards a conspecific. The mirror system in the monkey brain is an engaged system for detecting non-social intentions involved in object-oriented actions.

4.2 The mirror system, mimicry, resonance and imitation in humans

In monkeys then, the mirror system is automatically triggered by the visual processing of hand and mouth actions directed towards inanimate objects performed by others or by the execution of such actions. Arguably, it might well be the neural basis in the primate brain for a system of mimicry, whereby A's observation of conspecific B's action directed towards an object, compulsively causes A to form a motor plan that is isomorphic to the plan underlying observed movements, but whose execution is automatically pre-empted by inhibitory mechanisms. In the sequel, we shall distinguish between mimicry and imitation.

It is controversial whether monkeys and apes imitate at all (Tomasello 1999; Hauser 2001). As Hauser *et al.* (2002: 1575) write, 'what is suprising is that monkeys show almost no evidence of visually-mediated imitation, with chimpanzees showing only slightly better capacities [...]. Evidence for spontaneous visuo-manual imitation in chimpanzees is not much stronger'. But it is uncontroversial that, when mirror neurons fire in the brain of a macaque monkey upon his perceiving a hand action directed towards a raisin, the monkey is not involved in an imitative process at all. In our view, whether the duplicated behavior itself is intentional or not, imitation is an action and furthermore it may require some grasp of the intention involved in the duplicated action. True, the duplicated behavior need not itself be intentional: A may imitate B's non-intentional behavior, e.g. B's accidental fall onto the ground or B's non-intentional yawning. But for A to imitate B's behavior, A must *intend* to replicate B's behavior. Furthermore, if B's imitated behavior was intentional, then only by retrieving B's intention could A start to imitate B. As Hauser (2001: 147–8) writes, 'when humans imitate an action, they often infer the model's intention. Humans perceive actions as having goals and being guided by an actor's intention to achieve those goals. Thus, when we imitate, we are copying not only the physical action, but also the intentions underlying those actions'. What seems to happen in humans (and perhaps in dolphins) is a tremendous development of the ability to imitate, whereby anything—any noise, any motion—can become the target of an imitation in any modality. Again, as Hauser *et al.* (2002: *ibid.*) put it:

[...] even in cases where nonhuman animals are capable of imitating in one modality (e.g. song coyping in songbirds), only dolphins and humans appear capable of imitation in multiple modalities. The detachment from modality-specific inputs may represent a significant change in neural organization, one with a significant impact on not only imitation but also communication; only humans can lose one modality (e.g. hearing) and make up for this deficit by communicating in a different modality (i.e. signing).

Although mirror neurons found in the premotor cortex of macaque monkeys respond both when the monkey performs a specific action and when he sees another perform a different token of the same action, nonetheless it seems as if the presence of mirror neurons is not sufficient to ensure the ability to engage in genuine imitation.

By contrast with imitation, mimicry is not an intentional process. The process whereby the skin of a chameleon changes colors and mimicks those exhibited by its local environment is certainly not an intentional process. Moths are insects on which birds feed; they can be light or dark. Before the Industrial Revolution, light-colored moths used to proliferate on light tree trunks in England. With the advent of the Industrial Revolution, as tree trunks became darker, dark-colored moths became more difficult to spot than light colored moths against darker tree trunks and, as a result, dark-colored moths were selected. This is another instance of mimicry to be explained, not by any intentional process within moths' brains but, by natural selection. Some butterflies (the monarchs), which are the prey of birds (the bluejays), store a toxic substance from which they feed. Thus, they secrete a substance toxic to their predators. Other butterflies (the viceroys), which do not secrete the toxic substance, mimick the monarchs' colors, which misleads birds into 'believing' that they too are toxic. Such behaviors, which are clearly non-intentional and which are instances of mimicry, are ubiquitous in evolution (see Riddley 1995).

Thus, mimicry does not require the retrieval of the intention involved in the mimicked behavior, since there is none. Mimicry is the process whereby A's detection (visual or otherwise) of a property exemplified in A's environment, causes A to exemplify the property in question. Now, the mimicked property can be exemplified by pretty much anything: minerals or plants in A's environment, members of a different animal species or members of the same animal species. Arguably, if and when the mimicked property is a behavior instantiated by a conspecific, mimicry can fade into imitation. Thus, although it is triggered by sensory detection, mimicry is not a genuine action at all: if A's behavior is a case of mimicry, then A may have no intention to do what he does. As Hauser (2001: 20) notes of mimicry in fireflies, 'there is no evidence that the mimetic system is flexible, capable of matching any variant that comes its way. The capacity represents a highly specialized skill, one that is radically different from our own capacity to mimic or imitate'.

Flock and herd behavior in birds and mammals, school behavior in fish are instances of behaviors in which different individuals, which are part of large aggregates, synchronize their movements for some adaptive reason or other. For instance, it turns out that school behavior in fish minimizes the risk for individuals of being targets of predators (see Riddley 1995). Seeing an individual in the collection initiate a movement triggers in others the production of a similar movement. These examples are best thought of as examples of 'resonance' behavior: upon seeing an individual behave in a certain way, others 'resonate'.

Mimicry and resonance behavior are widespread in humans; and so is imitation. As common sense testifies, the mere detection (visual or non-visual) of some typically human behavior can cause the observer to engage irresistibly in a replication of the observed behavior: yawning, laughter and emotional contagion are all examples of human resonance behavior. A can be prompted to yawn, to laugh or to experience fear, respectively by seeing B yawn, by seeing him laugh or by detecting B's fear. Neither A's behavior nor B's behavior are intentional.

As neuropsychological and psychopathological clinical evidence shows (see Lhermitte *et al.* 1983), some cases of so-called 'utilization behavior' in human patients with lesions in the orbito-frontal cortex may be instances of mimicry, not imitation. Patients with utilization behavior either compulsively replicate the gestures they see other people perform or compulsively exploit the affordances offered by objects in front of them. On the one hand, the compulsive utilization of the affordances offered by an object is neither a case of mimicry nor of imitation. On the other hand, when frontal patients imitate other peoples' gestures, their own behavior is not guided by what Searle (1983, 2001) calls a 'prior intention' to do so.

Patients with so-called 'imitation behavior', by contrast, do not merely replicate the gestures of others: they mimick other people's goal-directed actions. Arguably, the compulsive duplication of others' goal-directed actions by an imitation patient requires the retrieval of the motor intention involved in the observed action and the patient's imitation behavior is presumably guided by his or her own motor intention. These 'imitation' patients, however, lack prior intentions: they do not form the intention to duplicate the intentional actions of others on the basis of a deliberative process. This is why their imitative behavior is compulsive. On the one hand, the imitation patient must be able to retrieve the motor intention present in the other's action in order to duplicate, not just the other's seen movements but, her goal-directed actions. On the other hand, although the patient has no prior intention to act imitatively, his movements are initiated and guided by his own motor intentions. In this respect, the imitation patient is like Searle's normal person absorbed in her thoughts who paces around the room: she has an 'intention in action' and no prior intention (see Chapters 1 and 6). Unlike a normal person, however, an imitation patient is driven to act by seeing others act. Such compulsive behaviors are explained by an impairment of the inhibitory mechanisms that normally preempt the execution of actions whose plans may be automatically triggered by the observations of others' actions in normal subjects. If there is a mirror system in humans, then it may well be the neural basis of human mimicry. Indeed, there is evidence that there is a mirror system in humans.

Using transcranial magnetic stimulation (TMS), Fadiga *et al.* (1995) tested the excitability of the human motor cortex in four distinct conditions: in the first condition, subjects saw an experimenter grasp an object; in the second condition, subjects saw an experimenter produce meaningless arm movements; in the third condition, subjects merely saw objects; and in the last condition, subjects detected the dimming of a small spot of light. The experiment revealed that in the first condition (in which subjects observed grasping actions), motor-evoked potentials (MEPs) induced by TMS recorded from the subjects' hand muscles, significantly increased compared to other conditions. Furthermore, an increase of excitability was recorded in the very muscles that would have been involved had subjects performed the grasping actions that they observed. This experiment suggests that, in humans as well as in monkeys, watching another perform an object-oriented action triggers the very cortical circuit involved in the performance of the action.

The functional anatomy of the human mirror system is currently under investigation with the help of neuro-imaging techniques. Using PET, Rizzolatti *et al.* (1996) and Grafton *et al.* (1996) compared brain activity when subjects grasped objects, when they watched an actor grasp an object and when they merely observed objects. They found that observation of objects being grasped activated a portion of the left STS. The observation of actions directed towards objects was found to activate other areas, most of which were located in the frontal lobe (where the SMA and lateral area 6 in the precentral gyrus were involved) and in area 45 in the inferior frontal gyrus. Importantly, area 45 in the human brain (otherwise known as Broca's area), which is active during the observation of object-directed actions, is widely taken to be homolog to area 6 in the ventral area 6 of the monkey brain, where Di Pellegrino *et al.* (1992) first registered the activity of mirror neurons. Areas located in posterior and ventral parts of the parietal lobe (e.g. area 40) were also found to be active during action observation.

Given that the information provided by the observation of an object-directed action performed by another can in turn be exploited in various tasks, the question raised by these findings is: which of these brain areas are involved in the different cognitive exploitation of these observations? For instance, a subject may observe an action for the purpose of identifying it or for the purpose of pantomiming it. It is likely that a subject's cognitive strategy can activate selective brain areas during action observation. In a PET experiment by Decety *et al.* (1997), subjects were instructed either to watch actions for the purpose of memorizing them for subsequent imitation or for the purpose of recognizing them. Observed actions were either goal-directed ('meaningful') or purposeless ('meaningless'). When subjects watched meaningless unfamiliar actions for the purpose of subsequent imitation, Decety *et al.* (1997) found an activation of the SMA and of the ventral premotor cortex. They also found a bilateral activation of the dorsolateral prefrontal cortex and a strong activation of the right inferior parietal lobule. When subjects watched meaningful actions for the purpose of recognizing them, Decety *et al.* (1997) found activations in the left middle temporal gyrus in the STS region, in the parahippocampal gyrus and in the ventral prefrontal cortex. Thus, areas in the ventral pathway turn out to be active during tasks of identification and recognition of object-oriented actions, while the dorsal pathway is active when the observation of object-oriented actions has mainly a technical (or executive) purpose. These experiments show that in humans, the observation of pantomimes triggers the cortical circuit involved in the recognition of action directed towards inanimate objects or non-social intentions. Thus, in humans, unlike in monkeys, pantomimes can trigger the response of the mirror system.

Arguably, the presence of a neural basis for mimicry is a necessay, though not a sufficient, condition for imitation. Meltzoff and Moore (1977, 1997) found out that newborn infants (42 min old!) are able to replicate gestures of mouth-opening, tongue-protrusion and lip-protrusion, which they see adults perform. These fascinating findings raise at least two questions. One question is: how can a human neonate manage to match her visual perception of another's facial movements onto a proprioceptive representation of her own face? A different question is whether neonates' replications of mouth-opening and tongue protrusion gestures are cases of genuine imitation or whether they are instances of mimicry (i.e. reflexive behavior). In answer to the first question, Meltzoff and Moore (1997: 180) offer the 'active intermodal mapping' (AIM) model, according to which 'the perceived and produced human acts are coded within a common (supramodal) framework, which enables infants to detect equivalences between their own acts and ones they see'. It is important to notice that an answer to the first question would leave the second question wide open. The reason for this is that for all cases of mimicry, the first question can arise: if and when a person is caused to yawn by seeing another person yawn, then the question arises of how visual information is converted into proprioceptive information. If neonates' replications of mouth-opening and tongue-protrusion gestures turn out to be instances of mimicry, then, until their orbito-frontal cortex matures, human neonates would be like patients with pre-frontal lesions. Against this interpretation, Meltzoff and Moore (1997) argue that 6-week-old infants do imitate facial gestures on the grounds that, in 6-week-old infants, the duplication can take place after a 24-h delay.

Meltzoff (1994) provides evidence that 18-month-old children are able to 're-enact' intended actions. In one condition, 18-month-old children saw adults engage in an action directed towards one of five distinct complex toys and fail to perform it. For example, they saw an adult pick up a dumbbell consisting of two wooden cubes connected by a tube, try to pull the two cubes apart and fail to do so. Children aged 18 months did not merely reproduce the seen gestures in the adults' failed attempt to perform the action directed towards an object. Rather, they performed a successful version of the intended action of which they had seen an aborted version. In another condition, 18-month-old children saw a mechanical device mimick the adult's gestures involved in a failed attempt to pull apart the two cubes making up the dumbbell. In this case, however, the children did not produce a successful version of the observed failed attempt on the part of the mechanical device. Meltzoff's (1994) last finding in the second condition is reminiscent of Rizzolatti et al.'s (1995) finding that mirror neurons in area F5 of the monkey brain fail to respond during observations of food-oriented actions performed with a tool. Arguably, in both cases, the kinematics of the tool motions differs from that of a biological motion, so that the observed action cannot be matched onto the observer's motor repertoire to allow automatic detection and attribution of a goal to the mechanical tool. Thus, on this interpretation, the kinematic structure of motion would fail to activate the motor preparation, which is hypothesized to be a representational resource shared by the perception and the execution of the action.

4.3   Infants' visual sensitivity to reaching and grasping

Gergely *et al.*'s (1995) and Csibra *et al.*'s (1999) findings, discussed in Section 2.2, seem to be corroborated by the results of experiments designed to investigate the visual responses of human infants to the presentation of human hand movements directed towards an inanimate object. In the habituation condition of an experiment by Wellman and Philipps (2001), 12-month-old infants see a whole person extend her hand over a barrier, reach and grasp an object (e.g. a ball) located behind the barrier. Then the barrier is removed and infants either see the person reach directly for the object or they see the person reach the object indirectly by producing the same curved arm movement as before the barrier was removed. Wellman and Philipps (2001) found that infants looked longer at the indirect reach event, even though they have already seen the same arm movement in the barrier condition.

In a series of experiments, Woodward (1998) and Woodward *et al.* (2001) presented 9-month-old infants with the display of two distinct toys, A and B. Infants were habituated to seeing either a human hand grasp—without lifting it—one of the two distinct toys, or a rigid rod with a sponge attached to it contact one of the two toys. Then, the positions of the toys were switched and the four following conditions were compared. In one condition, infants saw the human hand grasp the other (new) toy B in the location formerly occupied by A. In this condition, the hand grasped a 'new object' and moved through an 'old path'. In the second condition, infants saw the human hand grasp the same (old) toy A in a new position (the location formerly occupied by B). In this condition, the hand grasped an 'old object' and moved through a 'new path'. In the third condition, infants saw the rod contact B in the position formerly occupied by A. In this condition, the rod contacted a 'new object' through an 'old path'. In the fourth condition, infants saw the rod contact A in the position formerly occupied by B. In this condition, the rod contacted an 'old object' through a 'new path' (Fig. 7.6). What Woodward (1998)

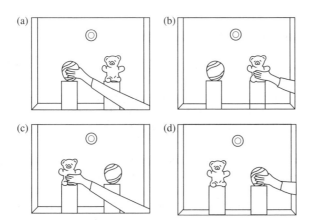

Fig. 7.6 Infants' sensitivity to goal of hand action. Human infants aged 9 months habituated to seeing hand reach ball (a) (rather than teddy-bear (b)) look longer at hand reaching a new object via same path (c) than at hand grasping same object via a new path (d). (Adapted from *Cognition*, **69**, Woodward, A. L., Infants selectively encode the goal object of an actor's reach, 1–34 (1998), with permission from Elsevier.)

found was that infants looked longest when the human hand grasped a new toy, whether or not the path was new. In the rod condition, however, this pattern of preference did not arise. Thus, this experiment revealed that infants' responses were stronger to the perception of a change of object or target of hand action, than to the perception of a change in the path, i.e. in the executive aspect of the hand movement. Woodward (1998) replicated these experiments with 5-month-old infants, who, unlike 9-month-old infants, do not yet engage in such social behavior as joint-attention. She found in 5-month-old infants the same pattern as in 9-month-olds: they looked longer at a human hand grasp a new toy by whatever path. When she replaced the grasp of a human hand by that of an artificial occluder, she found that neither 9-month-old nor 5-month-old infants showed the pattern of preference elicited by the grasp of a human hand.

One question raised by these findings is whether the relevant contrast is between genuine grasp as opposed to mere contact with the target or between the visual perceptual features (e.g. the texture), respectively, of a biological hand and of an artifact. When she replaced the grasp of a human hand by the grasp of an artificial claw, Woodward (1998) found that the preference for change of toy by whatever path disappeared. This result might be reminiscent of Rizzolatti *et al.*'s (1995) finding that mirror neurons specialized for grasping fail to fire if food is grasped with the help of a tool. Nonetheless, grasping and the finger-grip do play a role, since when 5-month-old infants saw a human hand land palm up on top of a toy, Woodward *et al.* (2001) report that the pattern of preference for new toy by whatever path also disappeared. Furthermore, Woodward *et al.* (2001) found that the visual texture of the human hand might play a role in infants' visual responses: in both 7-month-old and 12-month-old infants, the pattern of preference for the new toy by whatever path disappeared when the hand was covered by a 'metallic-gold-colored evening glove'. Finally, Woodward *et al.* (2001) report that, whereas they did recognize the goal of a grasping action, unlike 12-month-old infants, 9-month-old infants failed to recognize the goal of a pointing action.

5 The social perception system

Earlier in this chapter, we distinguished between social and non-social intentions, i.e. between intentions involved in actions directed towards conspecifics and intentions involved in actions directed towards inanimate objects. The former, unlike the latter, are intentions to affect a conspecific's behavior. In a social species, the ability to detect visual cues of social intentions is highly adaptive. There is growing evidence for the existence in the human mind of a cognitive structure specialized in 'mindreading', 'social cognition' or 'social intelligence', which involves the ability to intentionally cause mental states in the minds of conspecifics and to attribute mental states to them (for review see Baron-Cohen 1995).[3]

Human actions directed towards conspecifics involve specific visible bodily movements. What we call 'social perception' is the part of the human visual system specialized in the processing of cues of social actions and social intentions. The output of both

---

[3] Arguably, mindreading also involves psychological self-knowledge and the attribution of mental states to oneself. Whether knowledge of one's own mind and knowledge of other minds are acquired by the same path is a matter of intense scrutiny and discussion among psychologists and philosophers.

the mirror system and the social perception system, i.e. the visual perception of cues of both non-social and social intentions, serves as a visual input to the mindreading system, since both contribute to predicting and explaining what a conspecific is likely to do next—whether he is attending to, and intends to act upon, an object or a conspecific. In the previous sections, we have concentrated on the visual processing of cues of non-social intentions, such as the intention to grasp and manipulate an object. In the present section, we shall discuss the visual processing of a variety of human bodily parts and movements, which are rich cues of social intentions.

As we said above, human bodies are special visual objects: they play a special role in the human social perception system. Among human bodily parts, human faces carry special social information. More than the perception of any other human bodily part, the perception of a human face is likely to cause emotions in the perceiver, and no other human bodily part can convey as much information about a person's mental states, her emotional states, her intentions and the focus of her attention. Humans have a rich repertoire of facial gestures: in a human face, the eyes, the eyebrows, the forehead, the lips, the tongue and the jaws can move relative to the rest of the face. Not only can lip, tongue and jaw movements serve to convey a speaker's communicative intentions, but mouth movements and lip positions can be powerful visual cues of a person's emotional states: by opening her mouth and moving her lips, a person can display a neutral face, smile, laugh, grin or express grief. The movements and the position of the eyes in their orbit convey both information about the person's emotional state, the likely target of her attention and her intention.

In this section, we shall argue that the 'social perception' system in the human brain is a complex neural circuit that depends on several interconnected brain areas, including the superior temporal sulcus (STS) and the amygdala. In Section 5.1, we shall review visual cues of proto-social intentions extracted from the perception of the self-propelled motions of geometrical stimuli of the kind we discussed earlier in Section 2.1. In Section 5.2, we shall examine the perception of socially significant bodily movements including locomotion, hand movements, head movements, movements of parts of the face, such as eye movements, movements of the eyebrows and mouth movements. As it turns out, of all human bodily parts, the human face is arguably the richest source of visual information about human social intentions and emotions. Thus, in Section 5.3, we shall analyse the human face perception system.

5.1 Elementary visual cues of proto-social intentions

In Section 2, we argued that the perception of so-called biological motion is the primary level of the visual processing of human actions. Human actions directed towards conspecifics (i.e. actions with a high social component) may involve very subtle movements that differ in many aspects from the movements involved in object-oriented actions. In particular, they may involve locomotion, movements of the whole body and very subtle movements of the head and the eyes. In Section 2.2, we mentioned experiments by developmental psychologists Leslie (1988) and Spelke *et al.* (1995) showing that 7-month-old human infants expect that causal interactions among non-human physical objects involve visible contact or collision. In an experiment by Spelke *et al.* (1995), 7-month-old infants saw a video showing a man walk and disappear behind the left side of a screen and a few seconds later they saw a woman walk from behind the right side of the screen. After habituation, the screen was lifted and the infants were presented with one of the two following conditions. In one condition, the man walked towards the standing woman until he touched her. Then, she walked away from him. In the other condition, the man walked towards the woman, but when he stopped walking, she was distant from him and he remained at a distance from her. Finally, she walked away from him. Spelke *et al.* (1995) found that 7-month-old infants did *not* look longer in the second than in the first condition. Spelke *et al.* (1995) take these results to show that 7-month-old infants do not expect causal interactions between two human beings to be, unlike causal interactions between two non-human physical objects, limited to contact or collision.

Also in Section 2.2, we discussed Heider and Simmel's (1944) and Premack's (1990) evidence that seeing the self-propelled motions of geometrical stimuli can trigger judgments of proto-social goals and intentions. In Section 3.3, we discussed Woodward's (1998, 2001) and Wellman and Philipps' (2001) evidence that infants are sensitive to the non-social goals of hand actions, such as grasping, as opposed to the trajectories of the movements. There is an important difference between the experimental findings on infants' responses to hand movements directed towards inanimate objects and the findings on infants' responses to the self-propelled motions of geometrical stimuli. On the one hand, there is a clear asymmetry between the animacy of the human hand and the inanimacy of its target. On the other hand, seeing a human hand reach for and grasp an inanimate object is seeing a non-social action. It triggers in the observer an elementary judgment of non-social intention. By contrast, Heider and Simmel's (1944) animation and Premack's (1990), Gergely *et al.*'s (1995) and Csibra *et al.*'s (1999) experiments display the self-propelled motions of geometrical stimuli in relation to other similar geometrical stimuli of the same kind. Arguably, the visual cues of self-propulsion in the patterns of motion of geometrical stimuli directed to 'geometrical conspecifics' trigger in the observer elementary judgments of proto-social intentions.

As Woodward's (1998) experiment with a mechanical claw, and Woodward *et al.*'s (2001) experiment with a hand covered by a glove, show, neither the perception of self-propulsion nor the perception of biological motion might be sufficient to trigger judgments of non-social intentions directed towards inanimate objects. Furthermore (as mentioned in Chapter 4), pointing to an inanimate object, unlike grasping it, might involve an elementary social intention, i.e. the proto-communicative intention to demonstrate an object for the purpose of attracting another's attention. As Woodward *et al.*'s (2001) experiment on pointing shows, the visual cues sufficient to trigger the recognition of a non-social intention to grasp an object might fail to trigger the recognition of an elementary social intention such as the intention to attract another's attention onto an object.

It is no accident, we surmise, that Premack (1990) hypothesized that judgments of intention triggered by infant's perceptions of the self-propelled motions of geometrical stimuli in relation to other geometrical stimuli, serve as entries to the 'analysis of social behavior'. Nor is it an accident if Premack (1990) turned to the analysis of what he called BDR sequences of interactions between geometrical stimuli, where 'B' stands for base, 'D' for deflection from base and 'R' for recovery of base. A BDR sequence might consist of the display of two balls A and B, bouncing for 5 s (base). Then, B might get stuck in a virtual hole (deflection from base). Finally, as a result of A's contacting motions, B might resume its own bouncing motion (recovery of base). Seeing A's motion might automatically trigger an elementary judgment of social agency: A caused B to resume its bouncing motion.

Michotte (1950) himself argued that cues contained in simple patterns of motion (Premack's self-propulsion) can prompt responses of the 'social perception' system: 'in ordinary life, the specifying factors—gestures, facial expressions, speech—are innumerable and can be differentiated by an infinity of nuances. But they are all additional refinements compared with the key factors, which are the simple kinetic structures'. The view that the perception of the self-propelled motions of geometrical stimuli in relation to 'conspecifics' is an entry to the human system of 'social perception' has been recently corroborated by recent experiments. First, Herbelein et al. (1998) showed Heider and Simmel's animation, with three geometrical objects, to a patient with selective bilateral amygdala damage, who, unlike normal observers, did not attribute emotions and mental states to the stimuli. Second, Happé and Frith (1999) conducted PET studies using the same displays of motions of geometrical stimuli, contrasting random motions, goal-directed movements (e.g. chasing) and intentional movements (e.g. mocking), and found that the perception of the latter produced more activity in the temporoparietal junction, fusiform gyrus and medial frontal cortex than the perception of random motions. Finally, Castelli et al. (2000) report a PET study using Heider and Simmel's animation. They found an increased activation in four main regions: the medial prefrontal cortex, the temporo-parietal junction (superior temporal sulcus), the basal temporal regions (fusiform gyrus and the temporal poles adjacent to the amygdala) and the extrastriate cortex (occipital gyrus).

5.2 Processing the social significance of human bodily movements

In the section on biological motion, we discussed psychophysical evidence and evidence from brain imagery in humans, showing that the perception of whole-body movements, locomotion and Johansson-type point-light displays produced bilateral activation of the occipito-parieto-temporal junction, located at the posterior end of the superior temporal sulcus (STS), which, according to many neuroscientists, constitute a homolog area to the monkey MT/V5. Thus, as we mentioned in Section 2.1, PET studies by Rizzolatti et al. (1996) and by Grafton et al. (1996) found that observation of grasping actions activated the STS. Grèzes et al. (2001) found bilateral activation of STS during observation of meaningful hand actions, such as opening a bottle, compared with seeing a stationary hand. Bonda et al. (1996) found that seeing a point-light display of reaching for a glass, picking it up and bringing it to the mouth, activates a posterior portion of the left STS region.

Single cell recordings in the monkey brain by Perrett et al. (1982, 1985, 1989) show that cells in the STS respond selectively to a variety of bodily movements. Some respond preferentially to specific static postures. Some are tuned to particular bodily locomotory movements, such as walking or crouching, moving towards or away from the perceiving animal. Still others respond to hand actions made by the experimenter. Most cells that are sensitive to hand movements respond better to particular hand movements (e.g. grasping) than to others. STS cells respond to actions rather than to the targets of the actions. They respond to goal-directed hand actions, whether the performance of the action was fast or slow and whether the target was near or far. Some cells respond more when the experimenter opens his hand than either when he extends his index finger alone or closes his fist.

Head movements, head orientation and the direction of gaze in monkeys can convey important social cues of either domination or submission. Some neurons in STS will respond to ventral flexion of the head, not to dorsal flexion of the head. One cell responded strongly to ventral flexion, whether the head was viewed full face, in profile, from behind or inverted. In other words, such a cell codes a particular kind of head movement (i.e. ventral flexion) in object-centered coordinates, despite important changes in viewer-centered coordinates. That same cell responded also to downward movements of the eyelids producing closure of the eyes, but not to direction of gaze (see Carey *et al.* 1997). As Allison *et al.* (2000: 271) point out, 'this combination of responses is of interest because downward eye movement and ventral flexion of the head appear together as part of the behavioral response to breaking contact with another monkey during dominance interactions'. Furthermore, Perrett *et al.* (1982, 1985, 1990) found that, in general, cells that are most responsive to the perception of full face (as opposed to profile) are also more sensitive to eye contact (or mutual gaze) than to averted gaze. Conversely, cells that respond to the profile view of a face are also more sensitive to averted gaze (Fig. 7.7).

Sometimes, especially in cases of human deception, the direction of gaze can be dissociated from the orientation of the head. As noticed by Allison *et al.* (2000: 268–9), this is beautifully illustrated by a painting by Georges de La Tour entitled *The Fortune-Teller*, which exhibits the full face of a young woman located in between a young man and an old fortune-teller. In the painting, the young woman's gaze is averted to her right: she is carefully monitoring the gaze direction of the young man to her right whose jewelry she is stealing, while his own attention is being drawn towards the fortune-teller standing to his extreme left (see book cover).

In the painting by Georges de La Tour, we do not of course see the young woman's eyes move but, seeing her averted direction of gaze, we cannot but take it that she has just moved her eyes. This is an instance of what is called 'implied motion', i.e. the extraction of dynamic information from a static picture. In discussing biological motion, we referred to an fMRI study by Kourtzi and Kanwisher (2000), who found that seeing a static photograph of a athlete in action activates more of the area MT/MST than seeing a static photograph from which no implied motion can be extracted. Other PET studies have examined the brain activations related to perceiving eye movements and the direction of gaze. Some compared mutual-gaze condition, averted-gaze condition and no-gaze condition (closed eyes). Functional MRI studies have examined the brain activation caused by alternations of eye aversion and mutual gaze: they found activation in parts of STS anterior to area MT/V5. Although autistic human children are able to perceive the direction of gaze (whether it is directed to the perceiver or whether it is averted), they have been found by Baron-Cohen *et al.* (1995) to be unable to use such a perceptual cue to determine the target of a person's visual attention.

Developmental psychologists have found that 12- and 14-month-old infants use visual information about head movements, head orientation and gaze-direction to determine intentions and goal-directedness in perceiving object-oriented actions. In a series

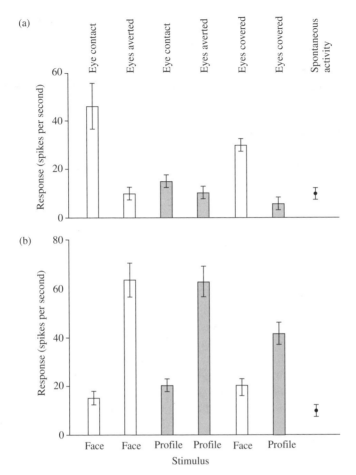

(a)

(b)

Fig. 7.7 Two cells from the superior temporal sulcus selective for gaze direction. (a) This cell responds better when the experimenter's face and gaze are turned to the monkey than when face and eyes are averted from the monkey (*white bars*). (b) This cell responds better when the experimenter's face and eyes are averted from the monkey (*white bars*). This is also true when the monkey saw the profile face (*shaded bars*). (From Perrett *et al.* 1985 permission sought.)

of experiments launched by Spelke *et al.* (1995) and pursued by Wellman and Philipps (2001), 12- and 14-month-old infants saw the head, shoulders, arms and hands of an adult sitting at a table on the top of which lay two stuffed kittens of identical shape and texture but of different colors. Habituation trials would consist of two stages. First, the adult would say 'look at the kitty!' while turning her head and looking towards one of the two kittens with an expression of interest and joy. Then, a curtain was drawn concealing both the adult and the toys. Second, the curtain was opened and the adult looked down towards a kitten and grasped it. Finally, the adult held the grasped kitten. After habituation, infants were presented with two conditions. In the consistent condition, infants first saw the adult look at the new toy (the toy that had not been the target of her attention in the habituation condition) and the screen closed. Then the screen opened and the infant saw the adult holding the kitten she had looked at. In the inconsistent condition, infants first saw the adult look at the same kitten as in the habituation condition and the screen closed. Then, the screen opened and the infants saw the adult holding the other kitten (she had not attended to). Infants aged 12 and 14 months looked longer at the inconsistent test event than at the consistent one.

Santos and Hauser (1999) replicated this experiment with cotton-top tamarins. They wanted to tease apart the relative contribution of head orientation and gaze direction to tamarins' appreciation of goal-directedness in human actions. Thus, they compared what they called a 'head-and-eyes' condition and an 'eyes-only' condition. In the former condition, the human actor would move sharply his shoulders, head and eyes. In the latter, he would only move his eyes. They found that tamarins looked longer at the inconsistent test event only in the head-and-eyes condition, not in the eyes-only condition. As Santos and Hauser (1999: 137) note, like the sclera of other non-human primates, and unlike the human sclera, the sclera of tamarins' eyes is gray, not white. It may therefore be harder for tamarins than for humans to detect the gaze direction of conspecifics without cues from head movements and head-orientation.

Among the movements of constituents of a face, mouth movements are socially important. In monkeys, Perrett and Mistlin (1990) registered single cells in STS and found some that respond more to an open-mouth threatening face than to a neutral face, a teeth-chattering face or a fear grin. In humans, some mouth movements are related to non-verbal communication; others are involved in speech and verbal communication. What is called 'lip-reading' or 'speech-reading' may contribute to linguistic understanding in a noisy environment. For example, the auditory perception of speech sounds can be influenced by the visual perception of lip movements, as shown by the famous McGurk illusory cross-modal effect: in McGurk and MacDonald's (1976) experiment, subjects see the lips of speakers in the process of uttering the syllable 'ga', while their auditory stimulus is the syllable 'ba'. As a result, they hear the compromise syllable 'da'.

5.3 The face perception system

The social perception system connects the visual system to a special purpose cognitive system: the mindreading system. At the heart of the social perception system is the face perception system. Arguably, perceiving movements of internal parts of the face is a crucial component of the system of perception of movements of human bodily parts, for at least two reasons. First, more than any other bodily part, the positions and movements of parts internal to a human face can carry emotional states and cause emotions in the perceiver. Second, according to one influential model (Bruce and Young 1986), a human face can give rise to two sorts of perceptual processes: the perception of the invariant aspects and the changing aspects of a face. The former contributes to the recognition of the identity of a person. The latter contributes to the perception of another's social intentions and emotional states.

In the previous section on the perception of the social significance of bodily movements, we discussed the perception of some of the changing aspects of a human face: movements and orientation of the head, movements and orientation of the eyes, movements of the eyebrows and movements of the mouth. More than the perception of any other human bodily part, the perception of a human face is likely to cause emotions in the perceiver and no other human bodily part can convey as much information about a person's mental states, her emotional states, her intentions and the target of her attention. Humans have a rich repertoire of facial gestures: in a human face, the eyes, the eyebrows, the forehead, the lips, the tongue and the jaws can move relative to the rest of the face. Not only can lip, tongue and jaw movements serve to convey a speaker's communicative intentions, but mouth movements and lip positions can be powerful visual cues of a person's emotional states: by opening her mouth and moving her lips, a person can display a neutral face, smile, laugh, grin or express grief. The movements and the position of the eyes in their orbit convey both information about the person's emotional state, the likely target of her attention and her intention.

Both the emotional significance of facial gestures and the emotions produced by perceiving facial gestures have been studied by cognitive neuroscience. We earlier mentioned Herbelein *et al.*'s (1998) finding that, unlike normal subjects, a patient with a developmental damage to the amygdala failed to attribute emotional and mental states to geometrical objects upon seeing a Heider and Simmel animation involving a circle and two triangles. Monkeys with large bilateral lesions, including the amygdala and the temporal neocortex, were still able to respond to visual stimuli but their behavior was emotionally inappropriate: compulsive manipulation of objects with the mouth, hypersexual behavior, tameness, lack of emotional response to seeing, e.g. snakes (cf. Kluwer and Bucy 1939). There is evidence that neurons in the amygdala in the human brain respond selectively to the sight of human faces, as opposed to any other stimuli. Studies using brain imaging in normal subjects, the observation of patients with damage to the amygdala and animal studies of the role of the amygdala, provide evidence that the amygdala is involved in extracting emotional states from facial expression. Finally, Adolphs *et al.* (1998) found that patients with bilateral damage to the amygdala were impaired in their social judgment in that they judged to be trustworthy faces that normal subjects judged untrustworthy and unreliable.

The visual processing of face patterns has been a topic of considerable interest for the past three decades. The neuropsychological investigation of the condition known as 'prosopagnosia' has revealed that patients with damage to the inferior occipito-temporal region are selectively impaired in visual face recognition, while their perception and recognition of other objects are relatively unimpaired. Developmental psychologists found out that newborn infants can reproduce facial movements of mouth opening, tongue and lip protrusion (Meltzoff and Moore 1977). They also found out that newborn infants (less than 1-h old) will turn their eyes and heads more towards a schematized white face (involving a pair of diagrammatic black eyes with a pair of diagrammatic eyebrows, a diagrammatic nose and a diagrammatic mouth) than to a scrambled face or a blank face (Goren *et al.* 1975). The evidence was not unequivocal, however: newborn infants did not show any preference for a schematized face over a face containing, respectively, three black squares instead of the eyes, the nose and the mouth, a linear vertical sequence including an eye, a mouth, a nose and an eye, and finally a scrambled face (Johnson *et al.* 1991). According to Maurer *et al.* (1981), 2-month-old infants look almost as long at eyes as at a whole face, while they look significantly less at other parts of the face (cf. Johnson and Morton 1991).

We shall presently review evidence in favor of the existence in the human brain of a specialized sytstem dedicated to the perception of invariant aspects of human faces and to the recognition of the identity of human faces. One thing is the ability to detect on the spot a conspecific's emotional states, the focus of her attention and her social intention (especially her intention to act towards oneself) by perceiving her face and facial gestures. Another thing is the ability to recognize and identify the face of an individual, whose visual appearance will change as she ages, across different facial gestures and expressions at different times.

According to a hypothesis variously dubbed the 'Machiavellian intelligence' hypothesis (Byrne and Whiten 1988; Whiten and Byrne 1997) and the 'social brain' hypothesis (Dunbar 1998), there is a correlation between mean group size among various primate species and the volume of their neocortex (i.e. the ratio of neocortex volume to the rest of the brain). According to this view, the volume of the neocortex in primates would be a function of the number of conspecifics that individual members would need to be able to identify, to recognize and memorize. Among other primates, humans have the ability to perceive and recognize the identity of a greater number of conspecifics' faces. The visual appearance of a human face is a pretty reliable index of a person's identity: only twins' faces may so resemble each other that sometimes they may be visually indistinguishable. Human adults are experts at face recognition because face recognition allows humans to keep track of the identity of a great number of conspecifics, who play important roles in their respective social lives.

As Sergent and Signoret (1992: 55) put it:

[...] face recognition is an effortless act performed as a matter of course and at a speed typical of an automatism. It is a function acquired very early during development and requiring no formal training, and it does not need to be cultivated or improved through special techniques as we feel no particular urge to achieve higher proficiency. It does not involve any thinking and it only occasionally fails us. There seem to be no limits to the number of faces that we can recognize and, as we make new acquaintances and as new actors or politicians become public figures, their faces are quickly learned and identified without obliterating the memories of already known faces.

Presumably, the perception of invariant aspects of faces contributes to the identification and recognition of persons. Thus, the perception of invariant aspects of faces is a crucial component of the human ability to build and memorize stable files about the identity of a great number of conspecifics. From an evolutionary perspective, it is likely to be adaptive for members of a highly social species to have a fast visual system for the recognition and categorization of kins, friends and foes, whose output can then be used by the mindreading system, one of whose tasks is to make decisions about whether to compete, to cooperate, to mate, to protect or to reciprocate. Earlier in this chapter, we discussed the system of human-face perception designed to provide information about the changing aspects of faces, i.e. to be used for the immediate understanding of others' emotional states and social intentions, not for the storage of stable information about the identity of persons. We now turn our attention to the processing of the face recognition system that must connect the visual system to memory.

The neural basis of the system for face processing largely overlaps with the whole social perception system. As emphasized by Haxby *et al.* (2000), face processing is mediated by a distributed neural system including three bilateral regions in the occipito-temporal visual extrastriate cortex: the inferior occipital gyrus, the lateral fusiform gyrus, and the superior temporal sulcus. There is growing recent evidence that the lateral fusiform gyrus might be specially involved in identifying and recognizing faces, i.e. in the processing of invariant aspects of faces. By contrast, the superior temporal sulcus might be more involved in processing variable aspects of faces. We shall presently examine brain areas involved in representing the identity of human faces.

Hoffman and Haxby (2000) conducted fMRI experiments to tease apart the sensitivity of visual attention to the identity of a face and to eye-gaze direction. In the first condition of their first experiment, subjects had to detect identity. In the second condition of the same experiment, they had to detect gaze-direction. In the second experiment, subjects either saw series' of faces whose eyes were all directed at, or all directed away from, the perceiver. First of all, Hoffman and Haxby (2000) found that the overall distributed human neural system for face perception includes bilateral regions in the lateral inferior occipital gyrus, the lateral fusiform gyrus and STS, all of which have been shown to respond more to the perception of faces than to other objects. Second of all, Hoffman and Haxby (2000) found that the perception of such a changing aspect of a face as gaze direction produced more activity in the posterior STS than in either the lateral fusiform gyrus or the inferior occipiral gyrus. Interestingly, the posterior STS in the human brain has been hypothesized to be homologous to a region in the superior bank of the STS in monkeys in which cells have been showed by Perrett *et al.* (1985) to respond preferentially to eye-gaze direction and facial expressions. Finally, they found that the perception of invariant features of face relevant to identity is based more on activity in the lateral fusiform gyrus and to some extent in the lateral inferior occipital gyri than in STS.

The existence of a specialized brain system for face recognition and identification was first suggested by the neuropsychological observation of prosopagnosic patients with bilateral lesions in the ventral occipitotemporal cortex (see Farah 1990): although these patients were selectively impaired in face recognition, their ability to recognize other objects was relatively well-preserved. Recent neuropsycholological and psychopathological investigation has revealed an interesting dissociation between two disorders: prosopagnosic patients and so-called Capgras patients. In prosopagnosic patients, the explicit visual recognition of faces is impaired, but their electrodermal reactions provide evidence of covert emotional response to faces. By contrast, Capgras patients' visual recognition of faces seems relatively unimpaired, but their emotional response to faces may be so severely impaired that the lack of emotional response prompts them to assume that very close members of their family are impostors (Ramachandran and Blakeslee 1998). Further evidence for the existence of a neural system specialized in face perception came from single-cell recordings in the brain of macaque monkeys that identified neurons in the superior temporal sulcus and the inferior temporal cortex that responded selectively to the perception of faces (Perrett *et al.* 1982, 1985). Subsequently, brain imaging studies have shown that the activation of the lateral fusiform gyrus in humans is stronger in response to the perception of faces than to the perception of non-faces, whether non-sense stimuli or different objects (e.g. houses, cars, tools or landscapes). Kanwisher *et al.* (1997) have called this area the 'fusiform face area', which has been hypothesized to be 'a module specialized for face perception'.

Further evidence in favor of the modularity of the fusiform face area comes from experiments showing that identifying a face turned upside down is a markedly more difficult task than recognizing some other object (e.g. a house) turned upside down (Kanwisher *et al.* 1997; Haxby *et al.* 1999). By contrast, the perception of inverted faces by prosopagnosic patients is not significantly worse than the perception of inverted faces by normal subjects, which suggests both that prosopagnosic patients use their intact non-specialized object perception mechanisms when they process inverted faces and that, unlike face recognition, normal subjects use their general perceptual mechanisms to process inverted faces (cf. Farah *et al.* 1995; Haxby *et al.* 1999). However, the results of fMRI studies (by Kanwisher *et al.* 1997 and Haxby *et al.* 1999) show nonetheless that the perception of inverted faces does engage the activity of both the lateral fusiform gyrus and the inferior occipital region. It may be that, although it is very hard to recognize the identity of an inverted face, nonetheless inverted faces are readily identified as faces and this generic recognition engages the face-responsive areas in the human brain. These results raise the question whether the face-responsive areas in the brain are modular mechanisms specialized for face recognition or whether they are areas engaged in human visual expertise that can be used to process different sorts of stimuli. According to the latter hypothesis (Gauthier *et al.* 1999), since humans are expert in face recognition, the so-called face-responsive regions serve face recognition as it would serve the expert recognition of individual members of any other category. Gauthier *et al.* (2000) found that, in an fMRI study of bird and car recognition, the face-responsive regions were more activated in experts at bird and car recognition than in non-experts. If so, then it might be that the so-called face responsive areas in the human brain would better be characterized as areas for the expert recognition of unique individual members of a category.

Epilogue: the two visual systems revisited

Much of the cognitive scientific research into human and non-human vision reported in this book provides ample evidence that human vision is not a unitary psychological ability. Seeing in humans is not a single kind of action. In this book, we have endorsed the dualist picture according to which, in many circumstances, one and the same stimulus can be processed in two fundamentally different ways: a tea-cup, for instance, can give rise to a visual percept and it can also be the target of a visually guided action of reaching and grasping. The semantic processing of a visual stimulus yields a visual percept, whereas basic pragmatic processing yields a visuomotor representation of a target for action. Our dualist picture of human vision owes much to two seminal contributions in the recent cognitive neuroscience of vision.

First, twenty years ago, Ungerleider and Mishkin (1982) showed that, in the primate brain, the projections from the primary visual cortex bifurcate into two segregated anatomical pathways: the ventral pathway and the dorsal pathway. The former connects the primary visual cortex to the inferotemporal cortex. The latter connects the primary visual cortex to the parietal lobes. Ungerleider and Mishkin performed lesions in the ventral and the dorsal streams of the brain of macaque monkeys. They found that the former disrupt identification and recognition of visual stimuli, but not the ability to use landmark information to localize a stimulus in space. Conversely, they found that the latter disrupt the ability to use landmark information to localize a stimulus in space, but not identification and recognition of visual stimuli (for review see Chapter 2, Section 1). The discovery of this double dissociation in macaque monkeys led Ungerleider and Mishkin (1982) to conceptualize the distinction between the ventral pathway and the dorsal pathway as a duality between an 'object channel' and a 'space channel' or what earlier writers (e.g. Schneider 1969) called, respectively, the What system and the Where system.

Second, in the early 1990s, neuropsychological research on brain-lesioned human patients led to the discovery of a significant double dissociation between apperceptive agnosia, caused by a lesion in the ventral pathway, and optic ataxia, caused by a lesion in the dorsal pathway. The examination by Milner, Goodale and collaborators of one patient with an apperceptive visual form agnosia, who could not perceive, recognize and identify the shapes and sizes of visually presented objects, revealed that she could still perform such accurate visually guided actions on objects as grasping them or inserting them into an oriented slot. Conversely, optic ataxic patients fail in such visually guided actions on objects as reaching and grasping, but they can still visually perceive, recognize and identify the shapes and sizes of presented objects (for review see Chapter 3). The discovery of this neuropsychological double dissociation between apperceptive visual form agnosia and optic ataxia led Milner and Goodale (1995) to conceptualize the segregation between the ventral stream and the dorsal stream in terms of a duality between vision-for-perception and vision-for-action (or the visuomotor transformation). In their view, the dorsal stream is not so much the Where system as the How system.

Thus, both Ungerleider and Mishkin's (1982) distinction between an object channel and a space channel, and Milner and Goodale's (1995) distinction between vision-for-perception and vision-for-action, are landmarks in the emergence of the contemporary cognitive neuroscientific view that the human visual system involves an anatomical segregation between two cortico-cortical pathways. In one fundamental respect, however, they diverge on the interpretation of the functional role of the dorsal pathway in the human visual system. Throughout Chapters 2, 3, 6 and 7 of this book, the related questions of the contribution of the dorsal stream and of the parietal lobes to human vision have recurrently arisen. In these concluding pages, we would like to return to these fundamental physiological and functional questions and show how our own dualist view of the human visual system relates to both earlier dualist models: the object channel vs. space channel model and the vision-for-perception vs. vision-for-action model.

As we pointed out in Chapter 2, there is little doubt that Ungerleider and Mishkin's (1982) dualist model belongs to a paradigm according to which both the chief function of vision in primates is visual perception and cortico-cortical pathways in the primate brain must underlie visual perception. Unquestionably, Milner and Goodale's (1995) dualist model is part of a different paradigm according to which neither is visual perception the unique (or the chief) function of vision in primates, nor are cortico-cortical pathways in the primate and the human brain restricted to perceptual functions. In this new paradigm, the visuomotor transformation is not relegated to subcortical structures but is fully part of the visual cortex of non-human primates and of humans. A first step towards this new paradigm was taken by Mountcastle and collaborators (1975) when they performed pioneer experiments in which they recorded the activities of neurons in the posterior parietal cortical areas of macaque monkeys involved in selective tasks of reaching and grasping. These initial insights were then further elaborated and refined by a series of experiments including the work of Sakata and his collaborators (for review see Chapter 2, Sections 5.1 and 5.2). Milner and Goodale's (1995) interpretation of the anatomical segregation between the ventral and the dorsal pathways into the psychological distinction between visual perception and the visuomotor transformation was the first systematic codification of the new paradigm.

Our own version of the dualist model of human visual processing falls squarely within the new paradigm, since in this book we insist again and again on the fact that one and the same visual stimulus can give rise either to a visual percept or to a visuomotor representation. Furthermore, we fully accept the thesis that the visuomotor transformation in humans is performed by cortico-cortical projections, i.e. by the dorsal stream. Our version of the dualist model of human vision, however, departs from Milner and Goodale's (1995) model in several respects and it accommodates some of Ungerleider and Mishkin's (1982) insights. In a nutshell, Milner and Goodale's model unduly restricts the role of the parietal lobes to the performance of crude object-oriented actions. We shall discuss our departures from Milner and Goodale's model under two main headings: first of all, we shall argue that the concept of action involved in their notion of 'vision-for-action' is overly narrow. In the process, we shall reflect on the complexities of the notion of a perceptual object. Second, we shall argue that Milner and Goodale's model underestimates the role of the parietal lobes, not only in the organization of high-level pragmatic visual processing (i.e. for action) but also, for the visual perception of spatial relationships.

1 The complexities of pragmatic processing

Milner and Goodale have usefully redirected the attention of the neuroscientific community on the importance of visually guided actions for a better understanding of human vision. But their opposition between vision-for-perception and vision-for-action captures only part of the relevant psychological and functional contrasts. All along, we made a distinction between what, borrowing from the tradition of linguistic studies, we called the 'semantic' and the 'pragmatic' processing of visual stimuli. While in normal subjects, the semantic (or perceptual) processing of visual inputs culminates in what we called in Chapter 5 epistemic vision, it involves a prior stage of processing, which, in the same chapter, we called non-epistemic vision. In the terms of Chapter 5, while non-epistemic vision leads to the visual awareness of perceptual objects, epistemic vision leads to the visual awareness of facts involving perceptual objects. Similarly, in humans, the visuomotor transformation is, in our view, but the first stage of the pragmatic processing of a visual target: the visuomotor transformation allows a normal human being to point or reach towards a visual target and to grasp it. Pragmatic processing of visual inputs in humans goes much beyond the visuomotor transformation because vision serves far more complex object-oriented actions.

In our view, it is characteristic of the pragmatic processing of visual inputs that it provides visual information for the benefit of what we call the 'intention box', by contrast with the 'belief box'. Unlike beliefs, intentions have a world-to-mind direction of fit. Unlike visual percepts, intentions have a mind-to-world direction of causation (for an extended discussion see Chapter 1, Section 5). Unlike beliefs, visual percepts have non-conceptual contents. Perceptual non-conceptual content is both more fine-grained and informationally richer than the conceptual content of beliefs. Visuomotor representations are the output of the visuomotor transformation: they represent the location of a target in egocentric coordinates, which is required to reach it, and they represent the spatio-motor properties of objects, which are required to grasp them. As both the comparison between the activities of AIP neurons and TE neurons in the brain of macaque monkeys and the comparison between perceptual tasks and motor tasks in psychophysical experiments in normal human subjects show, the non-conceptual content of visuomotor representations is quite impoverished relative to the non-conceptual pictorial content of visual percepts. In Chapters 6 and especially 7, we drew a distinction between the visuomotor transformation—which we labeled 'low-level pragmatic processing'—and higher level pragmatic processing based on the retrieval of action engrams (or schemas) for the skilled use and manipulation of complex cultural tools. Thus clearly, our concept of pragmatic processing is more inclusive than Milner and Goodale's concept of vision-for-action.

As the full discussion of Chapter 3 reveals, the psychological distinction between non-epistemic vision and epistemic vision is corroborated by the neuropsychological investigation of perceptual impairments prompted by lesions in the ventral stream.

As the discussion of Chapter 6 shows, it is also corroborated by the contrast between the individuation of 'proto-object' by location and the identification of objects by featural information.

On the one hand, visual-form associative agnosic patients fail to identify visual objects for they fail to 'extract the meaning' of the shapes and contours of a visually presented item. Thus, following this description of the perceptual impairment of associative agnosics, we used the linguistic term 'semantic processing' to denote the full process of construction of a normal visual percept: new pictorial information about a perceived object undergoes further conceptual processing and is matched against older information already stored in memory. As shown in the drawings of Fig. 3.2, associative-visual agnosics can still extract the basic shapes of visual stimuli. However, associative agnosic patients fail to extract the overall organization of the local shapes of objects. On the other hand, visual-form apperceptive agnosic patients are more severely impaired in that, as shown in the drawings in Fig. 3.4, they fail to extract any form at all. While associative agnosic patients fail to conceptualize the information encoded in a visual percept, apperceptive agnosic patients fail to form a visual percept. Apperceptive agnosic patients fail to represent the local shapes of objects, let alone their complex contours and overall organization. We might say that while associative agnosic patients fail to reach the level of epistemic vision, apperceptive agnosic patients fail to reach the level of non-epistemic vision.

In Chapter 6, we argued that perceptual judgments obey the 'constraint of contrastive identification', according to which, unless comparisons can be made between two or more instantiations of a given visual attribute (e.g. size) by two or more distinct objects at the same time, no perceptual judgment and/or recognition of a perceptual object can arise. There, we argued that the visuomotor representations of the targets of her actions formed by the apperceptive agnosic patient DF, examined by Goodale, Milner and their collaborators, fail to satisfy the constraint of contrastive identification for size and shape precisely because she can only represent the size and the shape of an object whose location is being coded in egocentric coordinates. As we argued there, only if the relative locations of at least two objects can be coded in an allocentric frame of reference can a perceptual comparison be made between the respective sizes and shapes of two items—something, we claimed, DF cannot do. DF's residual visual abilities can still provide her with the visuomotor representation of a target for reaching and grasping, located in egocentric coordinates. While her impaired visual system can still provide her with the representation of an object-for-action, it cannot provide her with the representation of a perceptual object because her semantic processing has been damaged at an early stage that prevents the visual perceptual information from ever reaching the level where it interfaces with conceptual processing.

In Chapter 6, we made a comparison between the visuomotor abilities evidenced by DF and the crude visual perceptual capacities of both human infants and human adults in tasks of multiple object tracking. In both developmental studies and multiple object tracking experiments, human infants and human adults are capable of individuating what Pylyshyn (2000a, 2000b) calls 'proto-objects'. Proto-objects in his sense are perceptual objects, not objects-for-action. They are individuated by their respective location coded in an allocentric frame of reference. They are perceptual proto-objects, not full perceptual objects, since they are not individuated by featural information: in such experiments, subjects fail to notice changes of shapes, textures and colors. Since they are located in allocentric coordinates, perceptual proto-objects are candidates for becoming full perceptual objects by means of further perceptual processing. Unlike perceptual proto-objects, the output of low-level pragmatic processing (i.e. the visuomotor transformation)—as evidenced by DF's visuomotor performance—are proto-objects in a different sense: since they are targets of reaching-and-grasping actions, they are proto-objects with spatio-motor properties located in egocentric coordinates suitable for the contents of motor intentions. Unlike perceptual proto-objects, unless their location can be recoded from an egocentric frame of reference into an allocentric frame of reference, they cannot be candidates for being turned into full perceptual objects.

As soon as one takes into account, as we did in Chapter 7, the fact that humans perceive not only objects that they can grasp and manipulate, but also human actions, then the notion of a perceptual object becomes very complex indeed, as do the neural circuits that underlie their visual perception. In Chapter 7, we explored a duality between two neural circuits, each in charge of processing two different kinds of human actions: object-oriented actions and actions directed towards conspecifics.

One system—the 'mirror system' located in the parietal lobe—is dedicated to the perception of object-oriented human actions. As the discovery of mirror neurons in monkeys and humans testifies, this system is at work both in the observation of object-oriented actions performed by others and in the preparation of one's own object-oriented actions. Because this system is at work in the preparation of one's own actions and in the perception of the actions of others, we argue that it is both a maximally engaged system for the recognition of object-oriented actions and a system for processing visual cues of non-social intentions. Thus, we called it a 'matching system' for the observation and execution of motor actions. We further argue that it is the basis of the human ability to imitate and thus to learn skilled actions by imitation.

The other system, 'the social perception' system (more ventrally located than the mirror system), is dedicated to the visual perception of human actions directed towards conspecifics. The social perception system processes visual cues of social intentions. It involves the superior temporal sulcus (STS) and its reciprocal projections onto the amygdala. The outputs of both the mirror system and the social perception system serve as input to the system for mindreading, i.e. the cognitive system in the human brain in charge of ascribing mental states to one's conspecifics and to oneself.

One and the same perceptual object can be processed by either the social perception system or the mirror system. A human face and a pair of human eyes are special perceptual objects whose processing by neurons in the STS and/or the amygdala are endowed with deep emotional and social significance. Now consider the perception of a human hand. If processed by neurons in the STS in the context of the perception of either an action of greeting or an action of fist-fighting, the perception of a human hand too will be vested with social and emotional significance. Alternatively, if processed by the system dedicated to the perception of object-oriented actions, the perception of an agent's hand engaged in a skilled action (e.g. painting) will trigger the preparation of a similar action plan involving the observer's hand. Arguably, no perceptual object other than a human bodily part can trigger such a rich variety of visual responses, including the observer's emotions and his or her preparation to plan an action isomorphic to the observed action.

Again, as we emphasized in Chapters 3 and 6, however surprising the remarkable residual visuomotor capacities of an apperceptive agnosic patient such as DF, they are nonetheless part of the low-level pragmatic processing of visual stimuli. As we emphasized in Chapters 1 and 7, human actions are always caused by intentions and humans are capable of planning impressively complex actions. They can entertain prior intentions with very abstract conceptual content directed towards invisible goals and involving a hierarchy of sub-plans and intermediary goals. Restricting ourselves to visually guided actions (actions whose goal is visually accessible), the skilled manipulation of a complex tool requires high-level pragmatic processing, not merely what is afforded by the visuomotor transformation. For example, grasping and manipulating a bow in order to apply it to the strings of a violin involve, but cannot be restricted to, the visuomotor transformation, since one could not know how to grasp a bow, manipulate it and apply it to the strings of a violin unless one had seen and observed many times other expert violin players perform the very same action. Thus, one could not learn how to apply a bow to the strings of a violin unless one could perceive the bow in relation to the complex contours of a violin and its strings. Nor could one learn to use a bow unless one could perceive the complex sequence of chin, shoulder, arm and hand gestures involved in the manipulation of a bow by an expert violin player. Arguably, learning how to use a bow also involves motor imagery and the ability to retrieve stored schemas for the manipulation of a bow.

As we discussed in Chapter 7, there are patients with ventral lesions, who can use tools and perform accurate skilled actions with tools, but who are impaired in the recognition of skilled actions and in the recognition of tools. These perceptual impairments stand in contrast with both basic visuomotor impairments and the higher level pragmatic impairments of apraxic patients. Since both low-level visuomotor and higher level pragmatic impairments are caused by lesions of the parietal lobes, we now turn our attention to the role of the parietal lobes in human vision.

2   The contribution of the parietal lobes to human vision

Optic ataxia results from lesions in the superior parietal lobule. Optic ataxic patients have basic visuomotor impairments: they cannot reach and/or calibrate the finger grip of the hand contra-lateral to the lesion side. Importantly, lesions in both the dorsal and the ventral streams, which produce either basic visuomotor impairments or deep perceptual deficits in visual form extraction are not lateralized: they can be bilateral. If a patient has a lesion in the superior parietal lobule (SPL) on whichever side, his or her hand contra-lateral to the side of the lesion will be affected by a visuomotor impairment.

By contrast, the effects of lesions in the inferior parietal lobule (IPL) are highly lateralized. As we discussed in the early part of Chapter 3, compared to the monkey brain, the human brain is strongly lateralized. Thus, from detailed knowledge of the function of the parietal lobes in the monkey brain, one cannot infer a detailed knowledge of the function of the parietal lobes in the human brain. Nor are accidental lesions in the human brains an entirely safe basis for inferring the function of a structure because their anatomical boundaries are rarely clear-cut. This is why much of our recent understanding of the lateralization of the human brain has been enhanced by recent neuro-imaging experiments in normal human subjects. The human IPL is comprised of two main gyri: the angular gyrus and the supramarginal gyrus corresponding, respectively, to Broadman area 39 and to area 40. Not only is human language highly lateralized in the human brain, but lesions in the IPL will produce significantly different impairments according to whether it is located on the left or on the right side. When located on the left side, lesions in IPL produce apraxic disorders. When located on the right side, lesions in IPL produce disorders in the perception of spatial relationships.

Apraxic patients with a lesion on the left side of IPL have no basic visuomotor impairments: they can reach and grasp objects. Rather, they are impaired in the visual recognition of tools and in the visual recognition of actions involving the use of tools. They cannot pantomime actions involving the use of an imaginary tool. Nor can they recognize pantomimes executed by others. According to Glover's (2003) recent model, while the SPL would be mainly involved in the on-line automatic control of basic visually guided actions towards objects, the left side of IPL would be involved in the higher level intentional planning of more complex actions involving the retrieval of complex engrams stored precisely in the left IPL. Thus, while lesions of SPL are expected to disrupt the automatic unfolding of the visuomotor transformation, lesions of the left IPL are expected to result in apraxic syndromes.

Importantly, as one moves from the automatic visuomotor transformation to the planning and execution of more complex actions involving the use and manipulation of tools, the distinction between action and perception loses much of its significance. On the one hand, as we said above, the ability to perform actions by using cultural tools and to pantomime the use of imaginary tools requires the storage of, and the ability to retrieve, schemas for tool manipulation. Such schemas are in turn formed on the basis of the observation of the actions of others. Thus, the ability to perform complex actions with tools relies on visual perception. On the other hand, schemas and engrams for the manipulation of tools are not only necessary for the appropriate actual or pantomimed use of tools but also for an understanding and the extraction of the meaning of actions involving the use of tools by other agents. Not only is what one can do shaped by what one perceives, but conversely what one can do shapes what one can perceive.

Unlike lesions on the left side of the IPL, lesions on the right side of the IPL produce various disorders in the perception of spatial relationships among visual objects, such as spatial disorientation, spatial neglect or simultagnosia (for review see Chapter 3, Section 5). Neuro-imaginig studies in normal subjects performed during perceptual and visuospatial tasks involving judgments of relative spatial locations and orientations of two or more objects consistently show activation of relatively posterior and ventral parietal areas in the fundus of the intraparietal sulcus (Haxby *et al.* 1994; Faillenot *et al.* 1999), as well as in the area of the angular gyrus in the IPL (Köhler *et al.* 1995). Such activations are thus predominantly located within the right IPL. Thus, Ungerleider and Mishkin's (1982) opposition between an object and a space channel, though based on electrophysiological and behavioral evidence gathered on the brain of monkeys, is relevant here. Crucial in this respect is the contrast between the localization of a visuomotor target for basic actions of reaching-and-grasping within egocentric coordinates and the localization of one visual item relative to others in a visual array within an allocentric frame of reference. An intact right IPL is required for coding spatial relationships among objects in an allocentric frame of reference.

Arguably, humans are not the only creatures able to code the relative localizations of distinct objects in allocentric coordinates, since the use of landmark information requires the ability to code spatial information in allocentric coordinates and many non-human animals build maps of their environment based on landmark information while they navigate. Nor presumably is the ability to perceive spatial relationships among different items in a visual array a sufficient condition for the artistic creation of pictorial works of art and the architectural design of models of buildings—something only humans can do. Arguably, the ability to create and appreciate such pictorial representations requires the ability to represent a representation as a representation, i.e. the ability to appreciate a representation opaquely and not transparently. But the ability to perceive spatial relationships is certainly a necessary condition for the creation and the enjoyment of pictorial representations.

In our view then, the contribution of the human parietal lobes and of the whole human dorsal pathway to human vision is more complex than can be captured either by the concept of a space channel (or a Where system) alone or by the concept of the visuomotor transformation (or vision-for-action) alone. It does contribute to the pragmatic processing of various levels of complexity. On the one hand, as visually guided actions become increasingly complex, the distinction between visual perception and visually guided actions collapses. Thus by contributing to higher levels of pragmatic processing, it thereby contributes to the perception of visual actions performed by others. On the other hand, it also contributes to the perception of spatial relationships. In fact, as far as is currently known from the neuropsychological studies of brain-lesioned human subjects and neuro-imaging studies in normal human subjects, the parietal lobes should be subdivided into three complementary areas, each with a fairly distinct role: the superior parietal lobe is mainly involved in the basic visuomotor transformation; the left inferior parietal lobe contributes to such higher level pragmatic processing of visual inputs as guiding the use of tools, the pantomimed use of imaginary tools, the recognition of tools, the understanding of actions using tools and the understanding of pantomimed use of imaginary tools; the right inferior parietal lobe contributes to the perception of spatial relationships. Unless one has an intact superior parietal lobe and an intact inferior right parietal lobe, one will not be able to switch from counting and/or drawing copies of objects lying on a table to grasping one of them.

Thus, we believe that Milner and Goodale (1995: 200) seriously underestimate the complexities of the human parietal lobes and the contribution of the human dorsal pathway to human vision when they write:

Visual phenomenology [...] can arise only from processing in the ventral stream, processing that we have linked with recognition and perception. We have assumed in contrast that visual-processing modules in the dorsal stream, despite the complex computations demanded by their role in the control of action, are not normally available for awareness. Attentional modulation of ventral-stream processing leads to conscious perception; attention modulation in the dorsal stream leads to action [...].

On the one hand, we would contend that much visual processing necessary for the elaboration of a visual percept, which takes place in the ventral stream, is as automatic and unconscious as visual processing required for the visuomotor transformation, which takes place in the dorsal stream (namely in the superior parietal lobe). On the other hand, we do claim that processing in both the left and the right sides of the inferior parietal lobes is required for some visual awareness: processing in the right parietal lobe is required for the conscious perception of spatial relationships of objects coded in an allocentric frame of reference. Processing in the left parietal lobe is required for high-level pragmatic visual processing involving the skilled use of tools. And as we have argued above, when it comes to high-level pragmatic visual processing, the border between pure perception and pure action becomes very thin indeed.

References

Adolphs, R. (1999) Social cognition and the human brain. *Trends in Cognitive Sciences*, **3**, (12), 469–79.

Adolphs, R., Tranel, D. and Damasio, A. R. (1998) The human amygdala in social judgment. *Nature*, **393**, 470–74.

Aglioti, S., DeSouza, J. F. X. and Goodale, M. A. (1995) Size-contrast illusions deceive the eye but not the hand. *Current Biology*, **5**, (6), 679–85.

Allison, T., Puce, A. and McCarthy, G. (2000) Social perception from visual cues: role of the STS region. *Trends in Cognitive Sciences*, **4**, (7), 267–78.

Andersen, R. and Mountcastle, V. B. (1983) The influence of the angle of gaze upon the excitability of the light sensitive neurons of the posterior parietal cortex. *Journal of Neuroscience*, **3**, 532–48.

Andersen, R. A., Snyder, L. H., Bradley, D. C. and Xing, J. (1997) Multimodal representation of space in the posterior parietal cortex and its used in planning movements. *Annual Review of Neuroscience*, **20**, 303–30.

Anscombe, G. E. (1957) *Intention*. Oxford: Blackwell.

Arbib, M. A. (2000) The mirror system, imitation, and the evolution of language. In *Imitation in animals and artifacts* (ed. Nehaniv, C. and Dautenhahn, K.), pp.00. Cambridge, Mass.: MIT Press.

Armstrong, D. (1968) *A materialist theory of the mind*. London: Routledge and Kegan Paul.

Armstrong, S. L., Gleitman, L. R. and Gleitman, H. (1983) What some concepts might not be. *Cognition*, **13**, 263–308.

Assad, J. A. and Maunsell, J. H. R. (1995) Neuronal correlates of inferred motion in primate posterior parietal cortex. *Nature*, **273**, 518–21.

Austin, J. L. (1962) *Sense and sensibilia*. Oxford: Oxford University Press.

Ayer, A. J. (1940) *The foundations of empirical knowledge*. London: Macmillan.

Baars, B. (1988) *A cognitive theory of consciousness*. Cambridge: Cambridge University Press.

Baizer, J. S., Ungerleider, L. G. and Desimone, R. (1991) Organization of visual inputs to the inferior temporal and posterior parietal cortex in macaques. *Journal of Neuroscience*, **11**, 168–90.

Balint, R. (1909) Seelenhammung des Schauens, optische Ataxie, raümliche Störungen des Aufmerksamkeit. *Monastchrift für Psychiatrie und Neurologie*, **25**, 51–81. (English translation by M. Harvey in *Cognitive Neuropsychology*, **12**, 265–81.)

Baron-Cohen, S. (1995) *Mindblindess: an essay on autism and theory of mind*. Cambridge, Mass.: MIT Press.

Barwise, J. (1989) *The situation in logic*. Stanford: CSLI Publications.

Bayliss, G. C. and Bayliss, L. L. (2001) Visually misguided reaching in Balint's syndrome. *Neuropsychologia*, **39**, 865–75.

Benson, D. F. and Greenberg, J. P. (1969) Visual form agnosia. *Archives of Neurology*, **20**, 82–9.

Bermudez, J. (1998) *The paradox of self-consciousness*. Cambridge, Mass.: MIT Press.

Berry, D. S. and Springer, K. (1993) Structure, motion, and preschoolers' perception of social causality. *Ecological Psychology*, **5**, 273–83.

Bertenthal, B. I. (1993) Perception of biomechanical motion in infants: intrinsic image and knowledge-based constraints. In *Carnegie symposium on cognition: visual perception and cognition in infancy* (ed. Granrud, C.), Hillside, New Jersey: Erlbaum.

Berthental, B. I. and Pinto, J. (1994) Global processing of biological motions. *Psychological Science*, **5**, 221–25.

Biederman, I. (1995) Visual object recognition. In *An invitation to cognitive science, Vol. 2 Visual cognition* (ed. Osherson, D), pp.121–65. Cambridge, Mass.: MIT Press.

Biguer, B., Jeannerod, M. and Prablanc, C. (1982) The coordination of eye, head and arm movements during reaching at a single visual target. *Experimental Brain Research*, **46**, 301–4.

Binkofski, F., Dohle, C., Posse, S., Stephan, K. M., Hefter, H., Seitz, R. J. and Freund, H. J. (1998) Human anterior intraparietal area subserves prehension. A combined lesion and functional MRI activation study. *Neurology*, **50**, 1253–9.

Binkofski, F., Buccino, G., Dohle, C., Posse, Seitz, R. J. Rizzolatti, G. and Freund, H. J. (1999) A fronto-parietal circuit for object manipulation in man: evidence from an fMRI study. *European Journal of Neuroscience*, **11**, 3276–86.

Bisiach, E. and Luzzatti, C. (1978) Unilateral neglect of representational space. *Cortex*, **14**, 129–33.

Blakemore, S.-J. and Decety, J. (2001) From the perception of action to the understanding of intention. *Nature Neuroscience*, **2**, 561–67.

Block, N. (1995) On a confusion about a function of consciousness. *Behavioral and Brain Sciences*, **18**, 227–47.

Block, N. (1996) Mental paint and mental latex. In *Perception, philosophical issues*, Vol. 7 (ed. Villanueva, E.), Ridgeview: Atascadero.

Block, N. (2001) Paradox and cross purposes in recent work on consciousness. In *The cognitive neuroscience of consciousness* (ed. Dehaene, S.), pp.197–219. Cambridge, Mass.: MIT Press.

Bonatti, L., Frot E., Zangl R., and Mehler J. (2002) The human first hypothesis: identification of conspecifics and individuation of objects in the young infant. *Cognitive Psychology*, **45**, 1–39.

Bonda, E., Petrides, M., Ostry, D. and Evans, A. (1996) Specific involvement of human parietal systems and the amygdala in the perception of biological motion. *Journal of Neuroscience*, **16**, 3737–44.

Booth, M. C. and Rolls, E. T. (1998) View-invariant representations of familiar objects by neurons in the inferior temporal visual cortex. *Cerebral Cortex*, **8**, 510–23.

Boussaoud, D., Ungerleider, L. and Desimone, R. (1990) Pathways for motion analysis: cortical connections of the medial superior temporal sulcus and fundus of the superior temporal visual areas in the macaque monkey. *Journal of Comparative Neurology*, **296**, 462–95.

Bratman, M. (1985) Davidson's theory of intention. In *Actions and events, perspectives on the philosophy of Donald Davidson* (ed. Lepore, E. and McLaughlin, B.), pp.14–28. Oxford: Blackwell.

Brenner, E. and Smeets, J. B. J. (1996) Size illusion influences how we lift but not how we grasp an object. *Experimental Brain Research*, **111**, 473–6.

Bridgeman, B. (1992) Conscious vs unconscious processes. The case of vision. *Theory and Psychology*, **2**, 73–88.

Bridgeman, B., Lewis, S., Heit, G. and Nagle, M. (1979) Relation between cognitive and motor-oriented systems of visual position perception. *Journal of Experimental Psychology: Human Perception and Performance*, **5**, 692–700.

Bridgeman, B., Kirsch, M. and Sperling, A. (1981) Segregation of cognitive and motor aspects of visual function using induced motion. *Perception and Psychophysics*, **29**, 336–42.

Bridgeman, B., Peery, S. and Anand, S. (1997) Interaction of cognitive and sensorimotor maps of space. *Perception and Psychphysics*, **59**, 456–69.

Brownell, P. H. (1984) Prey detection by the sand scorpion. *Scientific American*, **251**, (6), 94–105.

Bruce, V. and Young, A. (1986) Understanding face recognition. *British Journal of Psychology*, **77**, 305–27.

Bruno, N. (2001) When does action resist visual illusions. *Trends in Cognitive Sciences*, **5**, (9), 385–88.

Bullier, J. (2001a) Integrated model of visual processing. *Brain Research Reviews*, **36**, 96–107.

Bullier, J. (2001b) Feedback connections and conscious vision. *Trends in Cognitive Sciences*, **5**, 369–70.

Bullier, J., Girard, P. and Salin, P. A. (1994) The role of area 17 in the transfer of information to extrastriate visual cortex. In *Cerebral cortex*, Vol. 10 (ed. Peters, A. and Rockland, K.), pp.301–30. New York: Plenum.

Bullier, J., Schall, J. D. and Morel, A. (1996) Functional streams in occipito-frontal connections in the monkey. *Behavioral and Brain Research*, **76**, 86–97.

Byrne, R. W. and Whiten, A. (ed.) (1988) *Machiavellian intelligence: social expertise and the evolution of intellect in monkeys, apes, and humans*. Oxford: Clarendon Press/Oxford University Press.

Caminiti, R., Ferraina, S. and Johnson, P. B. (1996) The sources of visual information to the primate frontal lobe. A novel role for the superior parietal lobule. *Cerebral Cortex*, **6**, 319–41.

Campbell, J. (1994) *Past, space and self*. Cambridge, Mass.: MIT Press.

Carey, S. (1995) Continuity and discontinuity in cognitive development. In *An Invitation to Cognitive Science,* Vol. 3 *Thinking*, (ed. Osherson, D.), pp.101–29. Cambridge, Mass.: MIT Press.

Carey, D. P., Harvey, M. and Milner, A. D. (1996) Visuomotor sensitivity for shape and orientation in a patient with visual form agnosia. *Neuropsychologia*, **34**, 329–37.

Carey, D. P., Perrett, D. I., and Oram, M. W. (1997). Recognizing, understanding and reproducing action. In *Handbook of neuropsychology* (series ed. Boller, F. and

Grafman, J.), *Action and cognition,* Vol. 11 (ed. Jeannerod, M.). Amsterdam: Elsevier.

Castelli, F., Happé, F., Frith, U. and Frith, C. (2000) Movement and mind: a functional imaging study of perception and interpretation of complex intentional movement patterns. *Neuroimage,* **12**, 314–25.

Castiello, U., Paulignan, Y. and Jeannerod, M. (1991) Temporal dissociation of motor responses and subjective awareness. A study in normal subjects. *Brain,* **114**, 2639–55.

Chao, L. L. and Martin, A. (2000) Representation of manipulable man-made objects in the dorsal stream. *Neuroimage,* **12**, 478–84.

Chalmers, D. (1996) *The conscious mind.* Oxford: Oxford University Press.

Chomsky, N. (1965) *Aspects of the theory of syntax.* Cambridge, Mass: MIT Press.

Chomsky, N. (1980) *Rules and representations.* New York: Pantheon Books.

Chomsky, N. (2000) *New horizons in the study of language and mind.* Cambridge: Cambridge University Press.

Clark, A. (2001) Visual experience and motor action: are the bonds too tight? *Philosophical Review,* **110**, 495–519.

Clark, M. A., Merians, A. S., Kothari, A., Poizner, H., Macauley, B., Rothi, L. J. G. and Heilman, K. H. (1994) Spatial planning deficits in limb apraxia. *Brain,* **117**, 1093–106.

Colby, C. (1998) Action-oriented spatial reference frames in cortex. *Neuron,* **20**, 15–24.

Colby, C. and Goldberg, M. (1999) Space and attention in parietal cortex. *Annual Review of Neuroscience,* **23**, 319–49.

Craighero, L., Bello, A., Fadiga, L. and Rizzolatti, G. (2002) Hand action preparation influences the responses to hand pictures. *Neuropsychologia,* **40**, 492–502.

Crane, T. (1992a) The nonconceptual content of experience. In *The contents of experience, essays on perception* (ed. Crane, T.), pp.136–57. Cambridge: Cambridge University Press.

Crick, F. (1994) *The astonishing hypothesis: the scientific search for the soul.* New York: Touchstone Books.

Crick, F. and Koch, C. (1990) Towards a neurobiological theory of consciousness. *Seminars in the Neurosciences,* **2**, 263–75.

Csibra, G., Gergely, G., Biro, S., Koos, O. and Brockbank, M. (1999) Goal attribution without agency cues: the perception of 'pure reason' in infancy. *Cognition,* **72**, 237–67.

Damasio, A. R., Damasio, H. and Van Hoesen, G. W. (1982) Prosopagnosia. Anatomic basis and behavioral mechanisms. *Neurology,* **32**, 331–41.

Daprati, E. and Gentilucci, M. (1997) Grasping an illusion. *Neuropsychologia,* **35**, (12), 1577–82.

Daprati, E., Sirigu, A., Pradat-Diehl, P., Franck, N. and Jeannerod, M. (2000) Recognition of self produced movement in a case of severe neglect. *Neurocase,* **6**, 477–86.

Dasser, V., Ulbaek, I. and Premack, D. (1989). The perception of intention. *Science,* **243**, 365–7.

Davidson D. (1963) Actions, reasons and causes. In *Essays on actions and events* (ed. Davidson, D.), pp.3–19. Oxford: Oxford University Press.

Davidson, D. (1971) Agency. In *Essays on actions and events* (ed. Davidson, D.), pp.43–61. Oxford: Oxford University Press.

Davidson, D. (1978) Intending. In *Essays on actions and events* (ed. Davidson, D.), pp.83–102. Oxford: Oxford University Press.

Decety, J., Jeannerod, M. and Prablanc, C. (1989) The timing of mentally represented actions. *Behavioural Brain Research*, **34**, 35–42.

Decety, J., Perani, D., Jeannerod, M., Bettinardi, V., Tadary, B., Woods, R., Mazziotta, J. C. and Fazio, F. (1994) Mapping motor representations with PET. *Nature*, **371**, 600–2.

Decety, J., Grezes, J., Costes, N., Perani, D., Jeannerod, M., Procyk, E., Grassi, F. and Fazio, F. (1997) Brain activity during observation of action. Influence of action content and subject's strategy. *Brain*, **120**, 1763–77.

Decety, J., Chaminade, T., Grèzes, J. and Meltzoff, A. (2002) A PET exploration of the neural mechanisms involved in reciprocal imitation. *Neuroimage*, **15**, 265–72.

Dehaene, S. and Naccache, L. (2001) Towards a cognitive neuroscience of consciousness: basic evidence and a workspace framework. In *The cognitive neuroscience of consciousnes* (ed. Dehaene, S.), pp.1–37. Cambridge, Mass.: MIT Press.

Dehaene, S., Naccache, L., Le Clec'H, G., Koechlin, E., Mueller, M., Dehaene-Lambertz, G., van de Moortele, P. F. and Le Bihan, D. (1998) Imaging unconscious priming. *Nature*, **395**, 597–600.

Dennett, D. (1987) *The intentional stance*. Cambridge, Mass: MIT Press.

Dennett, D. (1991) *Consciousness explained*. London, Allen Lane: The Penguin Press.

Dennett, D. (1992) Filling in vs finding out: an ubiquitous confusion in cognitive science. In *Cognition: conceptual and methodological issues* (ed. Pick, H. L, van den Broek, P. and Knill, D. C.). Washington: American Psychological Association.

Dennett, D. (1994) Get real. *Philosophical Topics*, **22**, (1 and 2), Spring and Fall, 505–68.

Dennett, D. (1996) Seeing is believing—or is it? In *Perception, Vancouver studies in cognitive science*, Vol. 5 (ed. Akins, K.), pp.158–72. Oxford: Oxford Univ. Press.

Dennett, D. (2001a) Are we explaining consciousness yet? In *The cognitive neuroscience of consciousnes* (ed. Dehaene, S.), pp.221–37. Cambridge, Mass.: MIT Press.

Dennett, D. (2001b) *The fantasy of first-person science*. http://ase. tufts. edu/cogstud/papers/chalmersdeb3dft. htm

Descartes, R. (1644) *Méditations métaphysiques*. In Bridoux, A. (ed.) *Descartes, ocuvres et lettres*. Paris: Gallimard, 1949.

Desmurget, M., Epstein, C. M., Turner, R. S., Prablanc, C., Alexander, G. E. and Grafton, S. T. (1999) Role of the posterior parietal cortex in updating reaching movements to a visual target. *Nature Neuroscience*, **2**, 563–7.

DiCarlo, J. J. and Maunsell, J. H. R. (2000) Form representation in monkey inferotemporal cortex is virtually unaltered by free viewing. *Nature Neuroscience*, **3**, 814.

Dijkerman, H. C. and Milner, A. D. (1997) Copying without perceiving: motor imagery in visual form agnosia. *Neuroreport*, **8**, 729–32.

Di Pellegrino, G., Fadiga, L., Fogassi, L., Gallese, V. and Rizzolatti, G. (1992) Understanding motor events: a neurophysiological study. *Experimental Brain Research*, **91**, 176–80.

Ditchburn, R. (1955) Eye movements in relation to retinal action. *Optica Acta*, **1**, 171–6.

Dittrich, W. H. (1993) Action categories and the perception of biological motion. *Perception*, **22**, 15–22.

Dittrich, W. H., Troscianko, T., Lea, S. E. and Morgan, D. (1996) Perception of emotion from dynamic point-light displays represented in dance. *Perception*, **25**, 727–38.

Dokic, J. (1997) Introduction, issue on cognitive dynamics. *European Review of Philosophy*, **2**, 3–11.

Dokic, J. (2001) *L'Esprit en mouvement, essai sur la dynamique cognitive*. Stanford: CSLI Publications.

Dokic, J. (2002) Situated representations in language, thought and vision, typescript.

Dokic, J. and Pacherie, E. (2001) Shades and concepts. *Analysis*, **61**, (3), 193–202.

Dretske, F. (1969) *Seeing and knowing*. Chicago: Chicago University Press.

Dretske, F. (1978) Simple seeing. In *Perception, knowledge and belief* (2000) (ed. Dretske, F.), pp.97–112. Cambridge: Cambridge University Press.

Dretske, F. (1981) *Knowledge and the flow of information*. Cambridge, Mass.: MIT Press.

Dretske, F. (1988) *Explaining behavior*. Cambridge, Mass.: MIT Press.

Dretske, F. (1990a) The epistemology of belief. In *Perception, knowledge and belief* (2000) (ed. Dretske, F.), pp.64–79. Cambridge: Cambridge University Press.

Dretske, F. (1990b) Knowing, believing and seeing. In *An invitation to cognitive science*, Vol. 3 *Visual cognition* (ed. Osherson, D.), pp.129–48. Cambridge, Mass.: MIT Press.

Dretske, F. (1995a) Meaningful perception. In *An invitation to cognitive science, Vol. 2, Visual cognition* (ed. Osherson, D.), pp.331–52. Cambridge, Mass.: MIT Press.

Dretske, F. (1995b) *Naturalizing the mind*. Cambridge, Mass.: MIT Press.

Driver, J. and Mattingley, J. B. (1998) Parietal neglect and visual awareness. *Nature Neuroscience*, **1**, 17–22.

Duhamel, J. R., Colby, C. and Golberg, M. (1992) The updating of the representation of visual space in parietal cortex by intended eye movements. *Science*, **255**, 90–2.

Duhamel, J. R., Bremmer, F., BenHamed, S. and Graf, W. (1997) Spatial invariance of visual receptive fields in parietal cortex neurons. *Nature*, **389**, 845–7.

Dunbar, R. (1998) The social brain hypothesis. *Evolutionary Anthropology*, **6**, 178–90.

Efron, R. (1966–68) What is perception? *Boston Studies in the Philosophy of Science*, IV, 137–73.

Elliott, D. and Maladena (1987) The influence of premovement visual information on manual aiming. *Quarterly Journal of Experimental Psychology*, **39A**, 541–59.

Ellis, A. W. and Young, A. W. (1988) *Human cognitive neuropsychology* (augmented edition, 1996). Hove: Psychology Press.

Ellis, R. R., Flanagan, J. R. and Lederman, S. J. (1999) The influence of visual illusions on grasp position. *Experimental Brain Research*, **125**, 109–14.

Engel, A. K., König, P., Kreiter, A. K., Schiller, T. B. and Singer, W. (1992) Temporal coding in the visual cortex: new vistas on integration in the nervous system. *Trends in Neurosciences*, **15**, 218–26.

Engelkamp, J. (1998) *Memory for actions*. Hove: Psychology Press.

Evans, G. (1982) *The varieties of reference*. Oxford: Oxford University Press.

Fadiga, L., Fogassi, L., Iavesi, G. and Rizzolatti, G. (1995) Motor facilitation during action observation. A magnetic stimulation study. *Journal of Neurophysiology*, **73**, 2608–11.

Faillenot, I., Toni, I., Decety, J., Gregoire, M. C. and Jeannerod, M. (1997) Visual pathways for object-orientedaction and object recognition: Functional anatomy with PET. *Cerebral Cortex*, **7**, 77–85.

Faillenot, I., Decety, J. and Jeannerod, M. (1999) Human brain activity related to the perception of spatial features of objects. *Neuroimage*, **10**, 114–24.

Farah, M. J. (1984) The neurological basis of mental imagery. A componential approach. *Cognition*, **18**, 245–72.

Farah, M. J. (1990) *Visual agnosia. Disorders of object recognition and what they tell us about normal vision*. Cambridge (Mass), MIT Press.

Farah, M. J. (1995) Current issues in the neuropsychology of image generation. *Neuropsychologia*, **33**, 1455–71.

Farah, M. J., Hammond, K. M., Levine, D. M. and Calvanio, R. (1988) Visual and spatial mental imagery. Dissociable systems of representation. *Cognitive Psychology*, **20**, 439–62.

Farné, A., Roy, A. C., Paulignan, Y., Rode, G., Rossetti, Y., Boisson, D. and Jeannerod, M. (2003) Right hemisphere visuomotor control of the ipsilateral hand: evidence from right brain damaged patients. *Neuropsychologia*, **41**, 739–47.

Faugier-Grimaud, S., Frenois, C. and Stein, D. G. (1978) Effects of posterior parietal lesions on visually guided behavior in monkeys. *Neuropsychologia*, **16**, 151–68.

Fitts, P. (1954) The information capacity of the human motor system in controlling the amplitude of movement. *Journal of Experimental Psychology*, **47**, 381–91

Fodor, J. A. (1975) *The language of thought*. New York: Crowell.

Fodor, J. A. (1983) *The modularity of mind*. Cambridge, Mass.: MIT Press.

Fodor, J. A. (1986) Why paramecia don't have mental representations. *Midwest Studies in Philosophy*, **X**, 3–23.

Fodor, J. A. (1987) *Psychosemantics*. Cambridge, Mass.: MIT Press.

Fodor, J. A. (1998a) *In critical condition, polemical essays on cognitive science and the philosophy of mind*. Cambridge, Mass.: MIT Press.

Fodor, J. A. (1998b) *Concepts*. Oxford: Oxford University Press.

Fodor, J. A. and Pylyshyn, Z. (1981) How direct is visual perception? *Cognition*, **9**, 139–96.

Fogassi, L. Gallese, V., Buccino, G., Craighero, L., Fadiga, L. and Rizzolatti, G. (2001) Cortical mechanism for the visual guidance of hand grasping movements in the monkey. A reversible inactivation study. *Brain*, **124**, 571–86.

Fox, R. and McDaniel, C. (1982) The perception of biological motion by human infants. *Science*, **218**, 468–78.

Franz, V. H., Gegenfurtner, K. R., Bülthoff, H. H. and Fahle, M. (2000) Grasping visual illusions: no evidence for a dissociation between perception and action. *Psychological Science*, **11**, 20–5.

Franz, V. H., Fahle, M., Bülthoff, H. H. and Gegenfurtner, K. R. (2001) Effects of visual illusion on grasping. *Journal of Experimental Psychology: Human Perception and Performance*, **27**, 1124–44.

Frege, G. (1918–19) *The thought* (trans. M. Quinton). In *Essays on Frege* (1968) (ed. Klemke, E. D.), pp.507–35. Urbana, Ill.: University of Illinois Press.

Freud, S. (1891) *Zur Auffassung der Aphasien*. Leipzig: Franz Deuticke.

Friedman-Hill, S. R., Robertson, L. C. and Treisman, A. (1995) Parietal contributions to visual feature binding: evidence from a patient with bilateral lesions. *Science*, **269**, 853–55.

Frith, C. D. and Frith, U. (1999) Interacting minds—a biological basis. *Science*, **286**, 1692–95.

Gallagher, H. L., Happé, F., Brunswick, N., Fletcher, P. C., Frith, U., and Frith, C. D. (2000) Reading the mind in cartoons and stories: an fMRI study of 'theory of mind' in verbal and nonverbal tasks, *Neuropsychologia*, **38**, 11–21.

Gallese, V. and Goldman, A. (1998) Mirror neurons and the simulation theory of mind-reading. *Trends in Cognitive Sciences*, **12**, 493–501.

Gallese, V., Murata, A., Kaseda, M., Niki, N. and Sakata, H. (1994) Deficit of hand preshaping after muscimol injection in monkey parietal cortex. *Neuroreport*, **5**, 1525–9.

Gallese, V., Craighero, L., Fadiga, L. and Fogassi, L. (1999) Perception through action. *Psyche*, **5**, 21. http://psyche. cs. monash. edu. au/v5/psyche-5–21-gallese. html

Galletti, C., Battaglini, P. P. and Fattori, P. (1993) Parietal neurons encoding locations in craniotopic coordinates. *Experimental Brain Research*, **96**, 221–9.

Gauthier, I., Behrmann, M. and Tarr, M. (1999) Can face recognition really be dissociated from object recognition? *Journal of Cognitive Neuroscience*, **11**, 349–71.

Gauthier, I., Skularski, P., Gore, J. C. and Anderson, A. W. (2000) Expertise for cars and birds recruits brain areas involved in face recognition. *Nature Neuroscience*, **3**, 191–7.

Gentilucci, M., Daprati, E., Toni, I., Chieffi, S. and Saetti, M. C. (1995) Unconscious updating of grasp motor program. *Experimental Brain Research*, **105**: 291–303.

Gentilucci, M., Chieffi, S., Daprati, E., Saetti, M. C. and Toni, I. (1996) Visual illusion and action. *Neuropsychologia*, **34**, (5), 369–76.

Gergely, G., Nadasdy, Z., Czibra, G. and Biro, S. (1995) Taking the intentional stance at 12 months of age. *Cognition*, **56**, 165–93.

Georgopoulos, A. P. and Massey, J. T. (1987) Cognitive spatial-motor processes. *Experimental Brain Research*, **65**, 361–70.

Gibson, J. J. (1979) *The ecological approach to visual perception*. Boston: Houghton-Miffin.

Girard, P., Salin, P. and Bullier, J. (1992) Response selectivity in neurons in area MT of the macaque monkey during reversible inactivation of area V1. *Journal of Neurophysiology*, **67**: 1–10.

Glover, S. (2003) Separate visual representations in the planning and control of action. *Brain and Behavioral Sciences* (in press)

Goldenberg, G., Müllbacher, W. and Nowak, A. (1995) Imagery without perception. A case study of ansognosia for cortical blindness. *Neuropsychologia*, **33**, 1373–82.

Goodale, M. A. (1995) The cortical organization of visual perception and visuomotor control. In *An invitation to cognitive science, Vol. 2, Visual cognition* (ed. Osherson, D.), pp.167–213. Cambridge, Mass.: MIT Press.

Goodale, M. and Humphrey, G. K. (1998) The objects of action and perception. *Cognition*, **67**, 191–207.

Goodale, M. A. and Milner, A. D. (1992) Separate visual pathways for perception and action. *Trends in Neuroscience*, **15**, 20–5.

Goodale, M. A., Pélisson, D. and Prablanc, C. (1986) Large adjustments invisually guided reaching do not depend on vision of the hand or perception of target displacement. *Nature*, **320**, 748–50.

Goodale, M. A., Milner, A. D., Jakobson I. S. and Carey, D. P. (1991) A Neurological dissociation between perceiving objects and grasping them. *Nature*, **349**, 154–6.

Goodale, M. A., Jakobson, L. S., Milner, A. D., Perrett, D. I., Benson, P. J. and Hietanen, J. K. (1994) The nature and limits of orientation and pattern processing supporting visuomotor control in a visual form agnosic. *Journal of Cognitive Neuroscience*, **6**, 46–56.

Goodman, N. (1978) *Ways of worldmaking*. Indianapolis: Hackett.

Goren, C. C., Sarty, M. and Wu, P. Y. (1975) Visual following and pattern discrimination of face-like stimuli by newborn infants. *Pediatrics*, **56**, (4), 544–90.

Grafton, S. T., Arbib, M. A., Fadiga, L. and Rizzolatti, G. (1996) Localization of grasp representations in humans by PET: 2. Observation compared with imagination. *Experimental Brain Research*, **112**, 103–11.

Grafton, S. T., Mazziotta, J. C., Woods, R. P. and Phelps, M. E. (1992) Human functional anatomy of visually guided finger movements. *Brain*, **115**: 565–87.

Graziano, M. S. A., Yap, G. S. and Gross, C. G. (1994) Coding of visual space by premotor neurons. *Science*, **266**, 1054–7.

Gregory, R. (1978) *Eye and brain: the psychology of seeing*, 3rd edn. New York: McGraw-Hill.

Grèzes, J., Fonlupt, P., Bertenthal, B. Delon-Martin, C., Segebarth, C. and Decety, J. (2001) Does perception of biological motion rely on specific brain regions? *Neuroimage*, **13**, 775–85.

Grice, (1957) Meaning. In *Studies in the way of words* (ed. Grice, P.) (1989), pp.213–23. Cambridge, Mass.: Harvard University Press.

Grice, P. (1961) The causal theory of perception. *Proceedings of the Aristotelian Society*, **35**, Suppl.

Grice, P. (1975) Logic and conversation. In *Speech acts, syntax and semantics* (ed. Cole, P. and Morgan, J.). New York: Academic Press.

Grice, P. (1989) *Studies in the way of words*. Cambridge, Mass.: Harvard University Press.

Gross, C. G. (1973) Visual functions of inferotemporal cortex. In *Handbook of sensory physiology*, Vol. VII/3 (ed. Jung, R.), pp.451–82. Berlin, Springer.

Gross, C. G., Rocha-Miranda, C. E. and Bender, D. B. (1972) Visual properties of neurons in inferotemporal cortex of the macaque. *Journal of Neurophysiology*, **35**, 96–111.

Haffenden, A. M. and Goodale, M. (1998) The effect of pictorial illusion on prehension and perception. *Journal of Cognitive Neuroscience*, **10**, 122–36.

Haffenden, A. M. and Goodale, M. (2000) Independent effects of pictorial displays on perception and action. *Vision research*, **40**, 1597–607.

Haffenden, A. M. Schiff, K. C. and Goodale, M. A. (2001) The dissociation between perception and action in the Ebbinghaus illusion: non-illusory effects of pictorial cues on grasp. *Current Biology*, **11**, 177–81.

Happé, F. and Frith, U. (1999) How the brain reads the mind. *Neuroscience News*, **2**, 16–25.

Harman, G. (1990) The intrinsic quality of experience. In *The nature of consciousness* (1997) (ed. Block, N., Flanagan, O. and Güzeldere, G.), pp.663–75. Cambridge, Mass.: MIT Press.

Harvey, M. and Milner, D. A. (1995) Balint's patient. *Cognitive Neuropsychology*, **12**, 261–81.

Hauser, M. (1996) *The evolution of communication*. Cambridge, Mass.: MIT Press.

Hauser, M. (2000) *Wild minds*. New York: Penguin Books.

Hauser, M. D., Chomsky, N. and Fitch, W. T. (2002) The faculty of language, what is it, who has it, and how did it evolve. *Science*, **298**, 1569–79.

Haxby, J. V., Grady, C. L., Horwitz, B. Ungerleider, L. G., Mishkin, M. *et al.* (1991) Dissociation of object and spatial visual processing pathways in human extrastriate cortex. *Proceedings of the National Academy of Sciences*, **88**, 1621–5.

Haxby, J. V., Horwitz, B., Ungerleider, L. G., Maisog, J. M., Pietrini, P. and Grady, C. L. (1994). The functional organization of human extrastriate cortex. A PET-rCBF study of selective attention to faces and locations. *Journal of Neurosciences*, **14**, 6336–53.

Haxby, J. V., Ungerleider, L. G., Clark, V. P., Schouten, J. L., Hoffman, E. A. and Martin, A. (1999) The effect of face inversion on activity in human neural systems for face and object perception. *Neuron*, **22**, 189–99.

Haxby, J. V., Hoffman, E. A. and Gobbini, I. (2000) The distributed human neural system for face perception. *Trends in Cognitive Sciences*, **4**, 223–33.

Heberlein, A.S. *et al.* (1998) Impaired attribution of social meanings to abstract dynamic geometric patterns following damage to the amygdala. *Society for Neuroscience*, Abstr. **24**, 1176.

Hécaen, H. and Albert, M. A. (1978) *Human neuropsychology*. New York: Wiley.

Heider, F., and Simmel, M. (1944) An experimental study of apparent behavior. *American Journal of Psychology*, **57**, 243–59.

Heilman, K. (1979) The neuropsychological basis of skilled movements in man. In *Handbook of behavioral neurobiology, II Neuropsychology* (ed. Gazzaniga, M. S.), pp.447–60. New York: Plenum.

Hodges, J. R., Spatt, J. and Patterson, K. (1999) What and how: evidence for the dissociation of object knowledge and mechanical problem-solving skills in the human brain. *Proceedings of the National Academy of Sciences*, **96**, 9444–8.

Hoffman, E. A. and Haxby, J. V. (2000) Distinct representations of eye gaze and identity in the distributed human neural system for face perception. *Nature America*, **3**, 80–4.

Holmes, G. (1918) Disturbances of vision by cerebral lesions. *British Journal of Ophtalmology*, **2**, 353–84.

Holmes, G. and Lister, W. T. (1916) Disturbances of vision from cerebral lesions, with special reference to the cortical representation of the macula. *Brain*, **39**, 34.

Hu, Y., Eagleson, R. and Goodale, M. A. (1999) The effects of delay on the kinematics of grasping. *Experimental Brain Research*, **126**, 109–16.

Hu, Y. and Goodale, M. A. (2000) Grasping after a delay shifts size scaling from absolute to relative metrics. *Journal of Cognitive Neuroscience*, **12**, 856–68.

Humphreys, G. W. and Riddoch, M. J. (1987) The fractionation of visual agnosia. In *Visual object processing. A cognitive neuropsychological approach* (ed. Humphreys, G. W. and Riddoch, M. J.), pp.281–306. Erlbaum, Hillsdale.

Hyvarinen, J. and Poranen, A. (1974) Function of the parietal associative area 7 as revealed from cellular discharges in alert monkeys. *Brain*, **97**, 673–92.

Iacoboni, M., Woods, R. P., Brass, M., Bekkering, H., Mazziotta, J. C. and Rizzolatti, G. (1999) Cortical mechanisme of human imitation. *Science*, **286**, 2526–8.

Ingle, D. J. (1967) Two visual mechanisms underlying the behavior of fish. *Psychologische Forschung*, **31**, 44–51.

Ingle, D. J. (1973) Two visual systems in the frog. *Science*, **181**, 1053–5.

Ingle, D. J. (1982) In *Analysis of visual behavior* (ed. Ingle, D. J., Goodale, M. A. and Mansfield, R. J. W.). Cambridge, Mass.: MIT Press.

Jackson, F. (1977) *Perception, a representative theory*. Cambridge: Cambridge University Press.

Jackson, S. R. and Shaw, A. (2000) The Ponzo illusionaffects grip force but not grip-aperture scaling during prehension movements. *Journal of Experimental Psychology*, **26**, 418–23.

Jacob, P. (1997) *What minds can do*. Cambridge: Cambridge University Press.

Jacob, P. (2000) Can selection explain content? *The Proceedings of the Twentieth World Congress of Philosophy*, pp.91–102. Philosophy Documentation Center, Bowling Green State University.

Janssen, P., Vogels, R. and Orban, G. A. (2000) Selectivity for 3D shape that reveals distinct areas within macaque inferior temporal cortex. *Science*, **288**, 2054–6.

Jeannerod, M. (1981) Intersegmental coordination during reaching at natural visual objects. In *Attention and performance IX* (ed. Long, J. and Baddeley, A.), pp.153–68. Erlbaum, Hillsdale.

Jeannerod, M. (1984) The timing of natural prehension movements. *Journal of Motor Behaviour*, **16**, 235–54.

Jeannerod, M. (1986a) Mechanisms of visuomotor coordination: a study in normal and brain-damaged subjects. *Neuropsychologia*, **24**, 41–78.

Jeannerod, M. (1986b) The formation of finger grip during prehension. A cortically mediated visuomotor pattern. *Behavioural Brain Research*, **19**, 99–116.

Jeannerod, M. (1988) *The neural and behavioural organization of goal-directed movements*. Oxford: Oxford University Press.

Jeannerod, M. (1994) The representing brain. Neural correlates of motor intention and imagery. *Behavioral and Brain Sciences*, **17**, 187–245.

Jeannerod, M. (1997) *The cognitive neuroscience of action*. Oxford: Blackwell.

Jeannerod, M., Decety, J. and Michel, F. (1994). Impairment of grasping movements following a bilateral posterior parietal lesion. *Neuropsychologia*, **32**, 369–80.

Jeannerod, M., Arbib, M. A., Rizzolatti, G. and Sakata, H. (1995) Grasping objects. The cortical mechanisms of visuomotor transformation. *Trends in Neuroscience*, **18**, 314–20.

Johansson, G. (1973) Visual perception of biological motion and a model for its analysis. *Perception Psychophysics*, **14**, 201–11.

Johansson, G. (1977) Studies on visual perception of locomotion. *Perception*, **6**, 365–76.

Johnson, M. H. and Morton, J. (1991) *Biology and Cognitive Development, The Case of Face Recognition*. Oxford: Blackwell.

Johnson, P. B., Ferraina, S. and Caminiti, R. (1993) Cortical networks for visual reaching. *Experimental Brain Research*, **97**, 361–5.

Kanwisher, N. (2000) Domain specificity in face perception. *Nature Neuroscience*, **3**, (8), 759–63.

Kanwisher, N., McDermott, J. and Chun, M. M. (1997) The Fusiform face area: a module in human extrastriate cortex specialized for face perception. *The Journal of Neuroscience*, **17**, (11), 4302–11.

Kaplan, D. (1989) Demonstratives. In *Themes from Kaplan* (ed. Almog, J., Perry, J. and Wettstein, H.), pp.481–563. New York: Blackwell.

Karnath, O., Ferber, S. and Bülthoff, H. H. (2000) Neuronal representation of object orientation. *Neuropsychologia*, **38**, 1235–41.

Kitcher, P. (1993) Function and design. In *Midwest studies in philosophy*, Vol. 18 *Philosophy of science* (ed. French, P., Uehling Jr, T. and Wettstein, H. K.) Notre Dame, University of Notre Dame Press.

Kleist, K. (1934) *Gehirnpathologie*. Leipzig, Barth.

Kluwer, H. and Bucy, P. C. (1939) Preliminary analysis of the function of parietal lobes in monkeys. *Archives of Neurological Psychiatry*, **42**, 979–97.

Köhler, S., Kapur, K., Moscovitch, M., Winocur, G. and Houle, S. (1995) Dissociation of pathways for object and spatial vision. A PET study in humans. *Neuroreport*, **6**, 1865–8.

Kolers, P. A. (1972) *Aspects of motion perception*. London: Pergamon Press.

Koslowski, L. T. and Cutting, J. E. (1978) Recognizing the sex of a walker from point-lights mounted on ankles: some second thoughts. *Perception and Psychphysics*, **23**, 459.

Kosslyn, S. M., Alpert, N. M., Thomson, W. L., Maljkovic, V., Wiese, S. B., Chabris, C. F., Hamilton, S. E. and Buonano, F. S. (1993) Visual mental imagery activates topographically organized visual cortex: PET investigation. *Journal of Cognitive Neuroscience*, **5**, 263–87.

Kourtzi, Z. and Kanwisher, N. (2000) Activation in human MT/MST by static images with implied motion. *Journal of Cognitive Neuroscience*, **12**, 48–55.

Lacquaniti, F., Terzuolo, C. and Viviani, P. (1983) The law relating kinematic and figural aspects of drawing movements. *Acta Psychologica*, **54**, 115–30.

Lamotte, R. H. and Acuna, C. (1978) Defects in accuracy of reaching after removal of posterior parietal cortex in monkeys. *Brain Research*, **139**, 309–26.

Lauro-Grotto, R., Piccini, C. and Shallice, T. (1997) Modality-specific operations in semantic dementia. *Cortex*, **33**, 593–622.

Lê, S., Cardebat, D., Boulanouar, K., Henaff, M. A., Michel, F., Milner, A. D., Dijkerman, C. and Demonet, J. F. (2002) Seeing, since childhood, without ventral stream: a behavioral study. *Brain*, **125**, 58–74.

Leslie, A. (1988) The necessity of illusion: Perception and thought in infancy. In *Thought without language* (ed. Weiskrantz, L.), pp.185–210. Oxford: Oxford University Press.

Leslie, A. M., Xu, F., Tremoulet, P. D. and Scholl, B. J. (1998) Indexing and the Object Concept: Developing 'What' and 'Where' Systems. *Trends in Cognitive Sciences*, **2**, 10–18.

Levine, J. (1983) Materialism and qualia: the explanatory gap. *Pacific Philosophical Quarterly*, **64**, 354–61.

Levine, J. (1993). On leaving out what it's like. In *Consciousness: psychological and philosophical essays* (ed. Davies, M. and Humphreys, G.), pp.121–36. Oxford: Blackwell.

Lhermitte, F. (1983) Utilisation behaviour and its relation to lesions of the frontal lobes. *Brain*, **106**, 237–55.

Liepmann, H. (1900) Das Krankheitshild de Apraxie (motorischen Assymbolie). *Monatschrift fur Psychaitrie und Neurologie*, **8**, 15–44, 102–32, 182–97.

Lissauer (1890) Eine Fall von Seelenblindhiet nebst einem Beitrage zur Theorie desselben. *Archiv fir Psychiatrie und Nervenkrankheiten*, **21**, 222–70.

Loewer, B. and Rey, G. (1991) Editor's introduction. In *Meaning in mind, Fodor and his critics* (ed. Loewer, B. and Rey, G.), pp.xi–xxxvii. Oxford: Blackwell.

Logothetis, N. and Sheinberg, D. L. (1996) Visual object recognition. *Annual Review of Neuroscience*, **19**, 577–621.

Marr, D. (1982) *Vision*. San Francisco: Freeman.

Marshall, J and Halligan, P. W. (1994) The yin and yang of visuospatial neglect. A case study. *Neuropsychologia*, **32**, 1037–57.

Marteniuk, R. G., MacKenzie, C. L., Jeannerod, M., Athenes, S. and Dugas, C. (1987) Constraints on human arm movement trajectories. *Canadian Journal of Psychology*, **41**, 365–78.

Martin, M. (2002) The transparency of experience. *Mind and language*, **17**, **4**, 376–425.

Martin, A., Haxby, J. V., Lalonde, F. M., Wiggs, C. L. and Ungerleider, L. G. (1995) Discrete cortical regions associated with knowledge of color and knowledge of action. *Science*, **270**, 102–5.

Martin, A., Wiggs, C. L., Ungerleider, L. G. and Haxby, J. V. (1996). Neural correlates of category-specific knowledge. *Nature*, **379**, 649–52.

Matelli, M., Luppino, G., and Rizzolatti, G. (1985) Patterns of cytochrome oxydase activity in the frontal agranular cortex of the macaque monkey. *Behavioral Brain Research*, **18**, 125–36.

Matelli, M., Camarda, R., Glickstein, M. and Rizzolatti, G. (1986) Afferent and efferent projections of the inferior area 6 in the Macaque Monkey. *The Journal of Comparative Neurology*, **251**, 281–98.

McDowell, J. (1982) Criteria, Defeasibility, and Knowledge. In *Perceptual knowledge* (1988) (ed. Dancy, J.), pp.409–19. Oxford: Oxford University Press.

McDowell, J. (1994) *Mind and the world*. Cambridge, Mass.: Harvard University Press.

McDowell, J. (1998) Précis of Mind and the World. *Philosophy and Phenomenological Research*, 58, 365–68.

McGlinchey-Berroth, R., Milberg, W. P., Verfaellie, M., Alexander, M. and Kilduff, P. (1993) Semantic priming in the neglected field: evidence from a lexical decision task. *Cognitive Neuropsychology*, **10**, 79–108.

McGurk, H. and MacDonald, J. (1976) Hearing lips and seeing voices. *Nature*, **264**, 746–48.

Meltzoff, A. N. (1995) Understanding intentions of others: reenactment of intended acts by 18 months-old children. *Developmental Psychology*, **31**, 838–50.

Meltzoff, A. N. and Moore, M. K. (1977) Imitation of facial and manual gestures by human neonates. *Science*, **198**, 75–8.

Meltzoff, A. N. and Moore, M. K. (1997) Explaining facial imitation. A theoretical model. *Early Development and Parenting*, **6**, 179–92.

Michotte, A. (1950) The emotions regarded as functional connections. In *Feelings and emotions: the Mooseheart symposium* (ed. Reymert, M.). New York, McGraw Hill.

Michotte, A. (1946) *La perception de la causalite*. Louvain: Publications de l'université de Louvain.

Millikan, R. G. (1984) *Language, thought and other biological categories*. Cambridge, Mass.: MIT Press.

Millikan, R. G. (1993) *White queen psychology and other essays for Alice*. Cambridge, Mass.: MIT Press.

Millikan R. G. (1996) Pushmi-pullyu representations. In *Philosophical perspectives*, Vol. IX (ed. Tomberlin, J.), pp.00. Atascadero CA: Ridgeview Publishing.

Millikan R. G. (2000) *On clear and confused ideas: an essay about substance concepts*. Cambridge: Cambridge University Press.

Milner, A. D. and Goodale, M. A. (1995) *The visual brain in action*. Oxford: Oxford University Press.

Milner, A. D. and Goodale, M. (1998) The visual brain in action (precis). *Psyche: An Interdisciplinary Journal of Research on Consciousness*, **4**, 12. Available http://psyche. cs. monash. edu/au/v4/psyche-4–12-milner. html.

Milner, A. D., Paulignan, Y., Dijkerman, H. C., Michel, F. and Jeannerod, M. (1999) A paradoxical improvement of misreaching in optic ataxia: new evidence for two separate neural systems for visual localization. *Proceedings of the Royal Society*, **266**, 2225–9.

Milner, A. D., Harvey, M., Roberts, R. C. and Forster, S. V. (1993) Line bisection errors in visual neglect: misguided action or size distorsion. *Neuropsychologia*, **31**, 39–49.

Milner, A. D., Perrett, D. I., Johnston, R. S., Benson, P. J., Jordan, T. R., Heeley, D. W., Bettucci, D., Mortara, F., Mutani, R., Terazzi, E. and Davidson, D. L. W. (1991) Perception and action in 'visual form agnosia'. *Brain*, **114**, 405–28.

Mishkin, M. (1966) Visual mechanisms beyond the striate cortex. In *Frontiers in physiological psychology* (ed. Russell, R.), pp.00. New York: Academic Press.

Mishkin, M. (1972) Cortical visual areas and their interactions. In *Brain and human behavior* (ed. Karczmar, A. G. and Eccles, J. C.), pp.187–208. Berlin: Springer.

Miyashita, Y. and Chang, H. S. (1988) Neuronal correlate of pictorial short-term memory in the primate temporal cortex. *Nature*, **331**, 68–70.

Moore, G. E. (1942) Reply to my critics. In *The philosophy of G. E. Moore* (ed. Schilpp, P. A.), pp. 207–12. New York: Tudor Publishing Company.

Moore, G. E. (1993) Moore's paradox. In *G. E. Moore, selected writings* (ed. Baldwin, T.), pp.207–12. London: Routledge and Kegan Paul.

Morel, A. and Bullier, J. (1990) Anatomical segregation of two cortical visual pathways in the macaque monkey. *Visual Neuroscience*, **4**, 555–78.

Mountcastle, V. B. (1995) The parietal system and some higher brain functions. *Cerebral Cortex*, **5**, 377–90.

Mountcastle, V. B., Lynch, J. C., Georgopoulos, A. Sakata, H. and Acuna, C. (1975) Posterior parietal association cortex of the monkey: command functions for operations within extra-personal space. *Journal of Neurophysiology*, **38**, 871–908.

Murata, A., Gallese, V., Kaseda, M. and Sakata, H. (1996) Parietal neurons related to memory-guided hand manipulation. *Journal of Neurophysiology*, **75**, 2180–5.

Murata, A., Gallese, V., Luppino, G., Kaseda, M. and Sakata, H. (2000) Selectivity for the shape, size, and orientation of objects for grasping in monkey parietal area AIP. *Journal of Neurophysiology*, **79**, 2580–2601.

Myin, E. and O'Regan, J-K. (2002) Perceptual consciousness, access to modality and skill theories: a way to naturalize phenomenology?. *Journal of Consciousness Studies*, **9**, 27–45.

Nagel, T. (1974) What is it like to be a bat? *Philosophical Review*, **4**, 435–50.

Neander, K. (1995) Misrepresenting and Malfunctioning. *Philosophical Studies*, **79**, 109–41.

Noë, A. (2002) Is the visual world a grand illusion? *Journal of Consciousness Studies*, **9**, 5–6.

Noë, A. and O'Regan, K. (2000) Perception, attention and the grand illusion. *Psyche*, **6**, 15.

Norman, J. (2001) Two visual systems and two theories of perception: an attempt to reconcile the constructivist and ecological approaches. *Behavioral and Brain Sciences*, **24**, 6.

Nozick, R. (1981) *Philosophical explanations*. Oxford: Oxford University Press.

Ochipa, C., Rapcsack, S. Z., Maher, L. M., Rothi, L. J. G., Bowers, D. and Heilman, K. M. (1997) Selective deficit of praxic imagery in ideomotor apraxia. *Neurology*, **49**, 474–80.

O'Regan, J. K. and Noë, A. (2001a) A sensorimotor account of vision and visual consciousness. *Behavioral and Brain Sciences*, **24**, 939–1031.

O'Regan, K. and Noë, A. (2001b) What is it like to see: a sensorimotor theory of perceptual experience. *Synthese*, **129**, 79–103.

O'Shaughnessy, B. (1980) *The will*. Cambridge: Cambridge University Press.

O'Shaughnessy, B. (1992) The diversity and unity of action and perception. In *The contents of experience* (ed. Crane, T.), pp.216–66. Cambridge: Cambridge University Press.

Pacherie, E. (2000a) Conscious experience and concept forming abilities. *Acta Analytica*, **26**, 45–52.

Pacherie, E. (2000b) The content of intentions. *Mind and Language*, **15**, 400–32.

Pacherie, E. (2001) The causal theory of action revisited, mimeo.

Palmer, S. (1999) *The science of vision*. Cambridge, Mass: MIT Press.

Paulignan, Y., MacKenzie, C., Marteniuk, R. and Jeannerod, M. (1991) Selective perturbation of visual input during prehension movements. I. The effects of changing object position. *Experimental Brain Research*, **83**, 502–12.

Paulignan, Y., Frak, V. G., Toni, I. and Jeannerod, M. (1997) Influence of object position and size on human prehension movements. *Experimental Brain Research*, **114**, 226–34.

Pavani, F., Boscagli, I., Benvenuti, F., Rabuffetti, M. and Farné, A. (1999) Are perception and action affected differently by the Titchener circles illusion. *Experimental Brain Research*, **127**, 95–101.

Peacocke, C. (1983) *Sense and content: experience, thought and their relations*. Oxford, Oxford University Press.

Peacocke, C. (1989) Perceptual content. In *Themes from Kaplan* (ed. Almog, J., Perry, J. and Wettstein, H. K.), pp.297–329. Oxford: Oxford University Press.

Peacocke, C. (1992a) *A study of concepts*. Cambridge, Mass.: MIT Press.

Peacocke, C. (1992b) Scenarios, concepts and perception. In *The contents of experience* (ed. Crane, T.), pp.105–35. Cambridge: Cambridge University Press.

Peacocke, C. (1994) Content computation and exernalism. *Mind and Language*, **9**, 303–35.

Peacocke, C. (1998) Nonconceptual content defended. *Philosophy and Phenomenological Research*, **58**, 381–88.

Peacocke, C. (2001) Does perception have nonconceptual content. *The Journal of Philosophy*, **98**, 239–64.

Penfield, W. (1975) *The mystery of mind*. Princeton: Princeton University Press.

Perenin M. T. and Jeannerod, M. (1975) Residual vision in cortically blind hemifields. *Neuropsychologia*, **13**, 1–7.

Perenin, M. T. and Rossetti, Y. (1996) Residual grasping in an hemianopic field. A further instance of dissociation between perception and action. *Neuroreport*, **7**, 793–7.

Perenin, M. T. and Vighetto, A. (1988) Optic ataxia: a specific disruption in visuomotor mechanisms. I. Different aspects of the deficit in reaching for objects. *Brain*, **111**, 643–74.

Perrett, D. I., Rolls, E. T. and Caan, W. (1982) Visual neurones responsive to faces in the monkey temporal cortex. *Experimental Brain Research*, **47**, 329–42.

Perrett, D. I., Smith, P. A. J., Potter, D. D., Mistlin, A. J., Head, A. S., Milner, A. D. and Jeeves, M. A. (1985) Visual cells in the temporal cortex sensitive to face view and gaze direction. *Proceedings of the Royal Society of London*, **B 223**, 293–317.

Perrett, D. I., Harries, M. H., Bevan, R., Thomas, S., Benson, P. J., Mistlin, A. J., Chitty, A. J., Hietanen, J. K. and Ortega, J. E. (1989) Frameworks of analysis for the neural representation of animate objects and actions. *Journal of Experimental Biology*, **146**, 87–113.

Perry, J. (1979) The problem of the essential indexical. In *The problem of the essential indexical and other essays* (ed. Perry, J.) (1993), pp.33–52. Oxford, Oxford University Press.

Perry, J. (1986a) Perception, action and the structure of believing. In *The problem of the essential indexical and other essays* (ed. Perry, J.) (1993), pp.121–49. Oxford, Oxford University Press.

Perry, J. (1986b) Thought without representation. In *The problem of the essential indexical and other essays* (ed. Perry, J.) (1993), pp.205–25. Oxford, Oxford University Press.

Perry, J. (1993) *The problem of the essential indexical and other essays*. Oxford: Oxford University Press.

Pisella, L, Gréa, H., Tilikete, C., Vighetto, A., Desmurget, M., Rode, G., Boisson, D. and Rossetti, Y. (2000) An 'automatic pilot' for the hand in human posterior parietal cortex: toward a reinterpretion of optic ataxia. *Nature Neuroscience*, **3**, 729–36.

Poincaré, H. (1902/1968) *La Science et l'hypothèse*. Paris: Flammarion.

Poincaré, H. (1905/1958) *The value of science*. New York: Dover.

Poppelreuter, W. (1917) *Die Störungen der niederen und höheren Schleistungen durch Verletzungen des Okzipetalhirns*. Voss, Leipzig. English translation by J. Zihl (1990) *Disturbances of lower and higher visual capacities caused by occipital damage*. Oxford, Oxford University Press.

Pöppel, E., Held, R. and Frost, D. (1973) Residual visual functions after brain wounds involving the central visual pathways in man. *Nature*, **243**, 295.

Posner, M. I., Walker, J. A., Friedrich, F. J. and Rafal, R. D. (1984) Effects of parietal lobe injury on covert orienting of visual attention. *Journal of Neuroscience*, **4**, 1863–74.

Premack, D. (1990) The infant's theory of self-propelled-objects. *Cognition*, **36**, 1–16.

Premack, D. and Premack, A. (1995) Intention as psychological cause. In *Causal cognition, a multidisciplinary debate* (ed. Sperber, D., Premack, D. and Premack, A. J.), pp.185–99. Oxford: Oxford University Press.

Pritchard, L. C., Milner, A. D., Dijkerman, H. C., and MacWalter, R. S. (1997) Visuospatial neglect: veridical coding of size for grasping but not for perception. *Neurocase*, **3**, 437–43.

Putnam, H. (1994) Sense, nonsense, and the senses, an inquiry into the powers of the human mind. *The Journal of Philosophy*, **91**, 445–517.

Pylyshyn, Z. (1984) *Computation and cognition*. Cambridge, Mass.: MIT Press.

Pylyshyn, Z. (2000a) Situating vision in the world. *Trends in Cognitive Sciences*, **4**, 197–207.

Pylyshyn, Z. (2000b) Visual indexes, preconceptual objects and situated vision. *Cognition*, **80**, 127–58.

Quine, W. V. O. (1953) Reference and modality. In *From a logical point of view* (ed. Quine, W. V. O.), pp.139–59. Cambridge, Mass.: Harvard University Press.

Raffman, D. (1995) On the persistence of phenomenology. In *Conscious experience* (ed. Metzinger, T.). Thorverton, Inprint Academic.

Ramachandran, V. S and Blakeslee, S. (1998) *Phantoms in the brain, human nature and the architecture of the mind*. London: Fourth Estate Limited.

Recanati, F. (1993) *Direct reference, from language to thought*. Oxford: Blackwell.

Recanati, F. (1997) The dynamics of situations. *European Review of Philosophy*, **2**, 41–75.

Rey, G. (1997) *Contemporary philosophy of mind*. Oxford: Blackwell.

Ridley, (1995) *Animal behavior*. Oxford, Blackwell.

Rizzolatti, G., Camarda, R., Fogassi, L., Gentilucci, M., Luppino, G. and Matelli, M. (1988) Functional organization of area 6 in the macaque monkey. II. Area F5 and the control of distal movements. *Experimental Brain Research*, **71**, 491–507.

Rizzolatti, G., Fadiga, L., Gallese, V. and Fogassi, L. (1995) Premotor cortex and the recognition of motor actions. *Cognitive Brain Research*, **3**, 131–41.

Rizzolatti, G., Fadiga, L., and Matelli, M., Bettinardi, V., Paulesu, E., Perani, D. and Fazio, F. (1996) Localization of grasp representations in humans by PET: 1. Observation versus execution. *Experimental Brain Research*, **111**, 246–52.

Rizzolatti, G., Fadiga, L., Fogassi, L. and Gallese, V. (1999) Resonance behaviors and mirror neurons. *Archives Italiennes de Biologie*, **137**, 83–99.

Rizzolatti, G., Fogassi, L., and Gallese, V. (2000) Cortical mechanisms subserving object grasping and action recognition: a new view on the cortical motor functions. In *The cognitive neurosciences* (2nd edn) (ed. Gazzaniga, M. S.), pp.539–52. Cambridge, Mass.: MIT Press.

Rock, I. (1983) *The logic of perception*. Cambridge, Mass.: MIT Press.

Rolls, E. T. and Deco, G. (2002) *Computational neuroscience of vision*. Oxford, Oxford University Press.

Rosch, E. and Mervis, C. B. (1975) Family resemblance studies in the internal structure of categories. *Cognitive Psychology*, **7**, 573–605.

Rosch, E. Mervis, C. B., Gray, W. D. and Boyes-Braem, P. (1976) Basic objects in natural categories. *Cognitive Psychology*, **8**, 382–439.

Rosenthal, D. M. (1986) Two concepts of consciousness. *Philosophical Studies*, **99**, 329–59.

Rosenthal, D. M. (1993) Thinking that one thinks. In *Consciousness: psychological and philosophical essays* (ed. Davies, M. and Humphreys, G.), pp.197–223. Oxford: Blackwell.

Rossetti, Y. and Pisella, L. (2000) Common mechanisms in perception and action. In *Attention and performance*, XIX (ed. Prinz, W. and Hommel, B.).

Rothi, L. J. G., Heilman, K. M. and Watson, R. T. (1985) Pantomime comprehension and ideomotor apraxia. *Journal of Neurology, Neurosurgery and Psychiatry*, **48**, 207–10.

Rothi, L. J. G., Mack, L. and Heilman, K. M. (1986) Pantomime agnosia. *Journal of Neurology, Neurosurgery and Psychiatry*, **49**, 451–4.

Rothi, L. J. G., Ochipa, C. and Heilman, K. M. (1991) A cognitive neuropsychological model of limb apraxia. *Cognitive Neuropsychology*, **8**, 443–58.

Rubens, A. B. and Benson, D. F. (1971) Associative visual agnosia. *Archives of Neurology*, **24**, 305–16.

Rushworth, M. F. S., Ellison, A. and Walsh, V. (2001) Complementary localization and lateralization of orienting and motor attention. *Nature Neuroscience*, **4**, 656–61.

Russell, B. (1911) *The problems of philosophy*. London: Williams and Norgate.

Ryle, G. (1949) *The concept of mind*. London: Penguin Books.

Sakata, H., Shibutani, H., Kawano, K. and Harrington, T. L. (1985) Neural mechanisms of space vision in the parietal association cortex of the monkey. *Vision Research*, **25**, 453–63.

Sakata, H., Shibutani, H., Ito, Y. and Tsurugai, K. (1986) Parietal cortical neurons responding to rotary movement of visual stimulus in space. *Experimental Brain Research*, **61**, 658–63.

Sakata, H., Taira, M., Mine, S. and Murata, A. (1992) Hand-movement-related neurons of the posterior parietal cortex of the monkey: their role in the visual guidance of hand movements. In *Control of arm movement in space: neurophysiological and computational approaches* (ed. Caminiti, R., Johnson, P. B. and Burnod, Y.), pp.185–98. Berlin, Heidelberg: Springer.

Sakata, H., Taira, M. Murata, A. and Mine, S. (1995) Neural mechanisms of visual guidance of hand action in the parietal cortex of the monkey. *Cerebral Cortex*, **5**, 429–38.

Santos, L. R. and Hauser, M. D. (1999) How monkeys see the eyes: cotton-top tamarins' reaction to changes in visual attention and action. *Animal Cognition*, **2**, 131–39.

Schiffer, S. (1981) Truth and the theory of content. In *Meaning and understanding* (ed. Parrett, H. and Bouveresse, J.), Berlin: Walter de Gruyter.

Schall, J. D., Morel, A., King, D. J. and Bullier, J. (1995) Topography of visual cortex connections with frontal eye field in macaque: convergence and segregation of processing streams. *Journal of Neuroscience*, **15**, 4464–87.

Schneider, G. E. (1969) Two visual systems. *Science*, **163**, 895–902.

Scholl, B. J. and Tremoulet, P. D. (2000) Perceptual causality and animacy. *Trends in Cognitive Sciences*, **4**, 299–309.

Searle, J. (1983) *Intentionality. An essay in the philosophy of mind*. Cambridge: Cambridge University Press,.

Searle, J. (1992) *The rediscovery of the mind*. Cambridge, Mass: MIT Press.

Searle, J. (2001) *Rationality in action*. Cambridge, Mass.: MIT Press.

Sergent, J. and Signoret, J.-L. (1992) Functional and anatomical decomposition of face processing: evidence from proposopagnosia and PET study of normal subjects *Philosophical Transactions of the Royal Society of London, B.*

Servos, P. and Goodale, M. A. (1995) Preserved visual imagery in visual form agnosia. *Neuropsychologia*, **33**, 1383–94.

Shallice, T. (1988) *From neuropsychology to mental structure*. Cambridge, Cambridge University Press.

Shiffrar, M. and Freyd, J. J. (1990) Apparent motion of the human body. *Psychological Science*, **1**, 257–64.

Shiffrar, M. and Freyd, J. J. (1993) Timing and apparent motion path choice with human body photographs. *Psychological Science*, **4**, 379–84.

Shoemaker, S. (1994) The Royce Lectures: self-knowledge and 'inner sense'. In *The first person perspective and other essays* (ed. Shoemaker, S.) (1996), pp.201–68. Cambridge: Cambridge University Press.

Shoemaker, S. (1996) *The first person perspective and other essays*. Cambridge: Cambridge University Press.

Singer, W., Engel, A. K., Kreiter, A. K., Munk, M. H. J., Neuenschwander, S. and Roelfsma, P. K. (1997) Neuronal assemblies: necessity, signatures, and detectability. *Trends in Cognitive Sciences*, **1**, 252–61.

Sirigu, A., Duhamel, J. R. (2001) Motor and visual imagery as two complementary and neurally dissociable mental processes. *Journal of Cognitive Neuroscience*, **13**, 910–9.

Sirigu, A., Duhamel, J. R. and Poncet, M. (1991) The role of sensorimotor experience in object recognition. *Brain*, **114**, 2555–73.

Sirigu, A., Cohen, L., Duhamel, J. R., Pillon, B., Dubois, B. and Agid, Y. (1995) A selective impairment of hand posture for object utilization in apraxia. *Cortex*, **31**, 41–55.

Smeets, B. J. and Brenner, E. (2001) Perception and action are inseparable. *Ecological Psychology*, **13**, 163–6.

Smith, E. E. and Medin, D. L. (1981) *Categories and concepts*. Cambridge, Mass.: MIT Press.

Snowdon, P. (1980–81) Perception, vision and causation. *Proceedings of the Aristotelian Society New Series*, **81**, 175–92.

Snyder, L. H., Batista, A. P. and Andersen, R. A. (1997) Coding of intention in the posterior parietal cortex. *Nature*, **386**, 167–70.

Spelke, E. S. (1988) The origins of physical knowledge. In *Thought without language* (ed. Weiskrantz, L.), pp.168–84. Oxford: Oxford University Press.

Spelke, E. S., Gutheil, G. and Van der Valle, G. (1995) The development of object perception. In *An invitation to cognitive science, Vol. 2, Visual cognition* (ed. Osherson, D.), pp.297–330. Cambridge, Mass.: MIT Press.

Spelke, E., Philipps, A. T. and Woodward, A. L. (1995) Infants' knowledge of object motion and human action. In *Causal cognition, a multidisciplinary debate* (ed. Sperber, D., Premack, D. and Premack, A. J.), pp.44–78. Oxford: Oxford University Press.

Stevens, J. A., Fonlupt, P., Shiffrar, M. and Decety, J. (2000) New aspects of motion perception: selective neural encoding of apparent human movements. *Neuroreport*, **11**, 109–15.

Stroud, B. (1989) Understanding human knowledge in general. In *Knowledge, readings in contemporary epistemology* (ed. Bernecker, S. and Dretske, F.) (2000), pp.307–23. Oxford: Oxford University Press.

Taira, M., Mine, S., Georgopoulos, A. P., Murata, A. and Sakata, H. (1990) Parietal cortex neurons of the monkey related to the visual guidance of hand movements. *Experimental Brain Research*, **83**, 29–36.

Tanaka, K. (1993) Neuronal mechanisms of object recognition. *Science*, **262**, 685–8.

Tanaka, K., Saito, H., Saito, Y. and Moriya, M (1991) Coding visual images of objects in the inferotemporal cortex of the macaque monkey. *Journal of Neurophysiology*, **66**, 170–89.

Tanné, J., Boussaoud, D., Boyer-Zeller, N. and Rouiller, E. (1995) Direct visual pathways for reaching movements in the macaque monkey. *Neuroreport*, **7**, 267–72.

Teuber, H. L. (1960) Perception. In *Handbook of physiology, section I, Neurophysiology* (ed. Field, J., Magoun, H. W. and Hall, V. E.), pp.89–121. Washington: American Physiological Society.

Thorpe, S., Fize, D. and Marlot, C. (1996) Speed of processing in the human visual system. *Nature*, **381**, 520.

Tomasello, M. (2000) *The cultural origins of human cognition*. Cambridge, Mass.: Harvard University Press.

Tomita, H., Ohbayashi, M., Nakahara, K., Hasegawa, I. and Miyashita, Y. (1999) Top-down signal from prefrontal cortex in executive control of memory retrieval. *Nature*, **401**, 699.

Treisman,. A. (1993) The perception of features and objects Oxford: In *Attention Selection, awareness and control* (ed. Baddeley, A. and Weiskrantz, L.) Oxford: Clarendon Press.

Treisman, A. and Gelade, B. (1980) A feature-integration theory of attention. *Cognitive Psychology*, **12**, 97–136.

Trevarthen CB (1968) Two mechanisms of vision in primates. *Psychologische Forschung*, **31**, 299–337.

Turnbull, O. H., Beschin, N. and Della Sala, S. (1997) Agnosia for object orientation: implications for theories of object recognition. *Neuropsychologia*, **35**, 153–63.

Tye, M. (1992) Visual qualia and visual content. In *The contents of experience* (ed. Crane, T.), pp.158–76. Cambridge: Cambridge University Press.

Tye, M. (1995) *Ten problems of consciousness*. Cambridge, Mass.: MIT Press.

Ungerleider, L. and Mishkin, M. (1982) Two cortical visual systems. In *Analysis of visual behavior* (ed. Ingle, D. J., Goodale, M. A. and Mansfield, R. J. W.), pp.549–86. Cambridge: MIT Press.

Ungerleider, L. G. and Haxby, J. V. (1994) 'What' and 'Where' in the human brain. *Current Opinion in Neurobiology*, **4**, 157–65.

Vallar, G. and Perani, D. (1986) The anatomy of unilateral neglect after right hemisphre stroke lesion. A clinical/CT-scan correlation study in man. *Neuropsychologia*, **24**, 609–22.

Van Donkelaar, P. (1999) Pointing movements are affected by size-contrast illusions. *Experimental Brain Research*, **125**, 517–20.

Van Essen, D. C. and Maunsell, J. H. R. (1983) Hierarchical organization and functional streams in the visual cortex. *Trends in Neuroscience*, **6**, 370–5.

Viviani, P. (1990) Common factors in the control of free and constrained movements. In *Motor representation and control, attention and performance XIII.* (ed. Jeannerod, M.), pp.345–73. Hillsdale: Erlbaum.

Viviani, P. and McCollum, G. (1983) The relation between linear extent and velocity in drawing movements. *Neuroscience*, **10**, 211–18.

Viviani, P. and Stucchi, N. (1992) Biological movements look uniform. Evidence of motor-perceptual interactions. *Journal of Experimental Psychology, Human Perception and Performance*, **18**, 603–23.

Von Cramon D. and Kerkhoff, G. (1993) On the cerebral organization of elementary visuo-spatial perception. In *Functional organization of the human visual cortex* (ed. Gulyas, B., Ottoson, D. and Roland, P. E.), pp.211–31. Oxford: Pergamon.

Von Wright, G. H. (1998) *In the shadow of Descartes*. Dordrecht: Kluwer.

Walton, K. L. (1990) *Mimesis as make-believe*. Cambridge, Mass.: Harvard University Press.

Wang, Y., Fujita, I. and Murayama, Y. (2000) Neuronal mechanisms of selectivity for object features revealed by blocking inhibition in inferotemporal cortex. *Nature Neuroscience*, **3**, 807.

Wapner, W., Judd, T. and Gardner, H. (1978) Visual agnosia in an artist. *Cortex*, **14**, 343–64.

Warren, R. M. (1970) Perceptual restoration of missing speech sounds. *Science*, **167**, 392–3.

Warrington, E. K. and Taylor, A. M. (1973) The contribution of right parietal lobe to object recognition. *Cortex*, **9**, 152–64.

Warrington, E. K. and Shallice, T. (1984) Category specific semantic impairments. *Brain*, **107**, 829–53.

Weiskrantz L (1986) *Blindsight. A case study and implications*. Oxford: Oxford University Press.

Weiskrantz L, Warrington EK, Sanders MD, and Marshall J (1974) Visual capacity in the hemianopic field following a restricted occipital ablation. *Brain*, **97**, 709–28.

Wellman, H. M. and Philipps, S. A. T. (2001) Developing intentional understanding. In *Intentions and intentionality, foundations of social cognition* (ed. Malle, B. F. Moses, L. J. and Baldwin, D. A.), pp.00. Cambridge Mass.: MIT Press.

Wernicke, C. (1874) *Der aphasische Symptomenkomplex, eine psychologische studie auf anatomischer Basis*, Brolan: Cohn and Weigert.

Westwood, D. A., Dubrowski, A., Carnahan, H. and Roy, E. A. (2000) The effect of illusory size on force production when grasping objects. *Experimental Brain Research*, **135**, 535–43.

White, P. A. and Milne, A. (1997) Phenomenal causality: impressions of pulling in the visual perception of objects in motion. *American Journal of Psychology*, **110**, 573–602.

Whiten, A. and Byrne, R. W. (1997) (ed.) *Macchiavellian intelligence II: Extensions and evaluations*. Cambridge: Cambridge University Press.

Wilson, B. A., Clare, L., Young, A. W. and Hodges, J. R. (1997) Knowing where and knowing what: a double dissociation. *Cortex*, **33**, 529–42.

Wong, E. and Mack, A. (1981) Saccadic programming and perceived location. *Acta Psychologica*, **48**, 123–31.

Woodward, A. L. (1998) Infants selectively encode the goal object of an actor's reach. *Cognition*, **69**, 1–34.

Woodward, A. L., Sommerville, J. A. and Guajardo, J. J. (2001) How infants make sense of intentional action. In *Intentions and intentionality, foundations of social cognition* (ed. Malle, B. F. Moses, L. J. and Baldwin, D. A.), pp.00. Cambridge Mass.: MIT Press.

Wright, L. (1973) Function. In *Conceptual issues in evolutionary biology* (ed. Sober, E.) (1984), pp.347–68.

Wynn, K. (1992a) Addition and subtraction by human infants. *Nature*, **358**, 749–50.

Wynn, K. (1992b) Evidence against empiricist accounts of the origins of numerical knowledge. *Mind and Language*, **7**, (4), 315–32.

Xu, F. and Carey, S. (1996) Infants' metaphysics: the case of numerical identity. *Cognitive Psychology*, **30**, 111–53.

Young, M. P. (1992) Objective analysis of the topological organization of the primate cortical visual system. *Nature*, **358**, 152–4.

Zeki, S. (1993) *A vision of the brain*. Blackwell: Oxford.

Zihl, J., Cramon, D. von and Mai, N. (1983) Selective disturbance of movement vision after bilateral brain damage. *Brain*, **106**, 313–40.

Author Index

Subject Index